Lady on the Bridge

Memoir of a Nisei

Tadashi Kishi

CreateSpace

Cover page picture by Tadashi Kishi

Library of Congress Cataloging-in-Publication Data (Need to apply)

Tadashi Kishi 1921-
ISBN: 978-1461060703

TABLE OF CONTENTS

Prologue

Throughout all seasons
Hear the voices from the past
From this humble pen

The house I lived in

People lived here once
long ago
Lights were on
and voices heard
People scurry
here and there
I was there
long ago

Look upon that house
once more
No lights are on
no voices heard
Only shadows there
that tell the past
The rooms
dare I enter

A pen will be
my guiding light
Shine the light
into those dark corners
Live with me
the past so dear
Reveal the truth
that lay dormant there

Tell not simply
what I see
Shine the light
for in vivid colors
the pen will show
what's hidden there
Let the heart beat
pulse once more

Reach into the past
A Pen will show you the way
Find the heartbeat there

Why I write

Sometime ago, my daughter-in-law, Melanie and my son, Greg asked Yo and me if we would write about our past. Off and on, I tried to write or use a recorder but to no avail. Deep in my mind there was this bridge I had to cross that spanned over a deep gorge. I was afraid to take the first step, for emotions welled up. I envisioned below on the sharp rocks: Freedom, Liberty, and Justice for all – these and all of the words in the Constitution – dashed to smithereens and washed in the blood of patriots who believe in our America, the land of the free. There is always an eerie hollow voice echoing through the gorge in my mind: "I, Franklin Delano Roosevelt, do solemnly swear … preserve, protect and defend the Constitution of the United States."

I was afraid because some of events were too painful to think about, and my heart was torn. At times tears would form or my voice would fail. Then, one day, my granddaughter Isabel asked me to write about my thoughts about my incarceration at Manzanar during World War II. It was for her class report. It is a story that remains deep and something that most *Nisei*, second generation Japanese, never speak openly about.

My granddaughter, Isabel is an adopted child. My son Greg and daughter-in-law, Melanie had a hard time conceiving, but they still wanted to share their love with children. Finally, they decided to adopt. One day, when they were visiting us, I spent the day entertaining Isabel to make her feel at home and that she was part of the family. I remember when I was a child visiting my aunt and uncle with my parents, my aunt said, *"Maa, hontoni okiku natta ne"* (My goodness, how big you have grown). After that, they said nothing more. I stood mute by my parents all through the visit. That would never be the case with my grandchildren. On their visit, Isabel and I read books together, played hide-and-seek, said silly things, and we were having a grand time together.

Suddenly she stopped and looked at me with her blue eyes sparkling and smiling and said, "I am so happy."

Grandpa's heart melted.

On their flight home, the parents asked Isabel, "Did you have a good time?"

She answered, "Yes."

"Why do you look so sad?" they asked her.

"I miss Grandpa."

So you can see that I could not disappoint my granddaughter by not responding.

My response was not so much about the details of Manzanar and the life there but more what I had gained from that moment on - the family, grandchildren, especially Isabel, and the good people who had become a part of my life; none of this could have happened without my having gone through that terrible time in camp.

After I sent the letter to Isabel, I sent another letter about things that I had not said in the first letter. I called it "Things Unsaid." It was stiff and factual like a software manual. After writing the document, I always wondered, "Will anyone bother to turn to the next page and read?" Then one day, I saw an announcement of a writing class on "Writing From Life Experience" sponsored by the Livermore Park District and taught by *Sensei* teacher Linda Tacy. The class was scheduled for an hour and a half each week for six weeks. I have been taking the class for over three years. I am still learning.

It has been difficult to start because the story has been buried deep inside my psyche. By writing, I have begun to learn things that never would have come to light had I not started to write. It is a story of a *Nisei* growing up during the Great Depression who finds he is living in two worlds. Sometimes these two worlds are at odds with each other. Threading through this story is *Okaasan*: She is the glue that holds the family together. She bears, nurtures, and dotes on her offspring. She holds fast to her culture, for there is no other recourse for her. She resists the demise of a culture.

For each writings, I have written a haiku that embodies what follows.

I have written a poem "Penned" that was a result of a class exercise to take a word or phrase from an article and write something. I took "At the news on the radio …" to correspond to the news I heard on the radio, at my father's nursery on Sunday December seventh of the attack on Pearl Harbor. It is the pen that began to heal the torn heart.

Acknowledgements

I wish to thank the people who have helped to make this book publishable. First, my family, Gregory and Melanie, Glen and Margaret, who have encouraged me to write about my past, and especially, to my granddaughter, Isabel Kishi who gave me the courage to begin to write and overcome the roadblock of telling about my Manzanar experience.

The book could not have reached this stage without Linda Tacy, teacher of "Writing from Experience" sponsored by the Livermore Park District's Adult classes. And many thanks to the classmates who encourage and help me through those tough days but delight classes.

Even more important, it is my daughter-in-law, Melanie Kishi who, using her expertise in language, spent many days and hours correcting my writings and suggesting ways to for improvement.

I am indebted to Susan Uyemura (Shoho) who had initiated a committee to review the my memoir for possible publication by the Nikkei Writers Guild. Thus, I wish to thank the committee for their effort and I was pleased that they had accepted my story for publication. Again, I wish to thank Susan Shoho for having Professor Charlene M. Riggins make the final edit of my book.

Because of unforeseen delays and funding, I have decided to publish through CreateSpace.com, a Publish on Demand company. My special thanks to my son, Gregory for expediting the formatting, book assembly, and submission to CreateSpace.

Most of all, I am deeply indebted to Okaasan, mother who I come to know while writing my memoir and wish to dedicate this book in her honor.

Penned

Without telling anyone,
Going out before dawn,
Working all day by ourselves,
Shaking our heads in silence
At the news on the radio*

What happen to you?
After the news, "The Day of Infamy," on the radio,
You open your mouth,
And there is just a gurgle.
Your mind is racing to spew its data.
From one corner of your cranium,
Screams out a voice, "I want to be heard!"
Another and another reach out,
"No, listen, I want you to know."
There is chaos in your mind
For time and space have no meaning.
Yet, from your lips, a word, a sentence, may flow.
But the acid in your stomach eats away,
You feel your heart beat pulsing erratically.
A tear may drop for a voice screams,
"Remember how deep the hurt remains."
There are words but your voice is cracking.
You realize you are not making sense.
Silence is now a safe place.

Another time a granddaughter's voice is heard,
"Please tell how you felt about that time?"
You try your voice on a recorder
But that won't do.
You pick up a pen and begin to write.
The voices suppressed so long
All cry out wanting to be heard.
But your hand is now in control.
You will pick and choose your moment in time.
No acid can engulf the words you write.
Your heart beats strong and sometimes wildly.
You are in control and you write
A story that long remained so deep.
"The pen is mightier that a sword," they say.
But it is more than that.
It is a brush that can paint the story,
Give life to the feelings and hope that remained so deep.

Lady on the Bridge

It is more than sword and paintbrush too.
It is a light that reveals what's hidden.
It is an antidote that heals the wounds.

*"Telephone Repairman" by Joe Miller

Chapter 1: Beginnings

Fear of a dark place
Two worlds at odds in my life
Bridged by Mother's love

Letter to *Okaasan,* Mother

Okaasan, ogenki de irrashaimasuka, Mother have you been doing well?
Gobusata shite orimasu, I'm sorry I haven't written to you for a long time.

For many years I sat with you and reminisced about the past. I ask you to indulge with me once more.

Okaasan, for a long time I had been afraid to open a dark chapter for fear that it was not my place to ask you about your past. Now that I am older, I dare to write to you about what had bothered me for so long. It was one day when Frank and I were playing in *Otoosan's,* Father's nursery in Sawtelle, he said, "Did you know that mother held you in her arms as she stood on a bridge?" But I was too young to understand or even know what to ask about what he was saying. I had fears that it was not my place to even think or let alone to ask. A cold chill forever passed over my body as I dared to step into that past.

Time and again, I would always imagine a young Japanese mother holding a child in her arms and standing silently on a bridge. I wondered, "What brings her to this place and why am I here? Was this the answer to her despair, the hardship, the struggle, and the hopelessness she felt at this moment in time?" Silently the figure fades away as she turned away from the bridge. I was afraid to follow this dark path further to seek answers, for danger lurked there.

Okaasan, my fear was real for I lived in two worlds: American, and Japanese. But I had found the two worlds were frequently at odds with each other. It was a place of conflict and confusion. At home, I lived in your world, the culture you brought with you from feudal Japan. It was your place in the family to raise the children, while *Otoosan* was the authority and provided for our well being.

You were overprotective and indulgent with us, *Okaasan,* but you had never outwardly shown your emotions. You wore a mask. I had not seen you cry or shout. Your world was indirect. I had since learned that it was a way of life from a feudal era where one never showed weakness in the face of adversity. It was a world I could not penetrate easily, for I did not know how.

One step outside the home, I was in a different world. From these eyes, I could not see my black hair, my brown slant eyes, or my buckteeth. I knew who I was for I had chosen my world, America. I had read in my history books at school, that brave men had laid down their lives on this hallowed ground and on foreign lands to preserve freedom, liberty, and equality for all of us. I would not abandon that. It was only when someone insulted me with his slur "Jap" that I was reminded that I was not "*Hakujin*" (Caucasian).

Yet there were codes of moral conduct and honor that you had bestowed on us, *Okaasan.* Much of it agrees with the Judeo-Christian moral conduct that had made us "model citizens." For that, I was thankful. I know that you, with all *Issei,* held fast to a culture born in the feudal era. It had given you meaning and purpose in your lives since you, as it was with all *Issei* (first generation Japanese in America*),* had been denied at every turn the opportunity to assimilate into

American life. It was only after our internment at Manzanar in 1942 that I became aware that you could not become naturalized citizen, because of the Immigration Act of 1917. Then I learned that our Government had passed the Alien Land Law that denied Asians, especially Japanese, to own property. All of this was under the guise of "White only" that denied the *Issei* to realize the American dream. Even later, that dream of home has also been elusive for my generation. But you and *Otoosan* persevered, set roots in this hostile environment, and started our family.

The Japanese way of life defined who you were. But in my world, it is "we the people" who defined what our culture would be. I had chosen to discard those aspects of family culture that had no place in America's free society. But in both worlds, family was still the core of society. I have observed that esteem of family, diligence in work, and honorable conduct were the values of your life. Most of all, I had learned from you and *Otoosan* that "*haji*" (shame), and not guilt, was the essence of Japanese behavior. How often had I heard the words, "Do not bring shame to our family name?" Caught between two worlds, I had treaded lightly to preserve harmony, though I did not know how to do it or why I must.

Okaasan, what brought you to the bridge? Was it desperation that even your cultural value of *gaman* (endurance of pain) and *gambare* (ability to persevere) was not enough to see you through this troubling time? I know that both Shinto and Buddhism, nor Confucianism can give you any spiritual strength because they are the way of life, an attitude, and not religions. I had since learned that in the Japanese way of life that there was greater shame in asking for help than committing suicide. I only wonder if it was *haji* that prevented you from seeking help.

I would beg the question once more, but, *Okaasan*, I see that your cultural values brought you to this bridge. Over the years you have instilled in me those same values. Now I know that you had shown me one more, *Kodomo no tame ni* (self sacrifice for the sake of the children), for which I was eternally grateful.

We never open that chapter after Japan attacked Pearl Harbor, for it was too painful for us to talk about what happen afterwards. But we are not alone in our silence, because no *Nisei* wanted to open that betrayal and deceit by our Government. Most of all, you had suffered more than the rest of the family, because *Otoosan* was ripped out of our lives without knowing why and where he was being held. Then, after President Franklin D. Roosevelt announced Executive Order 9066, we lost everything that you and *Otoosan* had struggled for, our family nursery and our home. Our lives turned to dust just like Manzanar. But that was not enough punishment by our Government. Our loyalty was questioned and both *Issei* and *Nisei* were required to answer the same two loyalty questions, 27 and 28 even though you could not be a citizen under the Immigration Act of 1917. With Frank in the US Army, answering the two questions was heart wrenching and heart breaking. It was a time and place I did not wish to remember.

Okaasan, now that time has passed, a great tragedy has occurred within our family. It was as if a cancer had invaded our lives from which each of us could not fully recover from its invasive effect. In reality it was the seed from your culture, *chonan* that you planted and tended all through these years that had cast a dark shadow over *kyodai*, brothers. When I sat with you one day and we talked about the family, the past, and the future, I heard in your voice just a wish and not a commitment to do what was right for our family. Maybe it was your Japanese way that you could not usurp *Otoosan's* authority, for fear that you would shame his memory.

Unfortunately, each of your sons saw differently what that seed you planted meant. It pitted brother against brother in a civil suit that resulted in an untimely death of your son, Joe. I am saddened that much of what you and *Otoosan* had worked for and wish to pass on to us had been lost. Now, there is a great divide within the family and with the in-laws.

Okaasan, forgive me with great hesitation for being outspoken, but I have a heavy heart and I do not know how to heal this wound. There is so much I need to ask you about Joe and Frank and their relationship while they were growing up so that I can understand what has happen between the two *kyodai*.

I will write to you again as soon as I can recover from this tragic episode.

O-karada ni ki wo tsukete kudasi, Please take good care of yourself.

Your son Tadashi

Desperate time looms
Goodbye nostalgic Japan
Future to behold

Desperate Times

I look through the window of my mind to probe the ethereal shadows of our family to know the past. *Okaasan* and *Otoosan* brought with them a culture of an era, *Furusato* (old village) or nostalgic Japan. When Japanese talk about the *Issei*, they always say with reverence "*Furusato*", which means cultural purity, serenity in nature, and a way of life isolated from foreign influence. I often wondered why my parents would leave such a magical and idyllic lifestyle. It was, however, a chaotic period of economic hardship, national disasters, and even revolution that my parents lived in. For several hundred years, *Shoguns (Samurai warlords)* ruled Japan and kept domestic peace by isolating the country from Western influence, including Christianity, for fear of military intervention by foreign powers. Shoguns established a rigid social hierarchy where *Samurai* ranked highest, followed by farmers, artisans, and merchants. It was a period of renaissance when artistic advancement took place; in the theater, in musical instruments, and in the arts. It was a period stressing moral code and education. But the feudal system met its demise, not only because the farmers and businesses revolted against higher and higher taxes to support the Shogun's lavish life style, but also because the Shoguns failed to stop the military challenges of foreign intrusions. *Bushido* spirit (code of the warrior) and *Samurai* swords was no match against guns, canons, and frigates.

Otoosan was born in1882 and *Okaasan* was born in 1896 during the Meiji Restoration period (1868-1912) when the Emperor Meiji was reinstated as the ruler of Japan and the Shogunate removed from power. The deposed Samurais, who were better educated than most of the population, became teachers, police, and government officials. A major change was taking place to compete with Western Civilization. Emperor Meiji was faced with a revolutionary task to change from an agrarian economy to an industrial one. The Restoration process required large expenditures, leading to further financial crisis on the Japanese. Mass education and military conscription was introduced, and Shinto became the dominant ideology. It was also the time of America's Western Expansion that needed workers for the large plantations in Hawaii, for the construction of the railroads on the mainland, and for mining and manufacturing industries. First it was the Chinese who were recruited; they met with prejudice and were called the "Yellow Peril." Eventually American companies also turned to Japanese to fill the need.

I know that *Otoosan* was "*Chonan*" (first born son), who, like all first-born sons, shouldered the responsibility of the family during this desperate economic time. The time was ripe to seduce young Japanese men to immigrate to America to help their families back home financially. I do not know what promises were made to them, but when they arrived, they faced segregation and prejudice, just as the Chinese had. The work was backbreaking. But they endured.

I remember one year, *Otoosan* couldn't work outside in the nursery because it rained for several days. It was the first time that *Otoosan* had time to talk about his past. He was telling Joe, my eldest brother, that he had been a policeman as a young man, but that it had not earned enough to help the family. When an American company offered a labor contract to work on the railroads, he took the opportunity to gain more income for his family. His story was fascinating, but I was too naive at the time to understand the terrible working conditions, prejudice, and the hard work he endured. He said that when the contract ended, a handful of Japanese workers decided to move to Southern California near Palms/Culver City, and start farming. They used their knowledge of farming in Japan, where land is precious, and installed an intensive farming methodology: truck farming. The result was that they produced impressive yields for their crops. Farming was prosperous enough that *Otoosan* thought about marriage and raising a family.

I know that Japanese marriages were arranged through "*nakoodo or baishakunin*" *(*Matchmaker), and some marriages were arranged by exchanging photos or "picture brides," for those who didn't have the means to return to Japan to get married. I assumed that *Otoosan* was among these Japanese looking for a bride. But to my surprise, *Otoosan* had returned to Japan, to his village, Kishimura, Wakayamaken, Japan in 1911. *Otoosan* married *Okaasan* in 1912. The marriage was arranged through the traditional way of *baishakunin* (middle man). Her family was from Osaka but, at the time, she lived in Minamoto Mura, Wakayamaken, Japan. After their marriage, they both immigrated to American and landed at San Francisco, California on May 26, 1913. *Okaasan* first set foot on American soil at Angel Island Immigration Station that day. This was the start of our family in America.

It was mother's place to bear and rear the children. She gave birth to Mabel Shizuko in 1915, Joe Hitoshi in1917, Frank Ryuji in 1919, Tadashi in 1921, and Kazumi in 1925.

The farmers prospered during World War I by supplying food for the United States Army. But when the war ended November 1918, the government no longer needed the bulk of their crops. This was a desperate time for *Otoosan,* who faced less income from farming and with a growing family to support. He continued farming for several more years then turned to the nursery business as his next venture.

Today, *Otoosan* is busy moving the last of his possessions to a new home. It is nightfall and time for all of us to leave. Mother is in front and I am sitting with my brothers in the back of the model T-Ford truck. I hear the sput sputter and cough as the motor turns over. A sudden lurch and we are on our way. I am bundled up and facing backwards. I can only see the stars above as the car chugs along the road. I hear a faint sound that goes whhrroar, whhrroar, whhrroar. The noise gets louder and louder. Suddenly, to my right, the sky is filled with lights, and the high-pitched sound is deafening. It is scary since I can only see where we had been and not where we are going. Frank is peering over the side and says excitedly, "Did you see that? We just passed a midget car racing track." But then as we chug along, the noise slowly fades away.

While remembering Frank's excitement about the racetrack, I saw that his passion for fast souped up cars was always his first love. Even when he was married, he bought a fancy coupe instead of a family car. One day, I rode with him from Boyle Heights to West Los Angeles in his fancy coupe. At every stop sign, he would rev his motor, rrumph, rrumph, gun out of the starting block, and race to the next signal. Once again, he was stopped at the next signal and never gained an inch, but he was racing.

The trip seemed long, especially, looking backwards, and just hearing the chug, chug of the motor. Finally, the car slowed down: a chug, a cough, and a lurch. We were home at last in Sawtelle (West Los Angeles), California.

> *When the chugging stopped*
> *Desperate times left behind*
> *Life amid the plants*

Flavored with soy sauce
Dreams are what life is made of
So dream your heart out

My First Home

When one speaks of Sawtelle, Ca., one always thinks of an "Old Soldiers Home." In fact, now one can't find the town of Sawtelle because it was incorporated into greater Los Angeles as West Los Angeles in 1922. It had been famous for the Veterans Hospital built for the Veterans of World War I just north of Wilshire Blvd and Sawtelle Blvd. But I didn't learn about the hospital or World War I until years later when I was a teenager.

Now I'm just a tot growing up in this small town where my father has begun his nursery (plants) business. There are several Japanese families that moved to this town since Japanese are restricted from other areas in California. The Japanese are the working class doing domestic work. They are the railroad hands, laborers, gardeners, and nursery assistants.

I remember this house in Sawtelle through veiled memories. It is a single storied wooden framed house, steps leading up to a small porch, and the front door opens to a living room/dining area. All of the walls are wallpapered in a simple striped pattern. I see a sofa, an oak dining table with six chairs. I have a vivid memory of the living room not because of the décor but what happens here. One day, I see my eldest brother, Joe, having a birthday party with a few of his classmates in that living room. I also saw a yummy chocolate cake on the dining table for his birthday. Everyone at the party has a little cone shaped colorful hat on. One blond haired kid is pointing at Joe and laughing and says, "Joe your heads too big for that hat."

Joe puts both hands on his coned shaped hat and tries to push it back on top but the elastic is too loose to hold it straight. Joe's hat keeps falling sideways. "Aw gee, I guess I'll just wear it sideways," said Joe.

I recognize two of the kids from around our neighborhood, but the other two must be from his school classmates. His friends are laughing and talking and having fun, but I am too young to be invited. I think that one day I will have a birthday party like that though it never does (happen).

The kitchen was to the right and beyond it was a big screened in porch with a tub for laundry and a door leading to the backyard. While we lived in sunny California, the winters were cold on some nights. I remember seeing little metal spigots protruding from the floor near the walls and in winter Otoosan connected a portable gas heater to warm our house.

It was a cold winter night when I sat down on a small chair in front of our gas heater busily washing my feet in a basin full of warm water. I felt the nice glow of the fire from the heater warming me. The next thing I remember, I was in a bed with my parents peering down at me with worried looks. Otoosan said something to mother while he sat me up in bed. Mother, in the meantime, went to the kitchen. She came back with a small cup of dark liquid. Okaasan said, "Kore wo nomi nasai (Drink this)." I didn't know it was a cup of shoyu (soy sauce). The dark liquid tasted salty. I was about to refuse the rest, but father gave me a stern look and shook his head. I swallowed the rest when suddenly the shoyu gave my system a terrific jolt. My heart pumped faster and faster. I quickly snapped out of my daze. Even now, when I see someone cooking with soy sauce, I remember that salty liquid running down my throat. Then again, soy sauce is the way of life in a Japanese home.

Later I learned that the gas heater was not working efficiently and that I had been overcome by the carbon monoxide. When Otoosan checked the others in the house, he found they were being affected by the slow leak. Immediately, he roused them, herded them outside, and opened all the windows and doors to disperse the carbon monoxide.

While growing up in Sawtelle, I was my brother Frank's shadow. Frank was an adventurous kid and I followed him everywhere when I was big enough. One day, Frank decided to roam on the south side of town where there were some warehouses and factories. As we approached one of the warehouses, I saw a railroad siding with boxcars parked near the buildings. Frank said excitedly, "Let's go look at those box cars." It was hard walking because the empty lot was in rough terrain with weeds growing as tall as my height. I was just five years old. Frank, at seven, was urging me on when a group of bigger kids saw us, gave us dirty looks, and began shouting at us in a menacing tone. "Come on, let's get out of here," Frank said urgently. We both turned and high-tailed it back home. It was the last time we went near that place.

Another time, Frank wanted to visit Stoner Playground about five or six blocks away from our house. It was the first time I had slid down a slide. When I first looked at it, I was too scared to go up to the top. Frank just climbed up the steps to the top without hesitation and slid down quickly. "Come on, it's fun!" he urged me on. But I was not convinced that it was that easy to climb up so high. "Don't be a scaredy-cat," he teased me. He went back up and slid down headfirst. "See, it's fun," he kept saying.

As soon as he slid down, Frank rushed back to the steps and repeated his performance. Since the tall slide didn't seem to scare him at all, I meekly decided I would try. I hung tightly onto the railing and hugged the steps as close to my body thinking that I would fall off at any moment. I climbed up slowly one step at a time. I tried not to look down. The scariest part of going down is getting one leg at a time onto the slide before sliding down. It looked mighty far down from that top. I held tight to the side of the slide and slid down slowly, never letting go with both hands. Then, I decided to let go. Down the metal slide I zipped and landed at the bottom with a thump; I was surprised that it wasn't that hard to do after all. A few more times down the slide and I got braver and attempted to go down head first like my brother. It all happened so fast that I hit the sand at the bottom unceremoniously. By the time I got up from the ground and brushed myself off, Frank, always alert to new distractions, had already gone to play on the swings nearby.

"Sit down on the seats and grab onto the support chains and lean back and pull hard and with both your feet stretched out," he said. "Now, kick both feet back like this. Then lean back and pull again with both feet up," he continued. "See how easy it is to start swinging?" Frank was a great teacher showing me how to get the swings moving by myself. "It's all in the motion of your legs, pull on the swing supports to get moving," Frank said. We kept swinging higher and higher, but Frank soon lost interest in spending time at the playground and motioned me to head back home.

Booty of the past
Hazardous sloshing through life
Step through life's cycle

Tricycle

Until my brothers returned from school, I spent my days riding my tricycle in my father's nursery. The nursery hardly looked like a store because it was in the back of our home. There was a dirt path that ran through the middle of the yard that I could ride my tricycle on. There were so many plants growing in pots, tin cans, and in the ground in this yard; I never learned all their names. But I do remember a few special ones. One plant had pretty delicate green leaves and was just about my height. The stems branched out, and the leaves on top looked like an umbrella. When I was older, I found the plant was called "Heavenly Bamboo," except my parents called it *Nanten*. The delicate little leaves branched out like bamboo leaves. I imagined that I was looking through a kaleidoscope with a mixture of varying shades of red that turned green as it grew. There were lots of plants in clay pots of all sizes. I especially remember these pots because we had to clean the used ones in big galvanized wash tubs and set them out to dry. It was a dirty, messy job, and my hands turned white and lumpy. At the end of the yard, there were plants much taller than I. Father shaped the tops of the trees into big round balls. I learned later it was called Pittosporum tobira, a Japanese Pittosporum. These two, Heavenly Bamboo and Japanese Pittosporum, my parents planted in my garden when I had a home of my own, and they have been special to me. I always wonder if my parents brought some of these plant seeds with them from Japan so that they might have something of their homeland?

Every so often, I saw *Otoosan* digging plants that he had planted in the ground in the far corner of the yard. He dug with a funny looking shovel that had a short handle and a long and narrow spade part. I watched him dig all around the plant and scoop the dirt away until there was a big hole in the ground with the plant placed upright outside. Then he lifted the plant with the ball of dirt that enclosed the roots, placed it on a spread out gunnysack, wrapped it all up, and tied it. *Otoosan* cautioned all of us not to play among the plants, especially where he had dug out shrubs. But those holes eventually beckoned me.

One wintry season, my parents bought me a pair of yellow boots to wear to school on a rainy day. I was so happy to see those yellow boots that I had to try them out. I sat on the back porch steps and slipped them on. I walked around a bit and then looked for puddles of water to wade through. Sloshing through a few wet spots was fun for a moment, but I spied a nice puddle in the back yard. Slop, slop, and slop my boots sounded as I ran quickly to the puddle that was near some plants. On the first step into the puddle, I sunk down into a hole. Muddy water gushed into the top of the boots. I was standing in wet gooey mud inside my boots. I was startled. I managed to pull myself out of the puddle and slop, slop, and slop went my boots as I clomped and squished back to the house. *Okaasan* was watching me and came out of the house to help me take off the muddy wet boots. She didn't yell or scold me for my stupidity, but quietly helped take off my dirty socks and wet pants to clean me up. The boots were no longer bright yellow. Somehow, I can't remember wearing the boots after that or ever wanting another pair of boots.

I do remember one especially memorable day with my tricycle. First, *Okaasan* dressed *imooto* (younger sister) Kaz in a pretty dress and a hat. Next, she made me wear Knickerbocker pants that looked baggy and stopped at the knees, hightop button-hole shoes, a heavy coat sweater, and a cap with a brim like some golfers wear. *Otoosan* carefully put my *imooto* on the trike, and I stood next to her. "Watch over your sister so she doesn't fall off," *Okaasan* said to me. *Otoosan* set up a camera and took our picture. What I remember is the tough time buttoning up my shoes with a metal eyehook. I always took these tasks very seriously and tried to be thorough.

Sawtelle Nursery, younger sister, Kaz
On trike and Tad standing by

Music to my ears
School is fun but scary too
Learning the hard way

School Days

I remember my brothers sitting at the kitchen table doing their homework. I was curious about what Frank was doing since he was just a year older than I. I was anxious to go to school with them. Even though I would be five in December, I was still too young to go. I edged over where Frank was sitting and peered at his book. It wasn't a big book, but it had pictures of a boy and a girl. It had funny looking letters on the bottom of the page. Frank was trying to read. He was saying, "See Dick. See Dick run...See Spot run." I tried not to butt in. I quietly said the words he was trying to read. It looked like fun. Whenever Frank would leave his books around, I would grab them and try reading the stories.

One story I remember:
See It Go
"Look," said Dick.
"See it go."
"See it go up."
It was a picture of Dick watching an airplane in the sky. Soon, I was reading all of Frank's books from school.

It was the next year, and I was excited about going to school. On my first day, I walked with my brothers. They took me to the kindergarten room and left. Suddenly, I must have felt scared without my brother around. When I entered the classroom and saw all of the other children there, I began to bawl. The teacher tried to console me, but that didn't seem to matter. I was so disruptive that she decided to place me behind the piano. My crying must have been very loud because I could hear sound from the back of the piano becoming louder and louder with each song to drown out my crying. I can still see the back of that piano. The boards were unpainted or unvarnished and ran diagonally across the back. The boards vibrated with her playing. After a while, I became lonely and I stopped bawling. The last thing I remember about this embarrassing episode is a teacher coming around to the back, taking hold of my hand, and letting me join the children. Funny thing, I can't remember any of the songs she played. Even now, I can't carry a tune.

The next exciting event I remember during my year in kindergarten was the maypole dance. It was a big event for the school. Kids were everywhere on the schoolyard that day. At one corner of the yard was a tall metal pole with streamers of all different colors on it. We must have practiced weeks before because I remember holding onto a streamer and walking around the maypole clockwise while other children were holding onto streamers and moving in the opposite direction. We were supposed to sing songs as we moved in a circular fashion around the pole, but I think most of us were giggling. For the finale, the colorful streamers ended up wrapped around the pole. I looked for my brothers to see if they would be doing the same thing, but they were nowhere to be seen.

Lady on the Bridge

The weather was hard, cold rain that first day I started first grade. When I entered the classroom, almost everyone was huddled next to the heaters trying to dry off and stay warm. The floor was a mess with water puddles everywhere. You could hear the steam hissing and pipes banging as the steam expanded and contracted in the gold colored heater. With all of the commotion, it was a disastrous day for the teacher. I was in that class for only a few weeks because my father was moving his nursery to a lot in Santa Monica, Ca. I can't remember what my teacher looked like, but I can still hear the banging noise of the steam heater.

Chapter 2: Growing Up

Home, where the heart is
Nestled among the flora
Feel the ocean breeze

Santa Monica My Home

Around 1926, *Otoosan* moved his nursery just two miles from the Santa Monica Bay where the climate was mild, sunny most of the time, and cooled by the gentle Pacific Ocean breeze. Our new home was right in the middle of the new nursery located on Wilshire Blvd. and 25th street. An alley ran through the middle of the property and divided it into two pieces. There were two houses on this property; one was an old faded wooden green house on 25th street that remained empty for a time and our home was in the middle of the property adjacent to an alley that connected 25th street with 26th street. The house was a white wooden two-bedroom building. There was a large living room, kitchen, and a screened in porch on the west side. Two bedrooms were on the east side, and a large bathroom on the south side. My younger sister Kaz slept in one bedroom and Joe, Frank and I had the other bedroom. Joe slept in a bed and Frank and I shared a mattress set on the floor. Joe needed to sleep in the bed because he was recovering from surgery on his foot, the surgery was a result of a bizarre set of circumstances.

While playing at school, he had fallen and injured his knee. At first, he thought it was a minor cut and did not attend to it properly. His leg began to swell up and then turned reddish purple. At first, *Otoosan* called a family practitioner for help. He was not a qualified doctor, as I recall; he tried herbal ointments to cure the infection. I saw my parents pick holly leaves, scorch them over the stove, grind them up together with a liquid into a salve, and apply them to Joe's wound. They applied this holistic medicine for days to remove the infection. It did not work. The injury led to blood poisoning, and the poison settled down in his ankle. *Otoosan* finally took Joe to the hospital for help. The surgeon had to remove part of his ankle and was able to stem the infection. For some months, a schoolteacher was very kind to take Joe into her home until he could recuperate enough from his surgery. During his recuperation, she tutored him with his school studies so that he would not miss out in his schooling. Even after he returned home, it took a long time for Joe to amble around in crutches.

One day Joe let Frank and me try out his crutches. The first time, I felt silly and awkward trying to walk with one foot immobile and hopping along with the crutches under my arms. I almost stumbled. However, Joe could really zip along with them.

Several years later, after Joe had fully recovered, he built a clubhouse behind the house for a shop and a place to sleep. Frank and I still slept on the floor, while Joe's bed was empty. Then, my parents also slept on the floor with futons in the living room. This was nothing extraordinary for them because that is how they slept back in Japan. All of the bedding and the rolled-up mattress were placed in one corner of our bedroom. I usually had the chore of wrestling with the mattress, carrying it out of the corner, unrolling it for sleeping and, in the morning, jostling Frank out of bed and returning the rolled-up mattress back to the corner.

One of the big surprises I had in this house was meeting my older sister. I had gone through twelve or more years of my life not knowing I had an older sister. When my sister Mabel (her given name was Shizuko) was seven years old, my parents sent her to Japan to live with my mother's brother in Tokyo. It was my parent's wish to raise her to know traditional Japanese customs. Her return must have been a shock to my younger sister Kaz who had to give up the rights to her bedroom. My world too clashed with her world one day because she wanted me to do something and I balked. I saw the steam rising as she quickly went to *Okaasan* to let her know of *otooto's* (younger brother's) insolence. Later that day, *Okaasan* came to me and said that my sister was upset over me, but she did not scold me. She simply said, "*Neisan dakara yoku kikinasai*, she's your older sister so listen nicely to what she has to say." To this day, I cannot remember what the huff was all about; so much for assertiveness. After the encounter, I walked through life very gingerly with my older sister.

I always wondered why *Okaasan* would even think of sending her daughter off to Japan. Maybe it was the hard life of farming that she believed that she would be better off living with her brother in Tokyo. He was, after all, a prosperous stockbroker. I had no clue, only a question in my mind. Later, I chauffeured Mabel to her special school sessions to learn English and Home Economics. Soon on the weekends, she would share the kitchen with mother to try out her newly learned recipes. Instead of rice and *okazu,* it was the first time that I had macaroni and cheese casserole for dinner.

The green house on 25th street had one bedroom, small kitchen, bathroom, and a small porch. When I first saw it, the floor was in bad shape with rotten wood and the inside badly needed painting. The front door was on 25th street and it butted next to the sidewalk. At first, father used it for storage and later my parents moved into it together with my older sister Mabel. I am sure Kaz was relieved with the move since she had her bedroom back. Later, my parents following the traditional Japanese custom engaged a *baishakunin,* intermediary to find a suitable groom for Mabel. Soon, Mabel married a Japanese national who was a salesman for a Japanese dry goods store. Now it became clear why my parents sent Mabel Japan. Yet I never saw a closer daughter and mother relationship as I had seen between *Okaasan* and Kaz.

The property must have been out in the countryside because there was an outhouse next to the house. *Otoosan* removed and covered the place over. There were two apricot trees on the lot, but no one dined on them. One was huge because it was growing next to the old outhouse spot. I never ate apricots from that tree.

Mabel, Frank Tad, Kaz

Go reach for the stars
Take a spin on the airplane
What dreams are made of

Up, up into the Sky

Wroom! Wroom! "Frank, did you hear that sound?" I asked my brother, Frank. "Where did it come from?"

"I think the noise is from across the street!" said Frank.

"Come on Frank; let's go see what's happening over there."

We stopped what we were doing and ran to the front of our family nursery and looked.

"Wow! Look at that biplane! It's revving up its motor. I wonder if it's going to take off."

"Nah, the plane is just taxiing around the field," answered Frank.

"Look, it's going back to that building. Come on Frank, let's go across the street and see what's happening over there." I said excitedly.

I never imagined that the big empty field full of overgrown weeds we saw every day was an airfield. We climbed through the fence and started towards the buildings. It was farther away than we expected. We circled around several large buildings when we saw one that had a big sliding door open. Frank stuck his head in the big doorway. The inside looked like a huge warehouse. Several men were at their worktables working on plane parts. Someone noticed us and said, "Hi, do you want to look around?" Without hesitation, we climbed up into the building. Frank was wide-eyed and excited about everything the man showed us but I was too overwhelmed with the whole affair to understand what the person was showing us. Finally, when the man finished the tour, he said, " Wait here a moment." He went back to a workbench and busily cut and hammered something together. He returned and said to Frank, "This is for you." It was a wooden airplane. From that moment on, Frank was hooked on airplanes.

Frank was never enthusiastic about schoolwork, but his interest in airplanes was different. One day, Frank came home with a model airplane kit and an armful of balsa wood. I watched him while he carefully unpacked the kit and began making a model airplane. From that day on, the smell of banana oil permeated the bedroom. Like a little church mouse, I watched Frank work on his model airplane. The parts for the model were printed on the sheets of balsa wood. Each part had to be carefully cut with razor blades and sanded down. Sometimes Frank had to make his own parts from the schematic since the balsa was so fragile it would break easily. After several weeks, he was ready to glue the tissue paper onto the airplane skeleton. I was overjoyed when he asked me to help him. For the last stage, airplane dope and/or banana oil must be applied to strengthen and keep the tissue paper taut. As soon as the oil dried, Frank carefully carried his plane outside. The power for the airplane was supplied by winding the propeller that was tied to a large rubber band placed within the fuselage. Frank carefully proceeded to wind the prop, then lifted the plane above his head, and gently pushed it off into the blue yonder! It was a beautiful sight to see but, as soon as the rubber band unwound, the plane started to descend. For a moment, it was gliding downward nicely. Oops! It suddenly came down with a thud! I looked at the broken pieces and turned towards Frank to see his reaction. He just picked up the pieces and returned home to repair the damages. Occasionally, he was lucky and the plane would land without crashing. However, this was only a toy.

Lady on the Bridge

One day, we were at the Ocean Park Pier, an amusement park on a pier near Santa Monica. Among the many interesting things to see and do, you could pilot an airplane. Of course, you couldn't fly, but it was powered with a motor and allowed the pilot to maneuver the plane as if it were in flight. "Mother, can I ride that airplane?" pleaded Frank. At first, mother hesitated but she gave the quarter to Frank for the ride. The attendant helped him into the plane and gave him some instructions. At first, he powered up and tried a few maneuvers and suddenly a blast of air hit us as he let the motor go full bore. The plane rose up and he began banking right, then left, nose up and nose down. He was enjoying every minute of his quarter's worth of airplane ride. Frank would have flown off into the sunset, but the plane was bolted down. He had a magic glow on his face when he stepped out of the cockpit for he was an ace pilot!

Sounds bring thoughts of yore
Clickity clack of skateboards
Scoots through memories

Scooting around

It is tough growing up in the Depression years. That is, if you are not the first born male in the Japanese family. It's not that my brother Frank and I complained, "*Monku yuuna*, don't complain," as father would say, but we had to make many of our own playthings. I remember my brother Frank and I made our scooters from my big brother Joe's discarded skate wheels and lumber we found in the yard. Since *Otoosan* was busy setting up his nursery (plants) in Santa Monica, we borrowed Dad's tools, nails, and searched around for some boards for our project. Frank helped me saw the two-by fours for the L-shaped frame and a small stick for a handle. Pounding the nails was hard for me because the hammer was so heavy for a five year old. Most of the time, I used both hands to lift the hammer to pound. It was maddening because the nails wouldn't go straight in. Trying to pull out the bent nails was even harder. Finally, I would give up and pound the bent nails with all my might, in frustration, into the wood instead of trying to yank them out.

One Saturday, after we finished making our scooters, Frank and I hopped on our grand creations and headed from home in Sawtelle to *Otoosan's* nursery in Santa Monica. We traveled along the sidewalks on Sawtelle Blvd northward to Santa Monica Blvd. I can still hear the clicking sound of the skate wheels as they ran over the sidewalk cracks. I was excited and proud of my scooter as I pumped with my left foot to move it along. At every street, we would carry it to the next street's sidewalk and clickity clack our way until we reached Centinela Ave. We were careful to look both ways on Santa Monica Blvd and dash across the wide boulevard to the other side. Most of the houses were on the north side of Santa Monica Blvd with big empty lots on the south side. Going along for two blocks on Centinela Ave was tough because it was slightly uphill. Soon, as we reached Wilshire Blvd., we could zip down to 25th street to the nursery.

After the family moved to Santa Monica, I upgraded my scooter with a headlight in front. Actually, I took a coffee can, pounded it to the vertical board, and put a candle inside for a headlight. At the time, I thought the headlight was a neat idea even though I never rode the scooter at night. When I rode my scooter on 25th street, I ran into some trouble with some neighbors. A big bruiser of a fellow came dashing out of his house, cursing, and yelling at us to stop the noise. He didn't appreciate my scooter or the noise the metal skate wheels made rolling on the pavement. Luckily, he didn't attack us. It was then that Frank and I decided to give this great invention up and go on to bigger things.

Soap Box Derby was the craze around the 1930's. Frank and I decided we would try building one for ourselves. Again, we would scrounge around for the materials. We decided to take apart an old rusty red wagon for our wheels. We made our frames with two-by fours nailed cross pieces to hold our wheels in place except the front axle frame had to move or steer it. Since we had no great idea about a steering mechanism, we tied a rope to the crossbar of the front wheels. Stopping the car was another big problem for us. We could use our feet to stop the soapbox car, but our shoes would take a terrible beating. In fact, my parents couldn't afford to buy us new shoes all of the time because of the Depression. Sometimes, we would cut out cardboard inserts and stuff them into the shoes over the holes in the soles that would help save the socks we wore. Using our feet was simply ruled out. We decided to nail a board against the frame that we could pull on and let it scrape on the ground to slow down.

One day, I decided to test drive our new creation. Just north of Wilshire Blvd and near Centinela Ave., a new housing project was being developed. It was on a slight hill. I remember a water tower just above the project. I always wonder who was brave enough to climb up so high to maintain the water tower since I was scared of heights. I pulled my soapbox along Wilshire Blvd and up the street to the new houses. It seemed safe to try out the soapbox there since there was no traffic on the street. I readied my car at the top of the rise, sat down, held it steady with my feet, grabbed the ropes to steer it, and let go. Wow! It rolled down the incline faster and faster. For a moment I was elated. Then I realized if I didn't slow it down, I might end up on Wilshire Blvd. I grabbed the wooden stick for the brakes with my right hand. That caused an unbalance in my steering. The next moment I was ejected from the soapbox. It happened so fast that all I remember was my arm scrapping on the rocky pavement.

I saw my soapbox turned upside down. Besides a few bruises, I was bleeding near my elbow on the inside of my arm. Luckily, I didn't break any bones. I sat dazed for a moment, got up, turned the soapbox right side up, and dragged it home. When *Okaasan* saw my bleeding arm, she marched me into the house, cleaned the wound with peroxide, swabbed it with Mercurochrome and bandaged it. It seemed it took months for the wound to heal. Years later, when I look at the scar, a cold chill runs down my spine to remind me of that day on the soapbox. After that, I decided not to become a racecar driver.

No guarded moments
Dream with me of yesteryear
Nostalgia lives

Childhood Ties

It was inescapable, I was hooked for life after tasting vine ripened juicy red strawberries fresh from a strawberry farm. I had even picked them by myself. It happened one summer when Joe, Frank, and I were invited to stay for a few days at our parents' good friend, Mr. Nawa, who had a farm in Norwalk, California. Besides my Uncle's nursery in Glendale, California, the Nawas were the only other people that we visited and often stayed with for dinner. I had observed as a child that my parents' visits with them were unlike most social gatherings with other Japanese back home in Santa Monica. It was as if we were one big happy family. It was only later that I understood why. Mrs. Nawa had been *Okaasan's* schoolmate back in Japan in early 1900's before both of them got married and immigrated to America. The two must have been very close, because when they were together, I could hear laughter in their voice and a smile on their faces as they talked animatedly. In the Nawa family, there were two boys and two girls. Jiro was the youngest son who was a year younger than I was, Stella was about my age, and Mary was a little older than Frank and like a big sister to me. Their eldest son, Jim, was a few years older than my brother Joe was, and the two of them spent most of the time together.

What I remembered most about visiting their farm was that their neighbors were so far away that I could hardly see any homes nearby. It was so different from where I lived on 25th Street in Santa Monica. While our home was no mansion, we lived within the city limits with all of the utilities. However, on their farm, I was surprised to see that they had to pump water from a well with a hand pump. For me, it looked like fun to pump the water until I found out that there was no hot water on a cold day. Another surprise was the weather worn two-seater outhouse that I tried to avoid using as much as possible. When we stayed for dinner, I noticed that cooking dinner wasn't easy for Mrs. Nawa. There were no knobs to turn on the gas and she had to light it with a match to cook. She had to start by burning wood in a cast iron kitchen stove, and she had to be attentive to control the temperature for cooking. These were the challenges of living on their farm.

I remember Jiro showing us his family farm that one day. They had a big chicken coop not only to raise chickens, but also to sell eggs for their income. It was the first time I had seen an incubator, and chicks cheeping while busily feeding on mash. There were so many chickens clucking and squawking that it was very distracting. I was thankful that we didn't raise chickens, for it seemed to be lot of work to feed and keep the place clean. Worse still, I had to keep my eyes wide open and watch carefully where I stepped because I wasn't accustomed to walking around in a chicken coop,

Near the chicken coop, an old weather worn barn housed farm implements for maintaining the farm. What caught my eye was an old tractor that looked like fun to sit on and ride, but Jiro motioned me to follow him. We walked by a big open space that had been cultivated to grow their vegetables. I remember the soil on their farm because many years later, I found it was nothing like the soil I had to deal with when I had my own home in Livermore and wanted to grow vegetables.

A handful of their soil crumbled easily in my hand. It was easy to work with when Jiro, Frank, and I played in the dirt to make roads and hills for our toy cars.

In that tilled area, Mr. Nawa grew a number of Japanese vegetables that I didn't see in our grocery stores back home: like Japanese radish (*daikon*) and taro potatoes (*sato-imo*). I've seen Japanese radishes that were as long as two feet. However, cooked *daikon* is not one of my favorite vegetables even though *Okaasan* cooked them often during the Depression years. What I liked best was grated *daikon*, flavored with soy sauce, and added to a serving of sashimi. I remember Okaasan often asked me to grate the radish, but she told me once not to grate it feeling "*iya, iya ni suttara karai yo*. (Don't grate it as if you hate to or it will be spicy hot)." Mother also cooked the *sato-imo*, but not with any other vegetables because it had a unique consistency: gooey when cooked. She cooked them with dried shrimp or shaved dried Bonito fish for flavor. When I was a youngster, I usually had the chore of shaving the dry Bonito flakes because they did not come in a convenient package. Dried Bonito has the same consistency of a hard piece of board like iron wood. It was hard to shave because it wasn't flat.

Mr. Nawa also made a living by selling his oranges from his orange orchard. Every year, he would give our family several gunnysacks full of oranges. The oranges didn't last too long, because since the tree ripened oranges were so sweet, they would disappear quickly. His orange orchard was very special, because *Okaasan* once said that my father had helped Mr. Nawa start his orange orchard by grafting orange tree buds on citrus rootstalks.

On this day, Jiro pointed to their neighbor's land where we saw a strawberry patch. The farmer was driving his tractor tending to his crop, and was working on the last rows as he was heading away from us. Jiro said, "Let's sneak over there an pick a few strawberries before he turns around and comes back." I was anxious and willing. Without waiting, the three of us were hunched down close to the ground trying to look inconspicuous. We watched the farmer move further and further out of sight. The three of us were ready to dash towards a strawberry patch when Jiro said, "Come on let's go! He's way down there. He can't see us."

We rushed and picked a handful of ripe strawberries while hoping the farmer wouldn't see us. We dashed quickly back to Nawa's orange orchard, hid behind a tree, and started eating those sweet delicious ill-gotten strawberries. Each one was yummy. Strawberries had become my favorite fruit. I often wondered if it happened because of the excitement of snitching them from the farmer.

Meanwhile, Joe would tag along with Jim who was an adventurous individual. Jim had a Ford hard top coupe in which, we heard, he and Joe had taken a rip roaring ride across a big plot of land in front of their house. It was a bumpy ride as Jim sped across the field. Suddenly Jim hit a big ditch in the field and the car flew up and landed unceremoniously upside down. When the family heard the noise, they rushed out to see what had happened. Luckily, they only had a few bruises, but they both seemed to laugh off their risky car ride. One evening, Jim also took us on a ride through the open field to scare jackrabbits out of their burrows. Another time, while Joe drove the car, Jim would ride on the fender and take pot shots with his twenty-two rifle at the scared rabbits. I was always impressed with Jim's cavalier attitude. One year, when I was looking around the farm, I noticed a duck that was fenced in a small yard just outside the living room. It looked so lonesome by itself, I had to go into the yard and visit it. I would go "quack, quacking" like a duck just to tease it. The duck responded and kept quacking as it heard my call. Occasionally I did get to pet the duck. In addition, every time our family visited the Nawas, I would be sure to play with the duck. I had become attached to it because I never had a pet. Then one day on our visit, I didn't see my pet duck. I just thought the Nawas had released it outside rather than keep it penned up. Later that day, I was in for the surprise of my life. At dinnertime, Mrs. Nawa brought out the cooked meat from her oven. It was roasted nice and golden brown and set on the table. My mouth opened and eyes lit up. It was our pet duck! All of us, who had played with the duck, looked at each other and we all refused to have a serving of our pet. However, the adults didn't seem to mind and had a nice duck dinner. Later, every time I read Popeye in the Santa Monica Outlook newspaper's Sunday comic strip, I was always reminded of that day, for Wimpy would say, "Popeye! Let's have a duck dinner. You bring the duck!

Our visits continued until that fateful date December 7, 1941. Each family had their miseries to deal with, that consequently led to our ties being lost. I did not know what an awful fate the Nawas faced until after the war. Even when I saw Stella, Jiro, and Mary in Minneapolis, Minnesota, they never talked about what happened after that fateful day. They too were the "Silent Americans."

Ignorance is blind
Imbued in the human mind
Its voice mired in slime

Hatred's Ugly Head

This was my first day at McKinley Grammar School in Santa Monica. I had just taken one step onto the schoolyard.

"Hey look! There's a new kid. He's a funny looking Jap kid!" yelled a few school chums.

"Jap, Jap! Ha, ha, slant eyed Jap! Whatcha doing here? Go back where you come from!"

Nothing like this happened to me while I attended the grammar school at Sawtelle. I knew "Jap" was a mean spirited word against me even though I thought I was just like anyone else. That word and the taunting was enough to spur me into action! I charged at him, arms flaying - the fight was on. Quickly a crowd gathered, but, to the side, I saw my brother Frank watching to see that no one else would decide to pile on me.

I had the better of the tormenter. I was on top of him ready to hit him.

The crowd was yelling, "Fight, fight."

The noise of the crowd alerted the principal of the fight. Soon the principal rushed out, grabbed us, and marched us into his office.

"All right, why are you two fighting? Don't you know that fighting isn't allowed on the school ground?" the principal talked to us in a hard stern raised voice.

He looked at me and asked, "All right, why did you fight this morning?"

"He called me a Jap. That made me mad 'cause I don't like to be called that," I answered.

He looked at the kid and asked, "Did he call you a name first? Do you know what it means to call someone a Jap?"

"No," the blond haired, blue-eye boy, with tears in his eyes, said, "My friends pointed out the new guy as a Jap. So I repeated it."

"Jap is a mean word to call him by. We do not tolerate name-calling or fighting. Do not use that word again. Do you understand?" the principal said to the kid. "Now, shake hands and get along with each other."

When we moved to Santa Monica, the school year was already in session. It is confusing and scary to enter a classroom where you are the new kid. That was not the only surprise I was in for that day. The teacher introduced me as the new student in her class, but I did not last very long in her class. The teacher took me aside during the first week and began testing me to see if I belonged in her grade level. At the end she said, "I want you to go to this classroom and give the teacher this note." I had advanced to the second half of the first grade. The next teacher also tested me once more and decided I did not belong in her class either and sent me to another class. I skipped the first grade during my first three weeks in school.

Otoosan and Okaasan always encouraged us to study hard and to respect the teacher. They always reminded us, "They can take everything away from you but they can't take away what is in your head." I had no problem studying for school and behaving in class. Sometimes school was fun because we played baseball in class to learn arithmetic. The teacher chose two teams and marked off three bases. The teacher was the pitcher with flash cards on arithmetic. If you missed, you would go to the end of the line. Otherwise, you advanced around bases. The side changed when one team missed three problems. The team scored when a player advanced all the way around. I usually got on base because I liked math.

The most boring class was penmanship. Day after day, making those loops and slanting the letters to the right just was not fun. Somehow my dot for the "i" never seemed to be on target. Crossing the tee's just right seems such a waste of time. Some kids were very good at writing longhand. Others were painstakingly slow as they rounded those loops. I did try and I thought my writing was tolerable but I am glad the teacher did not grade us on our effort. I attribute this disappointment in penmanship to my stubby fingers.

Schooling went fine until I started fourth grade. To my surprise, Frank was at the same grade because his teacher wanted him to repeat the fourth grade. I remember seeing my parents disappointed when they received the note from the teacher, but they never admonished him. There were never any conflicts in our schooling because the school administrators made sure that we never shared any class together. No one made an issue about Frank and me being in the same grade, nor did I. He was my brother and I always looked up to him. He was always good to me.

It was in the fifth grade in my social studies class when a blond haired kid began to taunt me and dared me to fight him. I tried to ignore him. My parents never allowed my misbehavior in school. No sooner had I stepped outside then the kid began his bullying once more. He got hostile and called me a "Jap and a coward." The fight was on but the encounter was more about circling around each other for an opening to strike. School kids love a fight and began their usual chant, "Fight, fight" to roiled the water. More kids gathered, but I noticed once again, Frank was there. He looked around to make sure others did not gang up on me. He was truly my "*Niisan*, big brother."

In addition, once again, I met the principal.

Years have passed and I have forgotten the names, the faces are just shadows, but an echo reverberates, for hatred and jealousy never seems to go away.

Sun up to sundown
Mother's work is never done
Yet, O-somatsu (humble)

Worlds Apart

If the hostess said, "Please, won't you please dine on this ill-prepared food," how would you react if you knew how carefully the hostess had prepared a sumptuous meal for you.

While I was growing up, my parents instilled in me their customs through our daily living. Their world was Japanese: A life of humility that allowed them to survive in their hostile environment. While I could hold conversations or understand what was expected of me, I could not write nor read my parents' language. I often looked at the Rafu-Shimpo (Japanese Daily Newspaper) and glanced at the magazine they read, but I could not figure out any of the words on the pages. Everything looked like chicken scratches. It baffled me as well as intrigued me. Fortunately, my father and other *Issei* worked hard and donated money to establish a Japanese school in Santa Monica. I was a teenager when I attended my first Japanese class. As soon as my junior high school classes were over, I rushed to the Japanese school that was on 16th street near the Woodlawn Cemetery. I went to class every school day and on Saturdays.

The school building was a tall dark brown weatherworn wooden building that looked like a building for holding various performances because there was a stage in front of a huge high ceiling room. There were large tall windows on both sides of the building with the front of the building facing 15th street. The Japanese teacher's residence was behind the stage: a kitchen and a small room converted into a bedroom. When I first saw the rest rooms, I could not believe what I saw. They were two large outhouses but modernized later. When I first entered the school, I saw the familiar wooden desk with inkwells, book compartment, and slick wooden seat, ganged together with two or more similar desks placed in this big space.

It was a one-classroom school containing pupils of varying aptitudes. There was absolutely no fooling around in this classroom. I know because once when I acted silly, and the teacher walked over to me and slapped me across the ears. That knocked the silliness out of me forever. The Japanese regard the teacher, Sensei, highly. He is a god in this realm.

I found learning Japanese to be difficult because the written language incorporates archaic Chinese characters that have similar or equivalent meanings along with Japanese scripts derived from the Chinese characters. I have since learned that the Japanese had no written language in its early history; the Japanese imported and adapted the Chinese writing into their language. I found that learning to read the Chinese characters or find their meaning requires counting the number of strokes and looking up the word based on the count or by knowing the basic root in the characters and counting further strokes. It was a slow and painstaking process, tenderly thumbing through the pages of a dictionary.

In class, a student is required to stand at attention, hold the textbook with arms extended, and read aloud. At home, I practiced reading my homework by rising before sunrise, going out to the far corner of the nursery, with arms extended, and reading and rereading my lesson. Learning Japanese was a challenge, and I intended to meet it. When I woke up early, my parents were already up and busily starting the day's chores.

I am sure *Okaasan* saw me rise before the dawn and go outside to the far corner of the nursery with my Japanese textbook in hand. When I finished practicing, mother had prepared breakfast and was anxious to send us off to school. I can still hear her say, "*Osoku naru yo. Hayaku shinasai.* (You will be late. Hurry up.)" She had a smock on over her pretty dress, hair tied in a bun, and just waiting to put on her wide brim hat to start the day outside. Her day was never over. I never saw her standing idly by. When a customer entered the yard, she quickly greeted the person with a smile. With her limited English, she amazed me with what she accomplished. If a customer came in for a dozen plants, the person more than likely left with an extra dozen plants. Sometimes there were items that were more than she could carry and needed help. I know that the long day and the hard work took its toll on many occasions.

I remember one day after supper was finished, I saw *Okaasan* sitting on a chair, reaching with both her arms up to her shoulder trying to knead her tired and weary muscles. I asked that day if I could help her. *Okaasan* hesitated for a moment but she let me help her tend her weary muscles. When I put my hands on her shoulder muscles, they were as tight as an over wound watch spring. I carefully and gently massaged her muscles until they finally relaxed and loosened. Soon she said, "*Yoroshi,* fine." After that day, I made sure to ask her if she needed my help for I knew how hard *Okaasan* toiled. Yet, I never heard her complain.

All of us helped doing some of the housework. Saturday was laundry day. Mother's backbreaking job of leaning over the tub and scrubbing clothes using the old scrub board and wringing the wet clothes by hand was over because *Otoosan* had purchased a Maytag washing machine. However, washing clothes still took a lot of effort. First, we rolled the washing machine from the porch into bathroom, filled the tub with dirty laundry, added the hot water and soap, and started the washing. Nothing was automatic. The washer would bounce around as its clothes were agitated back and forth in the tub. And the noise ... When the wash cycle was over, you ran the soggy clothes through a wringer, dumped the sudsy water, reloaded wet clothes for rinsing the laundry, filled the tub with clean hot water, started wash cycle, and wrung clothes after the wash cycle. One day, when Frank was feeding wash through the wringer, he forgot to let go of the wet clothes. My eldest brother Joe moved quickly, hit the emergency release mechanism hard. He had saved the day; otherwise, Frank would have ended up in the hospital with a crushed arm. Most of the time we chose to rinse our clothes in the bathtub instead of cycling them through the washing machine. We put bluing in the wash cycle to make our white clothes look white. Except, when I looked at my hands, they were just as white but shriveled because they were forever in contact with water. Finally, we moved the washing machine out of the way and mopped the floor!

Before Okaasan went outside, she washed rice for our dinner. One day, she asked me if I would wash the rice in the morning for her. Very patiently, she taught me the following ritual: You wash the rice carefully several times until the rinse water is clear. Drain enough water and set the height of the remaining water by placing your hand flat on top and let it stand almost on top of the back of your hand. Sometimes, when I rushed the last step everyone grumbled because the hot rice was too tough. It was just as bad when I added too much water for soaking because the cooked rice turns into *okayu* (mushy).

When the rice was cooked and the main course prepared, everyone sat down to be served by mother. There was a certain pecking order at the table. Father was first to be served, then the eldest son, next the rest of the sons, and then the daughters in the order of age. Mother of course was the last one to sit down. Without exception, we all said "*itadakimasu,*" an expression of gratitude before meals, and began with the dinner. The main fare was the *okazu* that consisted of meat and vegetables. Dinner always ended with "*gochisoosama*," expression for thanks for the meal. No one left the table until *Otoosan* left first.

While we followed our parent's custom, dinner at home was, nevertheless, informal. Mother would always ask if we wanted extra bowls of rice, and we could eat *takuan* (pickled radish) or other *tsukemono* (pickled vegetables) on the side. *Chazuke*, tea poured over the rice, was always everyone's favorite. Extra servings were acceptable, but the rule was "waste not, want not!" If we left rice in our rice bowl, our parents would say, "Think of all of the hungry people in China!" I thought my parents were the only ones that said that about leaving food on the plate, but later my wife, Yo, said that her parents said the same thing. Looking back at the incident, I realize now that my parents left Japan when the country was going through economic hard times and it was the 1930s when the United States was in the depression years. Thus, wasting food was a cardinal sin. No harsh words were said to admonish us: only words that expressed "*haji*" (shame) for our action.

When mother served the meal, father, of course, served first and received the best portion. Then, "*Chonan*" received the same honor as father. Frank and I, of course made no issue about the servings since that was the way in the Japanese family. However, we could not, however, help but notice that Joe, the *Chonan* did not eat his cooked celery and pushed it aside on his plate. When Frank and I grumbled about why it was ok for him to be choosey, mother said, "*Niisan dakara*" (Because he is your big brother**).**

Shogatsu (New Year) is one of the most important holidays for Japanese as it is for most Asians. Preparation for this celebration begins before the end of December. The whole family would be busy cleaning up the yard and the house, and making sure that we started the New Year with clean clothes since everyone is supposed to start the New Year fresh without left over debts or duties. It was a busy time for mother who had to prepare all of the food that must last for at least three days. For the rest of us, the preparation for New Year meant that we would be going to "Little Tokyo," located in downtown Los Angeles, to purchase all of the ethnic foods. While mother was shopping, dad would take us to a café nearby and treat us to pie. What a terrible dilemma when you must choose between Boston cream pie, apple pie, cherry pie, etc., and, of course, there was my favorite: lemon meringue pie. I dared not choose apple pie because that was what my father would bake on very rare occasions, especially when it was a rainy day. That would be about the only time *Otoosan* would ever dare to step into the kitchen.

Meanwhile, mother would be busy preparing and cooking all of the food for New Year that must last for several days without refrigeration and without spoiling. I can still taste the rice vinegar and a touch of sugar mixed into the cooked rice for the *maki-sushi* that helped preserve it for several days. *Okaasan* not only prepared the food for the family but also she had to serve friends who visited on New Year's Day. I can still visualize and imagine all of the delicious food prepared by mother. If I timed it right, mother would let me have the end pieces she had just cut from her *maki sushi* roll. Although ingredients stuffed inside the *sushi* might vary, my favorite was *maki sushi* with *unagi* (broiled eel) as the main ingredient. On New Year's morning, breakfast started with *ozouni*, a kind of stew containing vegetables, meat, and the main ingredient, *mochi*. *Mochi* is a rice cake made from special rice that is much stickier than the traditional short-grained Japanese rice. Mochi results from pounding the cooked rice until it is of even consistency. There is a romantic fairy tale about a rabbit, the moon, and *mochi*. If you look at the face of the full moon during harvest time, you can see a rabbit pounding mochi in a mortar. In many Japanese communities, *Issei* would get together just before New Years to make mochi for all of the members of the group. The ritual, *mochi tsuki* is always a happy festive time. While men pound the rice into mochi, the women form rice cakes into round or square shapes. On a large table covered with powdered rice, the women quickly knead the *mochi* into thin sheets, snip a small piece of mochi and make delicious pastry by filling it with various flavorful ingredients. As a youngster, I observed that my parents would always take two round rice cakes of different sizes, stack them on a white paper, put a *mikan* or tangerine on top, and place them on the mantel in front of a miniature shrine. I thought it was just a New Year's decoration, but I was wrong! The *mochi* with the *mikan*, called *kagami mochi* was an offering to our ancestors. The shrine was a miniature Shinto shrine.

New Year's Day was very busy for *Okaasan* since she had to entertain friends that came to extend a New Year's greeting to the family. The table setting was always a work of art. Mother arranged the New Year's food around a centerpiece that was either a cooked *Tai* (Carp) or an *Ebi* (lobster). When a guest arrived, *Okaasan* would always say, "*O-somatsu keredo, doozo meshiagarinasai*, (It is ill-prepared, but please eat this.) It was an apology about the food she was about to serve her guest. "*Okaasan*, why do you apologize to your guest when I saw you work so hard to make the food taste good and look so appealing?" I asked her. She replied, "That is how I was brought up to say when I serve or give something." It was always upsetting to hear her say *o-somatsu* to the guest since she had gone through so much work. However, later, I noticed that my mother-in-law also made the same sort of apology about the food she was serving. The word my mother said was "*o-somatsu*" to describe the food she was offering. The word *somatsu* means humble or crude. The "*o*" is an honorific that added to the word to show respect to the person you are addressing. This was not the only occasion that Japanese women uttered such words. Even when giving a gift, this apologetic and humbling form of word is used. I noticed too, when *Issei* give something from the garden, they always pick the finest and best to share with their friends or neighbors and apologize at the same time. It is their way of saying thanks for everything: no handshake or overt show of thanks in their world.

It was many years later when my wife and I exchanged gifts with our close family and encountered a peculiar ritual during our joyous Christmas Holidays. Every Christmas, we would shop for gifts for the children. Like most families, we had to buy gifts within our budget. Trying to decide what to buy each child was always a big chore for this happy holiday season since we were not in daily contact with the families.

The scene would usually end up:

"What do you think about this dress?" my wife would ask.

"It's pretty but I don't know what color she likes," I would answer.

"Well, it's your niece!" would be her retort.

"Ok, let's buy it," I would acquiesce.

Later, we would notice that the niece never wore the dress. We had politely asked her, "Didn't you like the pretty dress we sent you?"

She would look at us and with a huff she said, "My mother buys my clothes at I Magnin (exclusive fashion store San Francisco, Ca). I never wear clothes from J. C. Penney!"

Immediately afterwards, I wrote to everyone saying that this would be our last Christmas to send gifts since we were having a hard time finding the right gift to please everyone. I added that I hoped the others would understand to do the same. The replies were unanimous, with a sigh of relief, and in favor of just sending Christmas Greetings.

Enough for humility, we are worlds apart.

Befuddled sometimes
At odds with my parent's world
Did I miss something?

A Hug Would Do

This could be my day of fame. I had always thought someday I could be a great actor since I was born near the MGM Studios in Culver City. Today was the end of our Japanese school year when our *Sensei* (teacher) planned a program for the parents to see how well we were doing in school. Everyone had some part to play in the night's performance. I was to play the part of a comedian. Tonight, my knees seemed wobbly as I climbed up to the stage since I had never performed in front of a large crowd. As soon as I said the first two words, I was in complete control and acted out my role of a comedian. My eyes swept over the audience for some reaction to my performance. I was happy to hear polite chuckles here and there, as they followed the act. What a relief that the audience did not hiss me off the stage. I was, however, disappointed at the end. There were no rousing cheers when I finished.

The last item of the program was the achievement awards. I waited anxiously as the Sensei called out the names. Finally, when I heard my name, I was flabbergasted. *Sensei* awarded me the title, *Yuutousei*, honor student. Out of the corner of my eyes, I looked towards my parents for any reaction – a slight smile, maybe. I was puzzled, no hurrahs. Even after I joined the family, my parents gave not one word of praise or congratulation: a handshake, pat on the back, or a hug. I remember in one of the stories I read in my Japanese text "Parents' love is higher than the highest mountain and deeper than the deepest ocean." Thus, I wondered if my parents were without any feelings. However, I have since learned that, in the Japanese culture, stemming from the feudal period, a show of emotion exposes one's weakness or vulnerability to others. Touchy feely" is not part of their culture. Therefore, it is *Shikataganai*, tough luck in my world.

Every December, our family went shopping at Little Tokyo in Los Angeles for our yearly *Shogatsu,* New Year food supplies. I noticed on several of our shopping trips to "Little Tokyo" a ritual that completely baffled me. This year was no exception. The whole scene reminded me of a documentary film about mating rituals of various animals. In particular, there was a scene where two large birds kept bobbing up and down and prancing around each other. The action I saw was as follows: Two women are across the street from each other and they notice that they know each other. The ritual begins. One or the other stops and makes a bow and then continues walking while still bowing every so often. Meanwhile the other person begins the same ritual while she continues her way. Who starts the ritual and who ends the ritual is beyond my comprehension. Can you imagine the scene if there are more than two people meeting in town at the same moment? The bowing by the *Issei* represents humility. That is, it is a sign of respect for the other person by humbling oneself by bowing. I guess the lower the bow, the greater the humility!

"*Okaasan*, why didn't you just wave your hand instead of bowing so many times? I asked.

She answered, "No, that won't do because you wave your hand to beckon the person or to gesture to indicate 'no.'" Then she proceeded to show me two different hand motions. "Now you see, the first bow was for greeting and the last was to say goodbye!"

I was going to ask her why they bowed more than twice and why they did not actually look directly at each other, but I thought I had better not ask.

This year, we were to meet her at a drug store near the market after she finished her New Years shopping for supplies. I saw her busy selecting some magazines for herself when she turned her eyes to an item in the display case. She motioned to the sales clerk and appeared to be dickering about the price. I tried not to stare, but I noticed that *Okaasan* had won the bargaining as the clerk carefully wrapped the item for her.

When we returned home, she surprised me with the item she purchased at the drug store. She said, "This is for you for your good work at school."

"Arigatoo, Okaasan (Thank you, mother)," I replied.

When I opened the package, I saw a bronze statuette of Ninomiya Kinjiro. I was astonished and thankful, but why the bronze statue? I knew he was a famous person in Japan because I read about his life story in my Japanese textbook. In his youth, he carried a bundle of firewood lashed to his back as he gathered firewood traveling throughout the countryside. By selling the firewood, he helped his family survive through the hard times of the Edo era. As he walked through the countryside, he would called out, *"Takagi wa naika? Takagi wa naika?"* (Do you have any firewood?). However, most important, it is the book he reads as he gathers firewood that shows him to be a dedicated self-educated man who never had the opportunity to go to school. He was born in a poor peasant family during Japan's feudal era, and he exemplifies the virtues of self-education, hard work, and dedication. Later, he became a successful farmer, philosopher, and went on to help revitalize the Japanese economy from the disastrous feudal period.

However, while I appreciated the statuette, I thought, I would have gladly accepted a pen and pencil set or a watch instead. Yet, Ninomiya Kinjiro must have been a great influence on mother's life and I see that this statuette is something very personal to her. Still, I am puzzled about my parent's custom when just a hug would do.

Once a grand old house
Time sheds the grandeur away
Like a molting bird

Old Green House (Wilshire Blvd and 26th street)

On a busy street
A forest green house stands
A dusty shadow of the past
Shedding its green
Like a molting bird
Two Italian cypresses standing proud
Guard the front stairway

Listen closely you can hear
Sounds of bygone days
Two lovely ladies on a carriage
Holding colorful lace parasols
Stop to visit this fine day
Sound of merriment is in the air
'Tis a tea party under way

Through the double oak door
Hostess greets them in
A circular staircase just ahead
In the parlor to the right
Young ladies sipping tea
White laced curtains
Accent the elegant decor

'Tis a busy night this very day
In leathered captain's chair
Whiffs of cigars fill the air
Six gentlemen talk intently
Three smoke rings waft upward
Gentlemen, a booming voice is heard
It's taxes that's killing us

Look around this land once more
Marching horde of stucco houses
Invade this bountiful avocado land
From this balcony view
Sea of red helmet roofs spread below

Lady on the Bridge

Cost of business just too high
Unload this land or die

Time takes its toll
Disorder is now supreme
Stately trees thirsting for care
Window shades all but gone
Delicate laces tattered and torn
Chipping paint belies its grandeur
Two green spires stand remnants of splendor

Frozen images
Cool facts of the past thawing
I Remember when

Remember When

When I was a youngster, I used to hear clinking milk bottles whenever our milkman made deliveries to our house. He parked his white truck in the alley that ran through my father's nursery. I was puzzled when I first saw the truck because it had no doors. "Isn't the driver scared that he might fall out?" I thought. I guess he never did fall out. He wore a white uniform and he carried his milk bottles in a wire basket. The bottles were rectangular, not round. A paper top capped the bottles and covered with another paper cap. The deliveryman moved so fast the bottles would hit against each other making their own little music. Quickly, he was off to the next house.

Mother never ordered more than two bottles since we only had an icebox to keep things fresh and cold. It was about four feet high. It was not pretty although it was made of solid oak wood like a nice piece of furniture. Metal sheeting lining the inside made it look dingy. Nothing looked appetizing inside this box. A musty smell always seemed to permeate the inside. You could not place anything on top because there was a panel door you opened to store ice for cooling and a drainpipe running from the top to the bottom of the icebox into a metal drain pan. Every so often, there would be finger pointing when someone forgot to empty the drain pan.

"It was your turn," one of us would say out loud.

"I did it last week," was the reply.

Meanwhile, *Okaasan*, without yelling or screaming, always in her quiet way, would get out the mop and begin swabbing the floor while the rest of us looked sheepishly at our foolishness. Quickly we fumbled around to help her.

We always had to remember to leave the sign out for the iceman to deliver our ice. Once, I remember when all of the ice melted and we needed to purchase another big chunk of ice from the icehouse before our next delivery. I rode with my brother to a big warehouse where he backed the pickup against the loading dock. A man in the office took our order and motioned us to follow him into the cold, cavernous warehouse. Big blocks of ice were stacked from floor to ceiling. A man, a big burly man looked at the order, picked up a pair of ice tongs, and walked towards a huge chunk of ice. Ice chips were flying around everywhere when the man began chipping at a big chunk of ice. Then I heard a loud clunk! A big block of ice slid off with a bang. Next, with a pair ice tongs, he picked up the piece we needed with one hand and hauled it over to our pickup.

It was several months later when *Otoosan* brought home an all white General Electric (GE) refrigerator. It was shiny white inside and out and had no awkward latches for doors or galvanized walls inside. When I first saw it, I was curious about the gadget on top of the refrigerator because it looked like a gun turret on the USS Monitor during the Civil War. It was about eight inches high and cylindrical shaped. I learned later that it was the cooling coils. It was a marvelous appliance. Even the *sashimi* (raw fish) slices stayed fresh for *Okaasan's* special Thursday dinner. Best of all, there were no more sloppy floors and no finger pointing.

Santa Monica, the town I grew up in, is a coastal town where the weather is temperate all year long. However, in the summer time, I could hear the cheery music sound of tinkle bells from the Good Humor man as he rounded the corner from Arizona Avenue onto Twenty-Fifth Street where my father's nursery was located. The sound of the tinkle bells was my signal to run into the house and ask *Okaasan* for some money to buy ice cream. When I ran as fast as I could back out into the street, I saw other children in the neighborhood stopping the Good Humor man for goodies.

There were several kinds of ice cream and flavors to choose from that made it hard to decide what to buy. While the chocolate-coated ice cream bar was one of my favorites, there was the ice cream sandwich, the orange bar with ice cream wrapped inside, the Popsicle, and the Tutti-Frutti. There were others, of course, but these were the ones that I liked most of all. Once in awhile, a different ice cream vendor would show up that changed my choice of ice cream. He sold a chocolate coated bar called Box Car. The chocolate bar was bigger than the Good Humor's bars. It became my favorite because I could savor it longer. What a shame, I can no longer hear the tinkle bells of the Good Humor man to entice me in my town of Livermore.

I remember too that Thursday was a special day for our family. A Japanese man would drive up to our house in a truck to sell fresh fish. He filled the truck bed with crushed ice to keep the fish fresh. Fish of various kinds and other seafood were nestled in the ice. The kitchen was *Okaasan's* domain. She would come outside and choose what she wanted for the evening meal. Sometimes it would be *saba*, mackerel. Sometimes, she would select *ika*, squid. However, she would choose a fish for *sashimi,* raw fillet fish. Not any fish would do for *sashimi*. The selections were active fish like *kamas* (barracuda), *maguro*, (tuna), and *hamachi* (yellow-tailed mackerel). We flavored the *Sashimi* with lemon, ginger, or grated horseradish, and soy sauce. Cut lettuce or cucumbers garnished the *sashimi* dish. That delicious meal is outdated since our parents are gone.

As always, there is a certain ritual for a Japanese family when mother served dinner. *Otoosan*, father is first. Then the *Chonan*, first-born son was next. *Okaasan*, always serve the choicest portion of the *sashim*i to the first two. The rest of us came in the order of our age with the custom that women came last. Rice is the main staple with hot green tea at dinner. It was a special treat for all of us.

Yes, I remember when.

Nature's wonder world
Beauty that nourished the soul
Lasting memories

Outing

This morning, I saw mother was busy in the kitchen fussing around cooking rice and making teriyaki chicken. She then made *hinomaru nigirimeshi*, cooked rice kneaded into a ball with a pickled salty plum colored red inserted into the center. The white background and the red plum in the center made an appearance of the Japanese flag. It also meant that there might be a picnic today.

"*Okaasan* are we going somewhere today?" I asked.

"*Ojisan* (uncle) is coming over today because he wants to show your *niisan*, older brother *sakanatsuri* (fishing) at night with a *yari* (spear)," she answered. "All of you are invited on this outing."

When she mentioned fishing, I was embarrassed to tell her about the first day I went fishing from the Santa Monica pier with Frank. I still cannot forget my disaster at the pier. Frank gave me his old fishing pole since Joe gave him one of his split bamboo rods that he was no longer using. My brothers did not tell me how to fish, nor did I ask since it seemed easy enough to do. All I had to do was put juicy bait on the hook and cast the line into the water. What could be simpler? That day, Frank and I walked from our home on Twenty-Fifth Street down to the Santa Monica pier. Frank was anxious to try out his new pole. "Hey, I'm going on the other side of the pier and try my luck," he said. I decided to find a place further away. I found a nice spot where the pier jutted out towards one side. I carefully baited my line and was poised to cast my line. I pulled back my pole high behind me for a full swing as I have seen others do. With a mighty heave ho, I arched the pole forward and released the line. Oops, I forgot to hold tight onto the pole. I was too stunned to be embarrassed at that moment as I watched my fishing pole sink into the ocean. I looked around sheepishly hoping that nobody saw my stupid act. I went meekly to where my brother was fishing. Frank was having some luck as he showed me a perch and a scorpion he had caught. For a while, I was too embarrassed to tell him what I had done. "Where's the fishing pole I gave you?" he asked. "I ... lost it when I cast my line," I said. He looked at me with his mouth open, disbelieving my words, and asked, "Why didn't you jump in after the fishing pole?" I had no answer for him. I was afraid to give him the excuse that it was twelve feet down to the water from the pier and that the water was probably fifteen feet deep. Besides, I did not know how to swim. Sometimes when I think back, I can still see that fishing pole slowly sinking into the ocean. If I had taken Frank's advice, the Santa Monica Outlook newspaper would surely have had a headline such as, "Young Japanese boy drowns trying to retrieve fishing pole lost while casting." I would die with *haji*, shame.

However, about night fishing: who fishes at night? Do the fishes ever sleep? How can you possibly spear a fish? When I had been fishing on the Santa Monica Pier, I could not see any fishes in the ocean even in the daytime. I was puzzled. I also felt some trepidation.

Mother kept on preparing the meals for the outing, putting the items in various lacquer boxes, wrapping them in several *furoshikis (*wrapping cloths) and pulling the diagonal ends of the cloth and tying knots to hold the boxes together. All of mother's *furoshikis* had lovely flower patterns, and she was careful not to have a sloppy package. She paid special attention to how she tied *furoshiki* together. She cooked her food *teriyaki* style, soy sauce, sugar and ginger, so the meals would not spoil on our outing.

About noon, uncle arrived, and soon everyone was busy packing up the cars for the trip. I was sure we would head for the mountains to fish in the streams, but we were traveling along the coast highway. I recognized some landmarks like Long Beach, and San Pedro since I had been there when some family friends left for Japan from the pier at San Pedro. However, we continued further down the highway until we branched off onto a narrow road. Then, Uncle turned onto a dirt road that headed towards the ocean. We were in the middle of someone's tomato field when uncle stopped. "Don't step on the tomato plants," *Ojisan* said. As I got out of the car, I could hear the ocean as the waves splashed onto the beach. Yet I could not see the water. We were on a cliff with trees near the edge that hid the ocean, and I could smell the tomatoes ripening in the field nearby.

Uncle motioned us to start unloading our supplies. First, I wondered how we were going to get down to the beach. I walked over to the edge of the cliff and looked around. A narrow pathway snaked downward. I decided immediately that I had better stick with the small items; otherwise, I would be in trouble navigating down that narrow, crudely carved pathway. I grabbed some light items and followed the big people down the cliff. Sure enough, I almost lost it on a turn that doubled back down. It took over an hour walking up and down the tricky pathway with the supplies.

On a high point of the beach, Uncle had marked out a spot for our outing. All during this commotion, I had not noticed the firewood that Uncle and my brothers had gathered and placed near our site. I was puzzled that we needed so much firewood. Then Uncle said, "Grab a shovel and dig a big pit where I marked off for our bonfire." I looked at the space he had marked off. It was big, big enough to bury all of us. Since most of our food was cooked, I was again puzzled. Why did he mark off so large a space for our small crowd?

Uncle and my brothers dug a large pit and carefully placed the firewood in it for a bonfire. It was still early, so we had time to wander around the beach. I could see that the beach was not a place for swimming. Close by were tide pools and, about fifty yards out in the ocean, I saw the waves smashing against large rock formations that protruded in the ocean. With each wave rushing shoreward, a burst of white foam would shoot upward. When the water would recede, I looked for seashells or picked up a string of seaweed and tossed it back into the ocean.

Meanwhile, Uncle had started the bonfire while mother had started setting out the *gochisoo* (dinner). At first, I heard the crackle of the fire igniting the logs. Soon the logs burst into a huge bonfire. I was scared that someone would come down to the beach and tell us to put out the huge fire. However, luckily this was a deserted beach. It was big enough to be a beacon to ships lost at sea. I stood my distance as the flames licked hungrily at the offering of combustibles. However, Uncle did not use the fire for cooking. He just let it burn down until only hot coals remained.

Uncle said, "We are going cover up these embers with sand and sleep on top of it tonight. You will be nice and warn through the night." As the sun slowly set in the west, it was definitely much cooler. When we bedded down with a blanket over the covered embers, it was nice and cozy. In the darkness, I heard the waves dashing on the shore, the sound of the water as it rushed shoreward, and then the sound as it receded back into the ocean. I felt the cool salt air waft over my face. There was no sound of traffic or lights from any houses to mar this serene moment. It was a clear and beautiful evening. The stars sparkled and twinkled ever so brightly I could almost reach out and touch them. I roamed the skies like the Greek Gods and Goddesses. I could see to the north the constellations Ursa Major, Big Dipper, Ursa Minor, and the Small Dipper with Polaris, the North Star, and Cassiopeia, near the Milky Way. Looking south, Sagittarius, Scorpios, and Aquarius were so easy to see without the haze of the city air. Even the planets Venus and Mars were bright objects in the sky.

Soon I was fast asleep, but I heard Uncle and my brother getting up for their night fishing. Uncle was carrying a lantern and gunnysacks, while my brother carried a pole that looked like a fork with a long handle. I fell back to sleep as they wandered off to the north.

When I awoke at dawn, they were both back from the night fishing. "Did you catch any fish?" I asked.

Joe smilingly answered, "Yeah, we sure did. Uncle and I speared several fish, including a sea eel."

Frank, the sleepyhead, heard his brother and asked, "Where's the fish?"

"Uncle put what we caught in the gunnysack and dunked them in the water in the tide pool to keep them fresh," Joe responded.

"What happened? Your trousers are wet," I asked.

"Uncle said, '*Abunai*, watch out!'"

"But it was too late. The rocks are really slippery and I slipped into the tide pool," said Joe. "Luckily I only scraped my leg."

How were you able to spear any fish in the dark," I asked.

Joe said, "The tide was way down, and the lantern attracts the fish."

Joe put his right hand up high and continued to say, "You're poised with the spear up high and "Wham" you plunge the spear at any fish you see. It sounds easy but the fish can dart away quickly. One time I speared a *unagi*, eel. I am glad that Uncle removed it from the spear because it is very ugly looking. It looks like a snake."

Uncle came by later and said, "Would you like to help me catch some *tako*, octopus?"

I had no idea what was involved in this adventure and, without hesitating, I said, "Sure, Uncle, I'll go with you."

We walked to the tide pool and Uncle got down on his haunches, leaned over a big overhanging rock in the tide pool, slowly put his right arm down into the water, and bent his hand underneath the rock. A few minutes past and he brought up his arm. There on his hand was a small round head and eight legs circling up his arm. He got up, moved to his gunnysack, and quickly took his left hand pushed the octopus into the sack.

"See how easy it is to catch an octopus," he said with a smile. "Come over here and follow what I did."

He stepped aside and let me take over the spot on the big rock. It was tricky at first with the algae, barnacles, and colorful anemones sticking out, making my footing precarious. I could not see very much in the tide pool since the cliff had shaded it. I got on my knees and put my hands down into the water and under the rock. Very shortly, I felt something funny on my hands. "Is this it?" I wondered. I pulled my hands up and there staring at me was two beady eyes on a fist size head. The beast had is eight tentacles wrapped around my arms. It was the queerest feeling. I was sure the octopus was sucking the lifeblood out of me. In a flash, my left hand was desperately clawing at the tentacles to release them from my arm. I looked and motioned to Uncle to take the *tako*.

Uncle was grinning and said, "*Ha, omoshiroi, neh*? Yes, how amusing, isn't it?"

I have never tried catching *tako* since that first lesson.

It's a scary life
That evil lurks in men's mind
Shadows on my mind

Scary

At one point in my young life, I think I was even scared of my own shadow. At night, I used to listen to a program on our radio called "Witches Tales." The program always started with a squeaky door opening, followed by a scary high-pitched voice saying, "Ha Ha, this is the Witches' Tales. Listen if you dare." One scary story I remember most vividly was the "Mummy's Hand." I've since forgotten most of story, but I remember the mummy hand disappeared from the casket and wandered around opening creaky doors and doing evil deeds. The hand was looking to murder the people who had unearthed the mummy from its tomb. In the dark, I could almost sense a hand crawling about the room. Every creaky sound in the house made me shiver. It was scary.

Stories about dead people were always scary when I was a youngster. Somehow, someone always told tales about ghosts appearing in the cemetery. Lucky for me, no cemetery was close to our home. They said the ghost appeared as a hazy cloud and turned into a fiery ball and chased after them. They told the story with such conviction that I believed them. Now that I'm older, I know the story has some merit -- no, not the ghost but the fireball. It's gross to know that a decaying body produces methane, a flammable gas. Even a static spark could ignite it easily.

On Halloween nights when I was a kid, older people used to scare small kids with weird stories. One night, a big kid in our neighborhood told my brother and me not to go near an old run down house because the man living there was a nut. "If the nut sees you, he'll shout and run after you. He doesn't like kids," said the older kid. "He's a weird looking big guy." My brother and I were curious just to see the weird man, but we were scared enough that we never wandered near that house.

I can't recall anyone wearing Halloween costumes, but we did go trick-or-treating. Maybe an apple or two was all we received for our troubles. Of course, this was during the Great Depression years. Some kids in the neighborhood wanted us to follow them to do tricking instead of looking for goodies. However, we knew our parents wouldn't tolerate us doing stupid things, such as pounding on someone's front door and running away quickly, overturning garbage cans, knocking down fences, or marking windows and windshields with a bar of soap. We followed them, but we didn't see a single witch riding on a broomstick.

Every day I recall the words of the radio show, The Shadow, "Who knows what evil lurks in the minds of men. Only the Shadow knows." It's a scary world -- no longer is it only the Shadow knows?

Floating out in space
Mind in total confusion
Round and round I go

Free Fall

So it seemed when I was eleven
Three was cheaper than one
It happened one day when Daddy said,
All three of you come with me.
Off to the hospital we will go
Your brother needs a tonsillectomy.
Might as well make it three,
Cost no more the doctor said.

Cold and foreboding the hospital scene
Hallways stark and uninviting
Scent of disinfectant in the air
Three beds await us in the room
Change your clothes for these wraps
Our modesty is left on the chair.
Mighty cold in the back,
As air streams through the wrap.

One by one we leave the room
Wheeled into the operating room
Doctor and nurses by my side
Brilliant light focused on my face
A cold nose cone on my nostril
Count backwards from 100
Did say the nurse so sweetly
Then carefully pouring the ether fumes
It smelt like oranges and freezing cold
One hundred, ninety nine, ninety eight...

Round and round I seem to go
Down into a cylindrical tunnel
My god, I'm falling freefall
No words are heard in this flight
It looks so dark below
Still falling, round and …
Suddenly, I am nothing

When I awaken I'm too groggy

Lady on the Bridge

Taste of oranges still prevail
Fire burning in my throat
Swap the clothes for the wrap
Back at home I am fed
Jell-O, ice cream, and mush too
Soothes my throat for while
Doesn't make three-for-one too great

Innocents of youth
Struggles on Taiko bashi
Loss of Innocence

Loss of Innocence

"Pssst. You want to see something hot?" a classmate came up to me and asked.

He was a freckled faced kid named Red in one of my Lincoln Junior High School classes who always tried to act like a big shot. He waved a small black package in my face. While my eyes were darting back forth trying to focus on the small book, he said, "You gotta peek at this French bible." He finally stopped waving it in my face and opened the small book. It wasn't a book but a set of three by four pages with crude cartoons and captions. On each page, a crude drawing of a man and woman depicting a sexual act appeared. If all of this was meant to excite me, I was too innocent to understand because nobody had told me about the "Birds and the Bees." I started to walk away after peeking at the disgusting piece of trash, but he kept after me. "Hey, I've got more books," he said. When I showed no interest, he hustled fast away from me looking to corner some other unsuspecting kid.

I was shocked, when another new kid named Red in my junior high school shattered that early intrusion into my innocence even more. His family had moved recently from Texas and had transferred into my class. Why he singled me out from the rest of the classmates I'll never know. He wanted to brag about his sexual encounter. He was smiling and half laughing when he said, "Let me tell you about what I did yesterday with my younger sister."

He continued, "My parents weren't home Sunday, so I snuck into their bedroom and stole a few of my father's rubbers." He reached into his right hand pocket and pulled out something rubbery and loosely crumpled up. "See," he said. "I got these. I used one on my little sister yesterday." At the time, I did not know what he was showing me, nor did I understand what he had done to his sister. Half grinning he said, "I went looking for my sister and finally caught her in one of the bedrooms. She was crying when I finished. I told her not to tell Mom or Dad." Then he smiled and said, "I'm going to do it again."

My life had been goody two shoes while growing up. Could it be that my parents did not hear the other shoe fall when I was bad? My world filled with feudal values, strict rules of social conduct. "Do not bring shame to the family name" was the onus place on us while growing up. I was so naive I did not know what some of the forbidden four letter words meant.

One day when I was at McKinley Grammar School, I was in our homeroom class eating lunch with everyone because it was raining hard that day. We were doing what little kids do, talking and joking around with some classmates while eating our bag lunch. One youngster was about to eat an apple, when someone said why don't you twirl that apple stem around and find out about your good fortune. The boy held the apple stem in his left hand and began twirling the red apple with his right hand. At the first turn he said, "A." He repeated another whole turn and said, "B." He continued twirling the apple until the stem broke off at "F." Then, somebody poked him while giggling and said, "You're going to F... someone!" Then I repeated the forbidden four-letter word, F..., too loud.

Suddenly the teacher, who was watching over us, came charging over. She headed right to me, pulled my ears, and marched me into the principal's office. She pushed me in a chair, went up to the principal, and whispered in his ear about what had happened.

The big brute of a guy got out of his throne and came over to me and said while glaring at me, "Did you say that bad F... word?"

I really didn't know what the word meant. I was about to say that I had just repeated what someone else said, but I was out numbered.

"We can't allow you to go unpunished for saying such a nasty word," he said. "I am going to wash your mouth out so you will remember never to say it again."

I was shivering in my boots.

I don't know where he managed to find a bar of soap, but he did. The teacher held me while he stuck that nasty thing in my mouth and swished it around.

I gagged.

Then he did it once more.

"There," he said, "that should clean out the dirty word."

I can still taste the soap, but I don't think it was 99.9% pure Ivory soap.

While the memory of the teacher's and the principal's faces have faded, the homeroom, principal's office, and the taste of soap remains clear in my mind. Looking back at that moment in time, I realize that I was still a naive kid, and the term, sexual abuse, and, worse still, incest, were not in my vocabulary. I learned at an early age that love had nothing to do with the "Birds and the Bees."

All through the years until internment, our home was always on the nursery property that my father leased. We lived near a middle class American neighborhood and not close to other Japanese families. Outside of those two immature and absurd incidences, I can't recall talking about sexual matters. Surely, there would be Hell to pay if I wandered outside my parents' strict cultural boundaries. Even while attending UCLA, my world was academics, and socializing wasn't a part of my world.

However, it was many years later on my GI duty in Japan when my strict world of moral values of Japanese was shattered.

Open minds and hear
Beautiful Christmas Voices
My two worlds now three

Voice of Christmas

When I was about eleven years old, something astonishing happened in my life. One day in December, my McKinley Grammar School announced a Christmas program. Our homeroom teacher made us form a double line and walked us to the school auditorium. When we arrived, the room was bustling with noise with everyone wondering what to expect that day. Our class sat on the left side towards the back of the room, making it hard for me to see the stage in front. After a few announcements, the principal said that we would be entertained by a group of children singing Christmas songs. The rear door open, and I saw young black children, all dressed up, enter and march in double row up to the front of the room. An adult, who led them into the auditorium, began to lead the group in Christmas songs. Suddenly all of the commotion in the room stopped as everyone listened intently. Their voices seemed in perfect harmony. I stretched my head this way and that way to see them perform. I had never heard such wonderful voices. When they finished, the audience gave them a warm applause. Quickly, they turned, marched down the aisle, and out of the auditorium. Again, there was a buzz of voices in the room.

Awed by the wonderful presentation, I wondered where those children came from. Their singing amazed me because I had a different perception about boy's singing. That's because one day, my big brother had said only sissies sing with a high voice. Then he proceeded to demonstrate with a low base sound. Well, I didn't want to be a sissy, so I mimicked him as best I could. As I think back, I might have strained my vocal chords because I can't carry a tune. I sounded like a frog croaking.

When I think back to my early childhood, I lived in a cocoon at first. I couldn't see, but I remember *Okaasan's, mother's* voice singing softly, "*Booya wa yoiko da nenneshina ...,* Little boy you are a good child, go to sleep go to sleep ..." Everyone looked like me. Mothers looked like my mother. As soon as I started to walk, my tiny world changed. There were blonde-haired people, brown-haired people, red heads, dark hair, white skin, freckled faces, short and tall, skinny and fat, and people wearing all sorts of clothes. I gradually learned that I lived in two worlds: at home, my world was Japanese; when I step outside, my world was American. At times, the two were at odds with each other. Now, with this astonishing experience of seeing the children whose songs were glorious, I added another world, Black.

I could only remember one black kid who was in my physical education class. While his hair was black and "kinky" (as the kids around me called it), he was skinny and always limped. Compared to the children in the Christmas program, he had a very light complexion. I can't recall anyone making a fuss over him being in school. He was just another kid in the schoolyard. My childhood exposure to the black people was indirect from reading the amusing book, "Black Sambo." Next, at night, I listened to radio programs such as The Lone Ranger, Sky King, The Green Hornet, Fiber McGee and Molly, Amos and Andy, and others. At the time, Amos and Andy was a very funny comedy with dialogue that was foreign to me since I had not lived in the world they portrayed. Looking back, I don't know if Blacks lived in the city of Santa Monica. That's why to hear them perform at the Christmas program was an eye opening experience.

Perched on Prospect Hill
A vista of the future
Samohi my school

Samohi Years

"Hayaku shinasai, Osokunaru yo, (Hurry up, you'll be late)." I could hear mother urging Frank and me to get going to catch the bus to school. I was an early riser and ready to go, but Frank loved to sleep in. *"Okaasan, ittemairimasu*, mother, I'm going," as I grabbed Frank's books and lunch and yelled at him as I half pulled at Frank to get the move on.

Our high school, Samohi was about three miles from home. Every school day we caught the city's municipal bus across the street on Wilshire Blvd and 25th street and rode to Fourth and Pico Blvd. Sometimes the traffic on Wilshire Blvd could be busy, and I would yell and hail the bus driver frantically to wait for us. If we missed the bus, it would be another twenty minutes' wait. I missed the bus only once. That day, I grabbed my books and lunch, ran as fast as I could down 25th street towards Santa Monica Blvd, turned towards 6th street, and up the grade to Pico. Every once in awhile, I would try to catch my breath by slowing down to a walk. I kept this pace up until I reached the school. I was completely exhausted when I reached my first classroom. After that one experience, I was determined not to miss the bus again.

Unlike McKinley Grammar School and Lincoln Junior high, "Samohi" was not a concrete buildings immersed in an asphalt jungle. The name Samohi was formed from the first two letters of Santa Monica High. I can only speculate about the short form for the school's name since I have not seen any official word about its origin. Maybe the school administrators were tired of writing "Santa Monica High School" in their reports and chose the short form. I would rather guess that the high school cheerleaders were tired of trying to rally the team using the four words of the name. Whereas, if the cheer leaders yelled, "Give me 'S.' Give me an 'A.' Give me a 'M.' Give me an 'O,' and an 'HI.' 'SAMOHI,'" it would bring the crowd in the stands to a rousing cheer.After the Santa Monica high school was built and rebuilt elsewhere several times, Samohi was finally constructed before the turn of the century (1900). Samohi had a beautiful high school campus with the main buildings built on Prospect Hill. Lovely mature trees stood on the lawns and near pathways leading down to the gymnasiums and athletic fields. Just north of the pathway, there was an open air Memorial Theater dedicated to the memory of Samohi students who had served in World War I. From the school you could see the Pacific Ocean since the school was just six blocks from the Santa Monica Bay. The school ground was between sixth and 4th Street (east-west) and to the north is Michigan Blvd, and Pico Blvd. on the south. Samohi students were not only from Santa Monica, but they also commuted from as far north as Santa Monica Canyon, as well as the nearby districts, Venice and Ocean Park. During my attendance, Samohi was a three-year high school: Sophomore, Junior, and Senior years. Left on site were a few temporary tent buildings set up for classrooms after the disastrous 6.2 earthquake in 1933 centered at Long Beach City to the south.

Unlike my experience in the grammar school and junior high, high school was the first time that I could be recognized for excellence in school. In contradistinction, my parents did not show any outward recognition of my doing well in school. Achievement was expected of you. Students had two academic choices: general education and academic curriculum for college preparation. I chose the latter because from the earliest time, my parents stressed that we should try to go to college. At times, they would hint to me to become a doctor or a lawyer. Neither of these options made any sense to me for I had no role model to inspire me. Looking back, I see that my parents saw these two careers as worthwhile goals because no other profession was open to Japanese. Again, when they said these words, "They can take everything from you but they cannot take away what is in your head," I did not appreciate what those words meant. Those words still rumbled in my head.

I loved math courses and geometry and trigonometry intrigued me. I was so caught up with geometry that I even carried the textbook with me, sat among the trees in the school grounds at lunchtime, and memorized the theorems and corollaries for the course. I did so well that the teacher on the day of the final called me to her desk and said, "I have already assigned your grade of 'A,' so you don't have to take the final. You may take the rest of the day off." I was flabbergasted and happy at those words. I took her advice, walked down to the Santa Monica beach, and enjoyed watching waves tumbling ashore, listening to the noisy seagulls flying about seeking food, and feeling the nice cool salt breeze against my face while my classmates struggled with the final exam.

I loved science courses too. One Christmas, I received a small science kit. It contained a mixture of a few chemicals, carbon tetrachloride for collecting insects, and a low powered microscope. I played with the science kit for a while but there wasn't very much to learn from it. I sloshed the carbon tetrachloride (banned) on ants, flies, and any insects I could manage to capture, but my interest waned in bug killing. Fooling around with the chemicals didn't help in my chemistry classes. In fact, the teacher of my chemistry course stressed dates and names that proved worthless when I was in college. Physics, on the other hand, was exciting because the teacher was dynamic in his presentation. Because I found physics to be a combination of math and the material world, I thoroughly enjoyed the class. Much of it was hands-on experience to see and understand how things worked. I learned that a new field of physics was emerging based on Einstein's $E=mc^2$. The text quoted that the energy in one cubic centimeter of water according to Einstein's law was equal to 20 kilotons of TNT. Amazing that this energy is approximately the energy of "Fat Man", one of the atomic bombs dropped on Nagasaki, Japan August 9, 1945. Some years later, I would stand at ground zero at Nagasaki and see what devastation occurs with that much energy released for destruction. I was horrified as I stood there, because I had read in my high school textbook that our world would have all the energy it would ever need if man could convert nuclear energy of water for peaceful use.

A surprising event happened for me in the physics class. One day, Mr. Roy McHenry, my physics teacher, asked me up to his desk and said, "I want you to conduct the physics class for students' day. Come see me after school, and I will give you all the information you will need to prepare for the class." I was surprised and didn't know what to expect. When that day came, I was a bit nervous for a few seconds but proceeded calmly with confidence through the rest of the hour. What the teacher said afterwards puzzled me until this day. He said, "You conducted the class well but a word of advice, 'I think you should seriously think about going into research instead of teaching.'"

While the English class was not my calling, I did work hard at the subject. Even though reading "Beowulf" was confusing, it did not discourage me to fumble through it. The teacher also assigned us the task of memorizing a stanza from some poem we read and recite it in class. If I were a bard then it would be quoting Shakespeare:

"Tomorrow, and tomorrow, and tomorrow,
Creeps in this petty pace from day to day,
To the last syllable of recorded time;
And all of yesterdays have lighted fools
The way to dusty death. Out, out, brief candle!
Life's but a walking shadow: a poor player
That struts and frets his hour upon the stage,
And then is heard no more: it is a tale
Told by an idiot, full of sound and fury,
Signifying nothing."
From Macbeth (V, v, 19)

Every once in a while, I catch myself mumbling, "Tomorrow, and tomorrow, …" I can't seem to get it out of my head.

In our civics class in school, we learned about individual rights and responsibilities, but in school I had a rude awakening. My parents have always stressed respect for *Sensei*, the teacher. "Do not bring *haji*, shame to the family by misbehaving," was the watchword. One day in my English class, I was paying attention to the teacher at her desk when someone whispered something to me from behind. Innocently I turned my head. The teacher saw me look backwards and motioned me to her desk. She said, "I want you to leave the room and stand outside till the end of the class." I stood by the classroom door hoping the teacher would let me return, for I was puzzled and hurt for something I didn't instigate. When the classroom bell rang, I quickly learned that democracy doesn't exist in school. Guilty as noted!

Yet, it was later in the semester when the same teacher was helpful and kind to me. I was one of three individuals that were selected to try for salutatorian during our graduation ceremony. The theme was "The American Way." Each of us would write a speech and present it before a selection committee. I spent many hours at night researching and wrote a speech "Hands across the Pacific." My English teacher spent her valuable time helping me with my work and preparing me for the presentation. I remember that I was quite nervous when I gave my speech, but I quickly got over the stage fright. While I was not selected as salutatorian, I learned how wonderful, dedicated, and without prejudice a teacher can be who helps and encourages a student. My parents were right, "Respect the teachers and maybe you will earn their respect for you."

In addition to the core academic courses, there were opportunities to take electives: print shop, woodshop, typing, and business math. All but print shop have been useful in my life. I always looked forward to sports after classroom hours. Since I was too small for varsity activities, I joined the B or lightweight activities. First, I tried basketball, but I didn't have the stamina for the game. Also, I found that I was so slow that I was always going against the flow of the game. I was, however, first string in warming the bench. I suddenly realized that Japanese have short legs. I decided to join the track team. I knew that only for the short 50-yard dash could I compete with other runners. Once, I tried hurdles but proceeded to knock every hurdle down as I ran towards the finish line. I ruled out all running events and I decided to compete for shot put where brawn counted, and not brains.

Since *Okaasan* always worried about Frank and me getting hurt if we went out for football, I delayed joining the football team in my sophomore year. I would have loved to be the star quarterback, but I have stubby fingers that make it impossible to grasp the football firmly and throw a pass. I had to be a lineman: guard or tackle. Playing on the football team was one of my enjoyable years at Samohi, and I learned some valuable things about sportsmanship.

My coach was Jim "Suds" Sutherland, a former USC football halfback, 1934-36. Like most football players I saw, his neck merged in a solid line from his head to his shoulder. He was a solid muscle mass from the top of his head to his toes. He suited up just like the rest of us and was always in the thick of our scrimmages. He was firm, showed us how to do our job better, but he never cursed or shouted at us. It was one day that I came to respect my coach even more. After one of our conference games, one of our teammates asked the coach if he would teach him some of the dirty tricks the opposing team was using. The coach looked at him and said, "I know all the dirty tricks of the game, but that's not what I am about. We play to win, but we play by the rules."

I always lined up as a tackle, and next to me, Leland Moody as a guard. We worked as a team and played our hearts out: "Hit high and hit low." In 1939, we ran over our neighboring rival, Venice and beat Leuzinger, Beverly Hills, Compton, and Redondo Beach. We were undefeated but had two tie games: Inglewood and Wilson (Long Beach). By virtue of the two ties we lost to the Wilson Bruins for first place. That year, Leland Moody and I were selected as the most valuable players. But football was a team effort and no nose was bent out of shape for recognition of our playing effort.

The locker room was something else: Sweat and grime, dirty smelly socks, bruises and scars, turf stained football shoes, football gear dumped on the locker room floor. Even after the shower, the smell of dirty socks and sweaty clothes is overpowering. I was thankful that some other poor soul would take care of the equipment and ready it for the next game. I can only dream now: If only I was young again to play the game once more.

Graduation Day

With pomp and ceremonies
All of yesterday
Has come to pass
For tomorrow, and tomorrow
Creeps in this petty pace
Day to day
But tomorrow and tomorrow
Is not just a shadow
It shines with hope
And brightness of the future
Step boldly into the light
Play the game
The American Way: Democracy

Zeros in the sky
Cast shadows on tomorrow
Dreams lost in red sea

Tomorrow and Tomorrow

High on the crest I saw the citadel of learning standing majestically against the skyline. Little did I know how formidable a task it would be climbing towards that dream. Today was an especially hectic and chaotic day in the girls' gymnasium filling in the lines to meet the task: Forms and more forms to fill out but when they asked me for my mother's maiden name; I was stopped in my tracks. What had *Okaasan's* maiden name have to do with learning? I probably would have gone through life not knowing that tidbit until my fourth grade teacher asked our class to draw our family tree. It certainly wasn't important to me at the time. Fortunately, I remembered. I often wondered if I put a wrong name down, would the Registrar know it was incorrect or even care.

I had this preconceived notion that college was the institution where I could focus on a career. No such luck! The first two years were crammed with requirements for advanced classes. ROTC was also a compulsory requirement that seemed to be of no use to me. At least I was fortunate enough to pass the "bone-head" English requirement. But then, I found out that I had wasted two years studying Spanish at Samohi because Spanish was not a requirement for a physics major in the College of Letters and Sciences. Only French or German was acceptable since many articles in scientific journals were written in these two languages. Sadly, I signed up for the German class that met five days a week. What a bummer. It seems that most of the students were there to gain an easy "A," for they all spoke German in the class with the professor while I stumbled with "*Das ist nicht sehr gut.*"

The UCLA campus was relatively new since it had been established near Westwood on more than 400-acres of land in 1927. Initially four buildings were completed in 1929. Almost everyone commuted to UCLA because there wasn't any student housing. Furthermore, UCLA was surrounded by affluent homes: Brentwood on the west, Bel-Air on the north, Beverly Hills to the east, and the famous Sunset Blvd that skirled the north campus area. There was a bus stop east of the Quad, but the bus only connected to downtown Los Angeles and not Santa Monica. I commuted with a *Nisei* whose family also lived in Santa Monica. He was a year ahead of me and majored in chemistry. The traffic was very light during 1939 as we traveled a total of five miles from his home. He drove along Santa Monica Blvd, turned north on Westwood Blvd, crossed Wilshire Blvd, passed through Westwood Village, and drove into the UCLA campus parking lot, which was a large unmarked open grassy field across from the men's and women's gyms and along Westwood Blvd. Sometimes we would end up far out in the grassy field since parking was catch-as-catch-can.

I remember my days started with a grueling walk from the mens' gym up three-tiers of Janss steps to the quad that sits high above the parking lot, Everyday, I lugged my heavy briefcase full of books and folders and struggled up eighty-seven brick steps. I stopped at each landing in order to catch my breath and switched the briefcase that was in one aching hand to the other one. At the top of the steps, I walked quickly across the quad to the math building and climbed another three flights of stairs to my classroom. I was flustered; my face flushed, physically exhausted, and my heart pounding hard. Because running up and down those eighty-seven brick steps was so demanding, I tried to schedule my physical ed and ROTC, both held in the gym, for 7:30 am, so I would not be faced with the Janss steps more than once a day.

I am not sure what I had expected when I attended college classes. The quality of teachers was a mixed bag. It seemed some professors were on an "ego trip" and others didn't put much effort into their class subject. One of my math teachers talked about raising chickens on his farm in San Fernando Valley everyday and never covered the material for the semester. On the last day of class, he said, "Read the next eight chapters for the final." Another professor railed against students, especially those who had received an "A" from a previous math class. He was picky about the students English in their presentation. I was even embarrassed to sit there and listen to his unprofessional ranting. It was so bad that a few students dropped out of his class. Another math professor had just written a calculus textbook and, in order to proof read the problems, he assigned all of them as classroom assignments. Fortunately, math was easy for me, but it was more homework than I cared for.

When I took the Chemistry 1A course, I found myself in a sea of students – all 500 of them. It's hard to find a vantage point to see and hear the speaker when you are late. The chemistry professor started his lecture saying, "Forget everything you learned about chemistry in high school." He was right. My high school teacher might as well have taught us alchemy instead of chemistry. I had a lecturer who wrote with his right hand and quickly erased what he had written with his left hand as he moved across the blackboard. I also learned that with so many students in the introductory courses, the professors go through a process of weeding out students. On the first day of the chemistry 1B class, the professor said, while waving a form for us to see, "All those students who received a "C" or lower in 1A, come down here for this form and sign out because you will not make the grade for this class." His words roiled the sea. What I remember most about the chemistry class was the smell of rotten eggs, hydrogen sulfide. The smell was in my hair, in my clothes, and anything I took to the chemistry lab. Sometimes I would walk outside just to get a whiff of fresh air.

I wasn't thinking about becoming an army officer as a career, but the university required all able-bodied male students to take ROTC. Most of the information was right out of the Army manual and boring. Probably the one thing I learned that was of any use was how to dig a cat-hole, that is, if I ever decided to go camping in the woods. Every week, we practiced close order drill, but we never seem to be in synch. We also practiced how to arm, disassemble, and maintain a World War I vintage Browning M-2, 50-caliber water-cooled machine gun. It had an awesome destructive power and an effective range of 1500 yards. One look and I hoped that I would never have to face that sinister weapon.

Meanwhile, in 1940, President Franklin Roosevelt signed the Selective Training and Service Act, creating the first peacetime draft.

"Greetings from your Selective Service: Register for Selective Service at your local Draft Office since you are now eighteen. Your classification is 1A. Please wait for your Draft lottery numbers."

My brother's number was selected for the draft lottery and, shortly afterwards, he was shipped out to Fort Ord, Monterey, California. I lucked out, and I chided him and said, "If you're going to win a lottery, this isn't the one to win!"

Lady on the Bridge

While there was a growing turmoil in Europe, our country had turned to isolationism following the costly involvement of the World War I. Congress passed a series of Neutrality Acts but imposed embargos while, at the same time, permitted the sale of materials and supplies to belligerent nations.

Frank was among the thousands of young Americans drafted but it did not appear that the United States was ready to be involved in the European conflict. The US Army was still varying of Japanese Americans in the military for he said that while at Fort Ord, he was assigned to drive an ambulance. Then, I was shocked and puzzled to hear from Frank that the Nisei soldiers stationed there were rounded up and held in a warehouse when the President's wife, Mrs. Eleanor Roosevelt visited Fort Ord.

"But you're a citizen, drafted and in uniform. What in the world is going on?" I asked him.

He just shook his head and nothing more was said.

While I missed seeing my brother after his visit home on his furlough, I was too busy attending UCLA to keep track of his deployment after his basic training. It was several years later that I would see him again.

After two years struggling to complete the basic college requirements, I never thought a dark shadow would cast over dreams of tomorrow, and tomorrow. It was December and the first half of the semester was almost through.

Chapter 3: Ringo-en

Red rays from the East
Strike our Pacific fortress
Future stained in blood

Japan attacks Pearl Harbor on December 7, 1941

The U.S. Navy took this photo of the *U.S.S. Arizona*
following the Japanese attack on Pearl Harbor on
December 7, 1941

CREDIT: Official U.S. Navy photograph. "*USS Arizona*,
at Height of Fire, Following Japanese Aerial Attack on
Pearl Harbor, Hawaii." December 7, 1941
Prints and Photographs Division,
Library of Congress.

War clouds to the East
Tsunami engulfed our lives
Dashed against barb wires

On the radio

It was eleven o'clock Sunday, December 7, 1941, our world collapsed.

"Come quick! Listen to what's on the radio," said my sister-in-law frantically.

Oh my God! Did you hear over the radio? Japan attacked Pearl Harbor this morning

Our jaws dropped and our eyes opened wide in disbelief of what had happened. All we could say was, *"Why? Why? Why did this happen?"*

Mother was at home while the rest of us were working at our family nursery in Santa Monica. We were stunned as the blood drained from our faces, and a disquieting silence fell. Little did we know that a *tsunami* would sweep over our lives very soon.

It was as if everything was preplanned when the FBI, in their black sedan, screech to a halt in front of the Nursery, seized *Otoosan, father,* who was working outside in the nursery, handcuffed him, and hauled him into their car. I rushed home worried about *Okaasan*, mother while Joe and my sister-in-law tended to the nursery.

Our nightmare was just beginning on that "Day of Infamy!" When I returned home, two agents ransacked the house looking for something or anything. They questioned *Otoosan*, father mercilessly, turned our house inside out, and left everything strewn on the floor. I saw *Okaasan*'s ashen face as we all stood by horrified by what was taking place. We watched but were unable to intervene, as agents acted like Gestapo. With smirks on their faces, they questioned *Otoosan* repeatedly using information they had gained months before by secretly wiretapping the phones lines.

This was no happenstance, for this same scene was taking place throughout the West Coast, a well-timed effort to round up and arrest every prominent member or leaders of the Japanese community.

Hate had raised its ugly head and the press, guardian of truth, began publishing lies that farmers tilled their land to point at military installations and airports; Japanese fishermen were Japanese sailors in disguise monitoring naval ships and passing information to Japan; the Japanese schools were training children to be Japanese soldiers who were ready to strike at America. It brought out the worst of our country; the vermin, including the "Sons and Daughters of the Golden West," who wanted to rid the "Yellow Peril" from California. Even clergymen spewed the vitriol at Japanese.

I remember vividly the panic we felt afterwards and tragic action we took to rid ourselves of everything Japanese. We threw everything into that bonfire: books, Japanese textbooks that I had studied so diligently, photographs by the armful that we had no time to sort out, Japanese sport fencing gear, papers, drawings, and list goes on. The fire reached hungrily for everything. I saw a photograph of smiling children begin to curl away from the heat. The faces turned grotesque and I heard a silent cry, "Why me? Why me?" Suddenly it burst into flames. Finally, there was a glow of burning embers consuming the last of our family's past. Only ashes remained. Yet, those watching the tragedy were still Japanese.

It was a disquieting feeling not knowing what was happening to my father. After a few days, we were allowed to see *Otoosan* at the Tujunga Canyon Compound, jailed with other *Issei*. I watched a confused and expressionless face of my father. No charges, just that he was Japanese. Ever after that day, we never knew where he was until he was finally incarcerated at the Santa Fe Federal Prison, Santa Fe, New Mexico as a POW. Then came our turn: curfew. The government issued a series of federal orders restricting the movement of people of Japanese ancestry from various Western Defense Zones designated by the War Department. A most famous quote by General DeWitt revealed the sentiment of many prominent people: "A dead Jap is a good Jap."

I returned to school to prepare for the end of the semester, but I moved like a mindless robot. I was apprehensive at first about what the situation would be when I returned to class, but nobody looked at me as the enemy. All I saw was worried faces among my classmates afraid of the draft. A few even talked about volunteering to serve.

I had to concentrate on my class subjects because December is the month for finals before the Christmas holidays. It is a grueling time filled anxiety about what the Professor would spring on you in the final exams. I went over and over the subjects and notes until I decided "What the heck, I can't cram any more into my head."

At last, the finals were over, and I decided to help at the nursery. I loaded up a wheelbarrow full of plants from the back of the nursery and started hauling them to the front. Suddenly the wheelbarrow slipped out of my hand as I blanked out. When my brother Joe heard the wheelbarrow drop, he came rushing out. He saw me on the ground and asked, "You ok?"

I mumbled something and got up.

"Hey, why don't you take it easy today?" he said to me.

I must have been too exhausted from cramming for the finals.

If we had been uncertain about our future, we would have seen our fate clearer when the vermin sprung out of their dark holes and began spewing their lies and hatred at all Japanese. The free press," guardians of truth," printed the same lies and characterized all Japanese as uncivilized beasts. Meanwhile, the President, Congress, and the Secretary of Navy were ready to act against all Japanese.

If I had been more cognizant that the world I lived in was not what it had seemed, I would not have been so shocked about what was happening. However, I remembered what I had learned in my Samohi civics class. After reading the Constitution, we memorized important names and dates, but never had any extensive discussion about the subject. However, the words of Patrick Henry still rings in my ears "… give me liberty or give me death!" I was always awed by those words and by our elected representative whose responsibility it was to preserve our freedom by upholding our Constitution. I cannot recall the teacher ever talking about discrimination.

I remember one night, I rushed outside when I heard the sound of ack-ack and saw searchlights crisscrossing and scanning the sky while illuminating puffy clouds here and there. I looked intently, but I neither saw nor heard any airplane droning high above. It went on for several hours, but no enemy planes fell. Only a weather balloon scared the Army anti-aircraft into action.

On February 19, 1942, President Roosevelt signed Executive Order 9066. Then, on February 24, 1942, the Army declared all of the West Coast a "strategic area" and imposed a curfew from 9 p.m. I had to drop out of UCLA since the curfew restricted me from traveling to school, especially at nighttime to utilize the library. That was the end of my dreams of tomorrow, and tomorrow.

Lady on the Bridge

Then the order for evacuation came. Hatred had begun the battle cry and governors of states where internment camps were to be constructed protested, "Not in my backyard." Forgotten are those words, "I ... do solemnly swear to uphold the Constitution.

However, that was to be the least of my worries.

FDR's Executive Order No. 9066

The President

Authorizing the Secretary of War to Prescribe Military Areas

Whereas the successful prosecution of the war requires every possible protection against espionage and against sabotage to national-defense material, national-defense premises, and national-defense utilities as defined in Section 4, Act of April 20, 1918, 40 Stat. 533, as amended by the Act of November 30, 1940, 54 Stat. 1220, and the Act of August 21, 1941, 55 Stat. 655 (U.S.C., Title 50, Sec. 104);

Now, therefore, by virtue of the authority vested in me as President of the United States, and Commander in Chief of the Army and Navy, I hereby authorize and direct the Secretary of War, and the Military Commanders whom he may from time to time designate, whenever he or any designated Commander deems such action necessary or desirable, to prescribe military areas in such places and of such extent as he or the appropriate Military Commander may determine, from which any or all persons may be excluded, and with respect to which, the right of any person to enter, remain in, or leave shall be subject to whatever restrictions the Secretary of War or the appropriate Military Commander may impose in his discretion. The Secretary of War is hereby authorized to provide for residents of any such area who are excluded there from, such transportation, food, shelter, and other accommodations as may be necessary, in the judgment of the Secretary of War or the said Military Commander, and until other arrangements are made, to accomplish the purpose of this order. The designation of military areas in any region or locality shall supersede designations of prohibited and restricted areas by the Attorney General under the Proclamations of December 7 and 8, 1941, and shall supersede the responsibility and authority of the Attorney General under the said Proclamations in respect of such prohibited and restricted areas.

I hereby further authorize and direct the Secretary of War and the said Military Commanders to take such other steps as he or the appropriate Military Commander may deem advisable to enforce compliance with the restrictions applicable to each Military area hereinabove authorized to be designated, including the use of Federal troops and other Federal Agencies, with authority to accept assistance of state and local agencies.

I hereby further authorize and direct all Executive Departments, independent establishments and other Federal Agencies, to assist the Secretary of War or the said Military Commanders in carrying out this Executive Order, including the furnishing of medical aid, hospitalization, food, clothing, transportation, use of land, shelter, and other supplies, equipment, utilities, facilities, and services.

This order shall not be construed as modifying or limiting in any way the authority heretofore granted under Executive Order No. 8972, dated December 12, 1941, nor shall it be construed as limiting or modifying the duty and responsibility of the Federal Bureau of Investigation, with respect to the investigation of alleged acts of sabotage or the duty and responsibility of the Attorney General and the Department of Justice under the Proclamations of December 7 and 8, 1941, prescribing regulations for the conduct and control of alien enemies, except as such duty and responsibility is superseded by the designation of military areas hereunder.

Franklin D. Roosevelt

The White House

Liberty bell rings
Born a Citizen now void
Crisis of the heart

Executive Order 9066

On February 19, 1942, President D. Roosevelt signed Executive Order 9066, authorizing the War Department to exclude every person of Japanese ancestry from prescribed military areas. The Government removed all people of Japanese ancestry from the Western coastal regions and deported them to guarded camps called "relocation camps."

When President Roosevelt issued the Executive Order 9066, the War Department initiated evacuation orders to Japanese families in all of the strategic defense areas. Some families had only forty-eight hours to move from their homes. The bigots, opportunists, vultures, and hate mongers descended on these hapless families and offered to buy their family belongings for pennies on the dollar or just take them away for nothing. We were more fortunate than they were, but to say fortunate is obscene here. Families in our area had several weeks before evacuation from our homes.

The Government set up several locations to allow families to store items. Of course, there was no guarantee that the items would be safe from robbery, nor was there any hope that families would be able to retrieve them. Yet this storage option was the best we could hope for because we had no other option.

With father incarcerated, and Frank already in the US Army, my brother Joe shouldered the task of taking care of the families, arranging for someone to take over the nursery, and deciding on what to keep, store, or discard. I had the responsibility of constructing wooden boxes to store some of the family belongings for storage. Mother and my younger sister, Kaz were busy sorting out the items. What to save and what to discard was no easy decision to make since storage space was limited. Except for the automobiles, we did not attempt to sell off any of the family excess belongings. My brother Joe offered other Japanese families the use of his Nursery truck and our backbreaking service to help haul any storage items free of charge.

Finally, on April 21, 1942, the announcement came for our day of assembly and evacuation. My brother and I transported not only our baggage, but also helped others with their family belongings. At the assembly site, Santa Monica Methodist Church, several old Greyhound buses were parked and waiting for us to board. Young soldiers armed with M1s and bayonets fixed ready for action watched the commotion very closely. Families tried to stay together, but youngsters tended to ride with each other. With all of the confusion, there was no time to cry. Silently we boarded the buses, the door banged closed and we were off to some far off desolate internment camp.

I recalled other times when I rode with schoolmates when we chattered and sang "Row, Row Your Boat" and "Ole McDonald Had a Farm" so loudly that the driver could hardly keep his sanity. This was a somber ride for we might as well have been draped in black and headed to a funeral. The riders looked this way and that while showing no emotion. Tears flowing? Nonsense! We were fresh out of tears. Our bus now headed towards the Mohave dessert on US 395.

As soon as we were out of Los Angeles City, the bus driver stopped, handed each of us a box lunch, and quickly started back on the road again. It was a gourmet lunch, consisting of one bologna sandwich, an apple, and a small milk carton. No one really had the appetite to enjoy the government's delicious meal. As the scenery passed by, my clouded mind was with gloom to enjoy the beauty of the desert. As we approached Owens Valley, I recalled that there was once a beautiful lake here but that Los Angeles County had usurped the water rights and dried up most of the lake. To the northeast was the Panamint Range bordering Death Valley, and just west of the highway was the Alabama Hills that I remembered where many Hollywood Western movies were filmed. I could almost picture Roy Rodgers riding Trigger here. Shortly, we arrived at a small country town among some scrubby trees. It was Lone Pine.

This is the place where the horror and humiliation of my life happened, which I have never overcome. The driver had stopped for fuel and said he would be here for at least a half an hour or more. He pointed to the restrooms behind the station. I joined the others in a single line and waited my turn. The men's restroom was a weather worn faded green structure, and the door seemed to hang and sag on its hinges. The door never closed during this procession. When my turn came, the scene was enough to make my stomach churn. The room was not just dusty, but dirty and unkempt. The basin was dirty with grease marks and rust stains. The faucet was green with age, and dirty water spots on the walls and floor signaled no paper towels here. Even a spider had abandoned a web that was in disarray with dust all over it. The toilet, ugh! Was it American-Standard? What ever make it was, the porcelain had yellowed with age and had rusted marks dripping down the interior. What joy; it was my turn. It was a long wait, but I stood frozen before the toilet. Try as I might, nothing happened. It was not just the stench that overpowered me, but the mental pressure from seeing the line of males waiting their turn. I was mortified and humiliated. I muttered something inaudible, buttoned up, and walk away from the crowd. From that day on, public restrooms have been the bane of my life.

The driver motioned us to return and board the bus. I often wondered why the driver had bothered to stop at Lone Pine since Manzanar was only seven miles further. We were now at the entrance of Manzanar, a guard gate manned by US Military Police. Barbed-wire fence surrounded the site and watchtowers "were erected for our protection," except that the searchlights and machine guns pointed inward. The sun was just sinking behind Mt. Williamson towering high in the Sierra Nevada Range. As soon as the MPs cleared us, the bus proceeded to a place for processing. There were a number of internees waiting for us to disembark. A dust storm must have just subsided because I could see dust on the internees' clothes and faces except for the clear area around their eyes where they had removed the goggles. This was our new home, a desolate and foreboding land.

Manzanar Entrance (Ringo-en)

"Library of Congress, Prints and Photographs Division, LC-A35-4M-10."

Watchtower with searchlight

Freedom left in dust
Sixteen by twenty foot room
My home, Ringo-en

Home, in the Land of the Free

After we unloaded our belongings, we lined up and received salt tablets that we gulped down with water spooned from a 50-gallon garbage can. The salt was to replenish what we might have lost from the hot weather. Next, we received our processing directions and assigned to our humble abode according to our family designation: ours was K4462. We picked up our belongings and trudged to our designated barrack. It was a long tar-papered building with batten boards hammered onto the tarpaper to hold them in place. There were tears and gaps here and there showing that they were slap to construction. There were six units per barrack, sixteen by twenty feet, with a bare bulb hanging from the ceiling, an oil stove, a floor made of rough green lumber that dried and exposed the ground beneath, and six metal beds (cots). Even the way of Japanese, *shikataganai* (cannot be helped) or even *Gaman* (endure it), the situation was hard to swallow. No tears shed and no words of horror uttered, just muted silence.

However, wait; there was a mix up in our assignment. There were six of us according to our family designation but another family also shared the room. Finally, the paper shufflers realized their error and assigned us to barracks in a new block. Before settling in, our next duty on the list was preparing our bed by stuffing straw into a canvas bag for our mattress. The event was new, humiliating, and a humorous experience all in one package. We were so eager to stuff the canvas bag that we forgot we had to sleep on top of this mountain of straw. I know that none of us slept that night.

The trip and the time for processing, registering, and quarter assignments had taken so long that we were too late for dinner that first day. We all waited for morning for our first meal in camp. As I watched the internees enter the mess hall on my first day for breakfast, I saw them move with somber expressionless faces like zombies marching across the serving line. Even mother had a somber look about her. If there were tears, they were dry. Mother had endured more hardship and humiliation than the rest of the family. However, she had an air of stoicism, a product of cultural heritage, "*Gaman*." Around the mess hall, the only noise I heard was the "slop, slop" of the food being spooned onto the plate or, somewhere in this large room, a young child crying or fussing. As best I can recall, the first breakfast consisted of a lumpy mound of oatmeal and burnt toast. With real butter rationed, apple butter was the choice of the management. No sugar was available to the internees since most of this ration went to the "*hakugin*" managers' (Caucasian administrators) dining room. The dinner special was a shock for even the bravest and daring. The tasty entrée was a reconstituted mummified beef liver. I definitely heard a clunk when the tissue mass hit the plate. One bite was enough for me! Later, I heard that some of the food consignment sent to Manzanar had stenciled on the package "Not for human consumption." I believe it!

Since our family was always isolated from a community of Japanese families, living among a camp full of Japanese and rubbing elbows day after day was a strange and new experience for me. Moreover, we were in a block full of strangers. Even though we were all in the same predicament, there was not even a sign of acknowledging one's presence from anyone. I sensed that everyone's mouth shut tightly. While historians claim that we are essentially a homogeneous ethnic society, I was surprised to hear when my mother said to my younger sister and me "Don't associate or become too close to the Terminal Island Japanese because they are very rough people. And don't mingle with the Boyle Heights people because some of them belong to gangs." The scuttlebutt that was floating about in camp about these two Japanese groups is the following: The Japanese who came from Terminal Island were mainly engaged in commercial fishing. It is true that the language spoken by fishermen is very course, if not crude, by any standard. It is not too hard to understand because, in the frenzy of landing the catch, you do not say, "Please hand me the gaff!" It is all about action now and politeness is dammed. As for those from Boyle Heights, the community had become predominantly Hispanic families with a few percentages of other races, such as, Japanese, Jewish, German, etc. During the 1930s' the young Hispanics were noted for their dress code as "Zoot-suiters." The other young people of that area, including the Japanese, were influenced heavily by the Zoot-suiters dress and tastes.

My sister and I had no reason to co-mingle with them, but to my surprise, I found out later that, while I was in Minnesota, my sister married a young man from Terminal Island in camp! Actually, he was not a fisherman. His family ran a small grocery store in that community.

I am embarrassed to admit that mother was also wrong on her second warning. In our block, there was a young man who had a ducktail hairdo, a mustache, and peg legged pants. All that was missing was a long chain hanging from his belt. He was indeed a zoot-suiter from Boyle Heights. He was probably one of the nicest guys I have had the pleasure of meeting. On Saturday nights, he shared his stereo system, his records, and introduced and taught social dancing, including jitterbug, to the young people in the block. Before the days of internment, my parents had had a negative view about American style dancing. The descriptive words they used were "*Shiri furi dansu!*" This is roughly translated as "Fanny shaking dance!" For all of the fanny shaking we did, we had many enjoyable Saturday nights that probably preserved our sanity and made camp life more bearable.

How could there be any culture clash in the camp? After all, we had burned or destroyed everything Japanese in order to shed our Japanese identity when the war with Japan broke out. Most of us had either lost our worldly possessions or stored them somewhere with the small hope of recovering them at some unknown future date. What we carried was what we were. However, no matter what we did, we were still Japanese. All of those cultural values that our parents had passed on to us through our daily lives remained; *gaman* (endure), *gambaru* (persevere), *giri* (duty), *oyakoko* (loyalty), *on* (filial piety), and *kodomo no tame ni* (sacrifice for the children).

At first, family members joined each other at mealtime but this in time became a meaningless exercise. However, family life in camp was no longer the same as it was before the internment. Mealtime that gave us a sense of togetherness and family structure had become a community affair. The home that gave us privacy and security was an open book. No longer was there a sense of pride, self-respect, or dignity in our life of confinement. Our daily life was monotonous, haphazard, and self-defeating motions just to fill the time that had no ending. It was truly a state of mind of hopelessness (*shikata ga nai*). How could we reconcile our predicament? How could we find solace or support from the family when explicit feelings were never expressed in a Japanese family? No, there were no cultural clashes per se within the family during my brief stay in camp. However, a storm was brewing among the internees.

Manzanar Street and Winter scene

"Library of Congress, Prints and Photographs Division, LC-A35-4-M-10."

Culture turned to dust
What was is no longer here
It met its demise

Demise of a culture

With one stroke of the pen, my parents' culture was left in shambles. *Issei* fathers, who were the breadwinners and authority figures of the family, were no longer relevant in the Internment Camp. Prior to the internment, prominent members of the Japanese community established Japanese schools and recreational facilities for their children in order to teach them the language and their culture. Other *Issei* donated from their meager income to help support the schools. However, successful businessmen and prominent members of the Japanese community were quickly rounded up after December 7 and incarcerated in federal prisons as "Prisoners of War." Their whereabouts were often unknown. *Issei* interned at Manzanar, were barred from participating in the local governing affairs. Day after day, I saw them sitting on their doorsteps dejected, rejected, and disbelieving what had happened to their lives and fortunes in America. I wondered often, "What are they thinking? Will they rise above their silence?"

For fear of infusing nationalism into the children, English only was strictly enforced within the camp discussions. Teaching Japanese within the camp was also disallowed. However, I found the Japanese language difficult and complex. How else would I, a *Nisei* understand my heritage? How else would I communicate intelligently with my *Issei* parents? The Japanese schools were looked at as hotbeds for subversive teachings. I found nothing of the sort. I attended Japanese school after attending public school and on Saturdays. I am grateful that I had that opportunity to learn about the heritage of my parents.

It seems worth noting that the US government would come to depend on our knowledge of Japanese. It was the knowledge of the Japanese language that we received by attending Japanese schools that proved to be vital to our country in war with Japan. It is ironic that prior to December 7, the US Army had set up a Military Intelligence School at Presidio of San Francisco to train *Nisei* in military Japanese in case we had a war against Japan. My brother, drafted before December 7, was later a member of the Military Intelligence School. Without diminishing the heroic action of the *Nisei* on the European front, the military recognized that the *Nisei* Military Intelligence Service (MIS) shorten the war in the Pacific by more than two years. Later, I would also graduate from MIS Presidio of Monterey, California and serve as an interpreter in Japan during 1947 - 1948.

Mother's role was in shambles too. We were now all wards of the US government such that her role to nurture, dote, and protect her children became a meaningless exercise. Her children scattered as soon as daybreak came. There was nothing here that reminded us of home. Back home our family had sat together for supper every day. There was a set protocol: *Otoosan* served first, *chonan* (first-born son) next, and the rest in the order or their ages. But we were family together as one. There was always the familiar scent of soy sauce in the air. And *Ocha*, green tea instead of milk, was on the table and rice was our main staple. *Okaasan* was always busy cooking and serving. She was always last to sit down with us. The kitchen was her domain. Even *Otoosan* rarely entered that sacred place. Now, the family that had been was no longer present.

The mess hall replaced her kitchen. Her children sat with their friends and sometimes ate at a different block mess hall. I too was guilty of that indiscretion. And why not join the crowd?

Especially when someone says, "Hey, the cook in Block 2 is serving beef tonight instead of the usual slop in our mess hall?" Life was just a game to survive in this hellhole.

Mess hall

"Library of Congress, Prints and Photographs Division, LC-A35-4-M-10."

Lady on the Bridge

From this desert bloom
Petals fall from cutting winds
Will it bloom once more?

The Room

Freedom lies in dust

A sixteen by twenty foot room
Squeezing in five or more people
Bussed to this desert terrain
It's for your own good they say
Too much hate for your safety outside
It's your patriotic duty in time of war
Silent are the words, Freedom and Liberty

Hanging blankets define my space
In this sixteen by twenty foot room
Tarpaper building gives no solace
Hastily built construction leaves a view
Desert land beneath and scorpions too
Starry skies above so cold and forbidding
Hollow are the words Justice for All

Barbwires and watchtowers your safety net
Searchlights your guiding light
For this sixteen by twenty foot room
The desert wind blows wickedly
Dust streams through the cracks
Ashen scenery has become this place
We are but one, dust

Silent faces in this room
Laughter a word unknown
Walls around me threaten to crush my will
It's only a sixteen by twenty foot room
No chairs to sit to catch my breath
No table to rest my disquieted mind
No open door brings freedom

Day by day, this is your space
Walls have ears for they are thin
No need to lock the door, for what's to lose
You lost your home and life-long dreams

Lady on the Bridge

Nothing left for this sixteen by twenty foot room
Take your time and enjoy the stay
No need to think what tomorrow brings

This the wasteland that I must face
The wind does blow whirling missiles
Etching its path across my skin
Shikataganai (It's fate) looms in my face
I vow I will not die on this reservation
By living in a sixteen by twenty foot room
For freedom lies beyond the gates

What will I remember?

On the first day of school,
A little girl runs home crying
Holding the child and comforting her, mother asks,
"You were so happy to go to school in your new dress.
I saw you skipping merrily on your way.
Why are you home so early and why are you crying?"
With tears soaking her mother's breast, she sobs,
"There's nothing Mommy.
No chairs, no pictures on the wall.
There's not even a flag I used to pledge allegiance to!
Oh Mommy, Mommy let's go back to America."
Child's naked truth: This sixteen by twenty foot room

In the dust your shot
Typhoid Mary's legacy
Angel voice, wake up!

Waking Up

Religion was never a big thing in my life. That's because my Japanese parents were never associated with any church. While the family on special occasions followed Shinto rites and Buddhist ceremonies, the two are not religions, in the sense of Judeo-Christian. However, I did attend the Methodist Church's Sunday school in my youth. Later, when I was older, I became a teenage Methodist. On Sundays, I listened to the pastor's sermon but he talked in a low monotone voice that droned on and on forever. If he had a message, I did not hear it. I was never baptized. Nevertheless, Christian faith was in my blood. At Manzanar, I had a wake-up call.

I remember the first day when our bus entered Manzanar. Dust never settles here. Tired from our travel, we staggered off the bus and met fellow internees waiting to process us for our incarceration. One handed us our schedule for processing. Another handed us three salt tablets and motioned us go to an internee standing near galvanized garbage. He dipped a big metal ladle into the garbage and said, "Swallow your salt tablets and wash them down with this." He shoved the ladle full of water towards us. I was astonished. He didn't even bother to clean the ladle for each internee. Then our fellow internees motioned us to a barrack for our first typhoid shots. However, it seems that I needed two shots to protect me from typhoid fever.

It was several weeks later that I had my second typhoid booster shot. Sunday the next day, a friend from my hometown said, "Our pastor is visiting Manzanar and he will be giving a sermon. Let's go hear what he had to say."

"You mean there's a church in this camp?" I asked.

"Yeah, it's a barrack building in block 15.

There was not much choice in what I could wear to church since all that I could bring to camp was about eighty pounds or whatever I could carry with me. At least I had a clean shirt and pair of slacks. I walked with my friend across the firebreak to block 15. When I entered, the room was nearly full of people, standing, for there was no furniture, only a makeshift pulpit in front.

Someone introduced the pastor and he began his sermon. I recognized him immediately. He was my soft-spoken clergyman from Santa Monica. I remember the day we assembled at his church. I saw him busily helping people who wanted to use the church facilities before boarding the bus for Manzanar. While I tried listening to his sermon, his voice didn't carry too far in the hastily built tarpaper barrack. But true to what I recall from his sermons back home, he proceeded to drone on and on as always. I was trying to pay attention when I noticed that my vision was changing. Darkness was gradually descending from the top of my vision downward. I tried forcing my eyes to open wider but a shade seemed to close over my eyes. Suddenly, my legs felt rubbery. I knew I was in trouble. I fought hard to stay erect but it was no use. I forced myself to gently squat down to the floor and slump between the people around me. I was halfway down but I cannot remember what happened after that.

If I was supposed to hear Angels, I do not remember. If I was at the Pearly Gate, I do not remember seeing Saint Peter. I cannot remember how long I was on the floor, but when I woke up, there, staring down at me, was my pastor.

He looked at me very concerned and asked, "Are you all right?" I was startled, if not totally embarrassed and didn't reply.

Then, someone yelled, "Move back and give him some air!"

I did not return for another awakening. But this was not the last of my enlightenment with religion. My brother Joe, his wife Yo, and his father-in-law had moved to their own lodging while, Okaasan, my younger sister, Kaz and I remained in our old room. We were all caught up in our miserable world trying to make the best of our situation. Okaasan, of course, had more than her share or worries. While I was busy with my teaching assignment, mother had spent her days at the Maryknoll Catholic Church established at Manzanar. She had heard that the Catholic father was helping wives locate their husbands who had been arrested and imprisoned by the FBI. Since I was busy preparing for my Physics class, I had lost track of her whereabouts. Then one day in our room, she told me she was spending her time at the Catholic Church. She said she was beholden to the Church father and accepted the Catholic faith and baptized. And she had encouraged my sister, Kaz to attend the Catechism classes to become a Catholic. She then asked me if I would attend the Catechism classes for her.

I was unprepared for her request and said that I wasn't sure that I wanted to be a Catholic. For all of the Sundays I attended the Methodist Church at Santa Monica, I never considered being baptized even though I accepted Christian moral values. Normally I would have consented to her wishes, but I told her I was sorry that I was too busy to take the Catechism classes. I thought the issue finished, but again a few weeks later, she asked me once more. This time she was more insistent. I reluctantly relented.

I had dubious feelings as I walked across the firebreak towards the Catholic Church located in the Recreation Building in block 25. After signing in, I listen intently to the first day session. I failed the Catechism instructions. When I saw Okaasan again, I said I was sorry but I was not interested in continuing. She quietly accepted my words; the subject of religion was closed forever.

Diabolic wish
Yes, Yes; No, No; I can't win
Nightmare of the Heart

Trouble in Paradise

"Hey you guys," someone yelled, "there's something big going on near the Administration building and the Manzanar police station. Come join us and see what's happening!"

It was Sunday, December 6, 1943 when a few of us were passing the time playing basketball. "Sure, why not," we called out and joined him. When we arrived at the scene, there was a crowd of people standing by looking towards the police station. Someone was shouting something, but I couldn't make out what he was saying, nor did I know why he or she gathered there. I looked over the shoulder of the spectators and saw a small group of armed soldiers facing the crowd. I was shocked to see one soldier sitting on the ground with a machine gun fully loaded – It was the exact model of machine gun (45 caliber Thompson sub-machine gun) that I had practiced with when I took ROTC at UCLA. At that moment, I knew this was not the place for me to be! The young recruits looked too trigger-happy for my money. I left the scene quickly and returned to my humble abode. It was later that day that I heard that a young *Nisei* was shot and killed at the scene where I had been earlier. A second person later died from his injuries. There were eleven other casualties. Most of the wounds were from the side or from the back. Of the twelve shot, four were *Nisei,* two were *Issei*, and five were *Kibei* (*Nisei* sent by their parents to Japan for education and later returned to the United States). Apparently the crowd had become unruly, and the guards responded by tossing tear gas grenades into the crowd. It was during this commotion that the soldiers panicked and fired into the crowd. How could such a terrible tragedy transpire?

There was enough guilt to go around for everybody for this terrible tragedy. The main factors that contributed to this confrontation were the degrading and hopeless camp environment and the suspicions, rivalry for control of the camp politics, and cultural differences between *Issei*, on the one hand, and the *Nisei* and *Kibei* on the other. Then there were the rabble-rousers who had no better things to do but to add to an explosive confrontation. The homogeneous ethnic society was no longer homogeneous.

This event began a day earlier. On December 5, 1942, violence broke out at Manzanar. The moment was ripe for conflicts between *Nisei* and *Kibei*. A month earlier, three *Nisei*, Fred Tayama, Joe Masaoka, and Kiyoshi Higashi, active members of the JACL, received permission from the War Department to represent Manzanar at a weeklong JACL convention in Salt Lake City. At the convention, they supported the resolution urging the War Department to draft *Nisei* for the American armed forces. Once again, the JACL, an organization never officially selected to represent the rest of the Japanese population, was making decisions that affected all of the internees. When Fred Tayama returned to Manzanar, many evacuees considered him an informer (*Inu*) for the FBI and the camp (WRA) administrators. On the night he returned, several masked men attacked him but he managed to survive. Tayama identified Harry Ueno, a *Kibei* as one of the assailants. Subsequently, Ueno was arrested and placed in jail, but not at Manzanar. Ueno, who had organized the Kitchen Workers' Union at Manzanar, was popular with the *Kibei* and *Issei* and with the anti-JACL crowd. He was also at odds with Tayama who had formed the JACL affiliated Manzanar Works Corps. But these two individuals were pawns of larger issues that were fomenting within the camp.

Who in his right mind could ever conceive of a diabolical set of questions based on the presumption that loyalty could be determined by a questionnaire? No other piece of paper (February 1943) could be more divisive between family members than the following two questions:

No. 27: Are you willing to serve in the armed forces of the United States on combat duty, wherever ordered?

No. 28: Will you swear unqualified allegiance to the United States of America and faithfully defend the United States from any and all attack by foreign or domestic forces, and foreswear any form of allegiance or obedience to the Japanese Emperor, or any other foreign government, power, or organization?

There was a buzz in the air, for rumors were running rampant about this announcement. The word was out that the questionnaire was labeled/presented/billed as an "Application for Leave Clearance" but in reality, it was clearly a loyalty oath to draft eligible *Nisei*, second generation Japanese Americans, into military service. The memorandum stated that a $10,000 fine and/or twenty years imprisonment would be imposed if an individual refused to answer and sign the forms. The *Issei*, who are non-citizens, were also required to sign off on the same questionnaire.

There was a meeting scheduled to discuss this new turn of events that had created a crisis within the camp. I was anxious to attend to find out what the government had in store for us. When the meeting started, I felt the tension in the air. It could explode at any minute. Mostly men and young *Nisei* and *Kibei* were there. There were no women attending this meeting. Only a handful of *Issei* were there for they had been relegated to non-participant in the camp's affairs.

I listened intently to the speaker's every words as he read the memorandum verbatim.

Someone shouted from the side, "What the hell is this all about? They take everything from us and now they want to do what?"

"Yeah, explain," someone voiced angrily.

I turned toward the agitator and nodded my head, agreeing with his protest.

The speaker waved his hand, "Let me finish," as he said loudly.

"Answering the questionnaire is necessary in order to determine who can be allowed to leave the camp," he continued.

Someone stood up and said, "I don't understand." He raised his voice: "They said that Manzanar was a Relocation Center from where we could leave eastward at anytime. There was never any Loyalty Questionnaire required. This is the same bull they fed us when they said leaving the Western Defense Area was our patriotic duty."

The speaker, looking flustered, spoke up, "I'm just here to tell you about this memorandum. I have no idea what the intent is except that it was given to me as an 'Application for Leave.'"

An older man stood up. "I'm an *Issei*. When World War I broke out, I volunteered to serve because they said I could become a citizen. I was a citizen until Pearl Harbor. They took my citizenship away saying that I'm an enemy alien, unqualified as an American. Now they turn around and hand me this crap. What do my answers mean anyway? 'Yes, yes' and I'm still a Jap - doesn't make much sense."

A young man in the back rose and spoke, "How can I forswear my allegiance to the Emperor when I have never been to Japan? In fact, I don't even speak Japanese." It seems I'm guilty because my parents are Japanese. Who drafted this anyway?"

At last, I stood up, found my voice and said, "I can't help but believe that the government is hell bent on destroying the Japanese family. *Issei* can only answer "No, no" because the law says they cannot become citizens. Thus if they answer otherwise, they become a person without a country or Persona non-Grata. For myself, the government has reclassified me 4-C, enemy alien. So am I alien or not? May I add that my father was arrested because he was a prominent member of our local Japanese community. There was nothing sinister about his service to the Japanese community. All he wanted to do was to provide *Nisei* the knowledge about the Japanese language and culture that defined who the *Issei* are. We have no knowledge of his whereabouts or even if we would ever see him again. On top of that, my brother is serving in the US Army Military Intelligence Service. I'm sure a number of you are in the same predicament. Rumor has it that "No, no's" will be sent to Tule Lake, a detention camp where these individual will become pawns for prisoner exchange. If I sign "Yes, Yes" while my mother can only answer "No, No" what's left of my family will be torn apart and never see one another again. What kind of justice is that?"

My voice was cracking. Others, around me were shaking their heads and agreeing. "Yeah, there's no justice here."

Another individual stood up and said, "Why don't the *Hakujin's* (Caucasians) come down here and give us some real answers?"

The speaker waved his hands and muttered something inaudible. The meeting ended shortly. Red faces angered at the confusing memorandum grumbled and headed back to their tarpapered rooms.

With a solemn face and heavy in thought, I joined the others and left. This was early February and I still had my physics class to prepare for the following day. Outside the night was cold but clear. As I walked between the barracks, I see the rooms within the camp dimly lit with the bare incandescent lights hanging from the ceilings. Suddenly, the searchlights swept across the camp reminding me I was not free.

Ringo (Apples), land is parched
Gnarled limbs, no fragrance in air
Please blossom once more

Lovely Apple Orchard, Manzanar

They were left to their own devices to survive this nightmare. One afternoon, I had a chance to wander around the camp. I saw the remnants of an orchard among the tarpaper buildings. There was no fragrance in the air, no white and pink blossoms of apple trees, only gnarled limbs on trees standing in what was once row after row of fruit trees. People from this valley told stories how this valley was a thriving apple and pear growing area. But the city of Los Angeles had sucked the lifeblood out of this thriving orchard by draining water from Owens Valley for its own use. Slowly the water table dropped, and the orchard succumbed to the arid soil. Sage and Manzanita brushes gradually set roots on this desert-like soil. Rattlesnakes, scorpions, tarantulas, and other desert life took over the land. Trees here and there reached deep for nutrients, but disease and insects ravaged those that were still standing. These desert dwellers had shown resilience to the ravages of time. As I looked about, it seemed so odd and yet ironic that this was an image of my parent's plight. The life of a proud and industrious *Issei* sucked dry of their energy and left without hope for the future. The fruits of their labor no longer needed. Their wisdom and help to participate in governing this camp no longer needed.

To the west and above the barbed wires and watchtowers, I could see Mount Williamson reaching high into the sky. Just five miles south was Mount Whitney, California's highest peak. White streaks of snow in the shadows of the sun graced the rocky tower. To the north of Mount Williamson, I saw an outline of a canyon that reached towards the west and across the Sierra range. Much of the foothills looked barren, but just southwest of the barbed wire fences, a streak of greenery snaked upward along the foothills. Dogwood and other shrubbery grew along this rivulet that fed water into the valley. As I panned the foothill further, I could see a few cottonwood trees lining both sides of a dirt road that led into the camp. The trail winds past a grove of trees with treetops and branches dead from the lack of water. A tinge of excitement rushed over me. Someday, I thought, I must follow that road over to that stream.

In my moment of reflection of the scenery, I forgot that this was late afternoon. To the north a whirling cloud appeared. Almost every day during the hot season, dust storms ravaged this valley. They moved with such ferocity that they caught every unsuspecting person unprepared to meet the disaster. Dust, pebbles, sand, and grit engulfed you in a moment's notice. I turned my back from the wind, rolled up in a ball, and tried to hold my breath as best as I could. The back of head was peppered with missiles and my skin felt like sandpaper had scrapped across it. My hair, oh my God my hair felt as if I have been sticking my head in a sand pile. I kept my eyes closed because I had forgotten to bring my goggles for this terrible reception. All I could think during that horrible moment were the stories I had read about nomads in the Sahara Desert that huddled against their camels until the sand storm subsided.

Every internee tells about the terrible dust storms at Manzanar, but none can match the experience of this man. It was one summer afternoon when the dust storm started to whip up across the valley floor, picking up everything that was loose. Suddenly the gust that was sweeping across the firebreak began to turn into a whirlwind. Its path now became unpredictable. It skirted a row of tarpaper buildings and headed directly at the block's latrine. A thunderous roar, a loud boom, a terrible shaking of the latrine, and the roof flew off and sides of the building fell away. There sitting on a toilet bowl was a man stunned, dazed, and shaken.

Dust storm

"Library of Congress, Prints and Photographs Division, LC-A35-4-M-10."

Liberty bell rings
Born a Citizen now void
Crisis of the heart

Decision

The time had come to make my decision. It was February 1943, and the US government demanded we answer two loyalty questions, Numbers 27 and 28, or suffer the consequence of a fine of $10,000 and imprisonment.

No. 27 Are you willing to serve in the armed forces of the United States on combat duty, whenever ordered?

No. 28 Will you swear unqualified allegiance to the United States of America and faithfully defend the United States from any and all attack by foreign or domestic forces, and foreswear any form of allegiance or obedience to the Japanese Emperor, or any other foreign government, power, or organization?

No other racial group members have been required to answer these questions in order to determine their loyalty. How could anyone conceive of a divisive and unjust questionnaire for both non-citizens and citizens? My life was a nightmare and my heart torn to shreds to answer these two questions that cut deep into our family's future. I was 21 years old, a citizen classified 1A before imprisoned here, but without due process, reclassified by the government as 4C, enemy alien. It seems that the reclassification was a convenient ploy to incarcerate me as an enemy alien. At no time did I have the opportunity to voice my protest, even though our Constitution guaranteed my "Rights" as a citizen. Now that government wants to draft all *Nisei,* my draft status is back to 1A, citizen. This fact alone made my answer "Yes, Yes" and "No, No" and enigma.

At first, my mother, younger sister, and I shared a sixteen-by-twenty foot room with my brother's family and his father-in-law. Later I lived with mother and my younger sister. Our furniture was stark, a potbelly oil stove for heat and an army cot with a canvas bag mattress filled with straw for each of us. There was no privacy. At night, I could see the stars through the torn tarpapered roof. Every day, every hour, and every minute, we were now wards of the government. The winds blew and dust invaded our privacy. Every bite at mealtime tasted gritty for dust was now a part of me.

Mother, sister, and I each faced a soul-searching decision that could separate us for life. My mother's only choice was "No, No." She could be deported and might never see her family because of her husband imprisoned elsewhere, and her son serving in the US Army. I would not make my decision frivolously for mother's life had been shattered and had suffered enough. I would not add to her misery nor will I leave her and let her bear this nightmare alone! I would decide not for myself, but I must try to stop this insanity and face the consequence. I sign "No, No."

What utter stupidity by the WRA. The Army realized that they had made a mistake in requiring all internees to sign off on the poorly worded questionnaire. However, the damage was apparent. It had caused great consternation and dissension among the people in camp. After realizing they made a mistake, they proposed an alternate set of questions for Japanese American women and for the *Issei,* but the powers-to-be realized this too would only lead to more uncertainties and did not push this change openly. Now that I had committed myself, what was the consequence of my action?

Take one-step forward
I will not die on this land
*For **Hate** brought me here*

One Step Forward

If I could go back and speak to Okaasan, I would tell her many things. I would tell her that there is more to our story in camp. I know that I was so busy trying to cope with my own dilemma that I didn't pay enough attention to her plight. After a few days of settling into the routine of doing nothing in particular, I needed to find a job within the camp. When I went down to the Administration office and studied the postings, I noticed that earlier internees had taken all of the office jobs. What was left was a posting for swampers.

When I went to apply at one of the warehouses, I saw several young *Nisei* inside the building sitting around chatting while a supervisor was busy at his desk shuffling papers. The supervisor explained that the job required someone who was strong enough to help unload merchandise delivered to the camp. He accepted my application and said I could start work that day. The job was boring since most of the time was spent waiting for orders to move merchandise. Unloading twenty tons of soap or cement can be backbreaking, but once everyone got into the rhythm of tossing these heavy items, the task would go rapidly. The work was sweaty, dusty, and everyone invariably ended up with cuts and scratches that looked like they had a fight with a wildcat.

At the end of an exhausting day, I felt that, at least another day had passed in this hellhole. But this job left something to be desired. Usually the day dragged on with nothing to do, and I often wished I could find something more productive than just sitting around waiting for the truck to come in. Then, one day, my prayer was answered. I saw a posting for applicants to train for teaching assignments under the Manzanar School Program.

On the first day, there were over 200 people interested in the program. After hearing the requirements for teacher accreditation, the number of applicants dwindled to about sixty college-trained evacuees. The program required applicants to take University of California Extension courses in education, psychology, educational psychology, American institutions, test and measurements, and secondary education to meet the minimum requirement for a provisional teaching credential. The extension courses were taught under the auspices of the University of California. Fortunately, there were enough qualified teachers among the school administration to teach the courses. Because the program required individual commitment to complete 24 units of educational courses, the number of applicants quickly dropped to 23. I was determined to meet the challenge.

One crisp and clear night, while I was crossing a firebreak on my way to a night class, I stopped for a moment and thought about my dilemma: teaching was challenging and a step forward, but was this all I wanted out of my life? As I looked all around me from the expansive firebreak, all I could see were the dim lights in the tarpaper buildings. I envisioned people in their one-room homes just trying to make the best out of their terrible predicament. It was an uneasy uncomforting thought. Once more I looked at this desolate place and said silently to myself, "I am not about to die on this reservation." I was angry. Then I looked around me. Manzanar personified Hate. Hate is what brought me here, and I vowed that "hate" would not be a part of my vocabulary.

For now, I had made a commitment to teach. I had something to look forward to, something good. I was determined to do my best.

I studied the required courses diligently even though some of the subjects were boring. I completed twenty-four units of educational courses. Finally, I was approved to teach high school physics. The school, from kindergarten through high school, was located in Block 1 along with the Project's Administration offices. My office was located in a laundry room that was modified for an office and space for science class supplies. On the first day, I met two *Nisei*, Mas Nakagawa and Hideyu Uyeda assigned to teach chemistry. We chatted a while and began looking over the supplies for our classrooms. There wasn't much to see. We had to improvise to make up for the lack of basic science equipment. My classroom was at the north end of a barrack. I knew the classroom would be no better than our own family barrack, so I didn't expect much. I could feel no warmth in this room; the walls were unpainted plasterboards, the floor was dark linoleum, a table in front of the classroom served as a desk, a blackboard stood along the front wall, but it was homemade and painted black. Throughout the semester, the blackboard was a challenge, a friend as well as a foe. At first, the chalk would show on the blackboard, but gradually the black paint would wear off. Finally, gaps in my writing would leave the student guessing as to what I was writing on the blackboard. Because even the required number of textbooks was missing, I spent many hours preparing for our classes and duplicating lessons on a ditto machine. This duplicating process was a nightmare: First, I had to write the information with a special ink-pencil; second, I would transfer the written material onto a soft gelatin surface, push a roller over it and embed the ink into it. Next, I had to place my blank paper and push a roller over it to transfer the ink to the paper. Each sheet would become progressively dimmer. Worse still, the gelatin would begin to disintegrate into one purple mess.

This was my first day: As I looked over my students, I didn't see happy faces, only puzzled looks wondering, "Who is this teacher who can't be much older than I?" However, they showed respect for me as their teacher, because *Issei* have always taught children to respect authority and, especially, a "Sensei." It is part of their culture. I was not nervous for I focused on my responsibility: teach them physics, a subject I was confident about teaching. As I looked at the students while conducting the class, I could see who was earnestly seeking an education and those who were simply occupying space. The latter usually sat in the back trying not to be seen or called on to participate. There were rumors that some parents wanted Caucasian teachers even though the *Nisei* were more qualified in the particular subject matter.

Try as I might, camp life was not an environment where you could motivate the students to study. Even the cultural pressure to study hard was nonexistent. I often wondered if I was too tough on the students or if the material was getting through to them. But I am no longer in doubt. It was fifty years later when I received a call from one of the students who had been in my physics class. He wanted to visit me. He told me that after he graduated from Manzanar High School, he had received a bachelor's degree in biochemistry at USC in 1951 and a PhD in biophysics from Cal Tech in 1955. He was ready to leave for a scientific project in Eritrea. He said he had just wanted to thank me for inspiring him to get a college education. I felt humbled by his words. Just one student inspired makes worthwhile all the effort of my teaching.

Our World – Manzanar School

Our World

1943 · 1944

Manzanar High

Science School Teachers

Science Teachers (left to right)
Mas Nakagawa, Chemistry, Tad Kishi, Physics
Hideo Uyeda, Chemistry
Photos from Manzanar High School 1944
Annual (Photographer, Miyatake)

Hold onto your seat
Hard to see clearly right now
What a spectacle

Myopia

Learning by the seat of the pants can be disastrous. For several weeks, after preparing the lessons for my high school physics class, I seemed to develop headaches. It didn't seem to go away.

I had always thought that my eyesight was ok. In fact, I assumed that I had inherited good genes from my parents. Father was the only one that wore glasses and that was after his cataract operation. Why should I have worried? After all, I had passed all eye tests for physical exams and for the Department of Motor Vehicles' driver license.

At the Manzanar School office bulletin, there was a notice about physical exams offered by the Manzanar Hospital. "Well, why not check about my headaches?" I thought to myself. At the hospital, a doctor examined me and said, "Everything looks fine. What you need is glasses. Let me make an appointment with the Optometrist for you."

This was my first trip to the eye clinic. The whole process went by ones and twosies. While sitting in a chair, the optometrist placed a contraption with a set of lenses in from of my face. He began with an initial lens setting and went through sequence as he changed lenses:

He asked, "Is one better than two?"

From each setting I chose as "better," he continued, "Is one better than two?"

The onesie and twosies stopped when I no longer could differentiate between the two sequences. From that point, he checked for astigmatism with the final lens setting in place and a new set of lenses to measure the distortion of the test pattern.

Satisfied with his examination, he said, "You are near sighted and you also have astigmatism in your left eye. Let me measure you for glasses and order you a pair."

I noticed that he was having trouble testing a sample pair of glasses. First, my nose is flat because my brother, Frank, occasionally gave me a bloody nose. I told that lame excuse to people. Second, I have no distinct bridge that will allow most glasses to seat properly.

The optometrist decided on the frame and said, "Come back in two weeks and pick up your glasses."

The day for my glasses arrived. The optometrist adjusted the frame to fit me. The whole event cost me nothing because I was a ward of the US government. After thanking the doctor, I proceeded to walk back to my humble abode wearing my spectacles.

It was weird! For every step I took, the hallway floor, seen through my new glasses, seemed to be somewhere else. My brain was signaling my leg that the floor was further down, even though my foot had already touched the floor. I walked to the exit as if I were walking on eggshells.

Then I was faced with a shocker. I had to walk down a short set of steps. My eyes would send signals to my brain but my foot and brain was not in sync. For each step, I hung onto the railing and carefully lowered one foot at a time until I could feel each tread of the step. For a moment, I knew I would have been embarrassed if any friend saw me in that awkward moment.

Lady on the Bridge

Back in our sixteen-by-twenty room, we had no cabinet or shelf to place or store things. I thought the safest place was to put them in the back pocket of my one and only good clean pants until I actually needed them. A few days later, I was tossing a football with friends from my hometown. We were going to form a team to play against another group of kids. Just as we were bending over in a huddle, I suddenly felt cold air coming through the seam of my pants. Oops, the seam had given out and my underwear was showing. My friend's had a good laugh but they were kind enough to gather around me and escort me back to my room.

I changed to my good pants and sat down for a moment. I heard a crunch.

Oh my God! I forgot I had my glasses in the back pocket! I reached back and pulled out my squished spectacles.

Capture its spirit
Life's hardship of Manzanar
Build Taiko Bashi

Taiko Bashi

I began to notice in this desert land that *Issei* began to heal their wounds by revealing what lives deep inside, the love of nature and its simplicity. I saw simple gardens, carvings from Manzanita, and most of all, a rock garden indigenous of this valley. Even apple trees blossomed. In the spring of 1943, life in the camp had returned to a more peaceful mood since that terrible period of strife and violence that had resulted in the death of young *Nisei*. School is in full session, and children and adults are participating in various outdoor activities. Health Services are available, religious organizations are very active, and the Project has allowed and encouraged industrial operations in the manufacturing of clothing, furniture, and farm products and created a Japanese garden within the camp grounds.

The old folks have captured the spirit of nature with the Japanese garden built among the apple orchard. A small stream meandered around through the garden. Boulders and rocks of various sizes picked from the hills nearby placed in varying patterns. The objects were not neatly stacked nor arranged in regular fashion, for nature is the ideal and regularity is not nature's way. A large boulder sat in the stream while another hung partially over the water. Look, a bridge spanned the meandering stream made from branches and limbs selected from trees outside the project. Each piece seemed to be selected carefully for the structure. The bridge arched in the traditional way of the *TaikoBashi*, Drum Bridge. Flat rocks of varying sizes were nestled in the ground, placed in a curved but irregular fashion, and led to the bridge. They were placed in such a way that suggested to the visitor to leisurely stroll along the path and even an invitation to pause to enjoy the wonders of nature.

When children saw the unique shape of the bridge, it was like a magnet drawing the youngsters to try climbing to the top. Two young girls would happily walk and skip into the garden. They would jump from one stepping rock to another until they came to the bridge. They giggled as they looked at each other and pointed to the bridge. Standing next to the foot of the bridge, they would try the walk but the circular arched path is too steep. Then they could face against it and slowly reach out with one arm to hang on while they brought one foot onto the bridge, put the other hand up to grab onto any part of the bridge, and pull and try to find a spot for the other foot. They would slowly repeat this ritual until they reach the top. They would be pleased with their success as they looked around the garden from their vantage point. They would seem puzzled about going down and might decide to turn around and face the bridge and climb slowly down, foot, hand, foot, hand until to the bottom. They might hold and slide down on the fanny, but there is no place to grab onto to avoid falling. Oops, a little girl slid unceremoniously down to the bottom with a thud, brushed off the dirt, joined her friend, and off they went.

The bridge was symbolic of life; arched to signify that life's journey is difficult to reach the other world. The *Issei* did not fill the entire garden with plants and flowers, but they sprinkled small trees and a few shrubs indigenous to this valley throughout the garden. This garden was the spirit of the valley but yet also Japanese.

Ringo-en Garden

"Library of Congress, Prints and Photographs Division, LC-A35-4-M-10."

In the darkest hour
Heart filled with anxiety
An Angel appears

An Angel Opens the Gate

It was now several months later. I had just completed one year of teaching physics, attended the first Manzanar High School graduation, and now was preparing for the next year's session. One day, I noticed on the Administration's bulletin board a posting for qualified individuals to teach Conversational Japanese to Army Reservists at the University of Minnesota. My heart beat faster. I read and reread the notice, for this could mean an opportunity to leave Manzanar - freedom beyond the gate. Quickly, I fumbled around for paper and pencil. This could be a dream-come-true. Immediately, I drew up my resume to send to the University of Minnesota inquiring about the language program. Meanwhile, I decided to go to the Manzanar school office and make an appointment to see the Superintendent of Manzanar Schools, Dr. Genevieve Carter, and inform her of my plans and request for a reference from her. For a few weeks, I waited for a reply. I kept telling myself, "If I don't get the job, it's ok. I'll manage somehow till another opportunity comes through." I kept hoping.

Then one day, I received an acceptance letter from the University of Minnesota detailing all of the travel arrangements. Then suddenly I felt a cold chill. I remembered the questionnaire 27 and 28 that I had agonized over repeatedly once again. I had not answered the two questions capriciously. But I realized that my leave now might depend on the answer to those two questions? Would the consequence of my answers to the loyalty questionnaire become a roadblock?

I returned to Block 26 to inform *Okaasan* about the possibility of leaving the camp. I waited for mother to return from her employment at the camp's sewing factory.

"*Okasan, Okaeri nasai* (Mother welcome home), " I greeted her.

"*Hai, tadaima*, yes I'm here, she replied.

"*Okaasan*, I have the possibility to leave camp to teach *Nihongo*, Japanese Language, at the University of Minnesota, but I am worried about the family for *Otoosan* (Father) is not home," I spoke with great hesitation.

"*Sorewa iikoto desu neh* (that's very good thing, yes it is), mother replied, "*Shimpai wa nai yo* (no need to worry), Kasorikku Huada (Catholic Father) *ni yotte* (according to), '*Otoosan wa sugu karimasu* (Father will return soon)'," she continued. *Koko wa anatano shorai de naiyo* (This place is not your future). *Shipaishinaide,kono ii shugyoukikai ni yukinasi* (Without worrying, go for this good job opportunity), she said with firmness.

With a sigh of relief to hear that *Otoosan* will be back with the family, I decided not to worry Okaasan about my answers to the loyalty questionnaire. I explained to her what the posting stated and that I would write to the University to apply for the job.

Okaasan said, "You studied Japanese with diligence and did well; I'm sure you will have a good chance for getting the job."

The next day, I hurried to meet with Dr. Genevieve Carter.

Dr Genevieve Carter came to Manzanar from the University of California to study and report on the impact of the evacuation for the department of sociology in May 1942. Soon the Project appointed her as the Superintendent of the Manzanar schools. However, she found that there were no plans for establishing schools at Manzanar. The evacuation had forced school age children to leave before the end of their school year. However, there had been no organized programs in the beginning to keep school age children focused and growing up in a normal way. The forced internment had torn the core of Japanese culture, family asunder.

The parents, concerned about their children growing up without any direction, pressured the administration to establish a summer program. Dr. Carter found that there were no guidelines for communication between project and evacuees, recruiting teachers, establishing supplies, adequate buildings for education, and housing on the site for the teachers. Dr. Carter faced this chaotic state with determination, negotiated for school grounds, and initiated an active recruiting process.

I first met Dr. Carter when she had announced the recruitment program for teachers among evacuees to augment the credentialed Caucasian staff. I had been impressed with her easy demeanor and sincerity towards education for the children in camp. I had taken an education course from Dr. Carter.

Now, while I fidgeted in my chair, Dr. Carter was calm and engaging that made me feel at ease. She remembered me as one of fourteen individuals of the original two hundred or more applicants who had succeeded in finishing the educational classes. She said she appreciated my effort to make the education program successful. I explained that I had an opportunity to leave Manzanar, a dream that I had had ever since I came to Manzanar. I said, "I am sorry I would have to quit as a teacher if I were to be accepted by the University of Minnesota. Would you write a letter of reference for me?"

Dr. Carter said she would gladly be a reference for me and not to worry about leaving the teaching assignment since the projects primary goal was to encourage evacuees to leave the camp.

I explained further that I had a special circumstance that might not allow me to leave even if the University of Minnesota accepted me. I said, "I answered "No, No" on the loyalty questionnaire." I explained my extenuating circumstance about the family: Mother who could only answer 'No, No,' Father imprisoned by the US government and his whereabouts unknown, brother in the US Army, and an underage sister in camp. At the time, if I answered "Yes, Yes," our family would be surely torn apart and possibly never see each other again. My answer had not been an easy one and had been a heart-wrenching moment. Since time has passed. I can without hesitation answer what I really believe, "Yes, yes," now that Mother will no longer be without her husband,

Dr. Carter said to me, "Write to the Administration what you have just told me. I am sure they will reconsider your answers. In fact, I am among the review staff and will support you in your request."

I was relieved and thanked Dr. Genevieve Carter for her time and support.

As mothers always will and always do, dote on their children, she said, "It's very cold where you are going. You will need some warm clothes for your trip." Unfortunately, we were behind barbed wires and there were no department stores, but only a one room canteen and general store. To my surprise, Sears Roebuck had received permission to set up a catalogue service in the canteen. We spent the day leafing through the catalogue for an overcoat, footlocker, and other items for my trip. Mother had to be selective since the internment had affected the family finances.

My departure was several weeks ahead, and while I waiting, I noticed, that *Okaasan* was not present during the evenings. I just thought that she was still busy with her commitment to the Catholic Church since she said they had accepted her into the faith as a sister. One day, just before I was packing my belongings for the trip, mother appeared with several pair's slacks in her arms and said, "These are for your trip." I was surprised and asked mother, "When did you buy these?" "Oh, I bought the material and sewed these pants at the sewing shop. The supervisor said I could use the machine at night to make these." All I could say was, "*Okaasan, arigatoo*, Mother, thank you."

A week before I left Manzanar, *Otoosan* returned from his imprisonment at the US Federal Prison Santa Fe, New Mexico. I did not see the proud and dedicated man of yesteryear. He was just an empty shell of someone I had once been so proud of back home. Try as I may, the words simply bounced off him. He was mute, oblivious to my presence. To say, "*Otoosan, okaerinasi*, Father, welcome home." Home? That would have been an insult to him.

After leaving Manzanar, I never talked much about the experience. Even with my immediate family, words always hidden deep inside. It was several years later when the camps were gone, I had returned from my job with the University of Minnesota back to California. Dr. Genevieve Carter was the first person I went to see and talk about the internment at Manzanar. I thanked her for her considerate support. Again, I found a warm, engaging, and caring person. She was my Angel that opened the gate to freedom.

Manzanar Graduation Celebration

Dr. Genevieve Carter, Superintendent of Education to my left

Stand at the Crossroad
No guarantees on choices
Life's a risk, be brave

Crossroads

After four days and three nights on an old Southern Pacific coach, there I was, at my destination, tired, numb, and grimy from sitting on the hard coach seat. Suddenly, I felt a cold dry sweat across my brow, for I was having second thoughts about this moment. Did I imagine or create my own crossroads a few months ago? Was my decision rash? I had an opportunity to choose: to stay or not stay in camp. However bizarre this thought might be, life in Manzanar was safe. There were no worries about tomorrow, and tomorrow, and tomorrow. I had all the comforts of home: a room, a bed, and three meals a day. However, the barbed wires and watchtower bounded my freedom. It was a life in a cocoon, carefree about what might or might not happen. But, who was I? Wasn't it time to come out of my shell?

I chose freedom over a safe haven. There would be unknowns, but I was not alone. When I had told my mother what I wished to do, she did not protest or shed tears. She, in her own way, prepared me for my journey. When it is time to leave, the mother knows and gently nudges her brood from the nest.

This was the last stop for this train. People gathered their things while ignoring a gum wrapper, crumpled newspaper, half-eaten sandwich, and anything that was too much of a bother to deal with in their haste to leave. However, I was raised to do. I left my seat as clean as I found it, left no trace of my presence, for it was the simple act of respect for others. I waited for a moment while the crowd thinned out, and then moved quickly towards the exit. I followed the passengers to the train station. Inside the building, I found myself in a huge open area where people were either milling around or sitting on rows and rows of oak colored benches. Everything appeared to be made of granite colored marble. The ample lighting within this foyer surprised me since I saw no massive light fixtures. Then up towards the ceiling, I saw sunlight shining through the large light wells. "Is this how it feels to be in a mausoleum?" I wondered as I waited for someone from the Methodist Church hostel to greet me.

I had arrived at Minneapolis, Minnesota's Great Northern Station on Hennepin Avenue. I was free once more.

Chapter 4: Minnesota

Whatever season
One room does not a home make
No heart no warmth here

Home away from home

I had never traveled outside of the State of California until I left Manzanar. Consequently, I did not know what to expect. Before leaving Manzanar, I had to declare a place to stay. I chose temporary housing at a church hostel in Minneapolis, Minnesota until I could find a more suitable place. However, where I would stay would be my choice and not the government's.

When I arrived at the hostel, I made my first telephone call since leaving Manzanar. Mother had told me before I left that her childhood friend, Mrs. Nawa, had written to her that Frank had married her daughter, Stella in the internment camp at Rohwer, Arkansas, and they had moved to Minneapolis where Frank was stationed. *Okaasan* had also given me Frank's address and phone number and told me to be sure to call him and visit him. When I called his home, my sister-in-law, Stella answered, and I asked her to notify my brother Frank that I had arrived in Minneapolis.

When Stella answered, she asked me where I was staying. I replied that I was staying at a church hostel in Minneapolis and that I had come here for a job to teach conversational Japanese at the University of Minnesota.

She said, "Why don't you room with my brother Jiro and share room expenses? By the way, my sister Mary and a close friend Fumiko that were interned at Rohwer, Arkansas, have come to live in Minneapolis. I'm sure they would love to see you when you find housing here. So, why don't I contact my brother Jiro and have him come after you if you don't mind staying with him."

Staying with him would be great because we always had fun together when we were growing up. It was a big surprise to find Jiro here in Minneapolis. I guess, once Stella was established in Minneapolis, she was able encourage her brother, her sister, and friend to relocate out of the Rohwer internment camp. I hadn't been in correspondence with Frank nor did I know his whereabouts until mother mentioned about Frank and Stella had married in Rohwer camp, Arkansas.

Jiro came to the hostel and helped me carry my things to his place that was a few blocks away. We walked past Loring Park towards Spruce Place between Nicholette and Hennepin Ave. I saw a series of older brick houses, but they were all in good shape. There were no yards in front of any of the buildings or fences between buildings. I noticed that almost all of them had basements with steps leading to the entrances. On some corners, I saw what appeared to be small stores situated in the basement floor. This was something new to me since I had never seen a house with a basement back home in California - let alone seen a store in a basement.

Jiro was staying at 1404 Spruce Street. It was an older gray wooden two-story house with steps leading up to the front door. As we entered the wide, dimly lit hallway, I saw the stairway to the second floor. Jiro's room was just off the stair landing. There was a bathroom near the stairs, and on both sides of the hall were two smaller units. Later, I noticed that these two units had a small kitchenette. The room I was to share with Jiro was formerly one big room that was both a dining room and living room. A large heavy dark brown stained sliding door separated the two rooms when closed. I imagined this apartment must have been part of what was formerly a four-apartment unit in a two-story building. The huge dark door was sealed shut, and our room was probably the former dining room. There was a dim light hanging from the ceiling and one window in the corner with the view of the back of the building. There was a small open closet and a double bed. The dark oak floor was well worn, and the walls covered with plain pattern wallpaper. There was no other furniture in this room. This was to be my home away from home but which home. Home that I longed for no longer existed since the one room in a tar papered building at Manzanar was hardly a home either.

Before I left Manzanar, mother made sure that I would travel with a footlocker for my personal items. It was a godsend because there was nothing here to store my things. The arrangement of the room, dim lighting and no furniture offered little hope of reading or studying for any length of time here. The makeshift wall that separated the original rooms provided little privacy. " *Kabe ni mimi ari*, Walls have ears," as mother would say.

Sharing the room was not a problem because Jiro was working the nightshift, and I would be busy during the dayshift at the University of Minnesota. Jiro said that every weekend, Stella asked everyone to come for Sunday dinner at her apartment. To defray the cost, everyone would share the expenses for the food. With only a room and a shared bathroom, I had to send my laundry out for cleaning. Without a kitchen or a refrigerator, I would be looking for a convenient and reasonable place for my meals. Fortunately, two main thoroughfares, Hennepin and Nicholette Avenues, were within walking distance.

Living here was quite an experience. It was not home. It was a place to hang my hat. I had not thought deeply about what it meant to be alone. Now I spent time sitting at counters in cafes, usually ordering the same meals day after day. During the week, I ate lunch in the University's cafeteria with the other members of the Japanese language programs. On the weekends, it was enjoyable to eat at my brother's place and be with family and friends. His apartment was a small one-bedroom unit with a small living room. I was surprised on my first visit to meet a new member of the family, a-six month old niece. On the weekends, my sister-in-law's sister and her girlfriend were always active with the USO that interfaced with the *Nisei* stationed at Fort Snelling.

Winter in Minnesota was cold and when it snows, it is hard for someone from California like me trying to navigate through the deep fluffy snowflakes. When the sidewalks were icy, it was even more hazardous. On one of those icy days, my foot shot away from me while my body hit the ground. I looked around sheepishly and tried to pick myself upright. It took two tries to stand up. After that, I learned to keep my center of gravity so I wouldn't keep falling down. It was even more miserable trudging through knee-deep snow when I was sick with chills and fever. I was alone. I couldn't even get up nor have the strength to go to work that day. Since I had no facility to cook or keep food in my room, I had to go out and trudge through the knee-deep snow to a diner on Nicholette Avenue to eat. Home was never like this.

While the snow was falling, it was a winter wonderland. It was the perfect picture of a White Christmas. I was disappointed that the snow's cape didn't stay white very long. The fireplaces, furnaces, and the factory smokestacks soon powdered the surface with soot. The scenery turns a dirty black mess. I thought I was safe from the soot until I looked at my collar and the shirt cuffs. They both had a disgusting black smudge on the edges. Then I wondered, "Are my lungs coated too?"

Summer was just as miserable because it was muggy, the clothes stuck against my skin, and the mosquitoes ate me alive. I wore long sleeve shirts, but that didn't deter the mosquitoes. I have a theory that the mosquitoes in Minnesota developed extra long proboscis' to draw blood from their victims. I had heard that Paul Bunyan had once roamed this land of ten thousand lakes. The land is green and pretty, but I would have rather been home in California.

Lovely autumn day
Here are Twenty-nine reasons
Frozen on this spot

Freeze the Thought

It was a beautiful autumn day in Minneapolis, Minnesota, and I was free as a bird to soar to any place I pleased. No dust storms or barbwires and watchtowers to remind me I was not welcomed in a land of mine. Just out of Manzanar four days ago, I was very lucky to be able to find a room with my family friend Jiro. Our friends, who lived in Norwalk, California, incarcerated and housed in Los Angeles Santa Anita Race Tracks, then uprooted, sent on a train ride across the US, and finally interned in Rohwer, Arkansas. Jiro had been able to leave the Internment Camp and live near his sister Stella. While I was still at Manzanar, *Okaasan* told me that she had heard from Stella's parents that Stella had married my brother Frank in the internment camp at Rohwer, Arkansas. I heard in mother's voice the happy news that Frank had married the daughter of her childhood friend. Then, her voice drifted into sadness that our family could not be at the wedding. Stella had moved to Minneapolis with my brother who was in the Military Intelligence Section (MIS) at Fort Shnelling, Minnesota.

Stella and Frank in Minnesota, 1944

I missed regular meals after riding three days and four nights by train sitting in an old coach car. I decided the first thing I would do is look for a bite to eat. While enjoying the freedom in this big city, I walked in awe and excitement along Hennepin and Nicholette Blvd. I read the signs in the windows and even stuck my nose into a few places that looked interesting but I could not quite make up my mind. Maybe I missed the familiar sound of the cooks in Manzanar banging on pot covers to tell me it was mealtime. Of course, the term "cook" was a euphemism for farmers, gardeners and laborers who took up cooking for the internees for something to do to occupy their time. Now I felt like a kid in a candy shop deciding on what to spend my five cents. At Manzanar, the only place I could spend my hard-earned money ($19.00/month) on goodies was the canteen. One-step into the canteen, I found nothing to tempt me.

While enjoying the freedom and the awe of this big city, something caught my eye. It was Bridgemans Ice Cream parlor. Twenty-nine flavors advertised right in the window. It struck my weakness. All I could think about now was the Sunburst malt shop back home in Santa Monica that I had missed while at Manzanar. I remember once my big brother Joe said, "I found a great malt shop. Come on, I'll treat you guys." After that first time, it became a regular treat for us. The malt and shakes were so thick that a straw would not do. Only a spoon could scoop the scrumptious freezing flavored ice cream into my mouth. The shop looked clean and inviting with bright fluorescent lighting and a horseshoe shaped counter with red vinyl stools for seating. I saw several customers already enjoying the shop's delectable ice cream treats. There were so many choices and combinations that it was hard to decide. I was up to the task. I savored a dish with five flavors topped with whipped cream. I still remember those lovely colors: red strawberry, lime sherbet, creamy rich yellow vanilla, deep chocolate, and a scoop of peppermint ice cream all sitting in a glass boat topped with whipped cream and cherry on top just waiting for me to dive in. In the summer my choice to abate the muggy summer climate of Minnesota was Orange Freeze, three scoops of orange sherbet, one scoop of vanilla, and a dash of soda mixed together. Bridgemans ice cream shop is forever in my mind.

The next day, I made plans to visit the University of Minnesota for my appointment to teach Conversational Japanese. My only mode of travel was by streetcar that connected Minneapolis with St. Paul. This was indeed a novel experience for me for I had never boarded one. I remember back home in Santa Monica, there was a streetcar line along Santa Monica Blvd. that connected Santa Monica and Sawtelle, but I seldom saw it running nor did I have occasion to ride one.

That morning, I boarded a streetcar on Nicholette Blvd. filled with passengers. I paid the conductor and looked for a place to stand and hang onto the straps to help steady my balance. I had no idea how far the ride was or how the ride would be to St. Paul. As the streetcar swayed a bit and stopped for passengers, a man with a rough weathered and flushed face came towards me. He appeared highly intoxicated, as he staggered from one strap to the next. As he came close to me, I tried to ignore him. Yet he came closer and looked at me as if not quite sure who he was looking for. Still unsteady on his feet, he said, "What tribe are you from?"

I was sure I was in trouble. I was unprepared for chitchat in the streetcar. I just looked at him and said nothing, nor did I raise my hand and say, "How." *Why would he single me out among these passengers?"* I thought. Then I realized it might be my black hair among the blond haired passengers, and besides I was dark tanned from living in the desert terrain of Manzanar. Besides, my skin looked leathered by the sun, etched with the dust and sand from the constant dust storms blasting through the camp. No wonder I must have looked like a Native American Indian. I wondered for a moment, *"Are we tied to a distant past where nomads from the Asian continent traveled across the Aleutian chain and migrated to North America thousands of years ago?"* I know I read that somewhere as I kept quiet and looked at him. Fortunately, the streetcar stopped and the man staggered off. "Whew!" was all I could say to myself.

Minneapolis and St. Paul, called the Twin Cities, lie on the opposite banks of the Mississippi River. The streetcar proceeded down toward the river, turned right to a bridge spanning the Mississippi river, traveled across the bridge and down 10th street to University Avenue. It was about a ten-mile ride to the University. What I remember most on this route was the garish billboard advertising "Honest George's Used Cars" and "White Castle Hamburger Hut."

The streetcars were always full because the government rationed gas during wartime. A few times, I had to wait for the next streetcar. The passengers seemed preoccupied with their own life, reading a paper, either gazing at the same old scenery, or looking at me with a blank face. I too learned to join the others with a blank face. It was my first winter, the most embarrassing thing happened to me when I tried to board the streetcar. If my earlier struggle with walking in snow was embarrassing, this was even worse. I never realized how slick the streets were after a snowstorm. That winter morning, I looked like a stuffed bear wearing a topcoat, hat, scarf, and gloves; this was clothing I never had to wear back home in good ole sunny Southern California.

Lady on the Bridge

My streetcar had arrived. I was standing in the street, reached out to grasp the streetcar's step railing, and suddenly I slipped and fell down forward flat on the street. Embarrassed at my clumsiness, I looked around to see if anyone had seen me, picked myself up, and reached once more for the railing. **Swish Boom**! I was down again a little sloppier. I picked myself up again, looked around to see if I had hurt myself. I was a bit ruffled, but none the worse. I looked up and was ready to try for the step railing but the streetcar was all ready a block away. I felt so stupid standing there frozen in the middle of the street.

University of Minnesota, Japanese Conversational Classroom (ASTRP)

Freedom day by day
Find beauty beyond the gate
Adieu, till again

Letters to *Okaasan*

October1944

Okaasan, while I was happy to leave Manzanar, there was sadness in my heart as I rode the Greyhound bus to Reno because I did not know when I would see all of you again. It was a long three days and three nights by an old Southern Pacific train to reach Minneapolis. I was just one of many people on the train beside young and old people including some soldiers riding with their friends. I never realized how vast this country was until you leave the towns and saw nothing but miles and miles of prairies, cornfields, and mountains. While people in camp tried to scare you about the hatred I might face outside of the camp, no one said anything, bothered me or even noticed my presence.

Okaasan, I want to thank you for packing some food for my trip. I will write to you again soon.

Your son,

November1944

Since I wrote to you last, several wonderful things have happened. I was very fortunate that Frank being stationed at Fort Snelling, Minnesota. You will be happy to know about your son, *Ryuji* (Frank). Frank and his wife Stella (Nawa) received me warmly into their lives even though they were struggling to make ends meet on Frank's meager army pay. The last time I saw Frank, the Army had just drafted him, and now he is married and is a father. *Okaasan*, you will love your lovely granddaughter Jo Ann. Just think I'm an Uncle. Stella's younger brother, Jiro, and older sister, Mary, are also here in Minneapolis. On the day I arrived, Jiro asked me if I would care to share his rented room. The room I share is in a two story older wooden home managed by an elderly couple. The room puzzled me because it was originally part of a large room separated by a dark stained heavy wooden sliding door. Now, sealed shut between the two rooms. It was nothing fancy: one window facing the next apartment, and we share the bathroom with other tenants. The place is in a nice neighborhood and is close to a park, Loring Park. With no kitchen facility, we both eat out. In fact, I hardly ever see him except when he returns at night. On Sunday, we usually get together and have dinner with Stella and with Frank when he is off-duty. We all share the expenses with Stella for the meal.

I have just started work and I travel every day by streetcar from Minneapolis to the University at St. Paul, Minnesota. When I catch the streetcar early in the morning, it is usually crowded. Everyone seems preoccupied with his or her own life, reading a paper, either gazing at the same old scenery, or looking at you with a blank face. I just sit quietly and join the others with a blank face.

I will write to you again soon.

Your son,

November 1944

Okaasan, I must tell you about some wonderful things that have happened since I wrote to you last time.

First, the weather has been nice but it is getting colder. I never knew how beautiful autumn could be because we had only one season back home. The leaves are turning to beautiful shades of yellow, green, and red all mixed, especially the *momigi* (maple), as the season changes. Then, I smiled because I knew that I didn't have to rake the leaves.

I faced my first day of teaching with nervous anticipation since my students were in the US Army Reserves. They marched in formation from their barracks into the building and peeled off one by one into the classroom. They were all college students, just about my age. The day went smoothly. They are all very bright, attentive, and show me respect as *Sensei*. I am amazed how quickly they pick up the language. The person in charge of the program prepared the lesson plan. She is a young Russian woman that was born and lived in Tokyo, Japan for twenty-one years. Her parents were "White Russians," the intellectual class, who fled to Japan during the Russian Revolution of 1917. She speaks fluent Japanese, very nice to all of us, and bubbles with enthusiasm about her Japanese language program. The instructors are all *Nisei,* and everyone is very friendly. Not once did I hear any complaining talk about the interment. We teach in the morning and meet in the afternoon to discuss about class work. Because I have some free time, I enrolled in a Math class at the University to continue my own education.

Okaasan, what I really wanted to tell you is about one of the teachers I work with. Her name is Ida Shintani. Her husband, Mas Shintani is a mechanic, and they live in the neighboring city, St. Paul, Minnesota. They have two lovely daughters. Her entire family, including her brothers and sisters, and her parents (Tanaka) moved to St. Paul from Los Angeles. Her brother Tom is also an instructor in the program. Ida is the most generous and nicest person I have ever met. She has taken me, a total stranger, into her family as if I were her younger brother. On several weekends, she invited me for dinner with the family, as well as, to go on picnics with them to see and enjoy some of the beautiful lakes of Minnesota. She never asks for anything in return.

I have been able to save some money since I have taken an extra job correcting homework and exams for the Physics Department. I hope you will be able to use the small sum of money.

Until next time,

Your son

January 1945

Okaasan, I experienced my first white Christmas. While it snowed at Manzanar, it is nothing compared to this. The Christmas spirit here is unbelievable. Even on cold winter nights, I hear carolers singing. Although there is a war going on, the stores are beautifully decorated, people bundled up for the cold weather, and scurrying to buy their Christmas gifts. The big Dayton Department Store is even more impressive. In front is a tall fir tree all decorated with lights and fabulous decorations that I never saw back home. There is a feeling of goodness and joy here.

I hope you enjoy the lovely handkerchiefs I sent you for Christmas.

Regards to everyone,

Your son,

May 1945

Okaasan, there is great joy in the streets because the war with Germany has ended, but because we are still at war with Japan, I will still be teaching at the University. I heard the good news that Ryuji (Frank) ends his Army commitment and will return to California very soon.

I have heard rumors that the Internment camps will be closing sometime in the near future. However, I am deeply worried where all of you will be returned to, especially when we have lost our home and nursery business in Santa Monica. Please let me know where all of you will be if Manzanar closes.

Your son,

July 1946

Okaasan, I hope everyone is fine and thank you for letting me know that the family can reclaim the houses in Boyle Heights, Los Angeles. I'm sorry that I have been of little help to the family in moving from Manzanar.

Okaasan, I hasten to tell you that I will be leaving Minneapolis because my job with the University is finished with the end of the war with Japan.

I thought it might be possible to continue my college education here at the University of Minnesota, but it seems that I will lose too much of my college credit from the University of California to make it worthwhile staying here.

I hope I won't be imposing on anybody by my return to California.

Till again,

Your son,

Flat out mistaken
No Zephyr breeze comforts me
Lost at Spanish Fork

Gouged at Spanish Fork

I was flat out mistaken to have thought I had a sweet deal to drive my friend's car from Minnesota to California instead of traveling home by train or bus. My teaching contract with the University of Minnesota ended, and I was preparing to return to California when my friend, Mas, asked me to drive one of his cars back to Monterey, California.

"What a great deal," I thought." It could save me time and money." However, his offer had a big surprise in store for me. Little did I know that he had bought an old Ford Motor Company's Lincoln Zephyr, a luxury car that Ford no longer manufactured. The motor was a twelve cylinder V12. Because he couldn't fix the Zephyr motor, he replaced it with a smaller rebuilt Ford Mercury engine. That caused a serious problem since the Mercury motor was a foot shorter than the Zephyr's V12. In order to cool the motor, he had to weld an extension of the fan shaft closer to the radiator. I didn't know about the change until after the fact. The car was a loser!

Mas asked me one other favor.

"Can you buy me at least twelve pounds of butter, pack it with dry ice, and bring it back on your trip since butter was still rationed in California?"

"Sure, that's no big deal!" I answered while not knowing how much running around I would have to do.

He also said that he knew a student at the University that could share the ride and expenses with me on the trip home. By the time the two of us rounded up the butter from several stores and found a place to buy dry ice, it was already noon. We decided to drive to California as quickly as possible. Since it was a two thousand mile drive, I had hoped to share the driving with my rider, but he declined the offer. I set my sights on Omaha, Nebraska, a 400 plus mile drive, for the first leg of the trip.

It was summer, it was hot and muggy, and we were driving through America's heartland. I had often heard of the great cornfields of the mid-west, that you could actually see the plant grow by inches. Indeed, it was mile after mile of cornfield, growing in checkerboard farmland as we sped through Ames, Iowa. Suddenly, there was a big "bang" sound in the rear of the car, followed by a **thump**, thumping of a blown tire against the fender. In a flash, I kicked my foot away from the pedals. It was a blowout on one of the rear tires. My reaction was automatic as I remembered one other time when a tire blew on a car I was driving.

It had happened one day when I was driving out on a country road, my father and uncle were sitting in the back, and my sister was in the passenger seat. Suddenly, as now, I heard **bang**, thump, thump, and thump! At the sound of the blowout, my sister yelled. I hit the brakes! It was the wrong thing to do! The car tried to pivot on the blown tire. I countered the pivoting and found myself correcting my first move. It was my lucky day! While the car tipped one-way and the back the other way as it pivoted, it didn't overturn. However, the car ended up on the wrong side of the road. In that brief moment of terror, everyone shaken by fear said nothing. It happened so fast my heart was pounding hard and my legs felt wobbly, but I tried not to show it. I drove to the side of the road, got out and changed the blown tire. That helped me calm my shaken nerves, but my legs were still shaking as I drove all the way home. "Never again," I said to myself, "will I hit the brakes when I have a blowout! I'll just jam my foot back and pray!"

My rider didn't lift a finger while I jacked up the left rear wheel, removed the blown tire, put the spare on, and cleaned up the mess. Luckily, there was no traffic on the road to be wary of danger. I finally reached Omaha, Nebraska, and I decided to drive further on to Lincoln to sleep in for the night. We were up early the next morning, ate breakfast, and were on our way again 650 miles to Cheyenne, Wyoming. While cruising at 75 miles an hour, I had another blowout on the same rear wheel. Thankfully, Mas had loaded the car with three extra spare tires, but they were all retreads. If Mas counted on having spare tires, he was in for a big disappointment. I thought that maybe the tires were blowing because they were defective retreads. I was miffed again at my passenger because he didn't bother to lift a finger to help change tires. I gritted my teeth and drove on while I did a slow burn inside and wondered, "Where in the world did this mute *Nisei* passenger come from?"

I drove more than 640 miles to Cheyenne, Wyoming without stopping. Even though it was late in the day, it was hot. I looked around and all I could see were granite hills. Not much vegetation was in sight in this stretch of the country. I worried that I would have another blowout on the hot roadway if I drove in the daytime. I decided driving across Wyoming at night was my best option. However, it was another 400 miles to go without resting. My passenger still didn't want to share driving.

I saw no outlines of shrubs or trees as I traveled at night across Wyoming, just bare shadows of granite hills. Finally, I stopped for a moment near Evanston just as the sun was rising. It was a beautiful sight of red and brown colors as the sunlight bounced off the granite face between the saddles of the hill. Quickly the landscape turned to a barren wasteland. I thought, *Thank god, Utah is only a few miles away*. Then, *"Oh no,"* the car began missing a beat every now and then. I was worried. Out here in this wide-open country, there isn't a garage in sight for miles. It was an anxious moment traveling with a sick motor. We limped into Salt Lake City early that morning. I thought we could keep going in spite of the car acting up, but I was wrong. The car finally broke down at Spanish Fork, Utah. I was in the Land of Brigham Young. The mechanic at the garage listened to my sad story and estimated it would take several days to fix the car. He pointed out a motel a block away that we should stay at while he worked on the car. There was not very much to do here in Spanish Fork to fill your empty hours.

After waiting one day, my passenger got impatient, boarded the Greyhound for Los Angeles, and left me stranded. After a few boring days of waiting, the mechanic finally said he fixed the car, lifted the hood and showed me his work. Then the mechanic said, "Let's give this one last shot. I'll rev the engine and see if everything was ok."

Vruum! Wham! Crunch! With a loud sound, the fan broke off and gouged the radiator! Water poured out onto the floor! Suddenly the blood drained from my face. I was stunned!

"Can you fix it?" I asked.

"Sorry, I don't have a spare radiator and I can't fix it right away because Ford doesn't make Lincoln Zephyrs anymore. I'll check around, but I'm sure nobody has parts for this car!"

I was in a panic! I asked to use his phone to call Mas in Monterey, California. He wasn't home, but his wife Ida answered. I told her the sad story. She said, "Mas was in Los Angeles and returning with a load of gasoline for his gas station. He'll be there as soon as he can."

I thought another day in Spanish Fork would go by since Mas had to drive over 1,000 miles from Los Angeles, California to Spanish Fork, Utah. I was surprised and relieved when I saw him later that day. He had driven all the way without stopping. After assessing the damage, Mas said he knew a mechanic in Salt Lake City where he could tow the car and get it fixed. However, he wasn't sure how long it would take. Once more, I was stuck in Utah a little longer. For what seemed like two weeks, I rode the bus every day to Salt Lake City to watch the progress. Even for a big city, there isn't much to do in Salt Lake City. At dusk, it seems, they roll up the sidewalk.

Finally, after waiting through many boring days, Mas had fixed the Zephyr. First, he said he would haul the car to Monterey and then take me home to Los Angeles. Afterwards he told me on the way to Monterey, "The reason you had those blowouts was from the tire rubbing against fender and not because of the retreads. I'm not sure why, but I found the car body wasn't seated correctly in the king-pin."

All through that anxious waiting, I never once thought about the butter in the trunk.

It's been a long time
Okaasan, tadaima
Wait, Draft Board wants you

Greetings from Your Draft Board

Even though Mas had worked so hard and long in order to fix the car and finally had towed it to Monterey, he said he wanted to get me home as soon as possible. After a brief rest, we soon headed for Boyle Heights and not Santa Monica. My home in Santa Monica no longer existed since the nursery was lost.

Except for Kaz, who was now married, the rest of the family lived in the four houses on this Boyle Heights property. I remember when we lived in Santa Monica; *Otoosan* had bought this property in the name of his married and eldest daughter, Mabel, who was of legal age, because *Otoosan* could not own property under the Alien Land Law. Even though the property was in Mabel's married name, there was a tacit agreement between *Otoosan* and the son-in-law, who was an alien, that the property belonged to our family. It was fortunate that the family was able to reclaim the houses in Boyle Heights before they left Manzanar.

We had arrived in Boyle Heights, and stopped at my parent's house

"Okaasan, Otousan tadaima, shibaraku deshta! (Mother, father I am home, It has been a long time since I saw you last)," I said as I entered my parents' house in Boyle Heights.

Okaasan, Otousan, I want you to meet Mas-*san*, my very good friend who brought me home from Monterey. I wrote to you about his family when I was in Minnesota. I am forever grateful that Mas and Ida took me in and treated me as if I were a member of their family.

"Okaerinasai (Welcome home)," greeted my mother.

"Mas-*san, arigatougozaimasu* (thank you so much)." Won't you stay and visit for a while?" continued mother.

"Arigatou, thank you, but I must leave soon to visit with another friend," said Mas. "Maybe some other time I'll be able to visit with you."

It was nice to be home again. Mother no longer wore the mask that hid her terrible ordeals that had started with that fateful day, December 7. The color of life had returned. She was once more full of energy. Father too looked different. When I left Manzanar, father had been a shadow of his former self. Today, he looked healthier, for his gaunt face had fleshed out, and I even detected a smile when I came home. Yet he was silent most of the time and never asked me about my absence. Mother, on the other hand, was busy trying to make my homecoming pleasant. Soon, she was trying to get everyone together to share our time together once more as a family. When I didn't see my younger sister, Kaz, I asked *Okaasan* where was she. She said that Kaz had married Yas Tatsumi in Manzanar on September 25, 1945.

I was home, but deep inside I felt out of place. Even though the house we had lived in on the Santa Monica nursery property was cramped for all of us living there, I missed the warmth and the memories it held for me. This wasn't home as I remember. I saw four white houses that were typical of stucco buildings constructed in the late nineteen twenties. Typical of the time, the houses all had hardwood floors, were well built, but the rooms were all modest in size. While the family was fortunate to be able to reclaim some of the stored items before leaving for internment, as I looked around, I was saddened to see that we had lost so many things. Only necessities saved. Things that were close to my heart and memories of the past were gone.

The war had brought a big change in the makeup of our family. Frank had married Stella while he was in the Army and lived in one of the houses in Boyle Heights. My younger sister, Kaz, had been married in Manzanar and lived with her in-laws. Joe, of course, was already married before he left for Manzanar. My older sister Mabel, the *Neisan*, raised in Japan, was also married several years before the war and lived in the main house, as she was a citizen and the legal owner of the Boyle Heights property. I was now the only single member of the family.

After Mas left, mother handed me an envelope saying that this must be very important because it was from the government. It was from the draft board. It read, "Greetings, you are scheduled for your Selective Service Physical on September 11, 1946. Please report to your nearest Military Entrance Processing Station for induction."

It seems that as soon as my employment with the University of Minnesota had terminated, the Draft Board was looking for me. What more contribution could I make beyond what I had given up by my internment at Manzanar and by what I had already contributed by helping the nation train Reservists to speak Japanese? With this letter, my hopes to reenter UCLA died. I decided that it would be silly to sit around and wait for the scheduled induction date, and so I volunteered for an early induction. At least, my military record would show that I was a volunteer rather than labeled as a draftee – if nothing else, it gave me some small control over my destiny,

Of course, *Okaasan* was always fussing over me. However, today was the day of my Army physical. Maybe there was still a ray of hope that I might skip induction for service. Would they reject me because of my flat feet? I wondered hopefully. My brother Frank dropped me off at the Army Processing building. Inside, there were about a dozen young recruits waiting to take their physicals. First, a recruiter pushed a form in my face and ordered me to fill out my life history. The questions were straightforward enough, but I saw a few recruits struggling with the questions. At this late date, surely there would be other *Nisei* or *Kibei* here, but I was the only Japanese American.

As soon as I finished, a rough looking sergeant barked out, "Take off everything except your shorts, socks and shoes and wait for your turn to see the doctor for your physical examination. You will have a chance to explain to a doctor about any physical disability that might defer you from the draft. Stand in line and wait your turn."

When my turn came, I explained to the doc that I had flat feet that hampered me from walking long distances. He didn't flinch. First, after performing a few indignities on me as part of my physical exam, the doc took out a piece of paper to test my flat feet. He told me to take off my socks. Then he leaned over and pushed the corner of the sheet of paper under the instep. The corner of the paper disappeared about a smidgen under my arch. Great, I thought the edge of the paper didn't disappear. Saved, I said to myself.

"No problem, move on," he said sharply.

The next event brought out the horror of my trip to Manzanar. All of us stood around a big tub with a paper cup to fill with our urine. I froze. I coaxed. I sweated out that horrible moment. Deep inside me, I felt that terrible embarrassing moment I experienced on the way to Manzanar while standing in front of that cruddy yellow stained toilet bowl at Lone Pine. Finally, while a cold sweat rushed over me, my mind convinced my body to do its duty. I moved on to the last station, the Oath of Enlistment.

Another officer barked out, "Raise your right hand and repeat after me. I ..., do solemnly swear that I will support and defend the Constitution of the United States ... So help me God. Now take one step forward."

He waited while we took that step forward.

"You're in the Army now!" he barked again.

Whereupon a gruff looking sergeant handed us our travel orders and motioned us to leave.

Basic survival
Let your sweat drizzle, drizzle
Yellow stain won't fade

It's Basic!

Today we boarded a train at the Los Angeles Union Station at dusk to travel to an Army installation for basic training. We headed 138 miles eastward to the small desert mining town of Barstow, CA. There was nothing out there in the heart of the Mojave Desert but a switchyard. When I boarded the train in LA, I didn't know what route we were taking. It was nightfall and it was difficult to see where we were going. At the switching yard, the train turned westward to Bakersfield, CA. The train kept switching back and forth, for I could see the end of our train now and then trailing us. Suddenly, darkness engulfed us for short spans as we passed through a series of tunnels. If only we were traveling daytime, this train trip would be an exciting one to remember. The train huffed and puffed slowly for 180 miles through the series of twists and turns through the Tehachapi Pass to Bakersfield.

From Bakersfield, the train headed northward through the central valley paralleling California Route 99. At sunrise, I could see the lush fruit orchards and vineyards of the San Joaquin Valley stretching to the east and west of the tracks. In the west, I saw the Diablo Range all brown and dry. My mind was a blank just waiting for something to attract my attention from this boredom. There was no chatter, for everyone was a stranger on this trip. I kept thinking, "The war was over. What possible need was there for me?"

It was almost noon, and it had been 300 miles of listening to the monotonous repetitious clickity clack of the train rolling along when we finally reached Sacramento and turned toward Davis, California. Then for some reason, when we stopped at Davis, our car moved forward for a moment, and then we were moving backwards onto a siding. I heard the hiss sound of the air brakes releasing the air pressure, the locomotive was abandoning us. Surely, this place couldn't be our destination because we were a short distance from UC Davis, an agricultural college. A sergeant came down the aisle and said, "We'll be here for awhile to we'll eat lunch. No one is to leave the train while we're here." Another soldier followed him and passed out a box lunch for everyone.

The motto of the Army was "Hurry up and wait." Waiting we did for a few hours, not knowing what was to happen next. Then I saw several buses coming to our rescue. We loaded our gear and piled into the buses. Yet, I still didn't know our destination. The bus driver headed southward on a country road and stopped along the side of the road near a stretch of hayfields. "OK, you guys, it's your pit stop!"

Soon we zipped back to the bus and finally arrived at Camp Stoneman, Pittsburg, California. This was still not our final destination, for Camp Stoneman was a "repo depot" for receiving, processing, and launching US troops overseas. I saw blocks and blocks of khaki-colored two story barracks and not much else. A corporal came, assigned us to a barrack, and led us to the mess hall. The army chow was even less appetizing than the meals I ate in Manzanar. At last, tired from the long day of traveling, I decided to sleep off the boredom.

I'm not sure what time of the night it was, but a non-com prodded me to get up. Still very groggy, I heard him say in a gruff voice, "Get up! You're on KP duty." The soldier roused a few more recruits for KP. "On the double," he barked. He proceeded to march us to a mess hall and handed us over to the cook. I got the job of peeling several sacks full of potatoes with another recruit. It seems that soldiers arrive here from overseas at unscheduled times of the day and must keep the chow hall open. Peel and cut the eye out, peel and cut the eye out, and on and on. I didn't want to see another potato for a long time after I finished. I dragged my butt back to the barracks, dropped on the cot, and sacked out.

Asleep, I felt someone prodding me again. "Get out of the sack! You're on KP duty," barked someone. Half asleep, I said grumpily, "I just got back from KP." The soldier ignored my protest. "Get up. On the double," he snorted. There was nothing else for me to do but get up because I was a raw recruit, and he had stripes on his sleeve. You can't get any lower than a recruit. That's the basics of army life. When I finished the second KP duty, I was determined not to be around for slave labor.

Our orders to move out came none too soon. We rode to Sacramento to catch our train for Tacoma, Washington. It was about 750 miles or more than thirteen hours by train. Again, our ride was at night with no scenery to enjoy. Finally, at Tacoma, we boarded army trucks to Fort Lewis.

The land was lush with greenery as we took the hard ride in the army truck. We entered through the archway into the army compound and stopped at our new home, a two story barracks. While we were unloading our gear, a tall, young, blond crew cut drill sergeant came out of the barracks. He had no smile, was no nonsense GI, and began giving us orders: "Pick up your gear and find a place to bunk and fall out here afterwards to receive your army uniforms."

This was a roof over my head and with pay for nine weeks of basic training. I decided to take the top bunk because, by some gut instinct, I didn't want something over my head. No sooner had I put my stuff on the bunk bed, than the Sergeant was barking orders: "Hustle up and line up outside. You need to check out your uniforms."

We rushed outside and formed a straggly line-up whereupon the sergeant yelled, "fall in and form a double line." Next, we marched to a building to receive our uniform and boots. When we returned to the barracks, the sergeant read out the rules and regulations and how to make the bed and about which inspections would take place. From that point "Yes, Drill Sergeant, No, Drill Sergeant" shouted aloud became my basic reply and never "Sir" or a recruit would be in deep trouble.

The next day after morning chow, we lined up outside, and the sergeant marched the group down the street to a one-story building. He ordered us in sets of three recruits to enter the building for a haircut that was a euphemism for sheep shearing.

When my turn came, I sat on a bench watching for the barber to yell "Next." Blond hairs, brunette, black, already covered the floor like leaves shed in autumn. I watched one recruit, who had neat wavy hair, looking sick as the barber sheared off his pretty long wavy hair. I watched as everyone left the room with a greenish sheared scalp showing. When the barber yelled, "Next," I didn't mind receiving a butchered haircut because I could never keep my hair combed neatly.

Next, we were required to get tetanus shots. The place wasn't the hospital or the dispensary, but just another building. I took my place in line while a GI, who surely wasn't a nurse or doctor, told everyone to take off his shirt for the shot. Just ahead of me stood a six-foot tall recruit about to receive the jab from the hypodermic needle. Suddenly his face turned ashen and he slumped like a wet rag to the floor. While two soldiers attended to him, the jabbing with the needle kept on.

I can't remember if I was required to write down my mother's maiden name, but the Army had paperwork for me to do just in case I ended up a casualty. Once these preliminary tasks were finished, the real grunt work began. My ears still ring from the gruff barking of the drill sergeant; Fall in, fall out, on the double, give me 20, hup two three four and the drill goes on and on through the day.

I know now why this countryside was so green. The normal weather report is rain. There was nothing more miserable than doing 20 pushups in the drizzle, drizzle, day after day in Washington. Of course, doing sit-ups with a wet fanny is just as uncomfortable. What was amazing after a few weeks was that the adrenaline flowed and the muscles hardened and grew in spite of the miserable weather. However, without chow, the next day would be hard to meet.

At the end of basic training, I was healthier, more solidly built, and twenty pounds heavier. It's a hard life without sustenance. The first thing I learned was to be the first in line for chow. The lesson came one day for breakfast. I must have moseyed over to the mess hall one morning, picked up the metal tray, and proceeded down the serving line. When it came my turn for French toast, there was nothing. They tossed me a piece burnt toast, and that was it! From then on, I was a chowhound – first in line.

Basic training was always on the double, discipline, and the drill sergeant had total control over the recruit. I soon learned how to cut corners to keep my space ship-shape army style. The Army wanted your bed neat and the bedding tucked tight enough that the drill sergeant could bounce a quarter on the bedding. At first, I took pains to meet the standard, but this cost time. I quickly learned to slip into my bedding without unraveling the blanket, sleep without moving, and slip out in the morning without a wrinkle in my bedding. A simple tuck here and there made it all nice and tight.

The Army taught me to kill. My weapon was a M1 rifle. If the drill sergeant heard the word "gun" for your weapon, you sleep with it. That happened to me one day when he misheard the word "gum" for "gun." The M1 became my 'honeymoon bride' for the night. There was no justice in basic training.

After the calisthenics, close order drills, marching miles on end, and night drill, our last exercise was bivouac. It was December in Washington and snowing. Our squad was readying for a twenty-mile hike and involved pitching pup tents for this last week training. What I worried most about were my flat feet for the long hike rather than pitching the tent and sleeping outdoors. Then we heard the good news, the army cancelled our bivouac exercise. It seems the group ahead of us suffered a dozen or more serious cases of pneumonia, requiring the Army to cancel all bivouacs until further notice. Mother Nature kept piling the white fluffy snow day after day for our benefit up to the end of our basic training.

It was time for "boot camp" to ship out. We headed back to Camp Stoneman, CA, an all-too-familiar place. This time I made sure, I wasn't available for KP. It was the Army's "hurry up and wait" process for we had to sit around for our orders. Some soldiers talked about slipping out and hitting the "hotspots" of Vallejo, a favorite town for the lonely GI's before shipping out. Then our travel orders came through.

All Japanese (recruits) received the order to leave for Presidio of Monterey to learn military Japanese at the Army's Military Intelligence Section (MIS) for the next six months. This was a strange fate indeed. Once hating me for being Japanese, now they want to pour more Japanese on me. The stigma of "Japs" did not end with the war. While I was in basic training at Fort Lewis, a

Nisei in our squad had told me the following: A young Caucasian recruit in the same barrack, kept pestering him and trying to pick a fight. George was a "*Yo-dan*," fourth-level black belt judo expert who was disciplined not to use his skill unless confronted with bodily harm. He was also smaller in stature than the Caucasian was, but he was solid muscle. Finally, it came to a showdown at the top of the stairs one day. When the bully tried to push George, he found himself at the bottom of the stairs. He kept his distance from then on.

Again, I found myself in a world with just Japanese and the surprise of my life began.

A long time ago
It happened in Monterey
Eyes flutter, heart wilts

It Happened in Monterey

"It happened in Monterey one day, I met her in Monterey ...," the words just keep buzzing in my head. Here I am with other *Nisei* and *Kibei* to the Army Language School at the Presidio of Monterey, Monterey, California to learn military Japanese. What a wonderful place to be. I was glad the Army moved the Military Intelligence Service (MIS) from Fort Snelling, Minneapolis, Minnesota to such a scenic place. If only I didn't have this drab uniform on, it would seem like a vacation. When I arrived, I saw the installation perched on a hill, and from the rise it had to be a breathtaking view overlooking the Monterey Bay. An old canon sitting on the crown greeted us at the entrance, a relic of the past, the Mexican-American war. Our barrack was the standard army two-story building, but well maintained, painted off white, and not at all like the drab buildings at Camp Stoneman. This was my new home, and I had my own space on the first floor, for there are no double bunk beds in this barrack.

When I understood that we were to learn military Japanese, I was worried. Not because of the language, but because I had heard from *Nisei,* stationed at the original MIS at Fort Snelling, that the training was intense, highly stressful, and required long hours of extra studying. I did not look forward to a stressful assignment. After all, the government had already taken five years of my freedom.

I was wrong about the stressfulness of the assignment, and my negative attitude changed. Once the language school started, the classroom pace was casual and relaxed. The original intensity to catch up with military language for the war with Japan was over. Now was the time for the occupation. However, I was not sure what the mission was for my training. I had heard from close friends and family members about the heroic deeds of the Japanese Americans, who graduated from MIS and served in the Pacific during World War II. They served in the Aleutians, South Pacific, Philippines, Indonesia, and even China, to name a few places. They translated, interpreted enemy documents, as well as intercepted enemy transmissions that caught the Japanese Army and Navy by surprise and led to their demise. Some *Nisei,* who were well versed in the Japanese language*,* infiltrated the enemy units, posed as their commanders, and successfully coerced enemy soldiers to surrender. Yet, I had not heard or seen their heroic deeds and contributions recognized or publicized openly. I felt a bit resentful about that. Now that the war was over, what possible contribution could I make? Would it even matter?

I was soon to find out and I was surprised. After two weeks of schooling, I received a request to help the section made up of *Kibei* with their English. This, indeed, was a bizarre circumstance; to come here to further my knowledge of Japanese and end up tutoring English.

This was still the Army life requiring roll calls, close order drills, marching, and occasional KP duties. At least, nobody came in the middle of the night to prod me to do KP. In addition, roll call was hardly up to army standard since some *Nisei* rushed down wearing their overcoats to hide that they were not dressed. This was one relaxed outfit, I thought.

Then one night I had the surprise of my life about fellow *Nisei*, people who looked like me but seemed to have a chip on their shoulders. One Saturday night, I decided to turn in early. If I wasn't careful this evening I thought, I could end up waking up to "**kotonk**." That's the sound of an empty coconut hitting the ground, according to Hawaiian *Nisei*, when they talk about knocking down a mainland *Nisei* in a fistfight. I had heard that infighting had occurred between the two *Nisei* groups, Hawaiian born and mainland, during the early basic training of the all *Nisei* 100/442 Battalion. The Hawaiian *Nisei* thought the mainland boys were putting them down with their Standard English versus the daily Pidgin English the Hawaiians used. However, that wartime animosity was to disappear. One weekend during basic training, a mainland *Nisei* invited a few Hawaiian *Nisei* to visit his former internment camps on a weekend pass. It was a revelation they would long remember. When the Hawaiian *Nisei* saw the plight of the Japanese-Americans, they learned what the *Nisei,* who had volunteered from the camps, were fighting to prove their loyalty. Quickly, they realized they were brothers fighting for the same cause.

However, the conflict reappeared for me.

That night in Monterey, after I had gone to bed, the bars in town had closed and three Hawaiian *Nisei* came rolling into the barracks singing away. Their voices were loud and annoying. I mumbled, "Knock it off!" That was the wrong thing to do. In a flash, the three Hawaiians converged on me and glared down at me looking for a fight.

"*Wat doing!* (What's going on)," said one Hawaiian.

"*Howzit, bodda you* (What's up, does it bother you)," said another.

"*Like Beef* (Want a fight)?" said the third Hawaiian.

I didn't like the odds: three against one. Especially when I couldn't move quickly tucked in bed. I just lay there doing a slow burn, looking for a way to even the odds if they decided to pile on me.

They kept staring down at me as if waiting for a fight.

The standoff went on for a while

Then, one Hawaiian said, "*Nuff already* (enough all ready)."

I was madder than Hell! Then, I realized I had made the right decision to stay cool headed. I couldn't understand how my fellow *Nisei*, whom I never treated disrespectfully and had trained with them here at the Presidio, could suddenly become uncivil and inconsiderate. One-on-one, they were quiet and non-belligerent. When in a group, they became aggressive.

When I was growing up back home, my mother had talked about people drinking and that it sometimes brought out the worst in people, especially those who were insecure. I heard the words, "*Shima guni konjo*" meaning small island complex. I learned that early Japanese and other Asians, who immigrated to Hawaii to work on the plantations, faced beatings and mistreatment by their bosses. I understand too that they could only communicate by means of "broken English." I had no quarrels with them.

The weekend passes were heavenly gifts. With the town of Monterey within walking distance, the weekends allowed me to enjoy the beautiful setting and the convenience of the shops in town. I walked down Cannery Row, made famous in John Steinbeck's novel. The factories were silent, for the runs of sardines had disappeared, but I did imagine the salty, fishy scent that remained. While I strolled along the shore, I felt the cool ocean breeze, breathed in the salt air, and saw seagulls, and heard their noisy cries as they swooped down here and there for food. This idyllic experience brought nostalgia for my days at the beach in Santa Monica.

The most rewarding thing about Monterey was the chance to visit my good friend, Ida. She was my angel who befriended me in Minnesota. Her husband, Mas restarted his gasoline station that they had to abandon here in Monterey after Executive Order 9066 was enforced. Her brother Tom had also moved his family here. Mas and Ida continued to treat me like a family member.

One weekend, Mas invited me to go crab fishing. I had no idea what was involved. When I went to their home, Mas was busy tying some chicken bones and scraps onto a circular net. He said, "We're going to do crab fishing off the pier." Go fishing for crabs off the pier? Surely, I thought, crabs don't swim. I remember that long ago night when my uncle had taken us to Laguna Beach for night fishing. In addition to the octopus, I had caught hermit crabs in tide pools and sand crabs on the beaches, but none of those had looked big enough to be edible. In fact, they looked like bugs I had squished in my father's nursery back home.

At the end of the pier, Mas now lowered two nets into the water. "We'll have to wait for awhile and check every so often to see if we caught any crabs," said Mas. Half an hour later, we pulled up one net, but no crab. When we checked the other one; two Dungeness crabs were feeding on the chicken scraps. Mas carefully picked them up and put them in a gunnysack. He lowered the net once more to catch a few more. That evening, I had my first taste of Dungeness crabs. I was hooked on their tender, delicious flavor.

It was after the first rainfall in Monterey, when Ida called me and asked if I would care to go mushroom hunting over the weekend. The only experience I had with mushrooms were with the dry *Shiitake* mushrooms my mother used as ingredients for her *makisushi*, sushi wrapped in seaweed sheets, or for her *chawamushi* , custard like soup. Over the years I had heard that some people, who harvested wild mushroom, thought what they found looked like the ones back home, ate their bounty and ended up with kidney failure or terrible poisoning by the toxins. The stories about eating wild mushrooms had always scared me away from trying my luck at plucking a few wild morsels. However, today the weather was delightful and refreshing after the rains, and this outing seemed like a fun thing to do. Maybe I could even learn about picking mushrooms.

We drove out along Seventeen-Mile Drive where a grove of Monterey pines and cypresses grow near the coast. The trees and shrubbery have a distinct appearance of windblown green hair formed by the prevailing westerly winds from the ocean. Jutting out on a cliff near the sea, a famous Lone Cypress was nature's own bonsai. Soon we came to a grove of pine trees. The March rains had produced a nice crop of mushrooms among the fallen pine needles. My friend handed me a small container to gather mushrooms, but I was unsure of what to pick.

"How will I know what to pick? I sure don't want to pick some poisonous ones," I said to Ida.

"Just follow me and I'll show you," she said, "You won't make any mistakes because the pine tree setting and the fallen pine needles have always produced "*matsutakes*."

Just to be sure, I stayed as close to my friends so I wouldn't mess up and pick something inedible. Just being outdoors in this delightful weather, feeling the salt ocean breeze, was worth every minute of this outing.

Lady on the Bridge

That evening, Ida prepared our bounty. She was an excellent cook. When I had met her in Minnesota, she said she helped prepare food at her father's restaurant in Los Angeles until Executive Order 9066 forced the family to leave California. Now this glorious day in Monterey, she cleaned and lightly sautéed the mushrooms in a light butter sauce. When I took a bite, it was delicious. It was firm and had a nutty cinnamon flavor. My mouth still waters when I think about that sumptuous meal. However, I wouldn't dare go picking my own wild mushrooms for dinner. After all, an angel or death cap always looks so pretty and inviting, but it is deadly.

My days at Presidio Monterey came to an end. I'm not sure how much I learned about military Japanese, but at the close of those six months in 1947, I received the generosity of my friends Mas and Ida once more. It was time to say goodbye, for our group was preparing for a graduation ceremony. Everyone in the barracks was busy spit polishing their boots, rubbing red rouge on belt buckles until it shined, and making sure the uniform was clean and pressed. Most important, we were busy sewing on our new stripes because we were now technical staff sergeant T-4 upon completing the six-month course. We prepared for the company parade to honor our graduation and our lieutenant chose me to carry the regimental color in the parade. For several days, we practiced marching and passing in review. We were not a precision drill team even after our practices. Finally, the day came for the grand finale.

Again, Mas and Ida had invited me and several other *Nisei* to their home to celebrate. On the day of the graduation, they came to view the ceremony with a young friend from San Francisco. I was very nervous that day carrying the regimental color. I couldn't remember why, but I was chewing gum all of the time. I mention the gum now because, time in years that followed, she (Ida and Mas' friend) reminded me of my gum chewing from time to time.

We assembled near our barracks and marched up the hill to the parade ground. I could see spectators lined up on the far side watching the ceremony. My friend Ida and some of her friends were watching too. This was a simple ceremony with no bands. "Attention, Right face, Forward March, …, Eyes Right (dip Regimental Flag), Ready Front (resume Carry), … Halt, At Ease, Dismissed. We were now officially graduates of the Military Intelligent Section Language School (MISLS), June 1947.

That afternoon, several of us went to Ida's home to celebrate our graduation. Ida was a gracious host and everyone was enjoying the get together. Then I received the surprise of a lifetime.

Ida said, "I want you to meet a good friend of the family who I invited to this party. Her name was Yoshiko (Yo), and she was the younger sister of Matsuko (Mat). I'm sure you remember Mat who worked in the same Conversational Japanese program at the University of Minnesota with us. In addition, Kei was her brother, who you met at my home in St. Paul, when he stopped by one weekend. Yo was single and lives and works in San Francisco."

I don't know what happened but, if this was about fire, then it was spontaneous combustion. Was it the twinkle in her eyes? When I said, "Hi, I'm pleased to meet you," something unexplainable happened to my psyche. I was not in control of my feelings. I chatted with her for a while as well as mingled with the rest of the people at the party. When the time came to leave, Ida said, "Why don't you stay and have dinner with us?"

The young woman, Yo, was also staying for dinner since Ida had her stay overnight at her home. Of course, I accepted. After dinner, Mas said, "The local young people are playing softball. Why don't all of us go and watch them play? While Ida and her younger sister did the dishes,

Mas's nephew and the rest of us, including Yo, piled into his car and went to the ballpark. It was night and the floodlights were on lighting a small playing field. All of us climbed up the bleachers to watch. However, when I tried to sit next to Yo, she interposed Mas's nephew between us. I tried to move closer, but it didn't work. Was she playing coy? If the bait was out, I was hooked. I couldn't remember who won the softball game since my mind was elsewhere. If anything, I was sure I lost the game. We did not speak that evening.

Eventually the day was over and I had to prepare to return to Los Angeles to be with the family on my furlough before being deployed to Japan. I was fortunate that a few weeks before the graduation, my brother was playing in an all *Nisei* golf tournament at Pebble Beach, and he had offered me his car to drive home instead of taking the Greyhound bus. I was stunned when I saw it. Frank, true to form, had bought a 1940 Ford convertible; low silhouette, painted powder blue and light brown, and shiny. It was an eye-catcher. I had arranged to travel with a friend, Tad Katayama who lived in Parlier, California. Meanwhile, Yo would be returning to her parents' home in Reedley, California. I decided to visit her at her parents' home since Parlier was just a few miles away.

My friend was a *Kibei,* a smooth talker, and a lady's man. We first stopped at his home and then went to see Yo. After meeting her parents, I chatted with Yo while my friend was charming her parents. She said that, after leaving Poston internment camp, she had worked at a Jewish preschool in Cleveland. She was very happy there because everyone was nice and the family she stayed with treated her like family. When the war with Japan ended, her folks wanted her to be closer to home. After a few days at home, she saw her future in Reedley was limited. Reedley was a small farming town, and her options were to help her parents on the farm, marry someone in town, or work part time at a packing shed during the harvest season. None of these appealed to her, for she wanted the opportunity to do more than be a farm girl. She was a very determined girl. Her older sister Mat, who lived in San Francisco, told her to leave home, come to the city, and find a job there. Yo took her advice and she now lived with several young *Nisei* girls in a boarding house on Octavia Street owned by a Japanese family.

I was happy I had stopped by. Somehow, everything seemed so at ease. To think, all this started one day in Monterey. Maybe I didn't lose the game after all.

Spanish Cannon guarding Presidio of Monterey, CA

Military Japanese Class at Presidio of Monterey, CA

Break from drudgery
Okaerinasai (Welcome home)
Home, where the heart is

Furlough

It's homeward bound again speeding south on Highway 99 after my army friend Tad Katayama and I had a nice visit in Reedley. I had agreed to give him a ride to Los Angeles to visit his family friend during our furlough. Once you left the "fruit basket" of California, the ride was truly monotonous between Fresno and Los Angeles. The scenery was even worse after you left Bakersfield. I remember one other time I had traveled along this route in 1939 to see the World's Fair at Treasure Island, San Francisco. I remember seeing "Burma Shave" signs that broke the monotony with the amusing quips:

IT WOULD BE FUN	IT WOULD BE NICE
TO GO BY AIR	IF LEFT ALONE
BUT WE CAN'T HANG	BUT UNCLE SAM SAYS
THESE SIGNS UP THERE	IT'S YOU I OWN
BURMA SHAVE	BURMA SHAVE

Each line was painted on a board, each board was spaced for easy reading, and the last word of the second and third lines always rhymed. Now coming home on furlough, I kept looking and hoping to see one more sign for a chuckle. Some signs end up holey because hunters love to shoot at them as they whizzed by. Then, any sign or post was an easy target for thoughtless shooters.

It was a two-hour ride over the winding Ridge Route. Passing through the Grapevine was always "iffy" because trucks could burn their brakes out and become dangerous runaways, car motors could overheat and stop dead in their tracks, and loose rocks sometimes cascaded down onto the highway. On our trip to the World's Fair in 1939, Ridge Route was not a divided highway, which almost cost us our lives. I remember vividly how we barely escaped a head on collision. That day, Joe had offered to drive one of his college friends from Santa Monica to UC Berkeley, and Frank and I rode with them. The other driver sped around a curve towards us. Suddenly his tire blew; he jammed on his brakes and swerved right at us. Joe, who was driving, veered our car towards an embankment, squeezed by two cars, and narrowly escaped the crash. It happened so fast we didn't realize until afterwards how lucky we were to be alive. Even today, I still see the errant car stopped in the middle of the road where we would have been.

The hillside was scorched now by the summer heat and turned golden brown. Without air-conditioning in my brother's car, the ride was uncomfortably hot as we passed by Lebec, Gorman, and Castaic. I was relieved after Castaic when I saw the San Fernando Valley below me. First, I would drop my friend off in LA and head to West Los Angeles to stay with my family.

When I was drafted and left for basic training, the family lived in Boyle Heights in houses that my father had purchased before the war. I remember father emptied our savings account to help pay for the property. I always wondered why he didn't buy a house near our nursery in Santa Monica instead of Boyle Heights where his son-in-law lived. Executive Order 9066 taught me the hard lesson that all things in America are not equal. My father could not buy his home because the Alien Land Laws (1913 and 1920) forbade Japanese ownership of land. In fact, all Asians

(Chinese, Japanese, Indians, and Koreans) were denied the right to become citizens. Their only recourse was to buy property in someone else's name, a citizen. When my older sister Mabel turned 21 years old, my father purchased the property in her name. However, there was an understanding in a letter from my father to the son-in-law and my sister that the property belongs to the family. Unfortunately, the right of ownership in a letter had no legal standing in court.

When Manzanar closed, the family was able to reclaim the property in Boyle Heights to restart their lives. Unfortunately, we lost our nursery in Santa Monica because the individuals, who took over the business, claimed inability to make payments. Interned and barred by Executive Order 9066 from leaving Manzanar, Joe could not return to take care of the financial and legal matters. When Manzanar closed in 1945, the family was now without the means of making a living. The heavy responsibility rested once more on brother's shoulder. Joe desperately wanted to restart a business and believed our Boyle Heights property could be used as collateral. He was mistaken. It was legally in our sister's name. The brother-in-law would not agree to let Joe use the property as collateral. Joe now faced a desperate situation to find finances to help our family survive. Joe was determined and he found the means to start a nursery in West Los Angeles. My parents now lived with Joe's family in a house on the nursery property. Again, I was coming home to impose on my family. Was this really my home? My home was gone. My home in Santa Monica no longer existed.

As soon as I stopped and walked up to the house, I greet mother, *"Okaasan, tadaima. Shibaraaku deshta.* (Mother, I have returned. It's been awhile)." This is what I always said when I returned.

*"Okaerinasai (*Welcome home*),"* answered *Okaasan.*

Okaasan looked happy to see me once again and quickly showed me a room where I would stay. I saw that my parents gave up their bedroom for my visit. I protested to *Okaasan* saying I could sleep on the couch because I was here for a short visit. She would have none of that. I also felt a bit uneasy for imposing on Joe and his family when they were struggling to restart their lives. Once again, Joe and his wife, Yo, welcomed me into their lives. Meanwhile, *Okaasan* was already thinking about how to spoil me.

Before the internment, one of the delicious treats the family enjoyed was Stern's Famous Barbecue in Culver City on Washington Blvd. The Texas style Stern's barbecued meat was so tender that it cut easily with a fork and melted in your mouth. The ribs were full and juicy. You couldn't eat daintily or you'd miss the flavor. I had gone previously with Joe several times to buy dinner for the family at

Joe Kishi's Family
West LA

Sterns. It was a small ranch style store-restaurant with a counter display of meats, beans, and potatoes for sale. The aroma of the mild chili and barbecued meats made my mouth drool. That day of my furlough, I saw *Okaasan* talking to Joe and I knew I would be spoiled for dinner that night.

When I looked around the nursery, I noticed that the business was not the same as we had in Santa Monica. At our former nursery, there was always a steady flow of customers. Ours had been one of the highest volume nurseries for bedding plants. I recall hearing this from the wholesalers who delivered plants. It was puzzling because only a few flats of bedding plants were on display.

"Joe, I don't see the usual customers coming in" I questioned him.

He said, "Our original nursery on Wilshire Blvd was in a good location and did well, but I realized that retail nursery business has high labor costs for the small amount of merchandise sold. I decided to start a wholesale nursery and make a profit on large sales. At first, I had to stock up from other nurseries, but now I grow my own plants. Mother has helped me hire several *Issei* women to start cuttings and seedlings for my own stock. I hope to expand and become a broker for nursery plants someday."

I thought back to something he said once when we still had the Santa Monica nursery during the Depression. One day, I delivered a few sacks of steer manure from Santa Monica out to Malibu. It was a nice long ride along the oceanfront, but just to satisfy a customer, the nursery lost money on the deal.

"How are the *Issei* doing," I asked. "Isn't it hard work for them?"

"They are very happy because jobs for *Issei* are hard to find nowadays, and it provides an income for the family," he replied.

At Joe's West Los Angeles nursery, I noticed back in the hothouse area, *Issei* women were talking, laughing, and having a great time working together. *Okaasan* seemed happier that I could remember by helping with the family nursery, and, especially, working with the other *Issei* women.

The days passed quickly and I had to return to Monterey for my next assignment. If you ever have to travel by Greyhound, do not if you have other options. It is cheap, but you stop at every little town. If you are lucky, the stop may be in a convenient place near stores. Sometimes it is located on the seedy side of town. Usually there was a small café counter, and restrooms. Why anyone would work as a waitress at a bus stop was beyond my understanding. The food was lousy, and the sandwiches taste like cardboard. You take a chance on the restroom because it could be filthy and disgusting with so many people using it. On one trip, the bus broke down and we all waited for Greyhound to find a spare bus. I lost a half-day waiting for the replacement. For insurance this time, I took this earlier bus. *Okaasan*, of course, loaded me up with goodies for my trip.

Finally, after ten hours, I arrived at Monterey. In two days, our contingent would move back to Camp Stoneman for our deployment. Now that I was a Tech Sergeant T-4', I did not have to worry about peeling potatoes on KP duties. My destination was San Francisco to board the troopship, General Hodges headed for Japan. It was a four-hour ride on a ferryboat from Pittsburg, CA and across the San Francisco Bay to one of San Francisco's piers.

Chapter 5: High Sea

*Off to parents' land
Sea gulls guide us out to sea
Hands across the sea*

High Sea

What would a GI be without his duffle bag? Mine was a dull olive green round cylindrical container jammed with all of my belongings and heavier than hell to carry. Here I was a soldier of the US Army on a tour of duty, a member of the Occupation Force headed for Japan. Today, I was shipping out for Yokohama, Japan from San Francisco, California on the troop ship, the USS General Hodges. The sergeant was barking out orders. One by one, we went up the gangplank, across the deck, down, down the stairwell through a maze of hatches, and down into the hold. It didn't go any farther down than this level for I

General Hodges, San Francisco, CA

could see steel plates that curved downward and even imagined I saw an outline of the welding. I was at the bottom of the ship. The paint on all sides was a rust-resistant bright orange, and a nauseating smell of diesel oil and paint permeated throughout the ship. I saw hammocks hanging row after row between metal posts. What a crowded mess this was. Was this my home away from home for two long weeks? Suddenly a master sergeant yelled out, "Find a place to stow your gear!"

Everyone hustled to find a good spot to hunker down for the trip. I wondered how it would feel sleeping in this webbing of ropes since I had never slept in a hammock. It did not seem at all comfortable. There were two or three tiers of hammocks strung a few feet above each other. I found a spot that was easy to get to and decided to take the top hammock. I prayed that this contraption would not dump me onto the metal floor in stormy weather! Yes, this was going to be home for the next fourteen days as we crossed the Pacific to Japan.

My friend was bunking in the bottom hammock but he looked worried. He was one of the many *Kibei* who had returned from Japan during the mid 1930's. Japan had been expanding its sphere of control by promoting the propaganda of the co-prosperity sphere for Asia, but this aspiration required military intervention. Back then, many Nisei, who went there to enter the Japanese schools, were soon eligible for military duty because of their dual citizenship. Consequently, the parents quickly called their children back to America in order to avoid military service. My friend said that on his return home, he had sailed on a Japanese passenger ship, but he was seasick and miserable all the way back to San Francisco. For the moment, he felt fine because the ship had not left the harbor. As soon as the sergeant saw that everyone had chosen their spot, he yell' "Everybody out topside."

On the deck, "Attention! At Ease!" yelled the sergeant. He then proceeded to give us the orders for what we could, and could not do on the trip. He said both officers and civilians were on this ship, but on different levels. There would be absolutely no intermingling between soldiers with these two groups on this voyage. Then he yelled, "Fall out!"

By nightfall, we were all down in the hold. While most of the men were just passing the time reading or napping, there was always a group of GI's on their knees crap shooting on a blanket. I heard the familiar phrase, "Baby needs a new pair of shoes," as someone rolled the dice for one more pass at winning the pot.

All eyes centered on one *Nisei*, the shooter. He pulled out a wad of money and placed it in front of him. Others, with money in hand, were ready to bet.

"Hey, I cover $5.00," someone shouted.

"I'll cover the rest," voiced another *Nisei*.

The shooter carefully raised his right hand up to his lips. With a quick whoof, he blew hard at the dice he was holding in his fingers.

"Baby needs shoes," he cried as though his ritual will bring good luck.

Quickly he tossed the dice onto the blanket.

"Nine's the point," someone shouted.

"Hey, I bet $2.00 he won't make 9," some piped up.

"$2.00 he makes it," quips another GI as he pulled out $2.00.

A GI gathered up the dice and handed it back to the shooter.

"Nine's the number. Come on baby," the shooter cried as he shakes the dice and tossed it once more.

"Eight, try again," said an observer and handed him the dice again.

"Come on baby," as he shook the pair of dice harder and throws again.

The dice rolled and turned up seven.

"Tough, seven out. Better luck next time," someone called out.

There was a quick exchange of money and the dice passed to the next shooter.

> *You'll die twice for this*
> *Gambling your life away*
> *For Baby needs shoes*

That first night, the dinner scene was big a surprise. Space was at a premium on the troopship. The chow line seemed endless in this crowded space. The lighting was bad enough that I didn't notice the slop. Then I looked for a place to eat with my tray full of food. There were no tables or chairs, but only a metal ledge to set my tray on and eat standing up. The smell of diesel always permeated the air and left a queasy feeling as I ate. As I gulped my food down, I tried not to notice a fellow GI, green in the gills, dashing out of the mess hall. Surprisingly, I notice that my friend, who had feared seasickness, had survived the evening meal.

The next morning, as I got out of my hammock, my friend said, "Hey, this trip may not be bad after all. The sailing was so smooth that I had no trouble sleeping." Soon we were back to face the endless line for a standup breakfast. Again, my friend seemed to stomach the breakfast fare without any trouble. Then we went topside.

The USS General Hodges was still at the pier! I saw an astonished look on my friend's face. He hadn't fared the ship ride on the high sea last night. The ship had not sailed out of port because of some minor problem with the ship's engine. As we looked over the side of the ship, men were preparing the ship to pull out to sea, anchors aweigh.

The tug pulled our ship slowly away from the pier and soon the ship started its voyage towards the Golden Gate Bridge. From topside, the view was beautiful, but down deep the tumultuous currents flowed. Violent action occurred when the fresh water from the rivers flowed into the bay and collided with the Pacific Ocean. As we passed under the Golden Gate Bridge, the ship shuddered against the current. My friend was turning green. From that moment on, he never saw the daylight for fourteen long days.

There was no romance to the high seas on this trip. It was a monotonous voyage punctured with an occasional fire drill, and we spent day after day just sitting around on the deck in the sun. I watched the seagulls circling above as they followed the wake of the ship, waiting for a few morsels as the crew dumped garbage off the ship's stern. I thought the ship, while it plowed through the water, would leave large wave patterns, but it just made a smooth series of 'v' shaped wavelets. I could hear the gulls crying as they swooped down for a morsel. Soon we were too far from land and the gulls had left. How did the birds know when to turn back? It was an eerie feeling, if not a lonesome one, when I was so far out to sea and heard only the drone of the ship plowing through the water and ocean waves lapping against the ship. Later on during this voyage, I saw days where the sea around the ship was so calm that it seemed we were moving across a pane of glass.

After seven days of monotony, I thought I would go stir crazy if I didn't find some activity to fill my time. Then, I realized that there were other GI's besides our group from MIS. Most of these GI's had probably never seen a Japanese, let alone knew how to greet one or speak any Japanese. I announced over the speakers that I was willing to introduce them to a few words of Japanese that might help them when they arrived in Japan. I pondered how I should proceed. I surely didn't want to bore them to death by lecturing like a teacher in a classroom. The next day, there was a large group of GI's waiting to hear what was going to happen. Of course, I had their attention since they were stuck on this ship with nothing else to do for the day.

After introducing myself, I called out, "Anyone here from New York?"

There was a loud cheer from a few GI's. I proceeded to ask about other places, and the response was always cheerful.

Then I asked, "Anyone here from Ohio?"

I saw two individual raise their hands and cheer.

Ohio! Did I say the name right? I asked.

They responded, "Ohio!"

"Wow," I said, "we have two GI's who speak Japanese already. You two are ahead of the class already."

In place of our "Good morning," Japanese will say, *Ohayo.*

So, let's hear Ohio.

The response was loud and clear, and I had taken a first big step.

Lady on the Bridge

For the next seven days I conducted a class for a half an hour teaching a few Japanese words, phrases, and greetings so that they could get around in Japan. It was fun for me, and they were all ears.

The troop ship sailed on for fourteen long days towards Yokohama, Japan. Deep in the hold, the gamblers were oblivious to the steady hum and throbbing of the diesel motor as they rolled the dice repeatedly. The gamblers would blow on the dice and mutter "Baby needs shoes" for good luck. For fourteen days, baby shoes won and lost many times over. Never worn.

> *My Parents' homeland*
> *This land of cherry blossoms*
> *What will be my thoughts?*

In the Land of Cherry Blossoms

The long monotonous journey was over and now I was a traveler wandering over my parents' homeland, not knowing what to expect. My eyes had many views for I was Nisei, an American citizen, but my parents were immigrants from Japan that had passed on their cultural values to me. What would my eyes tell me? Would I have a biased or slanted view?

A sergeant yelled, "Grab your gear, get your butt top-side, and disembark." On the wharf in Yokohama, a small group of musicians was playing a tune to welcome us to the land of cherry blossoms. I struggled down the gangplank with my duffle bags and other personal items and headed towards a line of passenger train cars that would take all of us to our next destination.

Disembarking, I was a mindless robot following the sergeant's barking orders and hadn't realized that I had just put

Disembarking at Yokohama Japan

one foot on my parent's homeland. However, this port harbor looked no different from San Francisco piers except that I saw a naked wall standing alone, an aftermath of the bombing. To one side, I saw a small crowd of Japanese standing around gawking at us while we debarked. The signs on the buildings were all in Japanese. As soon as our contingent boarded and stored our gear, the train headed for Tokyo, which was about twenty miles to the north of Yokohama.

However, the ride was a revelation of what had happen here. It had only been a year ago, May 1945, when the 39th US bomber group had destroyed the industrial area and razed the civilian homes with incendiary bombs in this region. While I saw the stark emptiness for miles and miles, I had never fully absorbed the horror and devastation that took place here until much later. Soon the train arrived at the Tokyo train station located near the center of town. Even though there were signs of bombing from the war, the cleanliness of the buildings impressed me. The station was an old red brick building and constructed many years ago. I waited for transportation to some Army facility, but our destination turned out to be the Nippon Yusen Kaisha (NYK) office building that was just three blocks from the station.

We gathered our gear and headed through the train station towards NYK building. Suddenly something caught my eye as we entered the waiting room. On both sides of the big open room, I noticed the public bathrooms but there were no doors for either the women's or the men's lavatories. Suddenly I thought, "This can't be the trip to Manzanar all over again. Was my world closing in on me once more?" I hurried hoping that my queasy feeling would go away. I moved quickly lugging my heavy duffle bag and suitcase to keep me focused on reaching the NYK building. Inside the building, we received our room assignments.

The Allied Translators Interpreter Service (ATIS) of the Military Intelligence Section (MIS) had taken over NYK's office building for its use as soon as America had won the war. I could not have been luckier than to be at these new quarters. It was a big room with windows and GI issued beds for four persons. What a gift. No spot could be better than this for my army assignment. This building was intact because America had spared the buildings surrounding the Imperial Palace from the Air Force's incessant bombings. The Tokyo Imperial Palace Grounds were across a wide avenue and was still majestic looking. Japan's famous Marunouchi Building, noted for its shops and offices, was on the next block. Across from the NYK building was the Kanda Building, which was the quarters for American women, both civilian and service personnel. Later, I learned that the Kanda Building had been the subject of many stories chronicled in U. S. Armed Forces newspaper, Stars and Stripes, about the nightly strip

MIS/ATIS, Nippon Yusen Kaisha Bldg. (NYK), Tokyo, Japan

Emperor Hirohito Imperial Pallace, Kyujo, Tokyo, Japan

tease acts observed by NYK GIs. The Army PX was located within walking distance near the Ginza District, famous for its bright, gaudy neon signs.

I had no idea about what my duties would be. Surely, the Army did not need me as cannon fodder since Japan had surrendered. On the first floor, I saw a huge room filled with a sea of desks, while other offices housed officers conducting, we later learned, special investigations. Our quarters were on the upper floors. The gods must have been looking down on me because there was no KP, latrine duty, and policing of the area. In fact, the Army served my meals in NYK's former dining room. Instead of picnic benches, I saw tables and chairs carefully placed and attended by Japanese nationals. I tasted fresh vegetables instead of the drab limp olive hued canned spinach they served during basic training back in Fort Lewis, WA that always tasted as bad as it looked. Our American military set up hydroponic farms in Japan to provide fresh vegetables instead of buying the products from the Japanese farmers that practiced questionable farming methods. Throughout Asia, including Japan, farmers used human excrement as the primary source of fertilizer for farming. The occupation forces had learned to give wide berth to "Honey Buckets," a familiar term for the containers of human waste, collected early in the morning from the local floor toilets in the residential districts. It was shocking to see a man trotting along a country road with a long pole over his shoulders with two buckets hanging by ropes on the ends of the pole on his way to deliver the "Honey Bucket" to someone's farm.

The only routine duty was guard duty, and that occurred once every two months. There was even a barbershop in the basement with young Japanese girls as barbers. During the haircut, I noticed that an older man (perhaps a father or other relative) sat to the side watching. I guess they were protecting the girls by making sure that no funny business occurred. Haircuts at the barbershop were unlike anything I had experienced back in America. The young barbers would clip your eyebrows, nose hairs, any loose hair in your ears, and end up with a nice warm towel soothing your face as part of the routine haircut. How fantastic to be pampered.

We were not the first *Nisei* contingent at the NYK building. The initial mission for ATIS, Allied Translators Interpreters Section, included censoring all written and published Japanese material including films, radio broadcast, telephone and telegraph. While we continued with the initial assignments, our team began to gather intelligence information from Japanese soldiers returning from Siberia. Our interpreters conducted war crime investigations for the American, the British Legation, and support for the US State Department.

Our contingent was separated into two groups: interpreters and translators. I became an interpreter. Today was my first assignment; interpreter for the British Legation at General MacArthur's Headquarters, the Daiichi Seimei building. As I walked along the wide avenue, across the avenue to my right, I saw the beautiful Imperial Palace grounds. There was no sign of destruction because America had also spared the Palace grounds from bombings. The beautifully maintained grounds around the Imperial palace were set far back

Daichi Bldg, General MacArthur's HDQ, Tokyo Japan

from the avenue. There was a large space where troops would march and pass in review during military ceremonies. In the distance was a stone bridge that spanned a moat surrounding the castle grounds. It would have been a wonderful setting to visit and take pictures, but, unfortunately, it was off-limits to commoners.

Lady on the Bridge

At last, I was at the Daiichi building. It too was an impressive sight: simple in design and built mainly of white granite. I climbed the steps and entered the foyer. There were so many desks, occupied by both civilian and military personnel that I hardly knew who to ask about the room for my assignment. When I went in a room that faced the Imperial Palace grounds, a British officer greeted me. He was conducting an investigation of war crimes in the South Pacific region where British soldiers, Australian, and New Zealanders, had clashed with Japanese forces. Several islands were involved. However, the main location had been Papua New Guinea. I was here as an interpreter. I left my feelings outside the door.

Soldier, read my lips
Face the Imperial Palace
Nothing but the truth

Soochishimasu (I will do so)

When I entered the room, a British officer was sitting at a big table while an ex-Japanese soldier in his old army uniform sat meekly across from him with his hands folded. The officer motioned me to sit next to him. There was no protocol or briefing about what was to follow.

"Tell the man to face the Imperial Palace and swear that he will tell the truth," said the Australian officer.

I quickly interpreted his statement while addressing the Japanese.

The ex-soldier bowed, turned toward the Imperial Palace, and said, "*Hai, soochishimasu,* Yes, I will do so."

I was the conduit for the interrogation of ex-Japanese soldiers. When the war ended, the British captured him and wanted information about war crimes that had been or might have been committed in the South Pacific. For the war in Europe, Australia had sent large military forces to the Middle East, leaving the South Pacific virtually undefended. Japan, meanwhile had attacked and entrenched themselves in New Guinea, Burma, Malaysia, and the Indonesia, and other South Pacific Islands. But the tide had turned and the Japanese army had found itself isolated from supplies, and struggling against the worst jungle conditions of weather, terrain, disease, leeches, insects, and the list of hellish conditions that goes on and on. Neither side, it seems, was exempt from the terrible circumstances that cause death and diseases. Moreover, I can only generalize about the events since I know very little about the war that went on in this hellhole.

"Did you see a missionary on the island?"

"No, I did not."

Did you hear about the missionary there?"

"Yes, I believe there was a missionary there?"

The ex-Japanese soldiers invariably end their reply with "*to omoimasu.* (I think or as I remember).' At which point, I was forced to state his reply as given or try a different approach to seek the truth.

"Did you hear that the missionary was captured by the Japanese soldiers?"

"Yes, I heard ...*to omoimasu.*"

"Were you there when he was beheaded by the *Kempeitai* (secret Japanese military police)?"

"No..."

On other days, I questioned prisoners about other islands and other atrocities, including cannibalism by the Japanese forces at Sananda, New Guinea when they were isolated from their own supply sources for weeks and starving.

I left my feelings at the door, but I live in two worlds. I was an American. I was Japanese. I was a soldier doing my duty and I was finding out that war was hell.

One day, I was on call, but I had no specific assignment. I entered the interrogation room and waited. Sitting with an Australian officer was a heavyset *Nisei* interrogating an ex-Japanese soldier. I looked at the flushed face of the Australian officer because he was having a hard time understanding, not with the ex-soldier but the *Nisei* interpreter.

"My bloody arse, I can't understand a bloody word my interpreter was saying!" blurted out the officer.

He saw me sitting, waved his hand at me, and said, "Will you take this man's place?" Apparently the officer couldn't understand his interpreter's Pidgin English."

The *Nisei*, whose place I was taking, must have come from a rural area of Hawaii where Hawaiian Pidgin English was the standard dialect. He got up and left quickly as I sat in his place.

The Australian officer looked directly at me and said in a heavy Australian accent, "Ask the ex-Japanese soldier, 'was the captured British soldier in "*Jaw-ile?*"'"

For a second, the word "*Jaw-ile*" threw me for a loop until I realized he meant "jail."

I did "jolly good" on that one. Then the next one came.

"Was the man a "*Nah e vee*" man?" the Australian officer asked.

What in the "*bloody arse*" was "*Nah e vee?*" I again hesitated for a second. Then it dawned on me he meant "Navy." I breezed through the rest of the interrogation after passing the first line of fire.

However, the *Nisei* interpreters had their own dialect problems. When the ex-soldier was from Okinawa, someone with standard Japanese would have a difficult time interpreting the words. Even on the main island Honshu; there were dialects that could result in mistranslation. Nevertheless, I had been lucky until then.

One day, I reported to the British Legation Headquarters to accompany a British Naval officer to interrogate an ex-Japanese prisoner in the Sugamo Prison. The prison built in 1920 by the Japanese government, incarcerated political dissidents who wanted to overthrow the government. With the Allied forces in control, Sugamo Prison held prisoners charged with war crimes committed throughout the war in the Pacific. One of the high profile prisoners was General Hideki Tojo, Prime Minister, accountable for all war crimes committed by the Imperial Japanese Army. Additionally, there were some two thousand war criminals held there.

I was to drive a jeep for the British Naval officer to the interrogation. Sugamo Prison was northwest of Tokyo in the town of Ikebukuro, Toshima Ward of Tokyo. When I arrived, I noticed that the US Air Force had spared the prison from bombing. As I approached the guard gate, I saw a guard tower that gave me a moment of rumination about the ominous guard tower at Manzanar internment camp. I was glad to be on the other side of the gate. From the guard gate, it was another short walk to the buildings. Each step of the way, guards were on duty. Once inside the big open foyer, the British officer submitted papers to a soldier to usher in the Japanese prisoner for interrogation. Soon, a Japanese in a plain navy uniform appeared. By his appearance, he was no common recruit. He moved sharply, head erect, and accompanied by a guard to our interrogation room. The guard removed the handcuffs and took a position outside our room but continued to guard.

The prisoner stood motionless until the British officer waved his hand for him to sit down at the table.

The British officer said, "Did you serve in Indonesia?"

"Yes, I did," the prisoner answered.

"Does he speak the Indonesian dialect, Bahasa," asked the British Naval officer.

"Yes, I know it," replied the prisoner.

Then a funny thing happened. The British Naval officer began speaking in this Indonesian language.

Immediately the ex-Japanese Naval officer smiled and replied in the same Indonesian language.

The whole atmosphere in the room changed. They were two people reminiscing about old times during the war. I did not understand a word they were saying. I needed an interpreter to follow the conversation!

The British officer stopped for a moment, looked at me, and said, "I won't need you for the rest of the day. Why don't you take off and come back for me at 4:30 pm sharp?"

I did not protest. I left quickly and went to our jeep to take time off.

At 4:30 pm sharp, I had returned to Sugamo Prison and waited for the British Naval officer to drive back to Tokyo. A week after I returned to my quarters at NYK, I came down with German measles and was hospitalized for two weeks. I must have been very sick because I cannot remember flirting with the nurses. However, there was a good side of being sick. The day I returned to the NYK building, the MIS soldiers were in full military uniform, lined up in formation, and ready to march to the Imperial Palace parade field to "pass in review" at some bigwig ceremony that day. I was not required to join them. I quickly got my camera, stood on the sideline, waved to them with a big smile, and "click, click" shot a few pictures.

| MIS/ATIS prepare for Mayday Parade | Mayday Parade on Imperial Palace Grounds, Tokyo Japan | Pass in Review, Mayday Parade |

Two worlds in conflict
This land's beauty was tarnished
Age-old profession

Off Base

My strict world of moral values that I had received from parents was shattered when I was a GI. One day, when it was my turn for guard duty of the Nippon Yuusen Kaisha (NYK) shipping firm building, I received my first view of the seamy side of life in Japan. For guard duty, you have to look sharp because the day starts with inspection. I made sure I had a haircut, spit polished shoes, shined brass buttons and belt buckle until I could see my reflection, and I made sure that my uniform was clean and the creases razor sharp. On that day, while the corporal of the guard conducted his inspection, I saw the building shake under a mild earthquake. It was the first time I had experienced the motion. Yet, nobody paid any attention to tremors in Japan since earthquakes were daily occurrences. On each watch, we were issued a helmet, a nightstick, and US Army 45-pistol and holster, but no bullets. Regulation for guard duty was two hours on and four hours off over a twenty-four hour period. My assignment was the front entrance of the NYK building. I stood at my post expressionless like a statue. I am sure a mannequin could have stood at my post since my forty-five was empty. I wondered, "What am I supposed to do in case of an attack? Do I scare him by waving my empty pistol? "I felt I was only window dressing and not much else."

The sight that shocked me happened during my night shift when I went up to the guard quarter for my four hours off to take a quick nap. I took off my helmet and gear, placed them on a chair, and glanced at the window to check the night scene. I could not believe what I saw out of the window. The quarters were on the second floor with only one window that overlooked the motor pool. It was a dark night without moonlight and no lights were shining from the buildings nearby. I squinted and peeked towards the motor pool. I could barely make out the outlines of trucks and jeeps in the yard. Then, I saw a cigarette with its hot red tip floating among the vehicles. I tried to focus my eyes to see clearer. There, I saw something. It was a phantom figure walking out of the motor pool while still adjusting his clothes. I saw another lit cigarette floating among the trucks. No vehicles were moving, but this was a busy night down at the motor pool. I surmised that the sight of the glowing tip of the prostitute's cigarette floating in the air logged the end of each encounter, yen for yen.

The next day, I asked my friends if they knew what about what was going on down at the motor pool. "Sure, they said, "but that's nothing compared to what happens at night down at the Shinjuku train station." This was hard times; family life in shambles, homes gone, and jobs vanished, so this was only one way that some Japanese could survive, especially, young girls. Many came from the rural areas, and many lived in shacks and lean-to's to survive. GI's were their targets because they had money and spent it lavishly.

Then he said, "If you're looking for action, be careful because many places were off limits. You can't miss them because the Army has posted signs, 'Off Limit, VD.'"

During the first days, I would stroll around the Tokyo district on the weekends just to familiarize myself with the neighborhood near the Palace grounds. One of places near there was Japan's famous Ueno Park. Thousand or more cherry trees that blossomed in the springtime attracted people just to see the beauty and breathe the delicate scent of the cherry blossoms. I would have loved to be here for that lovely event, but this was summertime. While I strolled along the paths, I saw several buildings, including a museum, but closed, probably because of the war and the poor economy. As I wandered around the streets near the Palace, I saw a stately brick building gutted from bombing. It was the Chief of Staff building. While the US Air Force spared the Imperial Palace, it had pinpointed strategic military targets.

Japan's former Chief of Staff HDQ gutted by US bombing

One weekend, I decided to go sight-seeing nearby. I kept walking until I came to a strange place. I was in a district with billboards that I had not noticed elsewhere. Hmmn..., I thought to myself. These were very exotic if not erotic pictures in front of these buildings. As I walked further past the buildings, I saw a few bars, but closed during the daytime. Then I saw the sign, Yoshiwara. I was strolling in the middle of Japan's famous, or rather, infamous Yoshiwara Red Light District. The buildings, right in the heart of Tokyo, looked like they were open for business at night.

I found myself in my familiar territory between two worlds. My parents taught me, "Do not bring shame to our family name." I had assumed all of Japan to be wholesome and proper. Yet, here I stood in the capital of Japan where Emperor Hirohito resided, and I found that Japanese tolerated a place like Yoshiwara District. What was I to believe? I had compassion and empathy for girls who felt they had to humiliate themselves by selling their bodies for this commercialism survival, but it was beyond my understanding. Once when I had been traveling with *Ojisan*, uncle, I had seen the purity of mind of the Japanese who unashamedly bathe together without deviant thoughts. All that my parents taught me seemed consistent with a fundamentally moral Judeo-Christian system, but now what I was seeing struck me as being without moral foundation. I was devastated.

Billboard in Yoshiwara District, Tokyo Japan

As someone of two worlds, I had always marveled that Japanese were able to accept certain human activities, such as public bathing and access to public restrooms, as normal acceptable actions. I had learned that when women smiled, they covered their mouths for modesty. When people met each other, bowing was the custom because physical contact was unacceptable, like a

125

handshake or a hug. Even in marriage, the married couple never displayed affection. What did love have to do with it? I was not sure. Thus, that day I presumed what occurred at Yoshiwara was acceptable, just another human event, part of Japanese culture. Now I know that there are red light districts all over the world, in spite of the disapproval of many cultures.

While the United States Far East Command did not condone such activity, they accepted the reality. In order to combat VD, the US Medical Corp set up prophylactic stations to service US GIs who solicited prostitutes. However, sometimes the act went beyond solicitation. When a rape was committed in Japan during the occupation, the authorities always looked for a US soldier as a suspect for the crime.

The hands of Japan's pre-World War II Occupational Forces under Co-Prosperity Sphere propaganda were not very clean either. The Japanese Army forced thousands of young women to serve as "comfort women" for the convenience of their troops. What irony, at the end of the war, the Japanese government set up comfort stations for Allied soldiers, a prize for the conqueror. I was deeply troubled. How was I to face the reality of "The Rape of Nanking" when I learned about heroic warriors who lived by the code of the *Bushido:* loyalty, justice, and honor? Even my work as an interpreter was forcing me to rethink my idealized image of the Japan that my parents exemplified by in their daily living.

Just as the people of Japan, forced to regard their Emperor as a mortal, the raw reality was that Japan was both beautiful and idyllic and at the same time, harsh and sad. Just like America, it became evident.

Out of the blue sky
A proposal to marry
Not kissing cousin

Proposal

It was the surprise of my life one day when the charge of quarters (CQ) came to my room and said, "There was a young lady downstairs wanting to see you."

What, I thought, a young woman waiting to see me? The only people I knew were Nisei GI's billeted here. He had to be mistaken, for I had not fraternized with any Japanese girl during my short time here. Puzzled as to who this person might be, I looked at the CQ and said, "I don't know any girls in Japan, let alone Tokyo."

"Well, she specifically asked for you by name, Kishi," replied the CQ. "She's waiting near the receptionist's desk." Quickly, he turned around and left.

My mind was blank as to why a girl would be asking for me by name. I had better get dressed anyway, I thought. I put on my tie and took one look in the mirror before leaving the room. "Always look sharp," I remember my drill sergeant at basic training used to hammer into us every day. Good enough, I thought, and I quickly took the elevator down to the first floor. In the foyer, I saw a young girl waiting near the receptionist. She could have been in her twenties, but I could not be sure. Her hair tied back in a bun, dressed neatly in a light brown jacket, and wearing a pantaloon bottom. Her clothes were not bright or flashy like many of the city girls I had seen in Tokyo. I imagined that she must have come from a rural village.

I went up to the information desk and asked the receptionist if the young girl sitting nearby was waiting for a Nisei GI.

"Yes, she's the person that was waiting to see you," he replied.

Still puzzled because I could not place her anywhere in my life, I went over to her and bowed stiffly and said, "*Konnichiwa, Kishi desu* (Good afternoon, I'm Kishi). I was told that you wanted to see me."

She got up from the chair, and she bowed several times, and she said, "*Konnichiwa, hajimemashite, watashiwa anata no itoko desu, yoroshiku onegaishimasu* ((Good afternoon, nice to meet you, I am your cousin, best regards to you I beg of you); She continued, "I'm one of your cousins on your father's side of the family. My family heard from your uncle that lives in Kimiidera, a town nearby that his sister in America wrote to him about her son in Japan. She wrote that he was an American soldier stationed at the NYK building in Tokyo. She hesitated for a moment and said, "The war and everything ... my father was killed in the war, and it has been hard for mother and the relatives to support all of us ..." She paused again and quietly said, "I thought if I could marry a GI and go to America, I would be so happy and my family would be so much better off without me since I am such a burden to them. That's why I rushed here without telling anyone I was going to Tokyo to see you." "Forgive me," she said as she bowed several more times. "But ever since I heard about you, I was hoping that I could marry you if you would have me."

Shocked at her bold statement, I could have busted out laughing or shouted at her in anger for assuming that I would marry her for her convenience, but I could not do that. As I looked at her, I thought, I do not even know you and, besides, I do not take the commitment of marriage lightly. However, I knew to say "No" so abruptly would bring immediate shame upon her. My

127

parents would not have wanted me to shame someone outwardly.

I said, "I' m flattered that you want to marry me, but I already have a girlfriend back in America whom I hope to marry someday. Therefore, you see, I have not been looking towards marrying anyone in Japan. I'm sorry you came all this way to hear this, and I'm sure you will find someone more suited to you than I am. I wish you a safe trip back home."

She bowed a little lower this time and said, "*Sumimasen, sayonara* (Forgive me I'm sorry, goodbye*)*.

I bowed and said, "*Sayonara*"

I was still in shock as I returned to my quarters. My head was reeling when I thought, "My god, we're not even kissing cousins." Then again, even if my parents had told me who she was, there was no way that I, a GI, could sit down and meet her socially. There is no fraternizing allowed with the Japanese.

For a Japanese girl who normally would be shy, I would say she had moxie. Nevertheless, the surprise visit of my cousin now began to make sense. I stopped for a moment and thought about the people that I saw when I walked in the city, the parks, and the shrines. There were women, young girls, young boys, and old men. Oh my god, it hadn't registered in my mind that most of the young men were gone. I heard that over a million and a half not only Japanese soldiers died in World War II, but also Japanese soldiers were hiding out in far off places to avoid surrendering. I had heard the desperation in her voice, a hope for tomorrow. I see now that her chances of marrying somebody were slim indeed.

**Cousin, who visited me in MIS/ATIS, Tokyo,
Japan, posed at Kishimura, Japan**

Mother's wish for me
Tour old Japan with Uncle
Doozo irasshai (Please come)

The Letter

Several weeks passed, and then I heard from mother saying that she would be sending a package that her brother had asked for. The request was a de-worming medicine called Santonin that he could not buy in Japan. As I read, I thought, "*What, a de-worming medicine? Why would anyone need that?* After all, there was no need to ask that question because GIs stationed in Japan did not eat raw vegetables grown in Japan. Like most Asian countries, this too was the land of "Honey buckets." Except for commercial buildings, Japan had no sewer systems. Fertilizer for farming came from human waste.

She asked me to let her know when I could take a week off to visit my uncle's home in Wakayama prefecture. She said that he would travel to Tokyo to pick up the package. She asked her brother for a special favor to take me on a tour to places that were part of her and father's life in Japan.

There were no priorities in my assignment at ATIS, and scheduling a week off was easy. I rushed off a letter to mother setting the week for my uncle to come to Tokyo. I declined to mention that my *itoko,* cousin, had asked me to marry her for surely the news would have shocked mother.

My uncle arrived at the NYK building on the agreed day, and we introduced ourselves in the traditional Japanese way. He was neatly dressed in a white shirt with a tie, gray suit, and vest tailored in a modest fashion. Traditionally, men present a stiff short bow from the waist. As we bowed formally, we each said, "*Hajimemashete, Yoroshiku onegaishimasu.*" My Uncle was a polite soft-spoken man but I could sense a presence of confidence in his voice. He was a businessperson who had made his living with the stock market. He lived in Tokyo but moved to Kimiidera when the war broke out. Greetings by handshaking were not acceptable in our culture.

My Uncle began, "I have been corresponding with your mother and asking her to send a medicine that was not available in Japan. I was surprised when my sister wrote that her son was an American soldier stationed at the NYK building in Tokyo. She thought it would be safer to send the package to you. In return, I wrote to her that, if you had time, I would take you to see your father's home, as well as to show you some of the sights of Wakayama."

"Uncle," I said, "Whenever mother spoke of Japan, she always said that she has been eternally indebted to your generosity, both when father came to Japan for his eye surgery and, most of all, letting her daughter Shizuko (Mabel) stay with your family. It was of little consequence for our family to be of service to you. I do have your medicine, and I am pleased that you were so generous to let me travel with you."

As I bowed, I said, "Excuse me, please wait a moment while I bring the package and my things and join you for the travel back to Wakayama."

"Yes, of course," he replied.

Quickly, I returned to my quarters to retrieve the package and pick up my small travel kit. Traditionally, *Omiyage*, presents, were customary for visitors to give to the host, but I was at a disadvantage since I was a GI in an unfamiliar territory to do any appropriate shopping for my travel to his home. The best I could do was to purchase a few things at the Army PX in the Ginza district. I had pondered what I could do with my meager GI salary. Money was out of the question since the Army paid us in special government script money instead green backs. I had really thought, "I'm shortchanged" when I received my first pay in the pink colored script money. It looked like play money and never felt like hard cold cash. Yet, maybe it was better than receiving Japanese yen. However, there were rumors that the first GI's had received yens when they landed in Japan.

At the PX, I bought candy and as many cartons of cigarettes as I could. Why buy tobacco? Cigarettes happened to be the commodity for trading in post war Japan. Buying tobacco was a new experience for me since I didn't smoke. When anyone asked why I didn't smoke, I would tell him or her the fairy tale that my father had a big stick in the house and not to smoke was well ingrained in my hide. The real story was that my brother and some neighborhood kids tried smoking once, and I was also there. We didn't have any cigarettes, but one of the kids had snitched his father's Bull Durham cigarette papers, and we decided the next best thing for tobacco was a tobacco weed. We looked all over the empty field for the tobacco weeds. We gathered enough to try to look like adults by smoking. I didn't have a clue how to make a cigarette with the tobacco weed and roll it into a cigarette using the paper. One kid said he knew how since he had watched his father roll cigarettes with his Bull Durham kit. I tried holding the paper, dumping some tobacco weed onto it, rolling the paper over it into a cylindrical mess, wetting the paper with my tongue, and crimping the end of the roll. Mine hung like a limp doll. The others were having the same problem. The boy who knew it all had some blue diamond matches and showed us how to strike the match head across the trousers to ignite it. It wasn't that easy. I broke my share of matches without igniting them. Finally, we managed to light our limp cigarettes. It was awful. If trying to suck the limp cylindrical mess to keep it burning wasn't bad enough, the sudden ingestion of smoke into my throat made me cough so much that I thought I was going to die. It wasn't the stick in the corner but the hacking and coughing from that smoke that had been enough for me to avoid smoking forever.

Now, preparing to leave with Uncle and meet the rest of my family, I checked my area around my bed and made sure it would pass any inspection while I was gone. I went downstairs and said, "I'm sorry to keep you waiting so long for me. This was the package my mother sent, and I have some things for you and your family."

"*Arigatoo, hontooni goshinsetsu desu* – Thank you, you were very kind," he said.

We walked three blocks to the Tokyo station where he purchased the *kippu* (tickets) for our trip. I couldn't help but remember the first time I had walked through this station and had seen the public restrooms. Both the men and women restrooms were completely in open view of the public. I was always amazed how modest the Japanese were in their daily affairs. The toilet was a very simple object: an elongated ceramic tile with an oval hooded piece at one end. I avoided looking inside because I would never intrude on someone's privacy if I were home. Eventually I came to understand that Japanese separate what was normal human function from what must require modest behavior.

This time I rode with my uncle and not in the double white striped Allied car. Because of the shortage of train cars, the cars could be crowded. However, we were lucky to find seats together. While some Japanese might have looked at us with a question mark, people were too polite to make an issue of me in my US Army uniform riding in this section. I never gave it a second thought. In addition, even though the train appeared to have been in service for a long time, it was clean, for no one would ever think of throwing trash on the floor.

I could hear the familiar clickity clack clickity clack of train wheels riding over the couplings of the tracks. Just outside of Tokyo, I saw the empty stretches of land where incendiary bombs had caused mass destruction to wood and paper houses. I was glad that my uncle had left before this destruction occurred, but I had heard that raids had demolished his Tokyo house. Soon we were traveling along the countryside, and here and there were familiar thatched roof farmhouses I had often seen in photographs and pictures. About forty-five minutes from Tokyo, my uncle, who was very quiet on this trip, motioned to me and said, "Look. Over there, far to your right, is Mt. Fuji."

Fuji Yama, Japan

The magnificent snow capped mountain rose majestically high in the sky as if to shout, "Come see me; here I am." Its conic shape looked so symmetrical I thought only the mountain spirits that Japanese revere so deeply could have created something as perfect as this. As the train kept chugging its way down the tracks, I remained glued to the scene in awe. We were passing Shizuoka when I saw the tea farms of Japan. If Fujisan was majestic, the tea farm looked like rows and rows of finely manicured carpeting gracing the hillsides. I saw the rice paddies, but each one seemed not much larger than a couple of acres. Many of the farms snaked up the hillsides. It was a sharp contrast from the miles and miles of cornfields that I saw in Iowa. I wondered how families could survive on such small acreage. Japan had at most six percent arable land, but the Japanese would not think of destroying nature by bulldozing to level the land for farming. Consequently, farmers used every usable open area. The hills and the low-lying mountains around the foothills soon obscured Fujisan. The ride was in sunlight except when we passed through long tunnels as the steam locomotive chugged its way from Tokyo towards Osaka. We were riding on the railroad lines called Tokaido Shinkansen (formally Japan National Railway).

It was a long six-hour ride from Tokyo to Wakayama. Uncle had brought along a bento for the both of us to share on this journey back to his home. It was a treat to eat rice instead of a sandwich or a hamburger. It was *a hinomaru bento,* the red pickled plum in the center of a bed of rice that I remember from my childhood back in Santa Monica. The rice and plum together looked like the Japanese flag, called *Hinomaru.* The sight of it brought back memories of eating *hinomaru* rice that my mother always prepared, especially with hot green tea. Finally, we arrived at Osaka where we boarded another train for Wakayama. Then we took a short ride towards Kimiidera on a streetcar.

We gathered our belongings and walked along a country road towards the west. It was a short walk to what seemed to be near a wooded area. There among the trees was a well-kept house unlike the farmhouses I had seen while walking along the dirt road. As soon as we reached the house at the entrance, *genkan*, and started to remove our shoes, his wife came out to meet us.

Uncle Tsutsui and family, Kimidera, Wakayama, Japan

She bowed and said, "*Hajimemashite,yoroshikuonegaishim asu. Doozo,Irashaimase* Please, come in."

"*Hai, Arigatoo* –Yes, thank you," I replied and continued while bowing, "*Hajimemashite,yoroshikuonegaishimasu.*"

To her husband she said, "*Okaerinasi* –welcome home."

He replied, "*Tadaima* –I am home."

Waiting inside was their son about twelve and a nine-year-old daughter who seemed puzzled to see a Nisei American GI. Simplicity is the way of life for the Japanese and the rooms were devoid of the massive furnishing that I was familiar with in the US. There were no pictures hanging on the walls, but there in a special corner was the *tokonoma*, an alcove where a beautiful scroll hung and where there sat a simple flower arrangement on a small low table.

Since it was near dinnertime, my aunt, his wife, quickly went to her little kitchen and busily began to prepare a meal for us. My uncle put some of his things away, returned, and motioned for me to sit on a *zabuton*, a cushion at a low table. The children did not join us, but then that was customary procedure when I was at home. The wife, after serving us, did not sit with us either, but waited in the background to serve us. While I felt that I was intruding into their life, I was going to enjoy the simple Japanese meal of rice, a bowl of soup, stir-fried vegetables, pickled *daikon*, radish, and green tea.

I knew that I was indeed in a Japanese home when my aunt said those familiar apologetic phrase, *Nanimo arimasen ga. Doozo omeshiagari kudasi.*- There was not much here, but please start eating." I still remember my mother without exception would say those very words after putting forth a great deal of effort to prepare a sumptuous meal for a guest.

I replied, "*Hai, doomo arigatoo gozaimasu* –Yes, thank you."

My uncle motioned with his hand and said, "*Doozo* – please."

I nodded my head and said, "*Itadakimasu* –I will receive meal thankfully."

When the wife was serving food, she did not stand above and place the food in front of us, for this would be a terrible disrespect to the guest and to her husband. She brought the food on a tray, knelt down next to us, and quietly served each dish. When she offered seconds, I said, "*kekko* – No, I'm fine." I had found that it was better to refuse rather than leave food on my plate. Food was a commodity not wasted, especially in these hard times.

After finishing a meal, it was customary to say, "*Gochisoosama* – thank you for the meal." However, it was nice to precede it with, "*Totemo oishikatta desu* – It was delicious."

While my aunt quietly removed the dishes, my uncle said, "We have a busy schedule tomorrow, so let's prepare for the night."

By arranging the shoji screens, they set up a sleeping room for the night for me. From the closet, she brought out a set of futons –one for the mattress and a quilt for a cover for me. It had been a long day, and I was soon fast asleep.

Early the next morning, I could hear the hosts getting ready for the morning. I dressed and excused myself to use their bathroom; I greeted them by saying, "*Ohayoogazaimasu*-Good morning."

In rural Japan, there was no hot and cold running water in the house. I washed up in the morning in a small area that had a trough with a cold-water spigot. In a small nook, I saw a ceramic toilet fixed to the floor. It was like the public toilets in the Tokyo Railroad Station. This was my initiation, and it was not easy to get use to this toilet. You have to squat over this gadget as you would do if you were out in the woods where no flush toilet was available. Pull your pants and shorts down below your knees, squat while facing a hemispherical cup and do your duty. Oh, how I missed American Standard.

Japanese breakfast was very simple, a bowl of rice and soup, either clear broth or *miso* with vegetables and fish.

This morning, uncle had scheduled us to meet my father's relatives and then was off on an excursion to a hot spring. From the gifts I had given him, he selected a few things including some cigarettes as *omiage* –gifts. The etiquette of gift giving was something I had never learned about when I was youngster. It seems that it was a social obligation; what to bring, what to wrap it with, even the choice of color, and what to say was just as important. I would have surely committed a terrible error and shamed my parents by relying on my own devices. Looking back, I was indeed fortunate that my uncle was taking care of the formalities of gift giving.

Again, it was customary and polite to say, "*Ittemairimasu* – I shall be leaving." First, the wife had our shoes at the *genkan* pointed in the right direction for us to slip on for our trip. We walked down the dirt road we had traveled earlier and headed to the village called Kishimura. The fields around us were all brown since the rice harvested earlier was gone. I could see birds landing near the rice stubbles picking out the grains left behind after the harvest. It was peaceful scenery as I looked to absorb all of what my parents must have experienced when they were young. Soon we came upon a row of farmhouses along the road. They stood the test of time of many years for they were sun bleached and weather worn but not dilapidated. Except for the *genkans*, I saw only eight-foot wooden fences standing between adjacent houses. The houses were traditional Japanese homes of wood and paper shoji's with gray tiled roofs. In front of one house, there was a big ornamental stone, a small pine tree, and a heavenly bamboo plant near the *genkan*.

Kishimura, Wakayama, Japan: Father's Village

    As we approached the *genkan*, uncle called out for someone to meet us. A young couple came out first and my uncle told him that a nephew from American had come to visit them. As we bowed and greeted each other in the traditional manner, an older man in an old khaki colored Japanese army uniform came out to meet us. For a moment, I thought I was looking at my father. The facial features were almost identical, and it was apparent he too had gone through hard times. I was speechless. Maybe they were unprepared to invite us in because we were outside all of the time. Even back home, when my parents visited close friends, neither my brothers nor I was ever in their conversations. I was completely unprepared for this encounter since my parents had never told me about my relatives in Japan. They just as well could have been strangers with whom I had no way of connecting. How I missed the good old handshake or a hug that would have given me some feeling of closeness. At times like this, I felt that bowing and smiling left guarded distance between people. My uncle saw that I was having trouble carrying on the conversation and stepped in to tell them about me and about my visit.

    The uneasiness lasted about an hour and we said our goodbyes. We doubled back to where I saw a streetcar. We rode the streetcar into town and transferred to a bus that headed towards a river near Oku doro, Wakayama. We walked a short distance and waited on a big rock jutting out into the water. My uncle explained to me that we were going river rafting and that a boat would pick us up at this spot. There was another couple also waiting for the boat. The river moved swiftly over the rocky river bottom and was clear but not very deep. Upstream I saw the boat with a man standing with a pole guiding the boat along the river. Soon he maneuvered the boat to where we were waiting and kept the boat stationary while we all boarded.

Lady on the Bridge

The boatman steadied the shallow bottom craft with his long pole as we gingerly stepped into the boat. He was a tall elderly man who stood behind us with his long pole. As soon as we sat down, he pushed hard with his pole and we were on our way into the river. I wondered how sea worthy this craft was as I sat quietly with some trepidation about this ride. I focused my eyes in two directions; where and how the boatman was doing his job. First, the scenery was beautiful with rocky shores graced in the background with green shrubs growing upwards along banks. The boatman deftly poked his pole in the water moving us along with the current. Sometimes the boat would scrape the bottom rocks but never against boulders jutting out. He was like a conductor orchestrating the movement of the boat; easy pokes here, a hard long push there away from a boulder and quick thrust movements as we rode down the rapids. Soon I was at ease and began to enjoy the scenery and the boat rafting.

It must have been at least an hour when we finally came to a landing – journey's end. My uncle ushered me to a bus station for a bus ride to an *onsen* –hot spring.

River Gorge, Wakayama, Japan

River boating Wakayama, Japan

Cauldron boils beneath
Enjoy with all nature's gift
Heals body and soul

Onsen

I followed uncle to a bus station where he purchased tickets for our travel to one of many hot springs in Japan. Back home, I had heard about some *Issei* going for a vacation at hot springs but never heard much about what it was like to spend time there. I remember one of the places they visited was a hot spring spa near Bakersfield, California. It must have been close to what they remembered about onsen in Japan because an elderly Japanese couple managed the facility. I always thought it was some sort of recreation place, but I had never had a chance to go there. Now I had an opportunity to see what *onsen* was all about.

When we arrived at our destination, my uncle headed towards a *ryokan*, a Japanese inn. It had the traditional wood structure and the familiar gray tiled roof. There were no shrubs or garden in front since the *genkan* was located just at the street. As we entered, a young woman in a kimono bowed and said, "*Doozo, Irashaimase*, Please come in."

We had already taken off our shoes and put on the slippers provided by the establishment. Uncle checked in and we followed the hostess to our room. As I was about to walk into the room with my slippers, my uncle motioned me to walk on the *tatami* in socks or bare feet. The room was exactly like the one I had stayed in at Nikko; *tatami* floors, *shojis* dividing the rooms, a small table with *zabutons*, cushions nearby, and a closet for storing the futons. The hostess showed us where we could stow our luggage. Later, a maid returned with tea for us to enjoy.

We had been on the go all day, so uncle said let's enjoy a soak in a warm Japanese *furo*, bath. I thought that was a great idea but I was puzzled about where we would take a bath since I didn't see one as we came to our room. Uncle handed me a *yukata*, a cotton robe that the maid had left for us, and he proceeded to undress completely and put on his yukata. When I was ready, he motioned me to follow him.

It was a short walk to a large public bath within the *ryokan*. There were several people already soaking in the large bath. I followed my uncle's motion of removing his *yukata*, folding it, and placing it with his slippers. Since I wasn't used to undressing in public, I was wholly unprepared for this display of my body to everyone to see, especially with women present. Then I remembered the public restroom at the Tokyo Station where the men and women's facility was located in one big room with each in separate sides of the room but visible to everyone. People went about their business as if it were just another normal event in their lives. It was a revelation continually to me how the Japanese could separate intimate human events from purely social encounters. I myself was having a difficult time weighing the Japanese attitude against Puritan view about nudity in public. Uncle was already dousing himself with water to cleanse himself before immersing himself in the hot bath. What the heck, I was not in my GI uniform and I looked Japanese, so I dropped my *yukata* and cleansed myself before entering the bath. I could see the steam rising from the water. No doubt, I was in for an experience of being tortured as a lobster immersed in a boiling pot of water.

Carefully, I dipped my toes into the water to test it. It was hot. How can anyone just slide into this without wincing? I inched my way in as my body began to accommodate to the thermal shock. Finally, I was fully in, and I began to enjoy the relaxing warmth of the bath. Only a small towel the size of a washcloth is allowable in the bath, for this was only a place for soaking and relaxing and not washing the body.

Sometime later, since my uncle started to get out of the hot bath, I prepared to emerge from the steamy bath. As I stood up, I felt the glow of my body, and it was red but thankfully not beet red. As we wiped ourselves with our cotton towels, we dried quickly because our bodies were still radiating the heat. We donned our *yukata*, and put on our slippers and headed back.

When we returned to our room, the maid was ready to serve our *yu gohan*, evening meal. We sat at the low table on the *zabutons*, cushions, while the hostess served dinner in our room. Rice, soup, and stir-fried vegetables were the usual fare during these hard times. I was somewhat puzzled because we were here to experience the onsen, the natural spring and as yet, I didn't know when that would happen. My uncle must have been reading my mind when he said that later we would enjoy the onsen that was just adjacent to our room. Now I was completely mystified because I had envisioned lounging outside in an onsen.

"Inside?" I asked.

He explained that there were many types of *onsens*, both indoor and outdoor. Each had different types of minerals that could help people's particular ailments. Of course, we had just come here to relax in the onsen. The water of the onsen bubbles came out of the ground into a pond, but fancier ones use a pool. Besides the various minerals, there will be a smell of sulfur because of the volcanic origin. He said he chose this *ryokan* because it removed most of the sulfur smell but kept the minerals for our onsen. Then he said, "We went to the bath first because we do not want to wash off the precious minerals from our body after dipping into the onsen." I was relieved about the loss of the sulfur smell because I certainly didn't want to smell like rotten eggs in the morning.

The ritual was the same as taking a bath. Wash and rinse yourself before you step into this liquid inferno. While we were enjoying our relaxing mineral bath, the maid had made our bed for the night.

Tomorrow we would head for Nara, the first capital of Japan.

Start of an Empire
Blessed by Sun Goddess Spirit
Nara Capitol

Nara

As we left the onsen, uncle said, "Today, I want you to see Nara and, if it were at all possible it would be nice to take you to Kyoto." But I had a train to catch later that day back to Tokyo, so we only had time to see Nara. He told me that Nara was Japan's first capital and therefore its history was very important to the Japanese. The Empress Gemmei established it in the seventh century.

"*Ojisan*, uncle, I said, "I thought only Emperors occupied the throne in Japan."

"No," he said, "According to Japan's ancient history, Japan was created by the Goddess Amatersu Oomikami many thousands of years ago. The Empress Gemmei was a descendant of Amatersu."

However, I was about to say that's nothing but mythology but decided to drop my words because the words might be contentious.

Nara was no longer the capital of Japan. During that period, Japan was marked with constant internal strife because various clans struggled to control the kingdom. First, the seat of the government moved to Kyoto and then to Edo, later called Tokyo.

I learned that day that the Shinto shrines and Buddhist temples in the park marked the humble beginning of Japan's Empire.

After a short walk from Nara station, we passed through the Torii into the park. The park was situated in a flat area with a large lawn area, and the shrines and temples were nestled among the trees and shrubs. We walked along on a wide array of gray rectangular flagstones that connected various historical sites. We headed towards Todai ji, the famous Buddhist statue, when I noticed a young boy struggling to feed a deer, except the deer seem to have the upper hand. I was puzzled why there were so many deer wandering about the garden?

Torii (Entrance gate for the Spirits) Nikko, Japan

I asked uncle, "Why are the deer allowed to wander about this historic garden? Won't they destroy its beauty?"

He said the Japanese believe that deer are sacred spirits; this is the Shinto belief. If anyone were to harm them, the Japanese would severely punish them.

As he was speaking, my mind wandered back to his statement about the Empress Gemmei being a descendant of Amaterasu. Deep in my mind, I recalled when I was learning Japanese; I had read the story of Amaterasu in my textbook. She was the Japanese Shinto Sun Goddess, ruler of the Plain in Heaven, and the shining light of the world. She had retreated into a cave because the thunder God had ravaged the earth and caused such commotion that it frightened her. She stayed there for sometime because no other Gods could persuade her to come out. Meanwhile, Demons ruled the earth and darkness prevailed across the land. One day, the Goddess of Joy and happiness lured her out of the cave; she saw herself in a mirror the Goddess of Joy had hung on a tree, and she returned to the sky. Suddenly there was sunlight throughout the land. Japan's flag with a bright red circle in the middle of a white background represented the sun and was a constant reminder of Japan's Shinto roots.

Rising high above me was the Todai ji, the temple that housed the largest bronze Buddha statue. At the entrance, uncle began removing his shoes to enter the temple, as he would if he were entering a home. I followed every movement he made to make sure I didn't violate any Japanese custom. Inside, I saw the massive bronze figure of Buddha.

"This is the largest wooden structure in the world," said uncle.

I looked up. Rather than beautiful, it was massive. It was fifty feet high. All I could do was wonder how they managed to build such a large bronze statue during the eighth century.

There had been a strong Chinese influence on the city. The Japanese had modeled their government on that of the Chinese, and Japan had also acquired the Buddhist religion from them many years ago. While Shinto remained the fundamental belief of the Japanese, the Imperial family took to Buddhism teachings so deeply that they decided to spread the religion throughout the kingdom. This was only one of many famous Buddhist temples in Japan. Next, I thought about Nara and noticed how the Chinese influence permeated Japan's culture. It was during the Nara era that Japan began to form its written language through the influence of the Chinese language. It was here that the mythology passed on by word of mouth preserved in treasured documents.

We returned to the entrance to put on our shoes and head towards Nara's Kasuga Taichu Shinto Shrine. Along the path, I saw stone lamps of many shapes and sizes. To enter the shrine without the ritual of cleansing oneself would have been a terrible breach of custom. Near the entrance, there was a structure where ladles with water were available to perform this rite. On each side of the shrine's entrance, I saw a pair of dog statues. I remember at another shrine that had lions instead dogs. Again, I followed my uncle's every move, starting with purification, removing shoes, making a small offering, bowing twice and clapping hands twice. We entered the main hall of the inner court. What captivated me were the rows of colorful lanterns housed in vermilion red paint. There seem to be lanterns everywhere.

"Uncle," I asked, "Do the lanterns mean something?"

"They were offerings by people who revere this sacred place," he replied.

We hurried the visit because it was time to head to the train station. Uncle said for me to ride the Allied car back to Tokyo. I thanked him for taking his precious time to *annai,* usher me, to nostalgic places of my parents' past. I extended my thanks to his wife for her generosity. He waited with me until my train arrived and we bowed and said our goodbyes. As I boarded the car, I was ready to wave goodbye as I would have back home, but I remembered my mother saying that waving one's hand was not to say goodbye but to come here or go away.

While the train sped towards Tokyo, the scenery whizzed by while I mulled over the once in a lifetime trip. However, I was ashamed that I hadn't made a connection with my father's relatives. Why didn't I take the time to learn about my father's past or my mother's, instead of caught up in my own life? I had found myself completely unprepared, and my Japanese had failed me.

Deer (Shika) Spirit

There was darkness everywhere
Thunder roars and lightning strikes
As *Susanowo*, God of Tempest, bellows
Fear and embarrassment cast a spell
Goddess *Amaterasu* cowers below

There was darkness everywhere
The mountains cast no shadows
Rivulets do not flow

There was darkness everywhere
The rivers turn to ice
Fishes do not swim

There was darkness everywhere
The rice fields wither and bend
Rice bowls empty stomach growls

There was darkness everywhere
The sun rise no more
Rooster will not crow

There was darkness everywhere
The Gods and Goddesses lure her out
Mirror reflects the way

There was darkness everywhere
The Goddess, *Amaterasu*, sees the way
Heaven above burst in brilliant light

There was darkness no more
Amaterasu embraces the land
Rooster crows and evil banished

There was darkness no more
A white deer perks up and cocks its ear
Keen like mother's ear hearing the cry of her child

There was darkness no more
Sunlight creates a harmony
Plants trees and earth sparkle with hue

Lady on the Bridge

There was darkness no more
The fields of rice begin to grow
Rice bowls full again

There was darkness no more
But who will bring this message to all
Amaterasu whispers to a deer

There was darkness no more
White deer Spirit of the forest
Spread the message "There was nothing to fear"

There was darkness no more
Let the light shine on this land
Hold fast to its beauty
Build a shrine at Ise to mark this day
Where Spirits, *Kami*, can live in harmony

Brilliance in the sky
Goddess of Sun not your light
Cry of death not life

Ground Zero

There was an arrow planted at "Ground Zero" where the atomic bomb burst 1600 feet directly above that spot on August 8, 1945. Without that arrow, I would have never known what had happen here on that day. The scene of destruction was familiar, for I had already seen the desolation of Japan's former industrial complexes as a result of Allied bombs. I had seen buildings left standing with structural steel hanging nakedly for one to see the destructive force of man against man. Here the same structural steel beams stood dangling, but grotesquely bent and melted and their protective shells strewn across the landscape like confetti. Gone were the bodies that were vaporized or scorched by the enormous energy imprisoned within the atom. Spared were the people outside of the city of Nagasaki that lay in a valley. Yet far to the right, I saw one wall of a church surviving man's anger and a stone *torii* standing alone, a gate for the spirits to pass through. What irony has man wrought to this place with that tiny atom?

Standing at Ground Zero, Nagasaki, Japan

As I stood there, I remembered reading about the wonderful facts about the atom in my high school physics class at Samohi. First, I had read about Madam Curie and her discovery of x-rays and that she had hypothesized that those gamma rays came from inside of the atom of thorium and uranium. I thought how beneficial this might be for mankind. Then I read about the brilliant mathematician, Albert Einstein, who was famous for his theory of relativity, which predicated the equivalence of energy and mass, $E=MC^2$. The text stated that if we could convert one gram of water to energy we would have the equivalent amount of energy of 3000 tons of coal. It was an eye opening statement of how much energy was contained in such a small amount of material. If somehow man could harness that energy, we would never lack power for factories or heating, and we would have electricity for our homes forever. Back then, before the war we were just entering the age of quantum mechanics and nuclear physics. As I stood there, I saw that man had found additional uses for such awesome energy and that there was no turning back.

What horror happened at the instant the electric charge ignited the high explosive (HE) and started the chain of reactions in the atomic bomb, Fat Man.

Japan's military leaders did not believe that America could deliver another atomic bomb after Hiroshima. Truman delivered the message loud and clear, "Fat Man." It was shortly thereafter, when Emperor Hirohito, in his address to the nation, said, "I am not God," and conceded unconditional surrender to the Allied Forces.

FAT MAN

A blanket of High Explosive (HE) hugs a shiny spherical shell
Hidden deep within a mighty Genie hides
The time has come to flex your muscles says Man
Electrons flow sparks ignite the HE fires with a mighty bang
Fiery blanket implode the shell with a mighty burst
Laws of Physics play their role, Mass, Energy, and Momentum

Shock wave and shock wave smash the shell towards the pit
Genie waits anxiously for its destiny, Critical Mass
Suddenly Einstein says it's time, E equal M C squared
Neutrons pierce the pit and all Hell breaks loose
Electrons protons neutrons gamma rays and unknowns mix
e to the x, e to the x, the Physicist shouts with glee

There was no blanket to cushion man's fate or time to flee
The intense flash of radiation pierces soft tissues
A fireball and shock wave move at supersonic speed
Scorching crushing and vaporizing blast their way outward
A mushroom cloud reaches towards heaven
Spewing its radioactive debris with half life unknown

This was Genie's gift to man but Hell be there just below.
A steel beam mangled and bent protrudes among the rubble
The fiery aftermath leaves only embers glowing
A scorched stone Torii stands naked awaiting *Kami's (Spirit)* presence
A broken church wall God's temple stands awaiting God's word
Only the smell of death, mangled bodies, cries of victims unheard

I stand here at ground zero trying to understand
Never to fully comprehend the horror of that moment
I feel revulsion within me of man's inhumanity
From these ashes let God's will be heard
Honor the dead and the brave young men
Let friend and foe come together and build a lasting peace

Kamikaze (Divine winds) failed
I'm not God Emperor says
People's voice be heard

Democracy

"Suto, Strike! *Suto*, Strike!" shouted by Japan's coalmine workers in protest against the establishment.

This was the first response to the new Japanese constitution that inaugurated democracy in action. Japan had surrendered unconditionally, and Emperor Hirohito was no longer the sacred ruler of Japan. General McArthur ordered the government section of his GHQ (General Headquarters) to draw up a model constitution, a nation ruled by the people. On November 3, 1946, the Japanese constitution came into effect that established that the will of the people, and not the military, nor the Emperor, would hereafter dictate the future of Japan. The constitution called for sweeping political, economic, and social reforms.

I wondered about the little people in this representative democracy. I saw no parade lauding the new constitution. Was it possible that the people would discard the icon, the symbol of being Japanese, the Emperor, whose ancestors dated back to the beginning of time? I had my doubts that the people would discard their culture because of words on a piece of paper. Most of the citizens were struggling to survive the aftermath of the war. The vast empty spaces, a stark reminder of firestorms from incendiary bombs on homes, were still visible throughout Japan. Many soldiers, who had surrendered and returned to Japan, found a desperate situation; their homes had vanished and family scattered or dead. The soldiers who returned were trying to adjust to civilian life, but the horrors of war; the futile *banzai* charge, the acrid smell of cordite and death, and the cry of the wounded and dying remained vivid and haunting for people every day. Democracy and freedom would mean nothing when struggle to survive was at their doorstep.

Home industries began creating merchandise to sell to the GI's. On the street corners in Tokyo, I saw trinkets, cameras, art objects, and anything that might catch the fancy of a GI to purchase. Every day I saw old men picking up the cigarette butts the GIs flicked into the streets because an American cigarette was a prized commodity in post-war Japan. A carton of cigarettes was gold on the black market. Stores that survived the war were struggling for business. At night, desperate young women loitering near train stations would sell their souls to survive the aftermath of defeat. The war had devastated the nation's fuel supply. Japan's meager coal supply was the only viable source of fuel. For many years, Japan's Parliament had thwarted the communist faction in organizing the coalminers. This was their moment in history. The communist dominated coalmine union wanted to seize the power. However, General MacArthur had other plans.

One day, I received my order for a new assignment to team up with another MIS GI, a *Kibei*. Our job was to assist in an investigation and evaluation of the coalmine industry in Kyushu, Japan for the US State Department representatives. Our orders instructed us to pack enough gear for a week or more travel and report to the Tokyo train station. We had no idea what was in store for us except that we were the interpreters for the State Department.

On the day of departure, the *Kibei* and I walked to the Tokyo train station and looked for the Army support personnel that would accompany us to Kyushu. As we approached the station, a young ruddy complexioned GI in fatigues, a corporal, hailed us to come with him. He looked no more than eighteen years old. He was smiling as if he were enjoying his duty. He raised his hands, waved, and motioned to us to follow him. I was surprised because he did not head for the regular train tracks but off to a siding. There in front of me was a separate train; two Pullman cars, dining car, supply car, and a flat car with two jeeps and a passenger car.

The corporal said, while beaming from ear to ear, "This is the train that you'll ride to Kyushu." He explained that he would be in charge of all of the logistics for our trip. This was a sweetheart deal. We had our own private dining car with a chef, waiter, and food supplies. He said we would have our first meal in the dining car tonight. Our quarters for this trip would be the Pullman. Then he said that we would not have to do anything on this trip because the porter would take care of it for us. Hey, we even had our own jeep to travel around in with no questions asked.

I had never traveled in a Pullman before. Even when I left Manzanar, California to travel from Reno, Nevada to Minneapolis, Minnesota, it was in a vintage coach. I spent three nights and two days on a seat, that was hard as a cement bench, and luckily, my mother had packed enough food for my travel. What a deal this was going to be! Each of us had a private compartment. At the Pullman car, a porter placed a footstool for us at the car steps. The interior was neat and clean, and the sleeping berths above were shiny wood paneling. I checked the sleeping arrangement to see what I would

GI Special train for Miiki Coal Mine Trip. Complete with Pullman car with Porter, Dining car with Waiters, and flat car transporting Jeep for our use.

experience at night. The beds had clean sheets, but I notice that the length of the bed seemed shorter than my bunk bed. Later that night, I was thankful that I was not six feet tall for I did not want to sleep doubled up in my Pullman bed through the night.

About suppertime, I felt a sudden jolt when a steam locomotive backed up into the siding and hitched onto our cars. Meanwhile, the State Department representative and his assistant boarded the train and settled into their quarters. The porter came through the Pullman car and informed us that dinner was ready. As I stepped into the dining car, I could not believe what I saw. The tables were set with white linen cloth, linen napkins, and a small vase with a flower set in the center, silverware, and real china. The waiter dressed in his white uniform ushered us to our table. The corporal outdid himself with the accommodations. The dinner was a small steak, potatoes, vegetables, served with hot rolls and dessert. It was a leisurely dinner. There was no distracting noise of dishes from the kitchen, and the waiter stood next to the kitchen door and looked attentively to see that everything was satisfactory. If this was army life, I should have signed on for four years instead of two.

After dinner, we sat in the lounge area of the dining car and introduced ourselves. The State Department representative was an elderly man, dressed in a dark gray suit with a tie, with thin graying hair but not balding. As I sized him up, I figured he was a career diplomat, for his manner was all business. His assistant was a stout young woman, not fat, with short brunette hair, and I guessed she was about forty years old. She had a pleasant personality, was friendly, and smiled a lot when she talked. The man in charge informed us that the primary objective of our trip to Kyushu was to establish the state of affairs of Mitsui Miike Company and the workers' conditions in the coalmines. He said, Japan's coalmines had a long history of labor troubles, and the socialist party was trying to establish a union for the workers but was thwarted in their effort. The mining company was undergoing hard times, and, in fact, was losing money. The socialist party wants to strike, saying that it is their right under a democracy. There have been attempts to strike at other industries, but General MacArthur would have none of that. It was our mission to insure no strike will occur. The man in charge said, "My assistant here has our tentative schedule of our meetings and a copy of the speech I will present to the workers". My *Kibei* friend raised his hand and quickly volunteered to do the interpreting.

On the way back to our cars, I said to my friend, "How can the workers even consider striking when the company was losing money? Is that what they think democracy is about?"

"It isn't necessarily the workers that were instigating this *Suto*, strike," he said. "The socialist party was really a communist faction that had over the years fermented labor unrest in Japan. The communists want to rule Japan."

As soon as we finished our conversation, a sudden jolt, the crunch of metal against metal of the train hitches let us know we were off on our way to Kyushu.

Once again, I was heading south on Japan's National Railways as the familiar sound of the clickity clack over the rails filled the air. Since the overhead light was too dim for reading, I prepared to climb into my Pullman bed. I pulled the cover panel up, turned the covers open, and for a moment I thought, I am glad I do not have claustrophobia. This thing was no bigger than a coffin. If the train gives a big jolt and the panel shuts, I am in real trouble. Tired and contented with a full meal, I fell asleep until morning sunrays woke me up.

What a joy to have breakfast in the dining car with full service again. I did not expect my meals served like this. This was something I saw in magazines when I was growing up. It was an untouchable dream. Never had I imagined I would step up to such a setting; linen tablecloth, linen napkin, silverware polished in placed, and a menu to select my choices. As soon as I sat down at my table, the waiter served coffee and handed me the menu for breakfast. Juice, small dish of fruit, eggs any style, hash brown potatoes, and toast was my choice for the morning. It was a leisurely breakfast as I watched the countryside pass by.

The train, pulled by a steam locomotive, had traveled all night and needed to refuel at Kobe, Japan. It was a relief to go outside and stretch our legs while they serviced the locomotive. The station was rather deserted, and what I could see around the neighborhood from the station platform was the aftermath of the Allied bombing of this industrial and port city. Only brick or metal buildings stood, but they all looked gutted. The conductor hailed us, and once more, we headed for Kyushu.

Kyushu was an island south of the main island of Honshu. Japan named the strait between the two islands, the Kanmon Strait. I wondered how we were going to reach Kyushu because I had heard there was a fast tidal current that flowed between the two islands, making it a dangerous passage. The train began slowing down and I sensed the train was descending into a tunnel. "What's going on?" I asked my friend. "Oh, didn't you know, Japan built an underwater tunnel connecting Honshu to Kyushu?" It was the first one ever built between two islands by any nation. Later, I would think of that train while I travelled on BART that connected San Francisco and Oakland under the San Francisco Bay. Our special train seemed to crawl through the tunnel until I saw daylight again. We arrived at our destination, Fukuoka, Kyushu train station but the porter motioned us to wait. We could hear the locomotive chugging as it moved forward and backward and the screeching of the metal wheels as it turned off the mainline into the siding. We heard a loud swoosh as soon as the engineer released the air pressure in the air hoses that connected the train cars. This Pullman was to be our home while we visited the Miike Company coalmines.

The corporal was busy unloading our transportation. The rest of us prepared to visit the Mitsui Corporation's Miike office and arrange our daily schedule. The coalmine was located at Ohmuta city in Fukuoka Prefecture, Kyushu.

We assembled this morning for our trip to the coalmine. The company tour guide handed us hard hats with lights attached for our excursion into the mine. On the way to the mineshaft, I noticed several people, men and women, working on a big mound of tailings. What brought this to my attention was that the women were pushing heavy carts along the tracks while most of the men were just standing around. I swear the men could have been members of the city maintenance crew I used to see back home who leaned on their shovels hours at a time.

At the mineshaft, we all entered the cage and down we went to a lower level of the mine. The guide told us that this mine has been in operation since 1868 and the current coal veins stretched under the sea for at least two miles. Here and there, I saw water dripping down from the ceiling of the mineshafts. Just the thought of all that seawater above me gave me the shivers. We walked and rode a tramcar through some of the tunnels. I saw men working at the coal veins, and it was a terrible working environment. Not only was the work dirty but also the coal veins of this mine were shallow and the men had to scrunch down to get at the coal with their tools. I thought it would get colder the lower we went, but the opposite was true. This was an experience I would long remember and a job I hoped I never would have to take.

All of us got a better understanding of what a coal miner must contend with day after day in this hostile environment. Of course, we saw only the most accessible part of the coalmines, for there were areas that posed greater danger to the workers. Not only was ventilating the areas difficult, but also, there was a greater danger of gas explosions. It was later that I learned about the horror stories of this particular mine. First, Japanese prisoners worked as beasts of burdens during the mine's early history. Next, during Japan's Co-Prosperity push, Japan captured Koreans, Chinese, and Filipinos and forced them to work in these mines under the same harsh treatment of the Japanese criminals. Later during WW II, Japan forced captured US soldiers, civilians, and British POWs to work the mines. They faced harsh and brutal treatment by cruel beatings. Even worse, they worked long hours and were given minimal food rations.

Without the forced labor when the war ended, the coal production drastically dropped to ten percent of its former capacity. Japan's economy was in trouble because coal was the most important fuel for Japan's industries. While returning soldiers helped fill some of the coal mining positions, the cost of Japan's coal was more than importing from other nations. The government subsidized the short fall, but the Allied Occupation Headquarters reduced or eliminated this aid to the coal mining industry. This was the era when the Japan Socialist Party organized and proposed a non-armed revolution strategy starting with the coalmines.

The Marxists started their movement after World War I; the government squelched their uprising, and imprisoned their leaders. The loss of the war, economic disaster, hungers, and, especially, ex-soldiers looking for jobs, made the time ripe for union action. At first, the U.S. Occupation administration looked upon unionism as the sign of democratizing force. The Miike mine was especially ripe for a strike by the workers because it was notoriously unsafe. The unfair practice of the supervisors showing favoritism in assigning work and wages further exacerbated the situation. When General MacArthur banned what he considered communist intrusion into the Japanese Cabinet, the union's demand for higher wages and a voice in the government died. The cry of democratic action, Suto, strike faded.

Entrance to Miiki Coal Mine Company, Kyushu, Japan

Coal Miners, Miiki Coal Mines, Kyushu, Japan

Chug-a-lug with you
The world was all a kilter
Fall off the wagon

Chug-a-lug

Except for a Shogatsu, New Year's toast, there had never been any liquor in our home back in Santa Monica. However, at New Years, my parents served *sake*, rice wine from a small porcelain decanter warmed in a pot, then dispensed into small thimble sized ceramic cups for each person to celebrate the New Year. Our family's *sake* set was white porcelain with delicate blue painting of a lily. When I was old enough, my parents let me join the toast to bring in the New Year. On my first sip of the sake, I felt a warm sensation as it trickled down my throat. After the first sip, I was not too anxious for more. The taste was something I could not describe at the time, but later, as an adult, it reminded me of warmed sauterne wine. A thimble size sip is not enough to leave you tipsy, but for the sake of any one's sanity, drinking enough *sake* can be devastating.

Because of my parents' abstinence from drinking, I never drank hard liquor and, in fact, I did not know the difference between rum, scotch, or bourbon. I was that naive. I had even written off drinking beer. That was after I saw the effect on a group of young high school students at one of our high school assemblies. One student heaved and left a mess that stunk to high heaven. It was disgusting.

I received my baptism of fire water when I was in the army in Japan. The act was just stupid and dumb. One day, my friends asked me to join a farewell party for a *Kibei* who was returning home to the US, after his tour of duty with the Military Intelligence Section, MIS in Tokyo, Japan. His friends arranged a party at a Japanese establishment in Tokyo. I was with a group of good friends at the party, and it was a rousing jolly time. Sometime during the course of the celebration, a toast to the honored guest came up. I joined them, Four Roses, 86 proof straight up. On the first swallow, I felt a burning liquid running down my throat. The euphoria of feeling good, laughing, and slurring words soon descended on me. Time span now escapes me. Did I have more than one Four Roses straight up? Did I try to keep up with the guest who was a seasoned drinker?

At some point in the evening, I needed to go to the bathroom. A Japanese toilet, as I have mentioned on a number of occasions, would always be a mental and physical challenge. However, in my intoxicated condition, getting to the *benjo*, bathroom was even more risky. Since we were sitting on the *tatami*, straw floor covering --no chairs in Japan -- it was hard getting up. As I left the room, I suddenly noticed the wall seemed to be at an angle, even moving, the ceiling seemed skewed. The end of the hallway seemed to disappear.

I woke up the following morning. My head was on the young host's lap. My good friend was nearby watching over me. I was miserable. I had learned a lesson. Chug-a-lug was not for me.

Farewell Ye Spirits
Nostalgia of old Japan
My two worlds can't mix

Sayonara

It was July 1948, in just over a month; my tour of duty would end. It meant that I would be on the high seas for fourteen long days of boredom. The smell of diesel fuel and fresh red paint on the hull of a ship still lingered in the back of my mind. I remembered holding back the queasiness in my stomach and the sour taste in my throat just enough to ride out the journey from San Francisco to Yokohama, Japan. I was not looking forward to the same experience.

Over the past few weeks, I had noticed others leaving ATIS for reassignment or discharge. I decided to find out from the company office what the procedure was for shipping out. The company clerk brought out my Army record and handed me a memorandum and a form to fill out. To my surprise, I could request a month early discharge. The memo stated that the War Department was actively seeking current members to "reup" or extend their tour of duty since so many *Nisei* were shipping out. The Army was offering a promotion in rank as an incentive to stay. Even promotion to second lieutenant was possible. There was even a hint that civilian jobs supporting GHQ, as a War Department employee, might be forthcoming soon.

All this sounded nice, but although my role as soldier was easy, this was not home. Every day when I returned to my quarters, it felt no different from space I shared with my family at Manzanar. Most evenings, I was the only one there for I had chosen not to become casually or deeply committed to life in Japan. Outside in the streets, there were always guarded looks from those who saw a *Nisei* GI. I missed the openness of people interactions that I found back home. The missed the simple informal greetings; "Hi there, Howya doing friend?" would be so nice to hear occasionally. A handshake, a hug, a pat on the back, a smile, a cry, and laughter all seemed to hide behind a mask. I looked Japanese, but inside of my head, I was still a stranger. On the other hand, one of my roommates, a *Kibei*, appeared to be having the time of his life stationed here. When I first met him, he said that he had just married two weeks before he shipped out from California. Yet, every night, he would change to civilian clothes and be out for the night. One day, he said that before the war, native Japanese did not fully accept him as one of their own because *Nisei* and *Kibei* were too outspoken. The tables had turned and now he was celebrating his good fortune.

I just wanted to go home. I picked up the redeployment form and started to fill it out. To my surprise, at the bottom, there was a choice to travel by ship or Army air transport. I had never flown on an airplane. It would be an adventure of a lifetime. All I needed to do was to provide some reasonable request for air transportation. "This was great," I thought. Quickly I wrote that I needed to return as early as possible to reapply at the University of California to continue my college education. I explained further that internment of Japanese by the U.S. government had terminated my college education. I submitted my discharge form and hoped for the best.

It was a few days later I received my answer. I could not believe it. The Army accepted my request for air transportation, as well as an early retirement date. The order stated I would transfer to the Redeployment Depot (RepoDepo) at Tachikawa Airbase, Japan. I quickly calculated the number of days of travel due to my good fortune. Under the best conditions, the air travel could be three days and the worst-case scenario could be six days if there were any unforeseen delays. What a relief to know that I would not be on that briny sea for fourteen long monotonous days.

Tachikawa Air Base was about 14 miles west of Tokyo and one of the busiest U.S. air bases. It was also located near some rural villages. My quarter was in a one-story bungalow near the edge of the compound. I tossed my gear next to my assigned bunk and read my traveling orders. The order stated to read the Air Base's daily bulletin board for my departure date. Since I was unassigned to any unit at Tachikawa airbase, my days were free. One day, I had a chance to wander around the neighboring countryside. I thought I would be conspicuous here since I was a *Nisei* GI, but no one paid any attention to me as I walked through the quaint little village. The streets were narrow dirt roads and all of the buildings had *genkans* next to the road just as I had observed when I visited the *onsen* with my uncle. The buildings were typical of Japan, made of wood and paper. This village must have survived the bombings because it still looked old and weather worn. As I wandered back to the airbase, I saw along the skyline, children in school uniforms skipping and walking among rows of pine trees. I sensed that they were happy because I could almost hear them

Tachikawa Air Base, Japan

singing and talking as they moved across that picturesque scene. I closed my eyes and thought, "Could I have lived that same idyllic moment if my parents had never immigrated to America?"

It was time to hustle back. At the base, I found my schedule for departure posted. The first leg of my journey home would be Guam, next Hawaii, and finally Travis Airbase, California.

Chapter 6: Homebound

Homeward bound my love
Fly far from land of Spirits
Flight back to Freedom

Heading for Guam

It was a sleepless night because I was anxious to be on my way home. After breakfast, a dozen or more GI's were packed and ready to ship out. I hooked up with another Nisei soldier who was returning to Southern California. I picked up my gear and headed towards the aircraft. There on the runway was a four engine Douglas DC-4 with cargo doors, a familiar sight from my hometown, Santa Monica, California. At least I was off to a good start. However, I was not sure what to expect once I was inside the aircraft. As I stepped inside the plane, I saw brown canvas bucket seats strung twenty-five on each wall of the interior. This was not going to be a luxury flight. There were no panels on the interior wall, and the center aisle was set up for transporting cargo. The aircraft's windows were behind us, and we would be facing the travelers on the other wall throughout the flight. Finally, when all the gear and cargo was stored, the captain announced, "Douse the butts and buckle up, we're taking off!"

The roar of the four motors was deafening throughout the plane as the pilot accelerated full power to take off. It was my first experience of feeling the acceleration of an airplane. It was an exhilarating experience even though I was in a bucket seat sitting sideways. I am not too fond of being high up in the air, but the power I felt as the plane took off was reassuring. Soon we were off towards Guam.

There was not much to see once we were in flight. At twenty thousand feet, you took your choice; it was either blue sky or blue water. The plane had the bare minimum in travel facilities. There was no "OCCUPIED" sign to the rear of the plane. The plumbing was Army basic; a funnel and a hose attached to it that snakes outside. We were about two hours in the air of our six-hour flight to Guam when the pilot came on the intercom, "Fasten your seat belt and no smoking. We're making an emergency landing to check our communication equipment."

Before I fastened my seat belt, I attempted to see where we were. There was nothing but ocean! "Where in the world was the pilot going to land this baby?" I wondered. "There's no sign of land down there," I thought. He did say emergency landing to check out his communication equipment, so he must know that somewhere near below was land. After we descended rapidly for fifteen minutes, he banked the plane to the right. He leveled off, began to rev the motors, and lowered the landing gear with a thump. There was a sudden steep descent with a definite jolt as the wheels touched down. I could hear the brakes screeching as the plane's nose tilted downward. We had arrived for our emergency stop. However, where in the hell were we?

The intercom came on, "We have landed at Iwo Jima. It won't take more than an hour to check out the instruments, so, in the meantime, I'll ask you to stay put." The passengers unbuckled their seat belts and looked out of the small windows. There was not anything to see. I thought, "Just maybe the landing strip was in an isolated spot. That's probably why we can't see anything."

I could hear the boarding ramps pushed against the plane. The freight door opened and two GI's in fatigues entered with tool kits and testing equipment. The pilot, who was waiting at the door, escorted the two to the cockpit. The rest of us just sat around and hoped for the best. It was almost an hour later when the pilot came over the intercom, "It looks like we will be here for a couple of hours more. You can get off the plane, but don't wander too far or we will leave without you."

It was nice to get out and stretch a bit after three hours in an uncomfortable canvas bucket seat. "So this was Iwo Jima." I mused. It was not that the landing strip was isolated, but that the whole place was devoid of vegetation, and there were no birds or animals in sight. I had read that volcanic action created this piece of land over a million years ago. I smelled a distinct odor of sulfur in the air common to volcanic regions. Someone said this island was about eight square miles. I calculated that was roughly three miles across in diameter. I knew why this god-forsaken place was so important to America. Iwo Jima had been the stepping-stone for the Allied Forces to invade Japan. In four days, two Marine divisions had invaded and conquered the island. On February 23, 1945, the Marines raised "Old Glory" on Mt. Surabachi, signaling victory after that horrendous battle. The costs: twenty thousand U.S. and Japanese soldiers lost their lives on this barren piece volcanic turf.

We were all standing around amazed at the emptiness of this island when the pilot hailed us to return to the plane. As we lifted off the runway, I could see "Old Glory" waving freely and proud. In a few minutes, the island faded into a mere dot in the ocean as our planed droned towards Guam. It would be at least another three hours before we touched down on my first leg of my journey home. Finally, the pilot came over the intercom; he said we would be landing at Guam in fifteen minutes. There were a few shouts of hurray as we began our descent to North Field (since renamed Andersen Air Force Base), Guam. However, Guam was not just another island in the Pacific for me. I remembered in December 1941, the day after Pearl Harbor, listening to the radio reports and reading the news that Japan had captured Guam. America lost the island because the military stationed only a small US contingent to protect it. When I stepped outside the plane, it was warm and muggy. Our orders were to billet here for the night. This was no barren island. There were trees and tropical plants, and I received a whiff of sweet smelling flowers in the air. Once inside the building, we received our assignment for our quarters and instructions for our flight schedule the next day.

What a shock it was in the morning to see my luggage piled outside the building. It was trouble. I saw no plane on the tarmac. There was no explanation, just "stand by for your next flight," the order stated. We milled around like sheep not knowing what to do with ourselves for the rest of the day. Rumors filled our heads as people speculated about why the delay and when to expect our next flight.

I had now lost a day of travel. The next was just another day of waiting. Then the rumor mill hinted that they bumped us from our flight because some brass wanted to transport his family and dog stateside. I was miffed because our flight status had become lower than dog priority. Then the other shoe dropped. It would be at least three more days before another plane would be available for us. I counted the unforeseen five extra dead travel days.

Five days lost but at least I had been on dry land in Guam instead of on the monotonous ocean voyage. Now I was on my way again. Hawaii was about 2800 miles southwest of Guam or ten hours of flight time to reach Hickam Field. We were about five hours into the flight when the pilot's voice came over the intercom: "I had to feather one of our engines, so I am making an emergency landing at Kwajalein Island to check it out. Don't panic, Kwajalein was just below us."

The pilot made a wide turn and descended rapidly towards an island. I heard the landing gears drop in place as the pilot put his flaps down and revved his remaining motors for the landing. No sooner had we hit the landing strip and bounced once, than the brakes were screeching until the plane stopped. As soon as we deplaned, a crew came out from nowhere and hauled the aircraft to a hanger.

"So this was Kwajalein," I muttered to myself as I looked around. There was nothing but ocean all around. I was sure a big wave would wash everything off this island. This island had been the key to Allied forces advancing on Japan. U. S. battleship guns and bombers had turned this island to stumps and dust before the soldiers assaulted this island. It took less than six days to overrun this strip of land. Other islands nearby suffered the same fate. Among the soldiers was a Nisei interpreter who, during the battle, coaxed Japanese soldiers and civilians to surrender without a fight. He was one of many Nisei who served in the war against Japan and whose stories of heroism largely remain untold. Kwajalein Atoll was part of the Marshall Islands and was an arc shaped strip less than three miles long and a half-mile wide. The landing strip was located in the midpoint of the arc but, as I looked down the runway, it did not look very long. I was thankful the plane's brakes had held, for I was unprepared for a swim in the Coral Sea now.

We assembled in one of the few buildings and awaited our news about the delay. It seemed like hours passed by until the pilot finally came in. He did not look too happy. "We have good news and bad news," he said. "The good news is that you get to relax and enjoy this island. The bad news is that two engines need overhauling and there are no replacement motors here. It might be a couple of days, but that's my best guess when the Air Force will fly the engines in."

With that sour note, a crew trucked our luggage to us. We had no idea how long we would be stuck here. I remember rumors I had heard about U.S. planes crashing during the war, not because the enemy shot them down, but because of poor maintenance by the techs or because the engines had exceeded their airtime. I guess we must have inherited one of these lame birds.

When I walked around the island the next day, I realized how small this strip of land was. Standing at the shore, all I saw was a beautiful turquoise colored ocean all around me, even though Kwajalein was one of many small islands that make up the Marshall Islands. Today was like yesterday and yesterday was like the day before. I had dreaded fourteen long days on a troop ship with nothing to see but water. Stranded on Kwajalein with nothing but sea around me, I now had time to look at that body of water; The Pacific Ocean defined who I was. If my parents had not had the courage to cross this ocean, I could have been an Imperial Japanese soldier stuck in a bunker on this island only to perish trying to defend it from the U.S. soldiers. Instead, I could leave the world in which people live behind a mask and return to the side of the ocean where I belong and can be free.

To the brave Uncommon Samurai

Face of foe but not
"Surrender," he shouts. "Live on."
Nisei voice his sword

Aloha Oahu
Swaying palm trees hula skirts
Enchanted Islands

Oahu, Hawaii – Hickam Field

It was another beautiful balmy morning. What could be more wonderful than finally leaving for Hawaii? The pilot made a wide turn south and informed us that the weather was clear and that we should reach Hawaii in about six hours. Soon boredom sets in as the plane droned on. It seemed silly but every once in a while I checked my watch to see how long we had been traveling. It was four hours of flight time. "No, not again, surely, this isn't another emergency," I thought when the pilot came over the intercom, And then the pilot said, "We're stopping at Johnson Island to pick up mail. We will be on the ground just a half an hour, so keep your seat belt on."

As the plane made a wide turn, I saw a small island about the size of a postage stamp. The closer we got, the island was just a landing strip with a control tower and one or two buildings to the side. The pilot made use of the entire runway to land. When he got out of his seat and opened the cabin door, I was horrified. There, just beyond the runway and in the water, I saw the tail of a plane sticking out of the water. Kwajalein Island may have been just a dot in the Pacific, but this spot would not show up on anyone's map. If I had to spend more than a day on this island, I would go stir crazy.

The pilot taxied the plane into windward direction. I felt the whole plane shaking as the pilot revved the motors full power to lift off this tiny runway. With a sigh of relief, we lifted off without ending up like the plane that was sitting in the ocean at the end of the runway. It was about two hours later that the pilot began his descent to Hickam Field, Oahu, Hawaii. This was a big airbase, bigger than Tachikawa, Japan. I saw hangers, all sorts of military planes, and soldiers walking along rows of barracks. Still visible on the main barracks were scars of the bombing and strafing by Japan's warplanes on December 7, 1941. I knew that when Japan had attacked Pearl Harbor, while Zeros swarmed Hickam Field at the same time. It was Sunday morning when

Hickam Field, Oahu, Hawaii

unsuspecting soldiers found themselves attacked by planes. They could not understand why, until they saw the "*Hinomaru*," emblem of a sun on the wings and fuselage of the attacking warplanes. The first wave struck at eight a.m. coming out of the northeast. The American soldiers completely unprepared had only small arms to fight the enemy. Then, a second wave hit them. It was hard for me to imagine the horror of the moment, where soldiers, looking towards another relaxing Sunday morning, found themselves under attack. While chaos reigned over this surprise attack, our service men rose to face the enemy with courage, heroism, and made the ultimate sacrifice on that fateful day.

"The Day of Infamy"

At the ancient shrine, Ise
A young man passes through the *Torii*
He walks with the spirits to the *Jingu*, Shrine
Silently he bows his head twice
His heart looks for *Amaterasu*, Sun Goddess
Twice he claps his hands and bows
Asks for divine guidance
Not for bountiful gifts
But loyalty to his *Bushido* spirit

To the East
Statesmen huddle around tables
Pontificate lofty ideals of peace
Each guard their secrets
Cloud of war disturbs the great white leader
A wish unsaid by the other
Silent words do not mix
Cauldron boils secretly in the seas
Suddenly the gates of Hell burst open

Aloha from Paradise
Brush cobwebs from your eyes
'Tis early Sunday morn
Pray to God and cleanse your soul
Take your weekend pass loll around
There's no need to worry
Oahu strongest fortress in the world
Bright red sunrays strike my door

Hawaii fate was sealed
The war in Europe was our priority
Move the ships and help the Brits
Our eyes are constant
The enemy was too far
Why then the blip from the north
Just our planes returning home
Bombs away warships belly up
Red sea tainted with diesel oil

In another place
A gold star glistens in the window
Tears fall to a mother's breast

Lady on the Bridge

A heart torn asunder
I raised the child to be a man
He chose the Flag his guiding light
Defend our shores from those who dare
Stood tall with brave young men
He was home a hero

Aloha Oahu
Swaying palm trees hula skirts
No wiki wiki (Not in a hurry)

Oahu-Vacation

I had often wondered what it was like to be a Japanese American in Hawaii when Japan attacked America. The same suspicion of loyalty of anyone Japanese, as I had experienced on the West Coast, was no different here. Historical records show that not one case of espionage ever traced back to local Japanese. It is ironic that at least eighteen Caucasians were charged with spying for Japan in Hawaii. While two thousand Nisei were in the armed services, many Japanese American civilians served as an indispensable work force for the military; they still met hate as "Japs." The War Department closed Japanese schools and religious temples but did not incarcerate all people of Japanese descent. Without a doubt, internment of Japanese people in Hawaii would have wreaked havoc on the workforce and economy because the Japanese made up fifty percent of the population. Many Japanese, as had my family, also carried out what turned out to be a useless act of burning Japanese language books, dolls, and other things Japanese to disconnect themselves from their culture. However, as they had in California, doubts about Japanese American loyalty had continued.

Nothing was going too well on this hurried trip home. At the terminal, I met with another disappointment about our flight schedule to the mainland. All military air transportation flights to the mainland were booked up for at least one week. I guess I was still lower than 'dog' priority. The boring ocean voyage I had avoided was now looking faster than my air travel. On the bright side, I had a chance to enjoy beautiful Hawaii, USA.

Unfortunately, my first breakfast in Hawaii turned into a nightmare. When I entered the mess hall, I saw a sea of service men already eating breakfast. The muffled voices of the crowd were almost deafening as I joined the line of men going through the serving line. I selected scrambled eggs, buttered toasted wheat bread, and, as I reached for coffee, I saw fresh milk served. When I had been at the NYK building, milk was a reconstituted white liquid that left your mouth tasting full of chalk. Once was enough for me. However, this looked like the real thing. I filled my cup and found a place to sit down and eat. I took a good swallow of that cool white liquid. It was the real thing. Then, as I was eating, the milk hit my stomach. My internal organs protested as I felt the churning. I had to move fast. I dumped my breakfast tray and headed for the latrine. I was however, new to this installation and panic set in. Where could I go? I rushed out and looked for any old barracks. This would be utterly humiliating if I had an accident. But the gods were with me, and I found relief. That was an awful close call. I decided no more milk from cows, contented or not. Normally milk had never bothered me, but I have heard that Orientals have lactose intolerance. Back home when I was doing my college homework late at night, I could sit and eat a quart of ice cream without any problems except my teeth would end up as icicles, and I might feel a sharp pain in the forehead from the cold ice cream. However, apparently this part of my Japanese identity had returned with me from Japan (and has been with me ever since).

Teruo, the Nisei I was traveling with, called his aunt who lived in Honolulu. He said, "My aunt was happy to hear from me and invited me to stay in her home until I am scheduled to leave

Hawaii. I told her I was traveling with another Nisei. She also welcomed you to stay since she has an extra bedroom. Would you care to stay at my aunt's home?" Without hesitating, I said, "Sure, this beats bunking in the barracks."

We gathered our belongings and caught a bus headed for Honolulu. His aunt's home was very close to town. Most of the homes were one story, set high off the ground, with a step leading to a porch in the front of the house. A low picket fence enclosed the small front yard. The aunt, who was probably in her early fifties, welcomed us warmly into her home. "You can stay in my son's bedroom since he was married now and living elsewhere." she said. "Please make yourself at home while you're here." We followed her to the bedroom and parked our baggage. I listened while Teruo and his aunt were chatting happily trying to catch up with the family history. It was surprising that the two were not conversing in Japanese, nor did she use the colorful pidgin or halting English that I had expected to hear.

Later, she said that she left early in the morning for work, and that we should help ourselves to anything in the refrigerator for breakfast. The big treat that night was a home cooked meal with hot rice in a *chawan*, a rice bowl and *okazu*, stir-fried vegetables, and broiled fish. It was a welcome change from bland GI food on our flight from Japan.

The next morning, Teruo and I decided to tour Honolulu and visit Waikiki beach. Every place was in walking distance from his aunt's home. As we neared the commercial district, I heard Japanese music playing. I was surprised for the moment until I realized that half of Hawaiian population was Japanese. Yet, when I had been in Tokyo, I had not heard music blaring away in the air even from the Japanese music store. Nor had I heard Japanese music playing loud back in "Little Tokyo" in Los Angeles, California. Then I heard people jabbering away in Japanese. They were not whispering, but loud enough for me to hear. This was all too new to me. As I walked past the familiar smells of soy sauce and deep fried tempura drifting out of cafés, I saw my favorite *manju*, pastry shop. I looked at Teruo and said, "Let's try a few *manju*." I have never been able to resist any of the Japanese pastries, especially, the *mochi*, chewy rice pounded into flour with the soft center filled with *azuki*, reddish purple beans. I remember whenever our family had gone to Los Angeles; my parents had always bought a box of *manju*. To give a box of *manju* is the Japanese practice of special *omiyage*, gift giving to friends and relatives.

While immersed in this Japanese atmosphere, it brought back memories of times in Little Tokyo, Los Angeles. While Okaasan did the Shogatsu shopping, Otoosan always took us for a treat at a café for pie. Yet, what marked that day in my life was the statuette of Ninomiya Kinjiro the Okaasan had purchased, and I did not grasp its significance. However, the war with Japan had crashed around me and during that terrible wartime injustice of internment, I had lost track of that precious gift.

If I had been in Japan, I would not have dared eat food while walking in public. But, here I was in Hawaii and I had just succumbed to the temptation of nibbling on my treats. Maybe my palate remembered the good old days at home with the family. Before every New Year's Day back in Santa Monica, the families would gather at the Japanese school and begin the ritual of *mochitsuki*, pounding sticky rice dough. This had been a time of togetherness; a time to celebrate the coming of a new year with hopes for prosperity and good fortune. This was the one time I saw no masks. I saw people laugh and smile. I saw men enjoying pounding the rice into a paste and encouraging each other to strike the rice mass one more time. Inside the school I saw *Okaasan* busy with the other Japanese wives cooking the rice and making the mochi pastry. They were chattering like chickens in the hen house, but the sound was gay and warm.

The walk to Waikiki Beach was longer than we expected, but we were going nowhere in particular anyway. What I expected to see did not exist. All I saw now was a narrow two-mile strip of sandy beach that could not have been more than thirty feet wide. However, the white shore stretched out into the ocean in a gentle slope that probably made surfing a pleasant ride. As Teruo and I walked towards the south, we saw Diamond Head proudly jutting out into the sky. Because Diamond Head seemed too far away to visit, we looked for a bite to eat and headed back.

One day, Teruo's aunt said we could use her car if we wanted to see more of Oahu. First, Teruo decided to check the status of our flight before heading out to see some famous spots of Oahu. The flight was still on schedule for Monday morning. We had time to do some sightseeing in Oahu, and finally, we would be leaving Hawaii for California. Aloha, Hawaii, may we meet again. I never did get a chance to go back.

There were no more islands between Hawaii and California. If anything happened on our flight, we would be in trouble because there were three thousand miles of ocean below us. Today, we boarded another Douglas C-54, but this time we did not have bucket seats. There were two rows of two seats abreast along both sides of the plane. "My God, it's a regular passenger plane. This was luxury." I thought as I entered the plane. Teruo and I found seats near the middle of the aircraft. We heard someone say that this same model Douglas C-54 was modified to fly both President F. D. Roosevelt and President H. Truman. However, ours had no luxurious interior finishing.

I hear the familiar coughing and sputtering sound of each Pratt &Whitney motor starting the warm up, then the sound of a smooth roar of the powerful engines. The pilot was now taxing and made the turn for the take-off, which it wasted no time doing as the plane's acceleration pushed me back against my seat. This time it was a big relief to be able to see where we were going without twisting my body or straining against the seat belts to see what was happening through the small porthole across from me.

Once in the air, I said to Teruo, "Thanks to you, I had a chance of a lifetime visiting Honolulu. Your aunt and cousins were very generous. I was curious that your aunt didn't talk to us in Japanese, nor did she have a Hawaiian accent."

"I had a great time too," replied Teruo. ""My parents will be happy to hear about my visit with the relatives. As for my aunt, my grandfather was one of the early immigrants to Hawaii and so she is really a *nisei* and her children are *sansei* just like me. But Oahu is a small island and the population is nearly fifty percent Japanese, and so they still retain much of the Japanese culture."

The flight home was moving smoothly until a flight engineer came out from the cockpit cabin. He was dressed in fatigues and wearing a bright orange Mae West life jacket. He looked nervous as he moved down the aisle. Then he opened his mouth, "Folks, don't worry, everything's okay. We just have a slight engine problem. It's nothing to worry about. I'll keep you posted." Then he scooted back to his cubbyhole.

There was a murmur among us passengers. We were perplexed although we did notice a slight vibration on one of the engines. The sight of the flight engineer wearing a Mae West floatation gear hadn't been too reassuring. Thank God the pilot didn't come on the intercom and tell us we had to ditch the plane. I looked through the window. There was an awful lot of water down there. Nobody panicked. We just sat waiting for another six hours. At last, the pilot came on the intercom and said, "Fasten your seat belt. We will be landing shortly at Travis Air Force Base, California." As we reached the California coast near San Francisco, the plane shook as the turbulent coastal currents jostled the plane. It was only minutes until the pilot landed our plane. Everyone yelled, "Hurray!"

I was home at last, but a little late: From 13 July 1948 to 4 Aug 1948.

Chapter 7: Civilian

Spark of life that glows
Tip toeing through life's dreamland
The heart grows fonder

San Francisco

Thoughts were running rampant through my mind as I waited to see someone I met only twice. When I asked myself, "What's my expectation? Will she even care?" I had no clue to what I was asking myself at that moment. As I thought back to our first highly unexpected meeting, I tried to remember what it was that attracted her to me. I suspected that my dear friend Ida's surprise was that meeting for me when she invited several *Nisei* to her home to celebrate our graduation from the Army's Military Japanese Language School at Presidio of Monterey.

I remember when Ida introduced me to a young woman sitting on the living room sofa. Ida said, "I want you to meet a good friend of mine, Yoshiko. She is the younger sister of Mat who worked with us at University of Minnesota in the Japanese language program. She is single, lives and works in San Francisco. I invited her to join me in celebrating you and others graduating from the Army Language School."

As I greeted her, I saw a lovely youthful woman about my age with high round cheeks, an engaging smile, and eyes full of life. She had curled hair that did not quite reach her shoulders, with rolled curled hair above her forehead that accentuated her lovely features. Ah but, the smile melted the sinews of my heart.

I had no idea that she was a close friend of the hostess. Now, I recalled one day when Ida invited me to her home in St. Paul, Minnesota, I saw a young *Nisei* soldier drop in for a brief moment to see her husband.

Ida had said, "This was Kei. He is Mat's younger brother who is stationed at Fort Snelling, St. Paul, Minnesota."

I remembered that Mat said her parents were farmers near Fresno, California and that Ida told me that her parents owned a restaurant in Los Angeles before the war. I was puzzled how Ida happened to meet Mat's family when the two places were four hundred miles apart. Ida told me that it was because of the war that she and Mas met Mat's family.

I learned of the following story from Ida. When the war broke out, the Army designated certain areas as Western Defense Area One and Defense Area Two and issued evacuation orders to move the Japanese out of the West Coast Defense Areas. There was a great deal of confusion and rumor about evacuation orders. Initially, some believed that moving from Defense Area One to the inland zone Defense Area Two would save them from leaving California. Mas closed his gas station in Monterey and moved inland to a farming town in San Joaquin valley, Defense Area Two. It was in this small farming town of Reedley that she met Mat's family. Unfortunately, their hopes that they were safe from further evacuation disappeared and they quickly moved to Minnesota.

The second time I saw Yo occurred when I was on my furlough to visit my folks in Los Angeles. My brother Frank, who had come to Pebble Beach to play golf with his friends, loaned me his fancy 1940 Ford convertible to visit my parents on my furlough. I was traveling with an army friend when I decided to visit Yo at her parents' home near Fresno. I remembered Ida mentioning that Yo's family had raised table grapes and peaches on two twenty acres of farmland. Their farm was on Manning Avenue, a major country roadway.

When I turned in on a dirt driveway, I stirred up a cloud of dust and stopped at the house. The building was an old one-story white wooden farmhouse that looked like it had been standing there since the early 1920s. As I looked around, I saw a tall old barn in the back near the orchard, a shed near a pump house, an outhouse, and small barn next to the house. Like older farms in this region, most of the structures looked neglected; some tilted at one angle or looked as if they would fall down at any moment if someone happened to lean on them

When she invited us in, her parents were also there to greet us. While bowing, we introduced ourselves to the parents saying, "*Hajimemashite, doozo yoroshiku onegaishimasu -* Pleased to meet you for the first time." My friend, who was a *Kibei*, kept the conversation going with the parents. Soon the parents politely left us with their daughter to chitchat with us. She was just as cheerful and friendly as before. However, I sensed that she did not belong there even though she had grown up in this farming town. Her complexion was no longer the sun tanned and ruddy face of a farm girl in this hot central valley. I noticed her hands were too delicate to be working outdoors. It was obvious that she had been away for some length of time from her family home after she had left with the family for internment at Poston, Arizona.

While we were chatting, she asked me what I thought about her sister Mat since I had worked with her at the University of Minnesota.

"Mat was fun to work with, but she was headstrong." I said. "She used to argue a lot with Tom, Ida's younger brother, but it seemed to be all in fun." I told Yo I also saw Mat's daughter, Sharon, who attended the University's preschool program while Mat worked. I told her that the army students that she taught enjoyed her as their teacher because she had a sense of humor.

I was surprised when Yo told me that she had visited Mat in St. Paul, Minnesota a couple of times when her sister was teaching there.

All I could think at that moment was, "Oh, really?"
The coincidence of meeting her brother and sister while I missed meeting her on her visits to see Mat was overwhelming.

We finished our short but pleasant conversation, and then it was time to go. At the time, I wondered if my visit made any sense since I was leaving for Japan. My friend and I left with an agreement with Yo to keep in touch. After I left, I thought, "Surely her parents sized me up when I visited her. I wondered what they thought about me."

During my stay in Japan, I corresponded with her regularly. I learned that she had, as I had left Manzanar, left Poston early to go back East. She wrote that she taught at the Jewish preschool at Shaker Heights, Cleveland. She liked her job and the people she stayed with, and might have stayed longer had her mother not insisted that she come home. She was the youngest of four daughters and there were four sons in the family. While three of her older sisters had spent their youth with their grandmother in Japan, she and her brothers later joined the sisters there to learn the Japanese language and the culture. In 1930, her father called them home because he could no longer support their lifestyle in Japan. The eldest daughter remained with the grandmother in Japan, whereas the rest of the children returned to America. The eldest son married in the Poston camp; the next older brother was inducted into the US army, sent to Camp Savage, and later to Fort Snelling, Minnesota to the Army Military Intelligence Section. He had been an officer serving in the Philippines and later in Japan during WW II. The other two brothers left home for school in the East but were inducted in the US Army shortly afterwards.

Her father, a prominent member in this Japanese farming community, was arrested with other Japanese and jailed in a Fresno, Ca. They were sent up north by train to Idaho, transported to Flagstaff, Arizona, then to Lordsburg, New Mexico, and finally imprisoned at Santa Fe, New Mexico. The story was all too familiar; it was the same as my father.

I smiled when she wrote that when she was anxious to leave Poston, several of her girl friends felt uncertain about their future and married hastily in camp. However, that thought was never her wish. She wanted to leave as soon as possible and try to enroll in college. When she found the opportunity to leave Poston, her friends thought she was crazy. "If you leave camp, you'll undoubtedly get hurt, even get raped," they said trying to scare her to remain with them.

Undaunted by her friends' scare tactics, she found work in Cleveland, Ohio. In exchange for caring for an elderly man, the couple provided her room and board. They also promised that she would have time to go to school. At first, she tried to carry out her task for the elderly couple, but they had misrepresented her duties. What they wanted her to do was the work of a full time live-in nurse and maid besides. Luckily, she was able to find another family who offered her a better situation. This time the family wanted her to be a companion for the grandmother. Here she found a warm and generous family that allowed her free time during the day. One day she visited Northwest University to inquire about enrolling in school. The school flatly refused to consider her. She learned that the University had a contract with the US Navy that did not allow Japanese to attend the school. Disappointed with the rejection, she decided to find full time work instead. At first, she found employment with the public school program, but the commute was too far. Then the family she was staying with told her about a teaching job with the Conservative Jewish Nursery School in Shaker Heights. She was one of two Gentiles working at the Jewish nursery school. While she had some doubts, she was happy that she found a warm reception by the nursery staff.

The war with Japan had ended and the Internment Camps were closing. Soon after her parents and family members returned home to Reedley, California from Poston, Arizona, her mother insisted she return home to be closer to the family. She reluctantly gave in to her mother's wishes but was very sorry to leave behind her newly found friends in Cleveland and the job she found so rewarding. After returning to this small farming community, she found her future prospects were not very promising. The choices were that she could marry, work in a packing shed during the harvest time, or help in the family vineyard. None of these options appealed to her. She decided to move to San Francisco and find her future there.

In San Francisco she found a place to stay, a boarding house run by a Japanese family. It was an old Victorian home typical of the San Francisco area. It was a two story wooden house with a basement for storage and laundry. The owners lived on the first floor while the roomers, young *Nisei* girls, shared rooms on the second floor. In her letters she wrote about her experiences in the boarding house. However, that is another story.

Now, I was home from Japan and out of the Army.

From the hotel I was able to contact her and we arranged to meet at my hotel. Since I had never dated anyone before, I had no idea what to expect. I remember our meeting very well. My anxiety melted away. We had embraced and kissed for just a moment but neither of us was accustomed to this sign of affection. I had never hugged anyone before, but it was a very special and happy occasion to see her once more. But we lived in two worlds, and we would never be able to shake off the culture and mores that our parents instilled in us.

Of course my room was strictly out of bounds for us. To bring shame to our family would be an unforgivable act in our parents' world. The hotel with its small foyer was also not a good place to continue spending our first time together. We left to stroll around Union Square while we chatted. Close by was Joseph Magnin where she worked in the credit department. She said that the Magnin family was very nice to their employees and she enjoyed her job there. She was surprised that even Cyril Magnin, the owner, would stop by to talk to the employees.

As we strolled further, we came to a coffee shop, Compton's Cafe, where we drank coffee and continued getting to know one another. She said she could not invite me to the house where she roomed because the owner did not allow any male visitors, and besides, there was no visiting room. Since she was working, we decided that we could meet on the weekends. I told her that I would be busy for a while because I needed to find housing and arrange to enter UC Berkeley under the GI Bill. I escorted her to the California Cable Car for her return to the boarding house.

The next day I rode the F-train to Berkeley and started looking for housing. I found a *Nisei* rooming house, but there was no vacancy and a long waiting list. After searching the local ads, I found one a block from the University, the Campus Inn. I shared a room with another student. I returned to the hotel to retrieve my belongings and checked out. I spent most of the following week filling out forms for the Veterans Administration GI Bill.

Budding love opens
Nourished by two hearts beating
Two worlds clash again

Dating Game

What a wonderful unexpected surprise when I went to the Admissions office at UC Berkeley and saw my academic standing. I had garnered 24 units of UC college credits for the UC Extension courses I had taken at Manzanar to teach high school physics and for the six months of Army Japanese Language School training at the Presidio of Monterey. In fact, there was enough credit to apply for a minor degree in education. Even more surprising, I could work towards a California teaching credential by taking just two more classes in education.

While the University was generous with credits towards a degree in education, I was disappointed that the University disallowed credits for the math class I had taken at the University of Minnesota. When I stopped attending UCLA in January 1942, I had had two and a half years of college credit. The windfall of the additional credits I received that added a full third year of college education surprised me. Time had not stood still. All I needed at this point were enough courses in physics to graduate for a BA in physics.

Living at the Campus Inn at Berkeley was a distinct advantage over the commuting I had done while attending UCLA. The UCLA campus was located on a huge 384-acre plot of land established in Westwood in 1929. Because the college had been relatively new, housing for students in the area was non-existent. Everybody commuted to the university. Here at Berkeley, my classes were within walking distance from Campus Inn. There was no need to lug all of my textbooks, and my classes were in nearby buildings. I did not have to rush around for meals because Campus Inn served breakfast and dinner Monday through Saturday, but not lunch. I was always amazed at breakfast time when the cook served cantaloupes, for I had never seen such scrawny looking melons. They were culls about the size of a tennis ball. However, I could not complain too vigorously since I had the luxury of eating in the dining room.

Since I had been away from heavy coursework, getting back to serious studies was a major hurdle. Most surprising, Physics had entered a new age, atomic physics. Coincidentally, E. O. Lawrence had successfully invented the first cyclotron at UC Berkeley. There were other mathematicians and scientists engaged in atomic physics who had, since the war, become known to the public: notably Bohr, Einstein, Heisenberg, Schrodinger, and de Brogelie, to name a few imminent contributors. Again, the events of World War II affected my life as it had so many others. My early education in physics was Newton's Classical Mechanics. These new age concepts and mathematics overwhelmed me because it was foreign to me. It was as if I had been wearing rose-colored glasses when I studied about atoms and electrons in high school physics and chemistry. Now suddenly everything looked different. I gradually began to realize that my mathematics understanding of this new era of atomic physics and quantum mechanics was seriously lacking. The intervening years, starting with the internment and extending through the Army commitment left me ignorant about the new age. I knew only the result: the Atomic Bomb, "Little Boy" dropped on Hiroshima and "Fat Man" on Nagasaki, Japan.

If my head turned in one direction, my heart looked elsewhere. Every day I was anxious to phone my girlfriend. I can still hear the clink, clink of the coins dropping into the coin eater of the public telephone on the second floor hallway. For both of us, domestic chores filled our Saturdays, and Sunday was our day to be together. I became a regular commuter on Key System's F-train from Berkeley to San Francisco's Transbay Terminal and back. My return trip was often on the last F-train from San Francisco across the Bay Bridge to Shattuck and University Ave. Berkeley. It would always be very early the next morning.

I was often the only person on the F train as I rode over the Bay Bridge to San Francisco. My mind was not usually focused on the scenery as the steady sound of the train sped on the tracks and the cantilever beams flashed by. I would be eagerly looking forward to seeing my girlfriend. At the terminal I would quickly board the Sutter line streetcar and ride to Octavia Street. My body bent forward while my legs reminded that San Francisco was hilly. I struggled uphill towards her boarding house near California Street.

We would always go for walks and just be with each other because there was no convenient place to sit together. Sometimes we would ride the streetcar on Geary Street to the beach. From the end of the line it was a short walk to the Cliff House. Near the Cliff House, we could see a cluster of seals lounging on Seal Rock as the waves crashed against the rocks and splashed upward onto them. I can almost hear the sea lions barking as they jostled each other for a better spot to rest. Behind the Cliff House was an odd structure that looked like a giant Kodak camera. I could never figure out why it was there since we found it always closed on our visits. It was much later I found out for $1 admission you could stand in the middle of parabolic disc and view the swirling motion of the rocky Pacific coast. They had named it the "Camera Obscura." I read Leonardo da Vinci first designed it in the 15th century.

From the Cliff House we would walk south, down some steps, and onto to the beach. It was always cool, if not cold, and nobody was in the water. I learned later that the tides were treacherous there. Riptides and strong undertows sometimes caught unwary swimmers into life threatening crisis. These were not like the beaches of Santa Monica. What I enjoyed most was our short walk from the beach across the Great Highway to Playland. It was an amusement park with a midway of games, a carousel, displays of mechanical gadgets, a nickelodeon, and best of all "Laughing Sal." Sal was a huge mechanical woman that would scream and belt out laughter that you could not avoid being amused by. She had red curly hair, a big freckled face, and a missing tooth. She moved back and forth while she bellowed her devilish laughter. I can always visualize that grotesque figure and boisterous laughter whenever I think about San Francisco's Playland.

As we walked down the midway, we could not escape the smell of stale popcorn, greasy food, and cordite from the rifle range all mixed with the cool salt air. In the background we could see the Big Dipper roller coaster, but I did not dare let us ride it since the structure looked like it would fall apart at any moment. However, there were plenty of fun things to do like the little game booths; knocking down milk bottles with balls or tossing rings to circle some item, all had their display of cheap glitzy prizes I could win by spending a small fortune just trying my luck or trying to impress my girlfriend of my skill. Above the din of the crowd we heard the sound of the thundering pipe organ playing. It was our cue to hurry towards the merry-go-round. There in front of us were chariots, gondolas, and animal figures: horses, lions, camels, and giraffes. The brightly painted figures were showing some wear and tear for their years, but it did not matter to us. Quickly we would get on the merry-go-round and choose the animals to ride on. The loud pipe organ would blast out its tunes as the carousel began its journey. I always made sure that I rode an animal that moved up and down so I could reach for the golden ring. However, the system was rigged. Most of the rings were not gold colored. As the carousel kept moving I waited to toss the worthless one into mouth of a big smiling clown. It was fun to be a child again.

On other occasions, we spent time in the city. Yo and I would sit down in Compton's Cafe for coffee, lunch at the Pheasant Restaurant, or a meal at Bernstein's on Powell Street. We were getting to know one another. One day I had a chance to sneak into her room while her girlfriends were giggling outside. She was rooming with one other girl who spent her weekends with her boyfriend in Berkeley. It was only a bedroom. They could heat something on a hot plate, otherwise, they had to go out to eat. The girls were served dinner in the dining room, but they did not eat with the owner's family. She said the meals were simple while the family dined royally.

I was surprised one evening while we were walking along Market Street and noticed a young couple kissing. We both turned our heads to avoid looking. I could almost hear my *Okaasan*, mother say, "*Mah, hontoni mittomonai*" "My goodness, it's truly shameful..." Our parents told us that kissing was not an appropriate thing to do in public. My two worlds were clashing once again. Yet my sweetheart did not mind that we held hands while strolling. Even when we visited our family, we never openly showed affection in our parents' presence. It would be disrespectful of their culture. Was it *haji*, shame, or a mask that I must wear to guard my feelings?

One evening, while we were sitting on a bench in Lafayette Park near her boarding house, she said, "When I was in Cleveland, I dated a young *Nisei* from California. One day he said he wanted to marry me, but I told him I was not interested. He said if I married him I wouldn't have to work because his family was well-to-do."

Then when she said, "His father owned a mortuary in Los Angeles," that struck me as funny because I remembered what *Okaasan*, mother had said about people who deal with dead things like a butcher or a mortician. There was a taboo about these people. I wondered how her parents would have viewed her association with a *burakumin*, pariah. Chidingly I said, "You missed your chance to marry a rich guy!"

Lafayette Park was the one place where we could sit and talk, even hold hands, and spend time together. It was on these occasions that I had to hustle home on the last F Train to Berkeley. It was always so difficult to say goodnight, but I had a two-mile hike to the Transbay Terminal. One day I changed my route home and, by luck, I found a bakery where I could buy donuts that were still warm to the touch. On the F Train I munched those delicious donuts all the way to Berkeley.

There was a huge difference between the campus life at UC Berkeley and UCLA. Since UCLA was relatively new, only professors taught all of the classes. However, at UC Berkeley, I was surprised to have teachers assistants (TA) conducting classes. The sheer number of students at UC Berkeley was overwhelming. I always felt I was just a number on an IBM punch card and not a human being. It seemed so impersonal. Some students would refer to UC Berkeley as the 'factory'. Basic 101 courses were so large that the lecturer looked like an ant down in front at the podium. Even getting from one class to the next, I had to zigzag through the crowd to reach my destination.

It was few months later when my sweetheart said with a sweet worried voice, "I look forward to your calls but I'm worried that it's costing you a lot of money. Why don't we talk about it this weekend?"

Love is forever
That's our hearts' wishes to be
"I do," and "I do."

The Toll of Wedding Bells

How naive Yo and I were when we began our wedding plans without involving our parents from the start. Both of us have been on our own since leaving our respective Internment camps in late summer of 1944: I left Manzanar, CA and Yo left Poston Camp-3, AZ. We were used to making our own decisions about our lives and accepting the consequences. We were completely unprepared for what would happen in our lives.

After we announced our engagement on December 19, 1948, we were busy and excited planning our wedding. Yo would be a June bride since the wedding date would be after my graduation, the second weekend in June. It would be a small wedding, ceremony, and reception because we would make our choices on what we could afford.

Yo, of course, would invite her friends at the rooming house, and her maid of honor would be her roommate, Grace. On the other hand, I had not even thought about a best man to stand with me at the wedding ceremony since I had neither kept track of my army friends nor kept close contact with my friends from Santa Monica. Ever since I was out of the army, I was lost in the clouds busily courting Yo and little else. A church wedding seemed unlikely since neither of us were affiliated with any church. Yo did say she knew a Reverend Wake from Reedley, CA who was practicing in the Bay Area. She thought he could perform the wedding ceremony, but we decided that also was too uncertain. "Where could we have our wedding?" was the first item on our list. We scanned the yellow pages and found an advertisement of a little chapel in Berkeley on Shattuck Avenue. We were eager to look and hoping for the best. When we visited the chapel, we were delighted. It was a lovely small white building, neat and well kept, and, in front of the altar, was a simple white decorative archway. The seating was enough for the small group we had in mind. Best of all, the cost fit our budget. It was also easily accessible by public transportation making it convenient for Yo's friends in San Francisco to attend the ceremony.

Next, we looked to see if we could find a place for our reception. Again, we had to think in terms of what we could afford. We remembered dining at the Claremont Hotel once, and found that the cost of the reception would be reasonable. We had the choice of canapé, soft drinks and dessert within our budget, but no hard liquor. For anyone who wanted wine, Claremont Hotel's wine fountain was open and free. Now that we were satisfied that all of this could be done from our savings, we decided to let our parents know of our plan.

This was not the beginning of a beautiful story. While we were busy continuing with our wedding plans, I received a letter from my younger sister, Kaz. We were stunned. We received word from my family to cancel our arrangements for the wedding.

She wrote asking us to hold off on our plans because my parents wanted to take over the wedding arrangements. According to Japanese custom, the groom's family hosts and pays for the wedding. Once again, our two worlds were at odds with each other. We were naive to believe that we had the choice of doing it all by ourselves. Because *Giri*, family obligation, is important in Japanese culture, I had no recourse but to concede to my parent's wishes.

The war, and therefore, the internment, had disrupted my parent's business and social obligation, *Giri*. My parents, bound by the Japanese cultural norm of social behavior, saw our marriage as the answer. The concept of *Giri* stems from the feudal period, and its manifestation demonstrates the debt of gratitude and social behavior held in the highest regard in human relationships. Thus, for our family not to observe *Giri* would be a *faux pas* and bring *Haji*, shame. A Japanese person cannot avoid their obligation for fear that *seken*, society, would view his or her behavior as a social blunder. We had no other alternative. Our wedding was the opportune time for my parents' to carry out that "*giri*." The family began to arrange the wedding place, the reception, and lodging for members of the wedding party. While Yo wanted to invite her friends, she felt that it would be a big expense for them to travel to Los Angeles from San Francisco. In fact, my parents did not ask for our input on the guest list.

The wedding date was to be set after my graduation; a church selected by the family and a firm date set, appointment with the pastor set, hotel accommodation set, and it was up to us to arrive at the set dates and time. During the interim, Yo traveled home to Reedley and I returned to West Los Angeles.

On the scheduled date and time, Yo and I met with the Pastor and sat quietly to hear his sage advice on marriage. Neither Yo nor I belonged to this beautiful church in the outskirts of downtown Los Angeles. The wedding party all stayed in our pre-assigned hotels in Los Angeles near the church.

It was as if attending anything but our own wedding. When the processional music began, I stood in front with my brother-in-law, Yas. The maid of honor, Grace, entered and marched down the aisle. I saw my lovely bride in her white wedding gown, escorted by her father, walking carefully together to the processional music. I stepped towards her, taking the place of her father on her right side. The minister began reciting the vows, "repeat after me," in several steps. Since we had agreed on exchanging rings, the Minister asks us to repeat, "With this ring I thee wed." Therefore, we followed the cue, "I do" and "I do," I lifted the veil, and kissed the bride.

The reception was a lavish several course formal Japanese affair held in Little Tokyo, Los Angeles. Yo and I were late for the reception because our driver took a tour of the city. When we arrived, O*kaasan* asked me, "What happened? We were worried." I replied, "*Okaasan*, we went riding around the city and didn't realize how far we had gone." When I entered the Japanese restaurant, I saw a sea of people already sitting and waiting for the bride and groom to arrive. I noticed that besides the family members and a few close friends, the rest of the guests were total strangers to me. I felt completely detached from the reception. I remember Joe made a toast, but everything else is a blur. We were both disappointed with the whole affair.

Weddings in our family came with a variety of marriage ceremonies. In our family, my older sister Mabel was the first one married according to traditional Japanese custom. The groom was a Japanese national, who worked for a Japanese dry goods store in Los Angeles. Mabel was a *Kibei*, who at seven years old, went to live with our uncle in Tokyo until 1933. They married in the traditional Japanese custom. I was surprised when Joe, the eldest son, married under Shinto Rites. His bride's family was Buddhist. I learned that a Shinto wedding is a private setting between members of both families. I watched in awe when the priest started with a purification process, shaking a paper-decorated staff, and chanting words I did not understand. The bride and groom exchanged sipping sake in a small cup three times, followed by more shaking of a staff with folded paper. The whole ceremony was interesting, confusing, and amusing all at the same time since I understood nothing about the Shinto rituals.

When World War II started, the war drastically affected weddings in our family. My brother Frank, who was in the US Army and stationed in Minneapolis, decided to marry Stella Nawa, our family friend's daughter. Because of the Executive Order 9066, the government forced the Nawa family out of Norwalk, California, interned them in the horse stalls of Santa Anita Race Tracks, uprooted them once more, and transported them by train to intern them at the Rohwer, Arkansas camp. While interned at Manzanar, *Okaasan* received a letter from her dear childhood friend, Mrs. Nawa about the impending marriage. I heard the sadness in her voice as she told the rest of us about the news because there were no way that any of us could attend the wedding. Yet, she had said she was happy that the marriage would bring our two families even closer together. *Otoosan*, of course, was still in the Federal Prison in Santa Fe, New Mexico without any recourse. Then, while I was in Minnesota, my sister Kaz married Yas Tatsumi in Manzanar. I guess my wedding was a last chance for my parents to celebrate their offspring's marriage proudly in front of their community.

Alternatively, to put it bluntly, our marriage was now a vehicle for the family to meet its long-standing obligations. Thus, our wedding bells tolled a sad tune for Yo and me.

Yo and Tad Wedding, 6/19/1949

It's a piece of cake
Starting a new slice of life
"I do" forever

Married-Honeymoon

As soon as we cut the wedding cake, Yo and I were anxious to leave and be on our honeymoon. We headed to her parent's home in Reedley, California while dragging tin cans tied to the back of our car. By the time we reached our destination, the constant dragging and tumbling on the highway tore off the cans. After our eye-opening wedding reception, we were relaxing at her parent's home. Yo was comfortable being with her family, but I had a hard time trying to catch her eye to leave and start on our honeymoon. I even wondered, "Does she have second thoughts about being married?" Finally she acknowledged my brazen hint and left with me to our Honeymoon Suite at the Fresno Hotel.

Okay, so it was not the Honeymoon Suite! In spite of our pre-registration, the Hotel had managed to bungle our request. However, it was acceptable. It was a night to remember for two people who were never alone and intimate together. The next morning we headed for Lake Tahoe for our honeymoon. We left none too soon because the summer heat of San Joaquin was rising rapidly. We passed the Mammoth Orange stand at Chowchilla and other roadside stands on highway 99. While there were other routes to Lake Tahoe, I decided to take the road to Sacramento and on to US 80 to Truckee. I turned south to highway 89 along the west shore of Lake Tahoe to Homewood where we rented a cottage for a few days. The cottage looked cozy, nestled among the pine trees, neat and clean, but not as beautiful as it had looked in the ads Our unit was a one-bedroom kitchenette with a small refrigerator and shower.

Every day the weather was so nice we visited Emerald Bay and walked along the North Shore. It was a beautiful vista seeing the blue water capturing a little Fannette Island in its midst. We walked across the road to Tahoe Tavern and enjoyed a leisurely coffee break in the dining room. The place was spacious and relaxing. When I looked out towards the garden, I was surprised to see Japanese lanterns hanging. I saw a pier that jutted out into the lake. Later, I was informed only rich patrons moored their boats there. In the evening, we spent several days in the Biggest Little City, Reno, Nevada. Neither Yo nor I believed in gambling. We did not have much to lose anyway. She told me her uncle was a habitual gambler who had to cry on her father's shoulder to bail him out of debt. When she saw her uncle come to their home for help from her father, she asked her father, "Why do you give him money? Why don't you let him suffer the consequence of his gambling?" Her father was *chonan* and he always looked after his younger brother even when he squandered his money away.

Both of my brothers gambled; Frank loved craps and Joe loved the horses. Neither one came out ahead in the long run. One day when I was in Minnesota, my brother Frank came knocking on my door and told me a sad story that he was in the hole for a large sum of money because of gambling at Fort Snelling. He asked me to loan him money to bail him out of his plight. I could not understand how, on his meager army pay, he would gamble when he had a wife and child to support. I was surprised that he and other army cooks at Fort Snelling operated a crap table on site. It seems that the temptation of being a sucker took over his good judgment.

172

I must admit that I gambled once. One day in 1939, while I was in the office of the new family nursery on Wilshire Blvd. I saw my brother Joe looking intently over several pages of data.

"What's that?" I asked Joe.

"It's a Racing Sheet," he answered. He told me that the data showed the performance of horses at various horse racing tracks as well as the condition of the track. He bet on the horses based on those cryptic racing sheets.

"I'm ready to phone in my bet," he said. "Why don't you try betting on one," he said.

I looked at Joe in disbelief. "No thanks," I said. "How can a piece of paper tell you which horse to bet on?"

"I try to keep track of the horses from previous postings," he replied. "I've been ahead so far with my choices. Sometimes, I drive to Santa Anita or down the coast to Del Mar for the last two races,"

When he saw my reluctance to bet, and he said, "Pick one and I'll pay a $2.00 bet for you."

Can't lose, I thought. I looked at his racing form: 'Good mudder, placed.' 'Not challenged' noted on another horse. I closed my eyes and picked one. "Here, I picked this one," and showed it to my brother,

The next day, Joe gave me $17.20. "You won!" he said.

I have never fed horses since that one time. After passing through the archway on Virginia Street, "The Biggest Little City in the World," we gawked at the splash of neon signs and finally entered Harrah's Casino that we had heard so much about on the radio. The lavish splendor inside was awesome. The whole scene was fascinating and mysterious at the same time. Elderly people were pulling on the handles on the slot machines with one hand, and feeding the slots with the other. Even when the slot machines regurgitated coins, the players showed little emotion and continued to feed the beast. Action at the big one-dollar slot machine was mind-boggling. I can still see a man with a fistful of silver dollar coins feed and pull the handle, feed and pull the handle of the hungry beast. Its appetite was insatiable.

With gambling revenues supporting the casinos, dining was inexpensive for us. Thus, we had come mostly to see the nightclub shows. Yo and I nursed our drinks as we watched the entertainment in the smoky room.

Soon our vacation was over and we headed southward to Reedley and Los Angeles. On our way up to Tahoe, I had my eyes on the Mammoth Orange Stand in Chowchilla. It was a Godsend in the hot San Joaquin summer weather to stop and watch the attendant squeeze and fill our cups with the cold fresh orange juice.

When we stopped and stayed at her parent's house, I had the chance to see what a farming life had been like for Yo. The house was an old wooden building with two bedrooms. We slept in the "cold room" named for its frigid temperature in the winter. However, this was summer and it was a sweatbox. Mosquitoes had free access to the house. While I was struggling to sleep in this hot room, I heard a high pitch "bzzzz" buzzing sound somewhere in the room. Suddenly it was upon my exposed face. "Whack, whack" I tried to slap the voracious beast. The buzzing stopped. "I got him,'" I thought. I turned over and tried to sleep once more, but that high-pitched buzzing came at me again. I frantically pulled the sheet over face to protect myself but opened the sheets up a bit, so I could still breathe. When I woke up in the morning, I saw where the mosquitoes had hit their mark.

I'm not sure how the next event came about, but my brother-in-law, Charlie asked me if I would help him pick some grapes. Apparently, the winter frost had damaged a section of his vineyard, and the summer heat had added to its demise. Charlie wanted to harvest the grapes on the vines and truck the grapes to a local winery. I should have said "No" since I was on my honeymoon vacation, but I didn't. I had never picked grapes. The vines suffered under severe weather conditions and were less than fifty percent productive. I learned that a seasoned grape picker will sit at one spot and pick all of the grapes on a vine then move to the next one. I had a hard time filling the lug boxes. I recall my action as a chicken with its head cut off running around a vine. When lunchtime came, I was never so exhausted. Charlie saw how beat I was, went to the refrigerator, and brought out a bottle of Budweiser beer. "Here, drink this. It will help you," he said as he handed me the beer. He was right. One swig of the cool amber colored hop tasting liquid moved smoothly down my gullet and invigorated me. My past loathing of beer vanished. I decided, at that instant, that beer was the nectar of the gods and a lifesaver forever.

"*Mata koi yo*, come again," my father-in-law said as he waved us on our way to my parents' home.

Before we visited my parents, I stopped by a liquor store for a six-pack of beer. When we arrived, I took my six-pack and started to put it in my parents' refrigerator.

"Tadashi, you drink beer?" was the first word out of my mother's mouth.

Otherwise, *Okaasan* fussed around trying to make us feel at home. However, we were still on our honeymoon vacation and wanted to visit Catalina Island. We drove to Long Beach to catch a ferry to Catalina. It was a twenty-plus mile ride into Avalon Bay. I had always thought that Catalina Island was owned by Wrigley Spearmint Gum and thought that only rich people visited there. On the radio, I remember the speaker saying, this is Tommy Dorsey or Woody Herman playing music at the Avalon Pavilion. I loved to hear the sweet melody of Benny Goodman playing his clarinet at the Avalon Ballroom.

The harbor was picturesque as our ferry entered the bay to dock. The first thing I recognized was the Casino Building where the big bands played. The town skirted along the shoreline with no roadways for auto traffic, because the Catalina officials allowed no cars. We booked a reservation for one night and spent the day like tourists viewing the beautiful island bay and enjoying the ocean breeze. Late afternoon, we picked up our luggage, boarded a shuttle bus, and headed to the airport to fly back to Long Beach.

Our next venture was a trip across the border to Tijuana, Mexico. We looked at the various shops and roadside hawkers but found nothing appealing as gifts. After seeing firsthand the sanitary conditions in Tijuana, we were leery of eating any food there. Since we had time to spend, we decided to see a bullfight we saw advertised in town.

When we approached the arena, we came upon a big green wooden stadium structure that looked as if

Casino Building - Catalina Island

it had seen better days. We climbed carefully up the wooden steps to a spot high enough where we could view the bullfight. The stadium was not crowded that day. This must have been amateur night for the bullfighter and the bull. The whole affair started with the bull entering the arena; the picador on a padded horses entered next plunging a lance into the bull's neck, followed by the banderoles that place hooked spears on the bull. With shouts of "oles," the matador displayed his skill moving beside and around the bull while flashing his cape. There was gore and more gore as a sword was finally plunged between the shoulder blades into the bull's heart. If there was finesse, the matador didn't show it. If it was exciting, I wasn't sure. Yo and I had not been prepared for this event because this cultural experience was foreign to us. Sometime later, I saw the movie "Blood on the Sand" on TV. The Bullfight was beautiful in its tradition, pageantry, and sadness in the ending. The movie left with a greater awareness and appreciation for the bullfight that I had seen in Tijuana, Mexico.

When we returned and spent time with my family, we headed for the Union Train Station to travel back to the Bay Area.

Chapter 8: My World

Time enough for Love
Dreams turn to reality
"I" had changed to "We"

Reality

No more drifting on blissful clouds, for our honeymoon had to end. It was time to get back to reality and continue the dream that I had started in 1939, ten years ago. However, the "I" had changed to "We."

Two young people, who lived on their own joined and live as one, Yo and I. Finally finding the home that had eluded me since that day of internment. Since housing was scarce for young people with a limited income in the Bay Area, I applied and received University of California housing for married veteran students. The University had acquired several World War II federal housing projects near the Cordonices Creek on the Gill tract for its use. Our first home was a one-bedroom unit on the second floor within the housing complex. The kitchen and living room were in one large open space. Behind this area was the bathroom on one side, open closet on the other side, and the bedroom next to these two areas. Our home was nothing fancy, but it was a humble start. Our furniture was avant-garde orange crate for we had none. Once settled, I enrolled in a graduate program while Yo returned to her job at Joseph Magnin.

When I applied to re-enter the University of California, the UC Extension courses I took to teach at Manzanar and the Army training at the Presidio of Monterey Language School had qualified me for a minor in education. The additional college credits I received from those two efforts allowed me to graduate with the BA in physics a year earlier. However, the gift of extra credits had its shortcoming. I realized my mathematics background was too weak to continue with graduate studies in physics. Thus, I decided to change my major to math in the graduate program to focus on applied mathematics or computational physics. Because of the change, I had to complete a few lower division math courses to satisfy the requirements for a major in math. When I had scanned the university class catalogue, I was surprised to see all of the courses listed that I needed, but no applied math courses offered in my first graduate semester that I could take. The first year was filled with the required courses like groups, sets, and projective geometry that had very little to do with numerical methods. The graduate courses offered in my second year were no better since professors required to teach many of the courses were not available. I had found the topics in the classes offered were esoteric and less applicable to numerical methods for applied mathematics.

An even more shocking experience I had was taking a test on differential geometry course. Rather than testing math problems, the teacher had prepared essay questions for her exams. The professor, a woman, called me in after the exam and told me she had to reduce my score because I failed to cross t's and dot i's in the right positions even though my answers were correct. Under time pressure, my writing became erratic and atrocious. Did it really matter if the dots of my i's were a few centimeters away?

The next discouraging experience I had was when I signed up for another graduate class. I sat through two sessions and dropped out. The lecturer's name was Pan, a visiting professor from China, who talked with a heavy accent and spoke haltingly in English. I leaned forward in my chair, pen ready to write, tried to catch his every word, but I could not understand a word he said. I quickly dropped the course and signed up for another class, set theoretical methods. I had begun to worry about losing eligibility. This class too was a loser. The subject was in fantasyland and not hard-core computational mathematics. At this point, my whole future looked grim indeed. The goal of reaching for a Ph.D. seemed more remote than I had hoped for now. Maybe I would have had the luxury of withstanding these setbacks if it had been five years earlier, but at twenty-seven, I was impatient to move on with my career.

Meanwhile, Yo, who commuted to San Francisco every workday, had provided most of our income. While the GI bill had provided the tuition and subsistence allowance for a married veteran, it was barely enough even though I had added additional income by correcting papers and working on a project for a professor. It was a struggle for both of us, but we were happily married. The reality of making a decision about pursuing the Ph.D. and requiring Yo to struggle with me was unfair. I decided to finish with a master's degree instead of continuing in the graduate program.

I had begun to apply for employment at various research laboratories and industries. However, graduates with science or math degrees in 1949 were not in high demand except at Army ballistic facilities, military government agencies, and aircraft industries. Since the UC Extension courses I took at Manzanar and the Army training at the Presidio of Monterey Language School had qualified me for a minor in education, by taking the additional courses in child development, student teaching, and a course in multi-media, I found that I could receive my California teaching certificate for secondary education. However, I remember my high school physics teacher told me not to teach, but go into research. I considered the teaching credential as my safety net and last option for finding employment. In order to have other opportunities for employment, I also had taken a Federal Science exam one Saturday and qualified for a GS-4 rating. Then one day at the university employment placement office, I had interviewed with the Los Alamos Scientific Laboratory representatives and received an invitation for a further on-site interview.

I vividly remember that day of the interview at Los Alamos. It was my first flight one summer afternoon in New Mexico on a small Cessna plane that commuted between Albuquerque and Los Alamos. The small Los Alamos airport runway was on a mesa. It was an "iffy" situation. If the pilot miscalculated, down we would go to the bottom of mesa. On our return flight to Albuquerque, I had notice an array of big puffy cotton ball clouds drifting across the blue sky. The pilot taxied the airplane on the small runway and gunned the engine faster and faster as the plane sped down the runway. The plane lurched downward for a moment after flying past the edge of the mesa. I hung onto my seat for dear life hoping that this was not my first and last trip. Quickly the Cessna lifted its nose upward and started a steady climb, when the pilot, steering the plane nonchalantly with his knees, looked towards me and said, "See those puffy clouds? Nothing to worry about, but we're in for a bumpy ride."

No sooner had he finished his warning, than we reached the puffy white clouds. The small plane rose up shortly, then down, sideways, forward, and continued to change its motion in random order. For a moment, I was worried that we were making less headway from these extraneous motions. For forty five-minutes I had endured the bumpy ride. My legs felt rubbery as I deplaned at Albuquerque. The combination of thermal currents and the summer storm clouds had given me the joy ride of my life. Thereafter, whenever I saw pretty white puffy cotton ball clouds in the sky, that bumpy day jostled in my mind.

I was happy to receive word of my acceptance; however, there was one condition that worried me. My hiring was contingent on passing the government's secret clearance. Once again, I wondered if my "No, No" answer on the Manzanar questionnaire would haunt me. Unsure that my secret clearance would come quickly, I decided to accept a math/science staff position with McDonnell Douglas in Long Beach.

I desperately needed to find a place to rent since I had just graduated from college, married, and taken a job in Long Beach, California. I scoured the want ads searching for a place close to work. Each time I answered an ad, the managers turned me down. Always in the back of my mind, I held the thought, "Can the aftermath of the war still linger this long against a Japanese?"

In one last desperate moment, I found a quaint cottage in Long Beach within walking distance of the beach. There were six cottages surrounding a small courtyard. Each had white stucco with a red tile roof, and they had probably been built somewhere in the 1920s. The manager kept the grounds and buildings in excellent condition although I could tell by the layers and layers of repainting that it had survived wear and tear over time. Long Beach had the reputation as a haven for retired people. Sure enough, all of the tenants were elderly persons, very polite but very curious to see two young people wanting to live there. By all appearances, the cottages were for vacationers since the unit that we rented had a small living room, tiny kitchen, and a closet-size bathroom. We were lucky that we did not have lots of furniture because our bedroom was a Murphy bed. This was going to be a real adventure. I was worried because Yo was petite and could easily end up in the Murphy bed that folded up inside the wall.

In the kitchen the stove was antique, white with sculptured legs, a metal back wall, and a shelf all in one, with a black vent running up into the wall. There was a small kitchen table just large enough for two people to sit, and a broom closet with a drop down ironing board and space enough for one broom. The bathroom consisted of a shower and a porcelain commode and washbasin on legs. This was home but it did not have any more space than the 16 by 20 foot room of the internment camp. It would have been adequate for a couple on a week's vacation near the beach, but it too cramped to relax in after a long day. Every evening we made a picnic lunch and walked to the beach. I still have fond memories of feeling the ocean air against my face, hearing the seagulls as they soared to look for food, and listening to the waves rushing in shoreward. However, we were living in a shoebox, so every weekend we continued the search for more space.

We went as far as Compton to inquire about a rental apartment in a housing project. I remember this town as having been a low-income area when I was a teenager. During my high school years, when our track team competed against Compton High, there were only a few blond-haired members on their team. While I was miffed that I was not good enough for this rundown location, quite a few blacks lived here. It was some years later in 1965 when California experienced the Watts riot. Six days of rioting ended with thirty-four people dead, thousands injured, 4,000 arrested, and 600 buildings destroyed at the cost over one hundred million dollars. The underlying cause of the riots was discrimination and lack of equal opportunity. What sad irony of refusal for housing even there.

In desperation for a place close to my work, I used my GI eligibility and applied for a government housing rental in Long Beach. Meanwhile, Yo found a job with the Fireman's Fund Insurance Agency in downtown Los Angeles. Every workday she commuted on the Pacific Electric Red Car from Long Beach to central Los Angeles.

Once settled, Yas and Kaz brought *Okaasan* to see our home and they usually visited us on most Sundays. Mother would fuss around in the kitchen trying to make our stay a welcome one. She had always hinted for me to find a job in Southern California and this was perfect for her because all of her children were close by. While Yo did not complain, I am not sure she was too happy to have her weekends tied up and have *Okaasan* pampering me. I remember Yo had mentioned that *Okaasan* had said something to her about me to which I would say, "Oh, she said that?" Of course, I am the last one to know about mother and daughter-in-law problems. Yet, I never sense any real tension in the air when *Okaasan* visited us.

Meanwhile, I was looking forward to my assignment with McDonnell Douglas, because my assignment was to learn programming for IBM's first electronic computer, the IBM 604. When I stepped into the work place I was in for a big surprise. There was no office space per se. Instead, engineers, draftsman, and other professionals occupied a huge open area in what seemed to be a modified hanger. There were no partitions to separate work areas of individuals. I noticed the din of people talking and shuffling aircraft drawings. I had no desk in that big space since I was new on the job. However, as I looked around, I had an unsettling feeling because the mangers office was on a mezzanine looking down on the open area. I had this bizarre picture in my mind of a prison with guards on the mezzanine watching the prisoners milling below in their cells.

For the moment, I did not worry about my desk because I would accompany the computing group to go to IBM's training class in downtown Los Angeles. Everyone seemed excited about the new age of computing and eager to learn. The assignment also required knowledge of numerical methods that I had learned at UC Berkeley. One individual, who was amicable, talked excitedly about the subject and went out of his way to suggest that I buy a numerical methods book for my work. I was not quite sure how to take the advice since I had never talked about my math and physics background. I presumed he was being helpful. However, I was annoyed when later he was persistent about me joining him and his wife at his Lutheran Church service. I kept declining his offer as I was not ready for another awakening. When I mentioned this offer to Yo, she was glad that I had declined the invitation.

Again, I had another surprise. As soon as I finished my computer class and we were waiting for IBM to install a computing system at the plant, the plant's blue-collar workers went on strike. No violence occurred on the project, but the working conditions became untenable since, as a professional staff member, I had to cross the picket line each day. When Yo heard about the strike, she was worried about me getting hurt crossing the picket line. One day, when the strike was still unresolved, the Los Alamos Scientific Laboratory sent me a letter informing me of my secret clearance approval. I waited patiently for Yo to come home from her work in Los Angeles and show her the good news. Again, I had to disrupt her life and move on.

This time, we needed a moving company to haul what little household furniture we had acquired. We had decided that I would drive first to Los Alamos, sign in, and arrange our housing. Yo would stay until the movers came to transport our household items, then arrange for an air flight to Albuquerque, New Mexico where I would meet her.

I looked at the map and saw that it was almost 700 miles from Long Beach to Los Alamos. I charted my route: Long Beach to Prescott, Arizona and stay overnight, Prescott to Flagstaff to Albuquerque, New Mexico, and finally to Los Alamos.

When I started out from Long Beach, I had no idea what to expect on my way to Los Alamos except that the trip would be across dry dusty desert land all the way. While I stopped at Blythe, California for gas, I saw an old fifty-gallon barrel near the gas pumps and I was curious to know why. I went to peek. Ugh! Cockroaches were everywhere: crawling on the sides, swimming in the water, climbing over the edges, and leaving a trail out into the dry desert. I decided this was not a place to loiter. I quickly filled my gas tank, paid my bill, and left in a hurry. It is hard not to remember that ugly scene. Cockroaches! Ugh!

As I left Blythe and approached the road to Prescott, the scenery began to change. For a moment, I had thought I was on the wrong road because I was gradually going uphill. The sagebrush, cacti, and other desert flora changed to scrubby chaparral and ponderosa pines as the roads turned and twisted up the mountain. Finally, at the top, I was surprised to see a light blanket of snow remaining on the shady side of the road. I saw a sign that noted the elevation as 5,356 ft. This was Prescott, the former capital of Arizona until the capital moved to Tucson and later to Phoenix. I spent a cold night there and started the next leg of my trip to Los Alamos, NM via Flagstaff, AZ.

The ride from Prescott to Flagstaff was unlike driving through the desert. I passed by Clarkdale, once a copper mining town, to Sedona, noted for its red rocks and a beautiful Tahoe like setting. However, Flagstaff remains primarily in my memory because many *Issei* worked on the railroads when they first immigrated to America. As I recall, both my father and my father-in-law mentioned that they were in Flagstaff at one time or another. Because Flagstaff was an important road and railway hub, my father and my father-in-law, whom the FBI rounded up after December 7, 1941, must have passed through this junction once again on their way for imprisonment at Santa Fe, New Mexico.

Years later, I had revisited Flagstaff several times when I went to Northern Arizona University to recruit potential computer scientists. On several occasions, snow covered Flagstaff because of its 7000-foot elevation. There was even a ski jump facility near the campus.

It was too bad that I could not stay in Flagstaff, because I saw two signs pointing out the historic meteorite site, and the Petrified Forest in the Painted Desert that I had read about in school. These two places remind me that Man is no match against nature's force and that we are just a speck in the ocean of time and space in our universe. It is hard to imagine that this desert land was once under the sea and the petrified logs were remnants of millions of years of nature's actions. Then the tremendous force of nature had uplifted the ocean bottom, thrust land and formed mountains, and left this desert five thousand feet above sea level. On my way, I saw the sign of a deep meteor crater that must have happened millions of years ago and left its mark in the desert terrain. Earthquakes and volcanic actions reminded me that the earth was in constant motion and we have little or no power to change any of it.

I had to move on with no time for sightseeing. The ride from Flagstaff to Albuquerque was dismal. There were miles of nothing until I neared Albuquerque. Of course, I saw a few tourist traps that hawked trinkets and souvenirs along the highway. The usual sign was an old wagon wheel hung on a fence, a white weather bleached skull of a bovine animal placed as decoration on the ground, and a store that had seen better days. However, the most desolate place I passed was

Gallup. It was no place to be. I thought it had an appropriate sounding name because, if you were riding a horse and came to Gallup, you would hightail off into the sunset. Albuquerque was, on the other hand, a thriving city. It was a relief to see civilization after driving across desolate scenery on Highway 40. To the east, I saw a beautiful mountain range, Sangre De Cristo that reminded me of the Sierra Mountain Range of California. From Albuquerque, the drive to Los Alamos was through Santa Fe to the northwest.

I had seen Los Alamos from the sky on my interview trip, but the sight of the mesa rising above the desert floor was inspiring. I drove up a steep two-lane road to the top of the mesa that was 700 feet above the desert floor. While I did not realize it at the time, I was 7000 feet above sea level where the air was very thin. The mesa itself was not one, but a finger of smaller mesas with canyons throughout the area, and it was part of the Jemez Mountains. There were conifers and not sagebrush – a welcomed sight.

Just before the summit, there was a guard gate where I had to sign in before entry to the site. Only citizens with prior permission can visit or live here. After I had completed all of the paper work at the guard gate, I headed for LASL's administration office to sign in for my security badge and housing.

Oh, Security
Like Jackals cornering prey
Unprofessional

LASL

Since I completed all of the information for my Personnel Security Questionnaire beforehand, signing in and receiving my ID badge went quickly. The first thing I wanted to do was check my housing that the Los Alamos Scientific Laboratory (LASL) had arranged for us. I was happy to see that our housing was in a new two-story apartment complex on Gold Street, and our unit was on the first floor. It was also within walking distance to the technical area. Next, I was anxious to sign in with T-5 Division to learn more about my assignment that they presented in very general terms at my interview. Although Los Alamos was a closed city, I noticed that my work area was also in a gated complex. I had assumed that my work area would be in permanent buildings, but I saw old wooden buildings that the government built during World War II. These were army styled structures built when America was on an accelerated program called "The Manhattan Project" to develop a nuclear weapon. I noticed that all of the windows had wired screens to discourage entry. When I peeked through the window, I saw a small pond next to the building surrounded with very little landscaping. It looked so out of place, I could not imagine anyone sitting there to relax. I even wondered if the pond was radioactive waste.

After signing in at the T-5 Division office, I met with two young staff members, Bob Aeder and John Lobato with whom I shared an office. Bob and John gave me a quick overview of the work I would be doing, but specific instructions for me would have to come from the Physicist since everything was on a "need to know" basis. While sharing small talk, John said, "A bunch of us are getting together to play basketball at the high school gym. How about joining us?"

I had just arrived and my apartment was still empty. I had nothing better to do so I agreed to join them. Playing basketball was not my greatest sport. Lucky the playing that night did not last too long, but I paid a price the next morning. I was not used to the thin air of 7000 feet above sea level, and besides, I was not in great shape. I hobbled into the office and began my assignment with T-5 Hydrodynamics group. The three of us were the interface between problem solving and computer application. There was nothing spectacular or challenging about the work. Our initial data was on a pink secret form. We keypunched the data, fed it into the computer, and waited for the computer system to spit out the data on a punched card. Next, we read the numbers off the card, did a few hand calculations using numeric tables, and fed the numbers back into the computer to advance the calculations. We were simply the external memory that supplemented the IBM 604.

While waiting for Yo to contact me about her arrival, I started my first assignment in T-5. I received the shock of my life. The Security Office informed me that I had had a security violation. I scratched my head and could not come up with an answer for my infraction. After all, I was new on the job and learned nothing secret while working. The Security Office told me that I had inadvertently left a blank pink form inside my unlocked desk drawer that had the word "SECRET" typed on it. I called Security and said, "But, there's nothing on the blank pink sheet of paper." There was a moment of silence on the phone until someone informed me that the word "SECRET" left unlocked was an infraction. Security then decided that since I was new at Los Alamos and it had been my first offense, they dropped the infraction.

I had managed to survive without furniture until the moving van arrived. Yo, in the meantime had informed me about her plane arrival at Albuquerque. Albuquerque was about eighty miles from Los Alamos with nothing but boring scenery along the route. On the outskirts of the city, I saw a divided and paved concrete stretch of highway that seemed to go nowhere. It puzzled me all the way into Albuquerque since there was nothing on both sides of the road. All I could think was, "It must be someone's boondoggle to put this road out here that serves no purpose."

Finally, at the airport, I watched Yo deplane at the airport terminal. She was not smiling because the dust was just beginning to kick up as it always did in the afternoon at Albuquerque. When we entered the terminal, the local people kept staring at her as if she were a long lost tribe member. The first thing she did was to hand me a package that was reeking with the wonderful smell of Stern's barbecue from Culver City, California.

Yo said, "Your mother insisted that I bring this food to you since it is one of yours and Kishi family's favorite barbecue meal. I was embarrassed on the flight because people kept looking towards me since the aroma was obviously coming from where I sat."

"Thanks," I said as I took the package and remembered that *Okaasan* was always thinking about my welfare and spoiling me.

As soon as I gathered her baggage, I said, "Let's go somewhere and have a bite to eat and relax for awhile." In town, we found a nice café and decided to order a snack. She looked at the menu and decided she wanted a big crispy lettuce salad like the one she always had back home.

While we were chatting, she suddenly looked horrified. There in her salad bowl, a big juicy worm stuck its head out slathered with dressing. She put her fork down; looking ashen, upset, and said, "Let's leave."

Our day was not over yet. I was back on the road to Los Alamos and I remembered a turnoff at Santa Fe that I needed to take. Somehow, I kept thinking that Los Alamos was north of Santa Fe. There, at a fork in the road, was a sign pointing north. Without a second thought, I moved along that branch while chatting away with Yo. It must have been about twenty minutes later, when she said in an excited voice, "Oh, how nice. Look, there goes a Union Pacific train."

"A train?" I muttered. "I'm lost," I said to her. "There's no railroad near Los Alamos. Let me drive back to the little store I saw on the other side of the road to find out how I can get back to Los Alamos." I made a U-turn back to the little store. Inside there were three men sitting around chewing the fat. I approached one that looked like he might know the way to Los Alamos. "I'm lost. Can you tell me how I can get to Los Alamos from here?" I asked.

He hesitated a moment while looking at me trying to size up this stranger and said, "You know, I heard about Los Alamos back during World War II but I'm not sure where it is. I think it's to the west of here. There's road a short ways from here that heads west through the desert. That might get you there." "Thanks," I said and returned to tell Yo what I found out.

The man's answer hadn't been too reassuring, but I decided to look for that road. Road? It was a dusty trail leading west. That one look was enough for me. Quickly, I doubled back to Santa Fe and found the right branch to take for Los Alamos. Later, I found out the road the man was talking about could have been a goat trail through some tough mountainous terrain.

Finally, at the main gate, we had to sign in because this was Yo's first access to the site. At first, Yo appeared to be apprehensive after all of the events that she had experienced in order to reach her new home. However, when we reached our apartment on Gold Street, she seemed pleased to see the newness of the apartment complex.

Soon she found out that the closed city had its advantage of being secure, for nobody needed to lock the front doors. For a while, she was busy arranging our apartment, as well as meeting some of the tenants near our unit. In fact, a lady in the same unit invited her to visit and share her Morgan David wine in the afternoon. Everyone we met was very friendly, for everyone came from all over the United States. It was a question of survival in this isolated community. I was not the first one in our family to live in New Mexico. During World War II, our government imprisoned both my father and my father-in-law along with other prominent *Issei* in the Federal Prison at Santa Fe. However, I had never heard their stories about that terrible period or where they had been.

Our new home was in a newly built U-shaped two-story apartment complex on Gold Street. The apartment was a one-bedroom unit on the ground floor with appliances already installed in the kitchen. It seems that no one locked the front door in this gated community. However, we soon learned what it meant to leave our front door unlocked. One morning, while we were getting up, we heard noises in our kitchen. When we looked, there was one of our neighbors making coffee.

"Oh, good morning, we just ran out of coffee and I hope you don't mind if I make coffee here," she said nonchalantly.

"Oh, sure." What else could we say?

Soon, Yo was anxious to find employment rather than staying idle at home. However, finding work outside of LASL was impossible, and not feasible for her to travel over thirty miles to Santa Fe, the nearest big city. Fortunately, the University of California had relaxed its nepotism rule because qualified clerical and administrative personnel were almost impossible to find from the surrounding communities. Because of her excellent record at Joseph Magnin in their credit department, and other experiences with accounting and interfacing with clients, she qualified for a position with LASL's payroll department.

Although I had already passed my security clearance, Yo needed to do the same for her employment. She was shocked when the past against Japanese showed its ugly head once more. She had told me earlier that when the government issued the Executive Order 9066 in 1942 and enforced curfew throughout the Western Defense Area, she wanted to return home immediately. When she boarded the Greyhound Bus for Reedley, the Fresno police arrested her for violating the curfew. Because she had been attending a Japanese finishing school in Fresno, she was afraid that she would be stranded there and not be able to leave with her family for the same internment camp. Fortunately, the family lawyer in Reedley was able to have her released from the Fresno Police Station jail. Yet, that infraction was still on the police docket. She had also told me that she worked at a variety store in Reedley when she was attending high school. With her earnings, she had purchased many things for her parent's home and supplies for her finishing school class.

For her security clearance, the FBI had wanted to clarify some points on her clearance form. She later described her experience to me, shaken and traumatized. She was in a big room with a dozen FBI agents ready to quiz her. First, they had questioned her repeatedly about the arrest at the Fresno Police station. Next, they began playing their game.

"You wrote that you worked at this variety store. That's a lie. There's no store there."

I did work there when I was in high school," she replied.

"That can't be. There's no store there."

For four hours, they kept brow beating her with the same question repeatedly trying to get her to change her story.

Lady on the Bridge

When she told me what happen that day, I felt ashamed that I had put her through that terrible inquisition. I had to control all of my anger at the bullies. First, I couldn't understand why it would take more than one agent to quiz her. Second, they had all the information or could easily determine whether a store had quit or moved without resorting to such brutal tactics. Lastly, why did they harangue her for four hours?

It seems they all had nothing better to do that day and wanted to play games like jackals preying on a defenseless creature. Then, I remember the day when the FBI came and took my father away after December 7, 1941. That scene too was brutal under the color of authority. After I heard what happened to Yo, I couldn't find any excuse for their inhuman, unprofessional, and childish performance.

IBM 604

185

Stranded on Mesa
Safe high up in a cocoon
The world spins on by

Mesa

In spite of that terrible inquisition by Security, Yo received her "Q" clearance immediately. She was excited about her new job with the LASL payroll department, because her assignment included learning to use IBM accounting machines and the IBM 604 for her assignment. This was the era of the IBM card input in place of pencil and paper. The job was a perfect match for her typing skills for keypunching data on IBM cards. Once she told me that she entered in a high school typing contest and she had typed 120 words per minute. I hesitated to tell her the best I could do was fifty words per minute. Yo learned her job so quickly and so dedicated with her assignment, her boss raised her salary twice within the year. It was an unprecedented action. But then, I remember when she was working at Joseph Magnin in their credit department, she was such a valuable employee, the owner, Joseph Magnin didn't want to lose her, especially after he learned that she had to quit because we were leaving the Bay Area for my job in Long Beach. He went so far to say to Yo, "I have a lot of favors owed me by the UC Chancellor, I am willing call the UC Chancellor to see if your husband can be hired for a job with the University; hence, you can stay with our store in the Bay Area."

When she had told me what Joseph Magnin had said, I told her, "No, Yo, I don't want to be indebted to anyone. I want to be my own person." and I ended the subject.

While we were probably the only Orientals at LASL in 1951, being Japanese was never an issue except for a young Hispanic girl working in the same department with Yo. She had a hard time relating what she had learned about Japanese in her school textbooks with the person she saw dressed like any other American. She undoubtedly thought Yo was a Japanese immigrant. The girl grew up in Espanola, a small town below Los Alamos, a town that would miss your eye if you drove by unknowingly.

For several months, the girl had kept bugging Yo about her coming over to see our apartment. Yo kept putting her off because she couldn't see why anyone would want to see our place. Finally tired of her constant inquiry, she asked, "Why do you want to see our apartment?"

"Oh, your apartment must be different from others: with lanterns, straw mat floors, and you sit on the floor with a cushion. You probably change into your kimono at home, cook rice with a hibachi, and eat with chopsticks."

My wife, completely flabbergasted said, "Our apartment is just like everyone else's unit. In fact, we didn't know where to put the refrigerator we shipped from California, so my husband put it in the bedroom and he keeps his beer in there." "Well, then, I guess I don't need to visit," she said shrugging her shoulders.

The closed city had unanticipated surprises for us every now and then. One day when we had returned from work and entered our apartment, our neighbor was busy using my wife's Singer Sewing machine. It was Yo's pride and joy that she had treasured since she had bought it for herself with her savings.

"I hope you don't mind, I just needed to sew this dress and your sewing machine is real handy," she said without flinching.

Also in our apartment complex, we had met a lovely couple, Ruth and Max from Michigan. Both of their parents were clergymen. One father was a Methodist Reverend and the other was a Reverend of the Episcopal Church. There was always a crisis when either of the parents visited them. The parents were teetotalers. One day, the couple rushed over carrying bottles.

"Can we leave these bottles with you?" they asked. "Our parents are visiting tomorrow, and if they see any liquor, they will pour it down the drain." Willingly, we became the keeper of their sin.

The entire countryside was rich with the history of the American Indians; namely, the Pueblo Indians. We spent many weekends with Ruth and Max scrambling up and down and in and out of old Indian caves and rubbles of dwellings in the surrounding mesas. When I peeked into a few caves, I couldn't help but notice the shiny red dirt floors that had darkened over the years. There were always questions, but no answers. It had seemed as if someone had smeared animal blood on the floor and polished it. I wondered, "Was it a ceremonial room or did somebody smear something to smooth the dirt floor?" On the small mesa, the walls of the dwellings had crumbled, but down near the bottom of the slopes, we found a few shards of pottery. We examined a few pieces, still wondering about their past, but we put them back where found them for others to see.

One day, we visited Bandelier National Monument that was a short distance from Los Alamos. It was a sharp contrast from what we had seen before. Along the sheer orange pink colored volcanic cliffs, I saw remnants of caves carved high up into the cliffs. Again, I couldn't help but keep wondering, "How did they manage to cut into the sheer cliffs, how did they survive, and why did they abandon this place?" The place looked like it could sustain a community since it was located in Frijoles Canyon. There was a stream, shrubs and trees, and I could see and hear birds. Surely, this place was more hospitable than the desert terrain nearby.

Down below Los Alamos, we visited an Indian community at San Ildefonso and observed an Indian ceremony. It was interesting to see the Indian dancers wearing colorful headdresses with feathers, leg bands, painted faces as they chanted and danced to the drumbeats. We observed these religious ceremonies with respect. When I was in Japan, I observed a fall Shinto festival in small town near Tokyo, but this ceremonial dance appeared to be very different from that. What I saw in Japan was gaiety and energy displayed by the spectators and the ceremonial dancers.

There were so many abandoned caves, but for us, none was worth revisiting. There were only a few Indian villages down in the desert valley worth visiting. There were only a few shops surrounding the Plaza in Santa Fe that were worth visiting. The "Big City" as the local natives called it, Santa Fe, was thirty-five miles away through desert land. I had heard that on Saturdays, the local people would go down to the Big Plaza and shop at the one and only "Big Sears Department store." There was really not much to do here on the mesa either: one theater, a few shops, a grocery store, a few bars, and not much else. It was Bob Aeder, a co-worker, who rescued me from this entire not much to do scene. Bob was one of those rare individuals that gave me hope about America. I would characterize him as one of those special persons who would give you "The shirt off his back," and he was above all, a friend.

High in the mountain
Fishes in the stream teeming
Mother Nature's day!

Bob

I remember Bob had told me that he grew up in Oregon where fresh water fishing was a way of life. One day, he said, "Tad, how would you like to go fishing up towards the Pecos this weekend with me?"

"Sure, but I have no fishing gear," I replied.

"You can have one of my old ones but you need a sleeping bag because we need to camp overnight to fish early. If you don't have a sleeping bag, I'll let you have one of mine for a few bucks." He replied.

That was the beginning of a trusting friendship.

Then one day at work, he said, "I heard of a real neat place for fishing up in Pecos. How about leaving right after work?"

Pecos was less than a two-hour drive from Los Alamos and there is not much to see in this sparse landscape. How sparse?

Bob said, "I've heard it takes at least 80 acres of grazing land to support one head of cattle."

Believe me it was true. The cattle I had seen were all skin and bones. Instead of a herd of cattle, only a few steers wandered about by themselves. Even the scenery was skin and bones. Besides sagebrush, manzanita bushes, and cacti, you might see a few adobe houses stuck in the middle of nowhere. Most adobe houses had strings of colorful chili hanging by the doorstep. Do they actually use that chili for cooking or are they just a decoration to fend off the devils? I had always wondered.

We had decided to take off early from work so we could set up a campsite before looking for a place to fish in the Pecos. Bob told me that except for the local Indians, not many people fished up in these mountains. As we approached the foothills, a large van with a Texas license plate pulling a trailer with a generator, roared past us on the narrow road.

"Did you see that car pulling that big generator?" Bob asked as he continued, "I've heard people from Texas come up to the Pecos to fish a lot but, with the size of the generator, those guys aim to stay for awhile with all the comforts of home!"

After having traveled along the narrow winding road, Bob found a camping spot where we could pitch a tent for the night.

"Let's take a look at the fishing spot before we unload our gear," he said.

It was a serene spot and we saw that nobody had been here in a long time since grass was growing over the pathway. Past the trees we could hear a stream running quietly beckoning our call. When we came to a clearing among the trees,

"Look at that stream and that pool of water over there!" Bob said excitedly. "This is great!"

We had to cross the stream in order to see what was further downstream.

"Hey, did you see those fishes breaking water?" he said. "It looks like we might be in luck here! Let's hurry back and set up camp site and try our luck fishing before the sun goes down!"

I helped Bob unload the tent, tent pegs, portable cooking stove, and the rest of the equipment for our night out in the Pecos. First, we found a level area to pitch the tent, smoothed the ground for the tent floor, pitched the pup tent and started to pound the tent pegs into the ground.

Then, suddenly a thunderous roar had startled us. It sounded like a thousand cattle stampeding toward us,

"What was that?" I asked Bob.

When I looked at Bob, his face had turned ashen as he said chokingly, "Oh my God, the stream! The stream!"

He dropped what he was holding and started towards the trees we had just returned from a short time ago. We rushed down the path to the clearing we had left not more than ten minutes ago. Muddy water was everywhere! The stream we crossed shortly before was now inundated with brushes, tree branches, and other junk that rolled down from upper tributaries.

"My god! It looks like a logjam from the headwaters broke! We're sunk!" said Bob

Mother Nature had its day!

Chapter 9: Livermore

From isolation
It's California or Bust
Uprooted again

California or Bust

Yo had taken a 180-degree turn from her first impression of Los Alamos. While the closed city must have been intimidating to her, it gave her security and good friendly neighbors. Every workday, Yo was anxious and full of energy to start because her job was challenging. She was always excited at the end of the day to tell me about the new things she was learning with Computer equipment, and what she was able to accomplish. Best of all, her boss was very friendly, supportive, and appreciative of her contribution so quickly to his group.

While Yo was happy with her work, my assignment had taken a drastic change in late fall of 1952. J. VonNeumann and R. D. Richtmyer to calculate "Hydrodynamic Shocks" had proposed a new computational technique. The numerical method eliminated the original assignment of Bob, John, and me in T-5 of using the IBM 605 and complemented with hand computing. It resulted in the breakup of our group; John Lobato decided to leave LASL, Bob Aeder transferred to the Card Program Computer (CPC) applications, and I had been assigned to join our Assistant Division Head, Dr. Harwood Kolsky, and staff member, Ruth Clark to begin programming the new computational technique for the IBM 701 stored program computer system.

Bob must have been anxious to leave Los Alamos, because shortly afterwards, he said, "There's a new Atomic Energy Commission (AEC) laboratory under the University of California starting in Livermore, California. I have applied and decided to leave LASL. I'll let you know more about the place after I transfer there."

I was sorry to see my friend Bob leave, but I thought no more about it since I was busy learning about the new IBM 701 computer. LASL had already contracted to buy the first IBM 701, and IBM invited our group to test out our programs at their facility in Poughkeepsie, New York. When I had learned about our travel to Poughkeepsie, I asked Yo to take a week off and join the three of us on our travel. We decided that this would be a convenient time for a few days of sightseeing in New York, for neither of us had been to the East Coast. However, before I could leave, Harwood asked Ruth and me to prepare our code for the assembly program. Like a fool, I volunteered not realizing how much time it would take. There were at least 4,000 IBM cards that I had to sort on an electro-mechanical sorter and then use the IBM 604 for pre-assembly. My nightmare began with the IBM Sorting machine because I had to sort by one column at a time, starting from the least significant position and work upwards. The beast feeds 650 cards per minute and spits out the cards into thirteen hoppers corresponding to the punches on the particular column. Next, I had to collect the cards from the hopper with the lowest digit on the bottom into a new stack, and then continue the process for the next significant digit.

Alphabetic information threw another twist into this sorting process, because an alphabetic punch consists of three zone punches: zero, eleven, or twelve punches and a numeric punch, which requires a second pass through the sorter to sort out the extra punches. The cards would zip, zip,

zip across the reading brushes and then plop, plop, plot into the thirteen hoppers; it was nerve racking. While I fed in two boxes of cards, the beast kept chewing them up at a rapid pace. My head was reeling from the noise and trying to keep track of where I was in the sorting process, and I needed to be careful not to drop the cards because the card hopper would not hold all 4000 cards.

I worried that I might not finish the task before our scheduled departure time. I had started from midnight on the day and finished the task around 8:00 a.m. the next morning. I didn't have time to catch my breath. Since then, computer companies made tremendous advancement. When I look back at that nightmare of a sorting process, today's stored program computer would complete the sorting as soon as it read the data.

When I returned home, Yo was anxiously waiting to catch our ride to Albuquerque in time for our flight to New York. We were newcomers to a city, and it was hard to tell if the cab driver that seemed to have taken a circuitous route was ripping us off. When we arrived at our hotel, I waited for the cab driver to unload our baggage as I had assumed would be the case as it was back in California. It seemed that wasn't part of his job description. A bit put out, I grabbed our luggage, paid the cab driver, and checked in at the hotel. Before we left Los Alamos, we had reserved a room, but when we arrived at our room, Yo and I looked at each other and decided we were not going to stay. One look was enough. It looked like a dungeon. We returned to the lobby, asked for our money back, and called a cab for another hotel. This time, we found one right at Times Square with a view of the street. It wasn't anything fancy. It wasn't new, but it was clean. It was early American with white cast iron legs on the bathtub and steam heaters. Our stay was a unique and memorable one since it was the first time we had stayed in a hotel where the neon lights blinked all night outside our window. When we see the celebration at Times Square every New Years Eve, we remember that we could see Times Square just outside our window.

We were tourists and we walked from our hotel, looked and gawked at the tall buildings, took in the sites: top of Empire State Building, Macy's Department store and its rival Gimbels, the RCA Rockefeller Center's winter plaza, and the Manhattan Financial District. We were not brave enough to try the subways. What I remember most about New York City was the incessant tooting of car horns, especially, by the taxi cab drivers. Jay walking seemed to be the modus operandi. Of course, I heard a few choice words hollered by irate drivers at the jaywalkers.

From Grand Central Station, New York, we were traveling along the Hudson River towards Poughkeepsie when Yo pointed towards a dull gray building complex and asked, "What's the name of the prison that I see over there?"

I smiled and answered, "That's West Point, the US Army Military Academy. Maybe the cadets feel it is a prison."

The next day, when we visited the IBM Center, IBM gave us a grand tour of the manufacturing facility, IBM electric typewriters and IBM card equipment. At the mainframe area where LASL's IBM 701 stood, I saw the side panels off, wires dangling inside, wires on the floor, and engineers testing the computer circuitry by using electronic scopes. What I saw was the computer undergoing major surgery. I had hoped that it would not die before we had a chance to test our program. IBM said that they would keep us posted on the progress of the system and the time for our trial run.

With the brief interlude, I decided to go sightseeing near Poughkeepsie to Vassar College and Hyde Park. Occasionally, I would hear someone say, "She's from Vassar," as if it was something special. I had to make a quick pass of Vassar College, but I found nothing special about the campus. Of course, it was for the rich. Next, we headed for Hyde Park and Franklin D. Roosevelt's birthplace. It was a beautiful estate with grounds kept well groomed. We walked through the garden and toured the buildings. I found that the buildings were not the original ones, but were remodeled and expanded by FDR's mother. In 1945 it became a National Historic Site donated by FDR, and additionally, his grave was located in the Rose Garden. While I stood there near the Sundial by his grave, I had mixed emotions about paying homage to someone who swore to uphold the Constitution, yet put me, a citizen, behind barbwires and watchtowers.

On our way back to the motel, we decided to shop in Poughkeepsie since Santa Fe had very little to offer and driving 80 miles to Albuquerque was too inconvenient. We found a nice department store in town, and we proceeded to shop for some things to take back to Los Alamos. At the cashier's counter, we noticed that they would ship our items free of charge within the United States. "Let's have them ship to our place," I said to Yo. "It'll save us from lugging the extra item with us." Yo agreed and asked the sales clerk for the shipping form. When the sales clerk looked at the address, she had a big question mark on her face. Then, she gave us the once over. She pointed to the address and said, "The store doesn't ship out of the country."

I checked Yo's handwriting and it was letter perfect. Then, I said to the clerk, "Los Alamos, New Mexico is in the United States. It's in the Southwest, next to Texas and Arizona." I added that New Mexico became the 47th State in 1912.

She listened to me, but I saw her doubtful look. She stood there for a few minutes and said she would ask the manager. It seemed like fifteen minutes before she returned. Then she told us the manager said that they could not send our package, because the address was not in the US. I looked at Yo with a frown and shook my head, picked up our items, and headed for the door. All I could think of on my way out was that only the original Thirteen Colonies must still be the greater USA. I could understand why someone from Espanola, New Mexico might not know about Japanese in America, but someone here in Poughkeepsie, with all the educational resources available, not be knowledgeable about the United States was astonishing.

When we returned to the motel, IBM had not completed their diagnostic efforts. Since Yo had taken a short leave from her work, we had to prepare to return to Los Alamos. Yo was happy to land at Albuquerque, because on one leg of our flight, we had experienced turbulence over the Midwestern states. It was uncomfortable, but I tried not to worry about it. When I looked at Yo, her face had not turned ashen white, but she tighten her lips and braved the rocking roller coaster ride until we landed.

When we returned from our trip, I had a big surprise waiting for me. Bob had sent me a letter informing me, "It's great out here and they need programmers. Come on out." He also wrote to use him as a reference, and enclosed an application form.

I was ready to leave LASL, but Yo didn't look too happy. She had fallen in love with Los Alamos. For me, in spite of the security of a closed city, the Mesa was total isolation from the rest of the United States, and no place to raise a family. Again, I had to set her world upside down. She wanted to stay; she loved her job.

I'm leaving if they accept me," I said. "You can stay if you want to."

I sent my application and waited for a reply. It came quickly and we were preparing for a transfer since the University of California managed both LASL and Livermore Laboratory.

Winter wonderland
Face Truth or Consequences
Crossroad in my life

Truth or Consequences

It was well past noon by the time the Mayflower Moving Company cleared security, packed our household belongings, and loaded the van. That morning, I had had hopes of traveling as far as Tucson, Arizona, but now, the best I could hope for was to stay overnight near Albuquerque and start early in the morning. Because I hate driving in snowy weather, I already ruled out traveling the northern route via Denver, Colorado and across Donner Pass, Nevada or take the alternate route on highway US 40 to Flagstaff, Arizona and then over Tehachapi Mountain, California. I remember clearly. It was December 1951 after a heavy snowstorm that I had the scare of a lifetime driving in snowy weather. It was our first winter in Los Alamos and Yo and I were going to Santa Fe for shopping when I drove down the back road from Los Alamos. There was still snow on the road, and, as I followed the ruts made by previous drivers, I suddenly hit a spot of black ice. The car began to slip and slide. Everything happened so fast that I had no time to panic. Instinctively, I took my foot off the accelerator, remembered not to hit the brakes, while my mind kept yelling, "Turn into the slide, turn into the slide." The car didn't spin out of control while I held tight to the steering wheel. Gradually I guided the car back away from the edge of the road. I had barely avoided skidding 300 feet down a cliff to the bottom of the mesa. That near death experience had been enough to discourage me forever from driving on any icy snow covered road.

We had plenty of time for our travel because the Mayflower driver said that he wouldn't arrive at Livermore until two weeks later. However, we had planned to omit any sightseeing because we were anxious to return to California as soon as possible. Truth or Consequences seemed to be the next best place for the overnight stay instead of the busy crossroad city of Albuquerque or further south to Las Cruses, New Mexico. I remember when I approached Truth or Consequences. I had noticed that most of the businesses were on both sides of the highway and not much elsewhere. There was just one café and one motel worth considering staying for the night. I wondered if I was again at a crossroads in my life. I could not understand why someone named this place Truth or Consequences, since I saw nothing here that I could associate the name with. Was this an omen that I had left the safe place of a guarded community of Los Alamos for an unknown future? Were there consequences for my decision that I would face soon?

Because it was long stretch ahead of us, we rose early in the morning. The sunrise was a beautiful sight, but it was no time for us to linger and savor the beauty of the red skyline. After a quick breakfast, we drove south to Las Cruces and turned westward on the highway US 10. Occasionally, we would see a weather beaten house standing far out in the dry forlorn landscape. I kept wondering, "How do they survive the harshness of weather? What do people do out here without water?" The first noticeable spot we passed by was Deming, a train stop perhaps, but little else that I could see. Further, on, Yo said, "Look! There's Lordsburg. My father said Lordsburg was one of the places he was held at after he was rounded up by the FBI." It too looked like just another train stop. "I remember *Okaasan* had told me *Otoosan* was also sent there with other *Issei* by the government after Pearl Harbor," I almost said aloud, but I let the words fade away from remembering that terrible time for our family during World War II. Soon Lordsburg faded out of sight as we traveled on our way to Tucson, Arizona. "Next stop 50 miles," a sign warned motorist to gas up or suffer the chances of the car stranded on the isolated road. "Buy authentic Indian jewelry, blankets, and mementos" would greet us at every water hole along the way. "Don't bother to turn those trinkets over and read the labels," I mused. Once, I stopped hoping to buy a gift, but when I turned the merchandises upside down, I noticed that label on many of the souvenirs had the words, "made in Occupied Japan" or countries other than USA.

At last we reached civilization, Tucson, Arizona, and decided to stay overnight. Although we were on the outskirts of the city of Tucson, the place seemed very busy because the Davis-Monthan Air Force Base was nearby. After an early breakfast, we were on the road again headed for the junction of Interstate 8 and 10 at Casa Grande. There were a number of little towns on I 8, but I noticed at Gila Bend a sign pointing, "Forty miles south to Ajo. I looked southward and I saw nothing but empty space. "What fool would want to go there?" I chuckled, because *ajo* in Japanese means 'stupid'. Later, I had heard that this town was the birthplace of copper mining in Arizona until the price of copper dropped drastically in the late 1980s. Along this route were low mountains and harsh desert lands until we reached Yuma where the Colorado River flowed through and southward to Mexico. It was also right at the border of Arizona and California. We crossed the Colorado River and continued on Interstate 8 to El Centro, California, then turned north on California Route 86 into the Imperial Valley. We stopped at Brawley to gas up at a station that had seen better days. As I got out of the car, I watched a man in blue coveralls come out of the garage, walk towards us to fill our gas tank while wiping his hands on his dirty greasy rag. I quickly decided that we would not stay and take a break. I headed north along the western side of the Salton Sea towards Indio.

I had never traveled this route before, but the names, El Centro, Brawley, and Coachella brought back memories from my years of taking *kendo*, Japanese fencing, at my Santa Monica Japanese School. I had participated in *Kendo* tournaments with *Nisei* from all over Southern California. I had advanced to second level, *Nidan* (comparable to second level black belt), and I thought that I was pretty good until my teacher sent me rolling backwards on my butt with one poke of his bamboo sword. I had practiced every Saturday night, and I wore the traditional outfit: *hakama*, the skirt like trousers of the kendo uniform; *keikogi*, jacket; *hachimaki*, head towel; *Bogu*, all of the protective gear; and *shinai*, bamboo sword. Like all martial arts, *kendo* was a well-disciplined sport and always required high respect for the teacher, *Sensei*. Unfortunately, every piece of my *kendo* equipment turned into ashes when our family tried to rid ourselves of our Japanese culture soon after December 7, 1941.

The weather was clear on this winter day, and I believed we would reach Reedley without anytrouble. Surprise! When we neared Indio, I saw dust clouds. I had thought it looked safe enough to proceed, but immediately a swirling and roaring thick dust storm engulfed us. The stripe on the two-lane highway had disappeared from sight. This was worse than when I was in midst of a dust storm at Manzanar. At least, when I was at Manzanar, I could roll up in a ball and wait it out. However, here, I could hear the dust, sand, and small pebbles scraping and blasting across the car's surface. While the inside of the car protected us, I couldn't stop, for I feared that someone behind me would smash into me from behind. I couldn't move to the side of the road, because I didn't know what was there. Besides, I could be stuck in a ditch or get lost out in the field without knowing how to get back to the road. I kept my eyes glued to the road, held my steering wheel steady to keep on my side of the road and prayed that we could survive this crisis.

Several minutes passed before I saw a red light moving ahead of us. I moved closer, and I saw it was a semi truck moving slowly and steadily forward. I stuck with him like a leech. I rode behind him more than an hour when the two of us finally saw daylight. I was relieved to see stores, motels, and landscaping. We had just passed Palm Springs, but I drove on to Banning to stop and assess any damage to the car. Except for dust all over the motor, I saw no problem, and we continued on our way. Even though it would have been late evening before we reached the in-law's home at Reedley, I had decided to keep going. Besides, it was a nice sunny day, and what else could happen to us in sunny California?

Dusk had fallen when we were well past the Grapevine on Highway 99. Suddenly, we had encountered the dreaded Tule fog of Central Valley. I slowed down, turned the lights to low beam, and kept my eyes glued to the centerline of the highway. I prayed that the drivers on the other side of the road would be doing the same. The fog rolled in, swirled around, and thickened up so much that the centerline disappeared. It was too scary and dangerous to continue driving against this white sheet. I kept looking out from corner of my eyes for a place to turn off and stop. Then, I barely saw what might be a motel sign through the fog. I turned in quickly with a sigh of relief.

We paid for the night and looked for our room. However, the fog had obscured the dilapidated condition of the motel. As we entered the room, we looked at each other disbelieving what we saw. The place must have been rooms for transients. The bed had an old iron post that was rusty where the paint had peeled off. It had long seen its days of beauty. When we pulled back the covers and looked, the sheets seemed clean but the lumpy mattress sagged half way to the floor. This was not going to a restful night for us. We had paid for the night, and driving through the fog was too hazardous to continue. We looked at each other and decided not to sleep in that horror called a bed. We chose to sit on the chairs until it was safe to drive on. We waited silently for several hours, and kept peeking outside to assess the foggy condition. The fog eventually began to ease up. The horrible night was over. As we drove back onto highway 99, we were shocked. Surprised, if not a big letdown, we saw a row of new motels about a half-mile down the highway. If only I had endured the fog a little further, we would have been safe for the night. The fog gradually faded away as we arrived at the in-laws' home in Reedley an hour and a half later. The next day, I decided to drive to Livermore to sign in at Livermore Radiation Laboratory, and to arrange for our housing while Yo stayed with her parents in Reedley.

I have often thought about our travel from Truth or Consequences and wondered if fate had all of the terrible events in store for us. But it was afterwards that I learned that a town named Hot Springs, New Mexico took on the name of Ralph Edwards' TV show "Truth or Consequences" on Edwards' invitation to promote the town into a national spotlight and not an omen foretelling the future. The truth was that we exchanged driving through cold icy snowy weather for the consequence of driving through dust storm and Tule fog.

A cold winter day
Flashing red lights welcomed me
Home away from home

Chief Michels' Welcome

On my first day, December 17, 1952, driving into Livermore, long before we moved into our own home, Police Chief Michaels had welcomed me. It happened on the day to arrange for our stay in Livermore. The road to Livermore had been a familiar sight. When I was still in college at UC Berkeley, I had traveled over Highway 50 and past Livermore to visit my in-laws down south in the Central Valley. I remembered Livermore as being just a bus stop at an old hotel at corner of P Street and Highway 50. There was an archway with the sign, "Livermore" spanned across P Street for travelers to recognize this sleepy town. I had noticed a few cottages behind the hotel that probably saw more action than in the hotel, and later when I lived in Livermore, such rumors abounded.

I entered Livermore from the east on First Street; I passed the fire station and ended at the flagpole, the Hub of Livermore. While stopped at O'Neil & McCormack gas station, I asked for directions to the Livermore Radiation Laboratory. Standing there, I saw the Bank of Italy building on one corner, Schenone Building with the Wells Fargo Bank and the State Theatre on the other corner. The gas attendant said to take a left and then turn onto East Avenue at the next five-way stop. This was the first time that I had driven into this town, and Bob Mainhard the Laboratory's Administrator had not given me any specific directions on how to get to the project. I was so preoccupied with reaching "The Lab" as an abbreviated name in the decades to come (sometimes "The Rad Lab" – a less appealing title...) that I didn't notice the red lights flashing at me as I turned into East Avenue. It was Chief Michaels. I was fortunate that he let me go on my way with just a warning.

From the five-way intersection, The Lab, what was once the Livermore Naval Air Station during World War II, was about three miles east down East Avenue. As I passed Nielson Lane, the city limit, the scenery changed from residential to hayfields. Large locust trees lined the side of roadway and a few residences and old farmhouses sat close to the road, but I saw no greenery except for Wente's vineyard to the south and a grove of eucalyptus trees near South Vasco Road. Finally, as I approached the Lab, the familiar sight of the government buildings reminded me of my days in the US Army. The badge office occupied a room in the World War II Naval Station hospital. Since my Q-clearance was already available from Los Alamos, the process for reemployment went very smoothly. The Lab had arranged for housing in Livermore's first housing tract built by H & L Homes, and I would start work as soon as we received our belongings.

I was anxious to see what and where my house would be since I had not seen any new housing when I first drove into this town. As it turned out, our house was located at the corner of Adelle St. and Elizabeth Court on a cul de sac. It was a single story one bedroom white house with an attached garage. I was happy to see that the yard had a fence that provided privacy that I hadn't had ever since I'd left Santa Monica. The house foundation was a slab floor, and throughout the entire house, the floor was covered with ugly brown and purplish asphalt tiles. The bathroom and bedroom were in the far end with very little closet space. Next to the living room was an open archway leading into one big area for the kitchen and dining room. There was a door leading to a single car garage. I was stunned when I saw that instead of a standard window, the builder used louvers and screens in its place. The builders must have convinced the building inspector to allow a quick and cheap way to build tract houses. Later, on every windy day, dust from the nearby houses under construction would swirl from the north through the louvers, and even between the slab flooring and the baseboards. The dark floor tiles coated with a dusty gray mess brought back the memory of days of misery of Manzanar. These hastily built houses would rank just a smidgen above the tarpaper shacks of Manzanar. Yet, I was thankful that the Lab had found me housing.

Now that I had officially signed in and had seen our rental home, I hurried back to Reedley and waited for the Mayflower Moving Company to notify me when our household goods would arrive. It was a few days before the New Year when we received a call from the Mayflower Moving Company stating that the van had already arrived at Livermore. The driver had been waiting for our instructions before he would unload our household items. He told us if we had delayed another day, he would have put our items in the nearest Mayflower storage at Oakland, California.

We were surprised that the Mayflower Company did not notify us of his arrival date earlier. We immediately rushed to Livermore in order to avoid the needless hassle of retrieving our belongings from storage. When we arrived, the mover was waiting with a helper that he had hired to unload our furniture. They unloaded and placed the big household items in the house and left the rest of the boxes in the garage. We noticed that only one item suffered damage during the moving. It seemed that the movers had placed a heavy object on top of Yo's sewing machine – her most precious belonging - and had not placed a protective padding, and that resulted in scratching the surface. While we were adamant about having the surface fixed, the moving van driver was reluctant to do so, but finally he agreed to have Mayflower restore it.

Closet space was at a minimum in this house and that made it difficult to place all of our belongings inside. Because this was a rental house, we had to be extra careful not to damage any of the walls. By the time we had fumbled around, New Year's was upon us. Yet, we still had boxes to unpack in the garage. I was sorry that I had to leave Yo to struggle with the rest of the boxes, but I was scheduled to start work at the Lab on January 3, 1953.

A few weeks later, Yo wanted to go back to work in the Lab's Accounting Department that she had worked in at Los Alamos. When she applied, they rejected her application because the University of California had a strict nepotism rule, which was strictly enforced. Even when her former Supervisor of Payroll at Los Alamos pleaded her case, the University held firm to its nepotism rule. Instead, the University of California offered her an opportunity to apply at the UC Berkeley campus. Unfortunately, Berkeley was forty-five miles from Livermore, and in 1953, she would have had to travel to and from work on two-lane roads. Since there was no public transportation during those early years, we would need another vehicle, an item that we could ill afford to buy at the time. Even worse, her commuting would have been during the rush hours, and extremely hazardous during the winter months. As a compromise, we had even considered a move to Walnut Creek, a halfway point, but that option was unattractive to either of us.

Disappointed with her options, Yo had decided to look for work in the Livermore Valley. However, opportunities were slim indeed, for the gravel industry was the main industry in the valley. Even the firebrick company had closed down in 1949, as well as the Coast Manufacturing Co. that made safety fuses during World War II. Like most small towns, most of Livermore's businesses were on First Street. On Railroad Ave, which was parallel to First Street, there was the

Lady on the Bridge

Livermore Train Station, a run-down housing complex called "Tubsville," and a plumbing shop. While Livermore was a small town, nearby Pleasanton was even smaller. Her options for work looked grim.

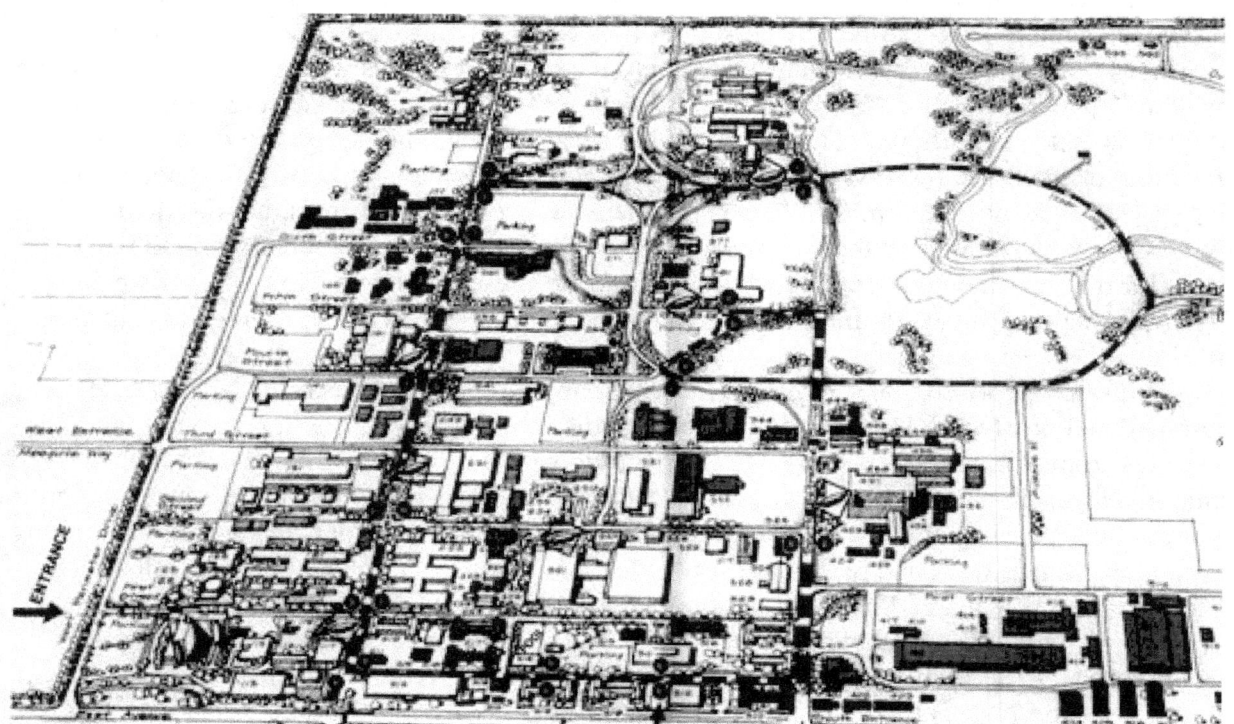

The Lab in Livermore

My World

Amaterasu,
Brilliance of the sun
Shine your guiding light
Your beauty
The colors of the rainbow
Birds sing
Land in abundance
Together as one
Warm and colorless
I look in the mirror
I see my world

I'm responsible
Bring out the best in people
Cast no color hues

Who am I?

I believed that I was no different from anyone else, and I treated others with the same respect. No matter who they were.

Once again, *Okaasan*, our two worlds were at odds with each other. The values that you instilled in us remained, but now that we were married, it was up to us to decide who we were and what we would pass on to our children. When I got married, graduated college, and started my career, I began on a journey that defined who I was.

Within a span of a year and a half, I had changed jobs twice. First, when I had taken a position with Mc Donnell Douglas, I found it virtually impossible to find housing; and then a strike by blue-collar workers made the working environment questionable. Next, I had looked forward to work at Los Alamos Scientific Laboratory in New Mexico because I thought the job involved math and physics, which were my strengths and interests. Yo and I had always talked about raising a family, but the longer we stayed, we learned that Los Alamos was not the place to reach our dreams. Worse of all, Los Alamos was a closed city that made it impossible for our parents to visit us since only citizens were allowed there. It had been a safe and friendly environment, but isolated. The job that the Los Alamos interviewers described was not my assigned task. I decided to transfer to work for the Lawrence Radiation Laboratory in Livermore. Once more, I had to uproot Yo from a job she was so enthusiastic about and found rewarding. I had faith that our roots eventually would grow deep here in Livermore and our journey of raising a family had just begun.

I had arranged to start work as soon as the moving company delivered our belongings to our new home, the house on Elizabeth Court, months before we were able to move into our permanent home. Boxes and boxes were still stacked in the garage waiting for us to unpack.

It was January 3, 1953 when I was stunned. It was my first day of work. I had just received a form to fill out from Mainhardt's secretary. Since her office was a cubbyhole and no space to sit down and write, she said that there were some unoccupied desks down at the end of the hall in the solarium (Bldg. 191 R190H) that I could use.

As soon as I entered the solarium, I found a desk to sit and was about to fill out the forms.

No! You can't sit there! That desk is taken!

That outburst took me by surprise since I had not noticed anyone in the room. Hmm… I thought, there is another desk on the other side of the solarium. I will just sit over there and fill out these forms.

No! You can't sit there either! That desk is already assigned to someone else! All these desks are already assigned to the UNIVAC group!

I thought, "It looks like Mother Hen is looking after her brood." From where had this woman suddenly appeared? She didn't have the courtesy to ask me why I was there. What a way to start my first day at LRL. In addition, there would be more surprises.

When I told the Mainhardt's secretary of my plight, she said, "Oh, you met Cecilia Larsen. She is in charge of the programmers for the UNIVAC group, but they haven't returned yet from

Remington Rand UNIVAC in Philadelphia, Pennsylvania." Then she told me that since the Laboratory was new, there were shortages of office equipment and furniture, and consequently secretaries were very protective of their office furniture and supplies.

She pointed to a room across from her and said, "You could use the cubbyhole across the hall from me since nobody was assigned to it."

Since the LRL site was a Naval Preflight Hospital during World War II, the room I was looking at must have been for Charge of Quarters (CQ) for a senior Navy Medical Officer because there was a connecting door to an adjacent room. When I finished filling out the form, Maindhardt's secretary informed me that the two people I would be working with, Bob Jastrow, the code physicist, and John Griffith, the junior physicist, were both in a project technical meeting that morning, so I would have to wait around for a while. The meeting would end at eleven o'clock, but, she said, they usually wandered back just before noon.

I had more than an hour to kill. With the big shots at the meeting, there really wasn't much to do here. The whole building had an ugly drab green paint job from World War II. Did I sense a faint odor of lingering disinfectant? After sticking my nose into a few rooms, I found my friend Bob, who had also transferred from Los Alamos Scientific Laboratory (LASL), busily working on an IBM Card Program Computer (CPC). The programmers and machines were all jammed into a small room. The noise of the printer banging away and the IBM cards that needed to be fed through the card reader to advance the computation was more than I could stand. Since he was busy, I waved and left the noise behind me.

It was near lunchtime when I saw a heavyset ruddy complexioned person approaching me. He was wearing faded GI issue green fatigues and had short crew cut that he probably managed to perform on himself with a clipper.

When he reached his office, he said, "I'm John Griffith, I'm sorry to keep you waiting. I just forgot that you were coming to work today. It's almost noon, so let's get together after lunch. In the meantime, I'll get you some copies of documents we need for the assignment."

He disappeared for moment and came back with three documents: a copy of the UNIVAC I Instruction Code (C-10) containing a list of instructions and execution times, finite difference equations, and a copy of "A Method for the Numerical Calculation of Hydrodynamic Shocks," by J. von Neumann and R. Richtmyer. That was it. I didn't even find a picture of the computer itself. While we were chatting, John said, "By the way, we're scheduling a flight to Washington, D.C. to run the code on the UNIVAC I."

Immediately, the gears in my head began to grind away. I just got here, the garage is filled with unopened boxes, and we're living out of our suitcases. At that instant, I was having a hard time trying to figure out what to say to Yo if this flight was really going to happen. Yo had had enough surprises, and, even though I knew she would accept the news as part of my job, it seemed unfair that John Griffith and Bob Jastrow had not waited for me before making the plans.

Showing that I was surprised at the news, I asked, "Oh is the problem already coded?"

John replied, "No, but you can code it on our plane flight to Philadelphia."

I raced through a quick mental calculation: I'd have at most fifteen hours to code this problem while on the airplane, and I didn't have a clue about preparing the code for the UNIVAC I.

"John," I asked, "Have you ever coded anything?"

"No," he replied.

Suddenly it dawned on me that neither he nor the physicist had any idea about what was involved in programming for the "Giant Brain."

In 1952, the UNIVAC I had predicted the landslide victory of Dwight Eisenhower over Adlai Stevenson, and had received the title of "Giant Brain." However, nowhere did anyone state what was required to program the computer. Somehow, everyone had the notion that the "Giant Brain" could solve any problem easily with very little preparation.

I scanned the set of equations and noticed several procedures that required a square root calculation. "John," I said. "Let's get together after lunch and see what would be involved in coding this square root as a subroutine."

I was still in shock while driving home for lunch. It hadn't been a very warm reception during my first few hours, but instead, a fiery one. In addition, I had to carry my two documents home since I was without a permanent office assignment. Yet John seemed so enthusiastic about handing me those two items as if they were all that I needed to know about my job. Because Yo had accompanied me to use the IBM 701 at Poughkeepsie when we were at LASL, I knew that she would understand that I might be required to travel. However, John's casual statement that we would be going back East to use the UNIVAC I without preparation was ludicrous. I knew I had to educate John that there was more to programming than just keying in a few numbers into the computer.

After I returned, we discussed some mathematical techniques we could use. Finally, we decided on a simple square root algorithm and proceeded with the coding. John was quickly learning that coding for a computer took more than writing the instructions on a piece of paper. I made sure that he was involved at each line of the coding in order to feel the pain. After we satisfied ourselves that we had a code for the square root routine, I had to give John another shocker.

"John," I said. "The UNIVAC I is a fixed point machine, and our method will work for normalized numbers. Otherwise, we'll be faced with divide faults in our calculations."

"Oh my God!" John yelped. "Jeezus, it looks like I have to come up with a set of strange numerical units for physical quantities. I'd better cancel the flight." Under my breath I said, "Thank God for little favors!" Now that the ground rules for coding were established, it was several months later that we considered running the code on the UNIVAC I.

It was during this period that I became acquainted with John. He was a person that seemed to know something about any imagined topic. Once we happened to focus on tea. John could tell the various nuances about tea culture. Typically, he would drag out a picayune cigarillo, light it, hold it with the end of his thumb and forefinger, take puff, and then bring it back down to his left side as he continued to give a full discourse on the topic at hand. Sometimes he would look upward and entertain me with a few smoke rings. He had been in the Air force during World War II, so his words were colorful.

When I would say anything, he would say something interspersed with of the following words: "Jeezus, No kidding, I'll be Gol dang, and Oh my God" as he thumped the side of his head with his right hand. He had a definite accent that I placed as from West Virginia. John was a kindly "fuzz ball" whose company you could enjoy while also admiring his professional talents. One day, he showed me a pamphlet on a series of technical seminars; Lifelong Learning sponsored by the University of California Extension Division, and held on Thursday evenings in Berkeley. John was keenly interested in computer applications even though he had stayed clear of programming. I had just embarked on the journey through the era of high speed computing, and any knowledge of applications would be important to me in the future. Well known scientists lectured on such topics as Monte Carlo, Finite Difference, Matrix, Game theory, Non-linear Problems, and Dynamic Programming, to name a few. I listened intently to the lectures, but some nights it was hard to keep focused after a long day at the Lab.

Meanwhile, the contingent of coders (the word "programmer" had yet to be coined), who had attended a technical class for three months on the UNIVAC I, returned from Philadelphia. Because they had been selected to receive this special training, they felt they were an elite group. It was like pulling teeth in order to get any information about UNIVAC I from them. Only one person, Jules Mersel, had heard that I had coded a problem for the UNIVAC I and offered to look over my work. A few days later I returned to see him. He said, "Your code won't work!"

For several days, I hand checked my work over and over and I found nothing that could cause a problem.

"Jules, I said," I've gone over this code several times and can't find anything wrong."

"Well it won't work," he said.

"Why?' I asked.

He hesitated for a moment and then said, "The first thing you must do is code in the first sixty words of memory as a bootstrap program to read the rest of the information from the program tape into UNIVAC I memory."

Making changes in a code was not an easy task because no assembler existed for the UNIVAC I. That is, the coder had to set each address. Any changes in the coding could result in modifying all of the addresses. I was not about to go through that pain. I resorted to patch coding: Branch to an empty area of memory, save registers, make the correction, restore registers, and branch back.

My woes were not over.

John and I made three trips back east to use the UNIVAC I at the U. S. Army Map Service. LRL was scheduled to use the computer from midnight to 8:00 am. I had the lowest priority. On the first two trips, I just watched. On the last trip, I watched the super-programmer at the console with a UNIVAC I engineer running her program at the console until 7:55 am. Then the engineer at the console said, "You're on!"

I hung my tape and walked towards the console. Suddenly the 8:00 o'clock buzzer rang, the engineer yelled, "That's all! Time's up!"

UNIVAC I – "Giant Brain"

When the sky looked black
I saw a silver lining
Paint with no color

Pits of Cherry Pie

Saved by the Bell, I thought. Little did John Griffith and I know what was in store for us.

The scientists and engineers at LRL needed more and more computer capabilities to design, model, and test their theories of weapon design. Dr. Edward Teller, founder of the LRL, and Sid Fernbach, Theoretical Physics and Computer Department Head, were constantly in negotiations and encouraging computer companies to build faster and more capable computers for the laboratory's computational needs. One day, Sid assigned John and me to evaluate the performance of two likely candidates to replace the UNIVAC I: Engineering Research Associates ERA 1101 and IBM 701. After detailed analysis, using hydrodynamic and Monte Carlo applications, we recommended IBM 701 as the best computer system to meet our needs.

When the UNIVAC I had arrived in March 1953, there had been concern that the laboratory could not keep it busy enough to justify its cost. There was also real fear among UNIVAC programmers: "Why in the world is the lab buying an IBM 701?" lamented a programmer for the UNIVAC I, "It's 10 times faster than the UNIVAC! We will surely run out of problems to run and we may soon be out of a job."

Meanwhile, Bob Jastrow contracted with LASL to use their IBM 701 for his code "Cherry Pie" because we did not have time on the UNIVAC I. The computational models for the weapons design had no simple answers. They were crude approximations of the real world, solutions of non-linear partial differential equations using grid systems and Monte Carlo for neutronics. Even the properties of materials, at high temperatures and pressures, were unknown. "Cherry Pie" was a tough problem by any standards. It was a two-dimensional Lagrangian hydrodynamics code requiring information from its nearest neighbors that changed as the computation proceeded. John generated the initial input and followed the physics: I did the programming.

I had asked John once about the name "Cherry Pie," but I didn't receive a sensible answer from him. It seemed that it was just a name, a whim of the moment. However, many of the computer codes for the Lab had strange sounding names since the name of codes were banned from reflecting the weapon's application. The names of wineries were good choices, as well as Greek Gods. One code used the name "Ghoti," but pronounced, "fish." The "f" sound from "gh" as in "enough." The "sh" sound from "oti" in "notion." Physicists had convoluted ideas about names.

Jastrow, John and I made three or more trips to LASL to debug and run the code. Each trip was more demanding than the last, both physically and mentally. Software was in its infancy; Assembly Language for programming and debugging by memory dumps. The IBM online printer at 150 lines per minute was faster than the UniPrinter typing output at ten characters a second, but we were still limited by our progress. John and I worked anywhere from twelve to sixteen hours and sometimes around the clock. On every trip, we stayed at the Los Alamos Lodge that had small cottages on site. Best of all, the rooms were equipped with a small refrigerator that we stocked with either Carta Blanca, Dos Equis, or Champale. We were so tired at the end of our computer run that with one bottle of the "nectar of Gods," we collapsed into bed until the next day's run. We were scheduled for three weeks at LASL, but we knew it was going to be more like five weeks (of course we told our wives three weeks), and we pushed for answers for Jastrow. The grand finale was the last day on the last trip to LASL in 1954. Jastrow was leaving LRL to work for NASA Headquarters in Washington, D.C. He was anxious to see the results of a series of runs with "Cherry Pie" before he caught his plane at 11:00 A.M. We had already worked around the clock, but Jastrow managed to run us into the ground until the last hour. With an armful of printouts and a sigh of relief, we shoved him off to catch his plane. When we returned to Livermore from our miserable computer excursion, John was so beat that he had to see a doctor for complete exhaustion. Later, when we chatted with Sid about our exhausting ordeal, Sid said, "Well, you didn't have to work that hard." Shortly afterwards, John decided he had enough and decided to join IBM in Yorktown Heights, New York.

As soon as John left for IBM in March 1954, Sid showed up at my door and said, "Tad, I want you to head the IBM 701 group." During the early history of the lab, programmers and technicians were associated with the large computer systems. In fact, we were classified by our particular major in college: Mathematician, Physicist, and etc. Also, the term "Computer Technician" didn't exist, nor did Computer Operator." The only comparable title for the latter was "Tab Operator," and that was too narrow in defining the responsibilities of a computer operator. Our salary paralleled the Federal GS pay scale when we first started at the Lab. Later, to my surprise, I found out that the GS rating affected my salary for advancement and imposed a ceiling on my salary. It was several years later that Sid was able to negotiate with the University of California to define new categories for computer personnel. For my new position as supervisor for the IBM 701 effort, there had been no posting of my title within the Department. There was no formal announcement in a meeting, or memorandum, nor what my responsibility entailed. If this was a promotion, it didn't come with more pay. I wasn't sure if the appointment was good news or bad news. Thus, I had nothing to show to Yo that I was in charge of the IBM 701. I was just it, but I found out that it was up to me to define my own role as supervisor. Numerous times, Sid would ask me for my input on what individual he should select as supervisor. This time, I was in charge of eighty or more employees, setting up around-the-clock computer operation, and conducting a programming class for new employees. The latter item was a big challenge: to teach programming when I myself had learned how by the "seat of my pants."

One night, I learned the scope of my responsibilities. The Lab's computer programs that progress to production mode were scheduled to run at night on the weapon's problems in one or two-hour intervals even though the total time required was many times larger. Computer Operators were hard to find since this was the early days of running a computer around the clock. What the Computations Department needed were responsible persons who could follow routine directions and do minor manual tasks. In our desperation to hire computer operators, I suspect that we had hired "butchers, bakers, and candle stick makers." Worse still, because of the Department's Full Time Equivalent (FTE) ceiling, the computer center was manned with a minimum of computer operators to cover the twenty-four hour shifts for seven days a week. It became a scheduling nightmare.

One night, Yo and I had decided to see Kurosawa's "Rashomon" in Pleasanton with our neighbor. As I entered our home after returning from the movie, our phone was ringing and ringing. "Who would be calling me at this time of the night?" I wondered. It was a frantic call from the IBM technician on duty for the IBM 701.

"There's no operator to run the computer," he said. "What should I do?"

"Did you try contacting the supervisor?" I asked.

"No, I only have your home phone number," he replied.

I reluctantly agreed to go back to the Lab.

I ran the 701 for eight more hours until the morning shift arrived. However, I couldn't return home because I had meetings all through that day. Finally, when I went home and dropped dead tired into bed, the phone rang. My mind was numb by this time and when a voice said, "I'm sorry there was a mix up in the operator's schedule…" I slammed the phone down and went back to sleep.

The IBM 701 was upgraded to an IBM 704 and then to a series of improvements as the technology advanced. The Laboratory became one of the world's largest computing centers, and my responsibility increased. It was during this era that I came to know Bob Hughes. When Sid asked me whom he might send to work with IBM on their FORTRAN Project with John Baccus at IBM World Headquarters, New York, I suggested that he choose Bob Hughes. Later, when he returned, I asked Bob to join me on meetings with users of IBM computer systems. In my role as supervisor, I looked for opportunities to recognize, to encourage, and to promote individuals for their contributions. Since monetary rewards were not possible, I asked individuals to join me in meetings, conferences, and interviewing appointments as extra benefits. One evening, when Bob and I were bending our elbows over the bar with other IBM users, Bob suggested our group be called SHARE. That name remained from that day on.

Bob Hughes was black. Once on my travel, he accompanied me to my family's home in West Los Angeles. Later I was surprised after Yo and I had spent a holiday down there. Yo told me my mother had started a conversation in the following way:

"Did you know Tadashi brought a Black person to our home?"

"My mother said that?" I asked my wife in amazement.

I remembered that particular day when I dropped by with my coworker Bob to visit my brother Joe's home at the nursery at West Los Angeles, CA. I never even gave a second thought that anyone in my family would be offended.

During that early period, a few members, who I had worked closely with, had dinner together at our respective homes. Bob was always a member of that group, and Yo had come to know Bob as a respected member of my team and cordially invited him into our home. In addition, Bob surprised me one day, when he visited my home with his girlfriend. He said he wanted me to meet her because they were going to Chicago to get married. I was honored that Bob valued my friendship enough to want me to meet his girlfriend. It was several weeks later when Bob dropped by to see me again. While I watched him get out of the car and help a young woman step out, my eyes opened wide and my jaws dropped a bit. The young woman he introduced me to this time was not the same person I had met before. Then he said, "I want you to meet my wife. We just got married."

Several years later, Bob and his wife had invited us to their house for dinner. Bob had purchased an Eichler home in Castro Valley that overlooked the San Francisco Bay. His wife was a nurse and they were enjoying their married life, but Mother Nature refused to let them start a family. At dinner, they were excited about introducing us to their two-year old adopted son. He was big like Bob and light complexioned like him and his wife. When I first met Bob, I always thought he was a former football player because he was about six-foot tall and with a solid build of an athlete. It was later that he told me, while in college, he said he was recruited by a football franchise, but he decided to continue his college education instead. With both of our children growing up, we had less time to socialize, but we remained friends until he retired from the Lab. Like my brother Joe, Bob was spending his time chasing that little white ball.

IBM 701

Left out on a limb
A lifeline with bits and bytes
Bit for an answer

Lonesome Spot

The age of large scientific computers began a never-ending journey and I was in for a bumpy ride. IBM modified the IBM 701 to meet the need of floating-point calculations for scientific and engineering calculations and designated it the IBM 704. Meanwhile Dr. Teller and Sid met with several computer companies to specify and design a computer for our specific needs. Only three computer companies had bid for this contract: IBM, Burroughs, and Remington Rand Univac. Burroughs could not meet our requirements, but IBM stated they could produce a computer for the Lab's requirements in forty-two months while Remington Rand stated that they could deliver a computer in twenty-nine months. Based on the shorter delivery schedule, the Lab signed the contract with Remington Rand Univac in September 1955. The computer was named LARC (Livermore Advanced Research Computer). However, when Remington Rand delivered the LARC in September 1960, it was two years later than promised.

Before the ink on the contract for the LARC dried, a few Computation Department and Electronics Department personnel left the Lab to work for Remington Rand. I was surprised because pirating people was not condoned, especially when The Lab had just signed a contract with Remington Rand Univac. However, as it turned out one member from the Computation Department did well with his move to Remington Rand, because he ended up retiring in Tahiti with nothing to do but play tennis all day, loll on the beach, and enjoy the Pacific Ocean breeze. I admit that I was a bit envious, for I could almost feel that cool ocean breeze. However, in reality Tahiti would have been no place for me to retire because I'd never see my grandchild.

At home, this period was filled with surprises. Greg was born with a bang on October 26, 1955. He arrived a month early when the Bay Area had an earthquake the night before. He was a hungry baby requiring twice as many bottles for feeding than a normal feeding routine. We were fortunate because my mother came to help for two weeks followed by Yo's mother. I learned later that it was the customary thing in the Japanese culture to allow the new mother to recover from childbirth. There were loads of cloth diapers that Yo presoaked, washed, and hung out on the

UNIVAC LARC

clothesline everyday followed that. Then the next year, an unexpected crisis came. In late November 1956, I had an unexpected surgery for a ruptured appendix. Yo indeed had her hands full to look after two babies at the same time. However, I did help with the chores whenever possible.

In 1957, about two years after the contract was signed, Sid came to my office and said, "I want you to give up your present responsibility and take charge of the LARC." He said I didn't have to worry about the software because Remington Rand Univac would provide all of it for The Lab. "Take charge of the LARC" was all that Sid said about my new assignment.

Additionally he wanted me to suggest whom I might select to take over my present responsibilities for the IBM computers.

I was happy to suggest: Han Bruijnes to manage the people and Clarence Badger for the technical support.

The next day Hans came by to tell me about his new assignment. "Tad, you had it easy in your job as supervisor. You really don't have much to do but attend meetings and talk to people."

Again there was no posting and no increase in salary, for it was just a change in my existing assignment. Hans was right that I didn't have much to do but attend meetings and talk to people. However, my responsibility for the new computer required studying how to best utilize the new computer architecture and keep track of the software promised by Remington Rand Univac Company.

The EE Department worked closely with Remington Rand on the LARC Project because EE would be in charge of maintaining the computer system at Livermore. My responsibility was to see that the LARC would have programs ready to run when it was delivered. The contract specified for system software and a FORTRAN compiler that would be provided by an outside software company, Computer Software Corporation (CSC).

Remington Rand faced a number of technical challenges: to require no vacuum tubes, to develop large drum auxiliary storages and a state-of-the-art ferrite core memory system, and to provide single error detection and correction for the system. The components that they based their contract on worked in the laboratory, but producing modules in mass quantities proved to be a difficult task. As a result, Remington Rand did not complete their design of the LARC in a timely manner, and the software effort suffered as a result. Finally in early 1959, Remington Rand requested a few programmers from The Lab to reside in Philadelphia, Pennsylvania to assist them in their software effort on the I/O processor. I was now faced with a dilemma, a tall order to fill, for I had been assigned to take charge of the LARC without any programming help. It was time to go on a scavenger hunt, for I was not prepared to leave the family and take on a prolonged relocation to the "City of Brotherly Love." I looked to our new hires that were waiting for clearances in the building designated as the "Cooler." I found two people, Pete Nickolas and Bob Brousseau, who were married but without children. I was relieved when they volunteered to relocate to Philadelphia for six months or more.

For months and months Remington Rand kept stating that the LARC was 90% on target. That last 10% never seem to materialize. Early in 1960, Remington Rand announced that the LARC would be delivered in September. Yet, there was no software in sight. I immediately pressed Remington Rand to provide minimally an assembler so that we could commence programming for the LARC. About six months before the late delivery, Remington Rand finally sent two programmers, Holt and Turansky to design an assembly program. They were an amazing dog and pony show.

When they arrived, I presented them our basic requirements for a symbolic assembler, with macro and pseudo instructions. Mr. Holt stood at the blackboard and began generating his interpretation of our request. I was amazed at the speed at which he was writing and how his chalk flew when he emphasized a certain point. It was phenomenal as he moved across the blackboard.

Then as I was watching, I said to him, "Wait, you have an inconsistency in your specification!"

He stopped. He stepped back, looked, thought for a moment and said, "You're right."

With an eraser in each hand, he moved across the two blackboards erasing all of the writing. His arms were moving like two propellers. Chalk dust flew everywhere as if a tornado were passing through. He sat down a moment with Turansky and appeared to be in a heated discussion. After a while, Holt said, "Let me think it over and get together with you tomorrow."

The second presentation proved no better than the first. This went on for over a week. Holt and Turansky had a grandiose scheme in mind. We wanted something more basic to get on with our programming. Finally, we agreed on a set of specifications. I asked them to copy what he had on the blackboard and send us an official document of our agreement.

After waiting for more than a week, the specification for the LARC assembler arrived. I was horrified. What they sent me was not what we had agreed. Time was running out for users to begin programming. I met with Sid and told him about our meeting and with Remington Rand's programmers and that they failed to agree on the LARC assembler. Then I said, " Sid, we have to write an assembler ourselves immediately or the LARC will be idle for a long time." Sid agreed but he said, "You can't have any additional programmers for the project."

That night I pondered, "Who can I get to write the assembler?"

The next morning, I looked in the mirror and there was my programmer. Fortunately, Pete Nickolas and Bob Brousseau, who had been working with Remington Rand on the I/O processor, had returned from Philadelphia. They were ripe for a new assignment. Neither one had any experience with an assembler. In addition, neither had I written one. There was one other person, Gretchen Glass, who had just received her "Q" clearance and had no assignment either.

I met and talked with them about a symbolic assembler that we needed to write for the LARC. I mapped out the specifications, and because of limited memory, I decided to write a two-pass assembler in order to eliminate an interim working file. I assigned the work as follows: Pete and Bob were assigned to the first pass to produce a table of symbolic references, Gretchen would evaluate the symbols generated from the first pass, and I would code the second pass and produce the executable code. We thought for a while and decided to name it SAIL, Livermore **A**ssembler **S**ystem written backwards.

We drew up flow diagrams, decided on the interface between each pass, and completed writing SAIL before the LARC was delivered. We had had to wait for the LARC to check out the assembler because we could not simulate our code on our UNIVAC I. When the LARC was installed, checking the SAIL was a nightmare for the three of us. While we were trying to check out the assembler, a user was trying to access it at the same time. It was a weather model that the code physicist, Chuck Leith, was running on the IBM 709. He was not about to wait for anyone to run, check out, and then run his code. He had converted the code for the LARC and had mapped out his storage allocation for the LARC. After talking to him, I concluded that if I could artificially produce a symbol table for his program, I could provide an executable file by means of my second pass.

Nothing could have been more stressful. Not only was I under the gun every second of the day, but also at night, for I had made a commitment to Chuck Leith. SAIL was successfully completed, but as I watched SAIL run, I noticed that processing the symbol table took an inordinate amount of time. For my second pass, I had used dual pointers and optimized searching for symbols by using "hashing" for both the mnemonics and the symbol table. When I asked the programmer, "How are you processing the symbols?" Gretchen said, "I keep running through the set of symbols until they are all evaluated." I pointed out to her that with her method, in the worst-case scenario, she would be processing the symbol table n-factorial times. I told her to use a system of pointers and link only those symbols that had not been evaluated. After she reprogrammed, Gretchen watched her program zip through the symbol table. For several months, CSC spent hours checking out their FORTRAN program. When the FORTRAN compiler was finally operational, the users were unhappy that the compiler was taking an excessive amount of time for code generation by FORTRAN. They pointed to our SAIL and asked, "Why can't you do the same?"

When Sid said, "You are in charge of the LARC," he had not told me that he wanted to eliminate the use of both IBM cards for input and printed-paper output. However, the users at LLRL were accustomed to IBM cards for code development and input. Input for the Remington Rand Univac computers was on tape that was typed by a UniTypist. Unfortunately there was no convenient way to make changes in the program without using the LARC system. Because the users complained, our EE Department suggested that we should install a punch-paper tape system as a compromise. When the equipment was installed, the users again complained because this scheme was not convenient to make changes.

EE had to modify a Remington Rand's paper tape synchro-punch system that would allow users to merge changes into a code and produce a new tape. I tried using this contraption and was completely devastated. While it was next to impossible to find the right place to make the correction, merging the corrections was absolutely impossible. Soon the punch paper tape unraveled in my hands and fell into pile on the floor. Sometimes the beast would fail to punch or the chad would not register correctly. I saw others come in, shake their heads, and simply walk out of the room. Frustrated with my results, I went to Sid and asked for a card-to-tape system. When the card-to-tape unit delivered by Remington Rand arrived, I was disappointed because it wasn't an elegant piece of equipment. It seemed to be an engineering prototype. Their solution for card-to-tape was both hilarious and dangerous, because the Univac system used round holes and the reader had to accept the rectangular holes of IBM punched cards. Everything was fine until I had a card jam. I was horrified when I went to remove the jammed cards. First, I had to lift up the cover, stick my hands into the guts of the system, and be careful not to touch an exposed 400-volt supply unit inside the card reader or face the danger of the high voltage.

In order to limit the paper output, the LARC was designed with a cathode-ray device called the Charactron built by Stromberg-Carlson. It outputted both alphanumeric data and graphics output onto 35-mm film. I had noticed the LARC technicians tinkering with it every day, but adjusting it for the best output depended highly on who was doing it. While Sid's idea of limiting hard copy output was laudable, the realization of his idea proved futile. Sid had to order special microfilm readers for users to select, mark the output, and only print those marked frames.

However, once the film was read through the microfilm reader, it was scratched and useless to the user. Soon the microfilm reader was shoved into the corner of the room and was gathering dust, because the users refused to use it. They simply printed everything.

Sid declared the LARC as an unclassified computer for non-weapons computer simulations. Once SAIL and FORTRAN were operational, I looked for ways to enhance the operation. First, I had specified a Master Control routine that was designed and implemented by Glen Hage who had become a member of my group. By software, program and hardware contingencies would be resolved, and allow pre-loading data or programs from the console. Next, I reviewed the Input and Output (I/O) program for the LARC in the I/O processor memory. I was appalled to find that program was not only coded in absolute addresses, but also worst of all, the programmers had used the physical location of the program as constants. This made the program virtually embedded in concrete. I dumped their code onto a tape and wrote a program to assign symbolic addresses so that the program could be modified to add further I/O capabilities. Then I extended the SAIL language to include the I/O processor instructions. Thus, the code could be more readily relocated and expanded for new requirements. Later, I was amused to hear someone bragging that he had made a symbolic I/O source code.

However, one day Sid brought along a programmer while I was in the machine room and said, "I have an assistant for you, Spenser Manlove."

I was stunned, for I had not complained to Sid about my assignment, "Take charge of the LARC." Then, Sid had an open door policy, and all I could think of at the moment was that this programmer wanted my job. While I had not been associated with Spencer in the past, I had no respect for him for his underhanded action. The time was ripe to think about other things, for I never had an eight-to-five workday trying to get the LARC into a twenty-four hour operation. I could relax and spend some time on my yard. I had already picked and shoveled the ground in front of the house, and I was ready to pour seven and a half cubic yards of concrete for my driveway.

Besides it was an opportune time since Greg was seven years old and attending the East Avenue School. Yo and I looked forward to seeing that our sons had a good start in school. Glen would be attending kindergarten the following year.

Meanwhile, about six months later when Hans Bruijnes dropped by my office, I asked him, "How are things going?"

Since he had commented that I didn't have much to do but talk to people all day about the supervisor's position that he had taken over from me, I thought it was a good time to elicit a reaction from him.

"I don't have any more time for myself," he said.

"Welcome to the club," I muttered. "It's lonely at the top."

Maybe the unexpected appearance of my assistant was an omen of things to come, for one afternoon in January 1963, Sid came to my office and handed me a blurred Xerox copy of what looked like a set of instructions. Sid said, "Tad, I want you to give up your LARC assignment and be responsible for the CDC 6600 computer system. You won't have to worry about the software because Seymour Cray and his staff will provide all of the necessary programs." In the back of my mind, I thought, "I've heard that story before, Sid!" However, I kept my mouth shut.

Shikata ga nai, I could have said to Sid. However, the first and last person had tried saying something similar, and Sid had replied, "I want you to clear your desk by 4:30 P.M. and resign from the laboratory!" That was the last I'd seen of him. I remembered that day because he came to me and told me what had happened: he was the computer operator supervisor for running the IBM 701 computers. From April 1954, the IBM 701 computer was operated around the clock seven days a week. Because the weapon's program wouldn't support more than one operator per shift, scheduling people for the operation was a nightmare. This doomed the supervisor who only wanted to keep his daytime hours and not help on the weekends or nights. Frustrated with the scheduling of operators, he went to see Sid, gave him an ultimatum for more people, and was fired. What the supervisor did not realize was that Sid did not have the authority to add more people, because the allocations of people and money for computer operations came from the Nuclear Weapons Program.

I looked at the two pages of Xeroxed instructions and I was confused, mystified, and baffled as to what the set of scribbling meant. It was worse than the UNIVAC C-10 code I received from John Griffith on my first day of work. There were no schematics, no drawings of the system architect, or detailed specification of the instruction set. I had no idea what Sid meant by the software that was being provided by Control Data Corporation (CDC).

I had never heard of CDC, but later I learned that a key computer design engineer, Seymour Cray, and Bill Norris, business manager, had formed the company to build computers for scientific applications. Seymour had previously worked for Engineering Research Associates and designed ERA 1103 computer system that competed with IBM's 701. Remington Rand had acquired ERA, and later Sperry bought Remington Rand, only to be later acquired by Burroughs Corporation. When Remington Rand took over, their focus for the computer was accounting applications. That's when Seymour left with Bill Norris and formed a new company. However, they needed support from the scientific community for a computer designed by Seymour Cray to succeed. They had come to Livermore because The Lab was the world's foremost scientific computer center. They visited The Laboratory with a proposal for new transistorized computer architecture called the CDC 6600. Sid worked hard to prod the Laboratory to support Control Data to build their 6600. The Lab directors agreed, and Cray's legacy was born. Since the CDC 6600 was still in design, the contractual agreement called for a 1604, followed by a CDC 3600, until the CDC 6600 could be delivered. Seymour designed the 1604, programmed the operating system, and wrote the FORTRAN compiler as well. The CDC 3600 was not Seymour's baby.

Since Sid said that Seymour and his staff would provide all of the software, I sent Pete Nickolas, my one and only programmer, to visit Chippewa Falls and see what was going to be available. Pete met two programmers designing software for the CDC 6600, but it was questionable whether they had Seymour's approval. This assignment was indeed full of surprises. I had not met Seymour Cray and did not know what to expect. However, as time passed, I watched as the CDC managers feared to tread where Seymour walked. Meanwhile, two groups of CDC's high management people from Southern California and from the Northwest came to talk to Sid about software support for this computer. It was obvious that each group wanted to provide software, but showed reluctance to deal directly with Seymour. I remember their hesitancy as they looked at Sid for him to persuade Seymour to consider outside software support. It was later that I discovered that Seymour was a man of few words.

Meanwhile, while Sid had assigned me the responsibility of the CDC 6600, there were several groups within the Computation Department that wanted to take over my job. First, the systems group for the IBM series computer wanted to install their batch operating system on the system. Then, there was one individual who was working on the IBM STRETCH computer system that wanted to program a compiler and possibly an operating system for the CDC 6600. I'm sure he also wanted to take over the system. The third effort was a time-sharing system proposed by Norm Hardy. Back in the early 1960's, Norm was invited to spend time at MIT on Project MAC (Multiple Access Computer)—CTSS (compatible time-sharing system) effort. Since Sid had an open door policy, it opened the door to all kinds of individuals to move into someone else's area of responsibility. After learning about all of the scuttlebutt that was floating around and no further word from Seymour, I went to Sid and said that I would only support the operating system proposed by Norm Hardy. Bob Abbot, who was working with Norm, was responsible for designing and implementing the system with a number of other programmers. The name he chose was GOB (Grand Omnificent Benefactor). It seemed that Seymour was not ready to provide specifications of any software, for the System itself would be delayed for several months.

From the beginning, Sid wanted a code to run production as soon as the CDC 6600 was delivered and accepted. Sid, in the meantime, had convinced A-Division to provide an unclassified version of one of its hydro-code. Since Seymour was reluctant to provide any information about the software, we didn't have a programming language for the system to write programs. When I talked to Sid and explained our dilemma, I asked him for additional programmers to help write some software.

Sid said, "Tad, we can't afford it. We have no extra FTEs."

"Sid, I need to start now to make an assembler available for programming, but I need extra help," I asked.

"Well, get started then," he said. "But the Department has no extra FTE's (employees who were Full Time Equivalent) to help you."

What could I do? Once again I looked in the mirror and there he was, the programmer for the assembly routine. For both the LARC and the CDC 6600, I decided I wouldn't go back to the Lab and spend the time designing, coding, and checking out my assembly programs, but work at home with family. For many nights during the Spring of 1963, I sat the kitchen table with Greg and Glen while they did their homework or reading, but I programmed until midnight. Greg was eight years old and Glen was in kindergarten but he enjoyed sitting and reading with us. All of this work had to be done in addition to my supervisory position and as a staff member assisting Sid with his participation in the government's Coordinating Committee (COCOM) dealing with strategic embargo of computers. Under COCOM's evaluations and recommendations, the United States wanted to restrict the access to and the selling of advanced scientific computers to the Soviet Bloc nations. My responsibility was to study and evaluate computers of all sizes and make my recommendations to Sid. My detailed evaluations were based on the computational procedures of large-scale scientific programs for the weapons program.

I needed two programs: an assembler and a 6600 simulator to run on one of The Lab's computers and not face the disaster I had on the LARC to debug my code. Since I had the basic assembler specification from the LARC effort, I changed the specification for the CDC6600 operations and included Macros capability. I met with Norm Hardy and Bob Abbott, proponents of the GOB operating system, and Bill Mansfield and Jeannie Martin, who wanted to write a compiler for the computer. Out of that meeting, further specifications of the assembler came from Bill Mansfield, who wanted complete flexibility for every field in the assembler statement. Only the symbolic location and the pseudo-operation codes were fixed. The assembler was required to allow dropouts, symbolic assignment of registers, and all forms of arithmetic within each field, and allow continuation of the coding line. The cost in processing one line of code was enormous as compared to a fixed format, and because of Bill Mansfield's compiler, it never materialized; the flexibility was a deadly trap causing endless grief for the programmers. However, that was what I had agreed upon when I started.

After reviewing my specification for the code output, I decided that it should be relocatable code consistent with existing compiler output. On our IBM systems, there was already a well-defined relocatable format. I thought "Wouldn't it be nice to be compatible with their format?" I contacted the IBM support group for their advice and specification. The door was shut -- absolutely no cooperation.

Pete Nickolas, who was the only person left in my group, and I began discussing the task before us. My assembler would provide Pete's simulator with an absolute code and data. The simulator would then allow the programmer to execute and print out each instruction, the contents of the registers, and set any flags within the code. Pete wisely chose to use double precision to retain exact comparison with the targeted CDC 6600. The Lab's CDC 6600 contract stipulated a CDC 3600 and a Cray's 1604 as interim computers until the CDC 6600 were installed and operational. We decided that the CDC 3600 was the computer we should use to implement the simulator since it was already available in the local area. However, I needed to generate programs for Pete to simulate. I went to the system programmers on the IBM STRETCH and asked if they could input a restricted specification of our assembler and generate object code for us to run on the CDC 3600. Clarence Badger and Garret Boer quickly modified their Assembler to output CDC6600 code.

There were four separate programming efforts for the computer that were going on in parallel. The GOB group had decided to generate Peripheral Processor Unit (PPU) code using The Lab's DEC PDP1. Pete was generating CDC3600 code for his simulator. I was busy writing the assembler, which I named VIVID. Meanwhile, William Bennett, who was recently hired from The University of Arizona, Tucson, started programming an unclassified version of one of our main hydrodynamics code.

Bill Bennett was a bright, unique individual, and a super programmer. I remember Bill when I went on a recruiting trip for programmers in 1963 to The University of Arizona in Tucson. Right at noon, Bill came dashing into the Recruiting Office wanting an interview. Bill was not on the recruiting schedule, but I proceeded to talk to him during the lunch hour. He said he was a graduate student in the Physics Department, but he was financially in a crisis and needed a job quickly. He was a rare find, and I told him I would send him an application as soon as I returned to Livermore. He was so anxious, he wanted to join the recruiting team immediately and join them going back to Livermore.

I faced the dilemma of using the simulator that was being debugged while attempting to write and check out my assembler. I kept close track of Pete's progress and changed my code as he progressed with his effort. Thus, much of my code retained the coding of my earlier simulator experience. As all programmers experience, Pete had his share of debugging errors. On one occasion, he ran his simulator and looked at the results. There was nothing. He scratched his head and, as all programmers will do, he ran it again. The same result happened. I asked, "Did you make any changes to your simulator?" He said, "I wanted to be sure to have a clean memory and so I wrote a clear memory program before running the simulator." Somehow, his program thoroughly cleared memory for him. We laughed off what had happened, but, of course, I had my share of blunders.

Although Sid had said, "Tad, we can't afford any additional programmers for the CDC6600," several programming efforts had already begun. I didn't have the veracity to tell Sid that I had lured people out of the "Cooler (place where people waited for security clearance)" to work on the GOB effort. There may be other explanations of how we managed to acquire programmers for the large GOB effort but this is my story. The Computation Department always anticipated the programming needs of the Laboratory. Sid, therefore, allowed the Department to hire programmers to fill this need since security clearance took six months to a year to complete. I found that no supervisor was in charge of training nor did any supervisor even bother to visit the new recruits assigned to their group while they were waiting in the "Cooler." I went on a scavenger hunt. Each person I talked to in the cooler was eager to do something besides playing bridge. I explained to the new programmers that I had an unclassified programming project that, if they were willing, could begin immediately for the CDC 6600 on GOB, the operating system. The response was overwhelming. I had my help: Cliff Plopper, Ed Nelson, Shig Tokubo, and one other programmer quickly joined the Gob effort. As it turned out, they proved their worth by their valuable contributions to the project. Yet many years later, people still had the notion that Sid had provided all of the extra help for the GOB effort.

Meanwhile, Seymour and his assistants were busy on the CDC 6600 back at Chippewa Falls, Wisconsin. Very little information came out of their effort. In fact, Seymour had changed the logic of one instruction that I used, but never let me know of the change until I tried VIVID on the computer. Pete Nickolas's simulator proved its worth, for he had done a superb job. I had watched Bill Bennett check out his hydro code using the simulator on the CDC 3600. He was a perpetual motion machine assembling and simulating his code. He had produced a stack of simulator printout of his code and carefully checked his results. When we were back at Chippewa Falls to try out the 6600, his code became a valuable checkout tool for Seymour. Seymour would sit at the 6600 console with Bill to debug the 6600, run Bennett's hydro code, and compare the 6600 results against the simulator output. I saw Seymour jump out of his chair and disappear among the wires of the 6600 bays. It appeared that there was a discrepancy between the 6600 result versus the simulator value. I learned then that timing of bits through the system depended on wire length. As a result, snipped wires fell on the floor and the check out would restart with Seymour back at the console. There was one other action that personnel had to be careful when near the computer. If somebody leaned against the covers of the 6600 computer bays, errors could occur because the capacitance in the system could be affected. When the 6600 was debugged, all of us had a notion that Bill's hydro-code was hard wired into the 6600. One of the most amazing thing I saw happening with the 6600 was, when Seymour decided to go home, he would simple flick the power off switch and walk away as if he was turning off the room lights. The next morning he would turn the power on and continue where he left off the day before.

It was during this period that I became acquainted with Bill Bennett. He told me that he was fifty-fifty American Indian and that his father was a high-level person for the Bureau of Indian Affairs back in Washington, DC. However, Bill was an all-American guy: outgoing, full of energy, and smart. In addition, when he arrived at Chippewa Falls, the first thing he did was to fill his washbasin with the local Leinenkugel beer. How could I not like him?

Seymour was a man of few words when I was assigned to the CDC 6600. At more particular meeting when Bob Abbott joined me to visit Chippewa Falls, he asked Seymour about the disk system. I can't recall the question, but Seymour's answer was clear. When Bob asked about the disk, Seymour said, "I haven't thought about it." There was absolute silence for several uneasy moments. Poor Bob was left hanging and swaying in the wind and I couldn't throw him a lifeline. After the CDC 6600 was checked out and accepted, Seymour asked me if I had any thoughts about the system. While writing VIVID, I included a timing output of the object code such that a programmer could optimize critical loops by rearranging the coding sequence. I had a good understanding about the timing of programs and so I said to Seymour, "If you had one more register to pre-fetch data including instructions, you could gain twenty percent in executing a code." He smiled for the first time and said, "I thought about that too and it will be in my next computer."

Sid Fernbach, Tad Kishi
6600 Acceptance Test

One could easily get used to the easygoing life in Wisconsin, especially, around Chippewa Falls. While waiting for the final checkout of the 6600 and running the acceptance test, local beer and Colby cheese can be a tough combination to match. It seems that each town has its own home-brewed beer and if you mistakenly order another burg's beer, they will look at you with disdain and simply ignore your order. Leinenkugel Brewing Company was established in 1867: finest beer ever in Chippewa Falls.

The Lab's contract called for a set sequence of tests for acceptance. Pete and I, who had set up the tests, were diligently following the contract requirements when I received a call from Sid. "Tad, quit running the acceptance test and get the damn computer out here!" Sid said in no uncertain terms.

The CDC 6600 brought a new era in computer usage and finally in the Computation Department supervisory structure. First, during the check out of the 6600, Seymour learned firsthand how the Lab runs large-scale scientific calculations on computers. He and his staff had written his version of the operating system and his FORTRAN compiler. He believed that the on-line printer was sufficient to handle the results of computations. Everyone tried to convince him that we needed to write output to tapes for our high-speed tape system (HSP). Seymour was adamant about his understanding of large-scale scientific computations. As soon as Bill Bennett's hydro code was running production, the on-line printer never stopped. His super CDC 6600 was running at printer speed. Seymour finally conceded that we were right about high-speed output.

As soon as the 6600 was accepted, Bob Abbott and his crew began debugging GOB. Meanwhile, I was tracking down the last bug in VIVID. While all of this was going on, I noticed that the programmers working with GOB would suddenly disappear and come back with changes to their code. When I asked what was going on, they said they were using the DEC PDP1 to reassemble their PPU code. I must have been brain dead when I wrote the specs for VIVID. The

CDC 6600 consists of the CPU instruction set and the PPU (Peripheral Processor Unit). I said to the GOB programmers that I can introduce a pseudo-op to assemble PPU coding and output punched cards for them right on the system if they would provide me with specs. The changes only required setting up a hash table for the PPU instruction set and providing punch card output. I'm sure the addition of PPU code saved a lot of shoe leather.

The second major change came when Norm Hardy programmed the GOB system to interface with teletypes as input to GOB. Where upon time-sharing became a reality at the Lab. Hans Bruijnes and his staff was also busy trying to install their IBM version of the Batch System Monitor 400 on the 6600. There was a power struggle for the system resources between GOB and Monitor 400 if not the control of the 6600.

The following is Bob Abbott's quote:

"Hans Bruijnes wanted it all for the Monitor. And I said, 'Do what you want, but I'm taking it.' Indeed, his Monitor was incompatible with what we had done. After we were up and running, Hans had to change his Monitor so that it used GOB. He reverted to being one of the programs serviced by the round robin method of GOB."

Meanwhile Abbott had made an agreement with Sid that he did not wish to continue maintaining and upgrading GOB forever. GOB was written in a series of macros, available in VIVID that was as close to FORTRAN as possible. The era of System Development versus Application Programming began to take form. Hans and his team began taking charge of the GOB system and reprogramming it into FORTRAN with the Lab's extended language capability. The result was a new acronym was born: FROST (FORTRAN Resident Operating System for Time Sharing). Later, LTSS was the follow up of FROST. But the credit goes to Norm Hardy's proposal and Bob Abbott's implementation of The Lab's time sharing system with the help of many individuals who were waiting for clearance, left unwanted, and unassigned, happy to have something to do, and I was happy to give it to them. While Sid left me holding the empty bag, I met each deadline: assembly program called SAIL for the LARC and VIVID for the CDC 6600. In the end, and to my delight and relief, the production codes were also running upon delivery.

By the end of 1960's, the Lab had acquired so many computers, other computer installations were envious and called LRL as a "Museum of Computers." However, museum was a misnomer. It was not a repository for computers but a place where the state of the art was advanced to meet every challenging need for the seamless access of compute power, storage, and output. After all, there was a war on with the Soviet Bloc, cold but real. Even the Computation Department was morphing into a new organization flowing with energy of change. The computers, output, storage, and remote stations were networked together and made accessible at a user terminal. The concept was called the Octopus system that was home grown and evolved over the years. Timesharing was born on the CDC 6600 and a FORTRAN, compatible across the large-scale computers, was designed and implemented on the IBM computer systems.

Supervision by computer system no longer made sense. Sid decided that Computation Department reorganizes into Systems and Applications. From that day on, a constant struggle between the two branches of the Department was born: Who is more important, who is more valuable, and who should be rewarded during the salary discussion? I observed that a broad brush was used to paint an individual's worth and it was inversely proportional to the distance to the Department head. Therefore, the Systems group believed that they were the anointed ones and everyone, regardless of their assignment, was better than any Application programmers were.

At our next supervisor's meeting, Sid told us that the Department was changing the Supervisor's assignment. Then he told us what are new assignments would be.

I was apprehensive because I was always involved in both of the parts that he mentioned by the nature of my past and existing assignments. As I looked around, all of the supervisors were looking at each other with questioned looks, and just waiting for what would be in store for each of us. The Lab prided itself for its matrix structure where various departments had been supporting projects and programs, and now, following Sid's changes, people in Applications would become an integral part of that matrix system. However, the matrix system was never pure, and more often, used when it was convenient for the Programs and Projects. Previously, the assignment of people centered on computers came from the scientist that each work for. Thus their direct supervision and performance evaluation were always indirect leaving much to be desired for the employee's welfare. Sid had divided the supervision of personnel into an equal number of people by examining the number of people supporting each of the Lab's Departments, Projects, and Programs.

I was no longer in charge of the CDC 6600 where my assembly program, VIVID and Time Sharing were born, but now in charge of programmers and technicians for Earth Science, Test Programs, Bio-Med, and High Energy (Laser) programs. However, support for my VIVID never died since it was written for a major user, and Sid's COCOM participation still remained as one of my responsibilities. All of the assignment of "you are in charge of" never came with a posting, or a formal title, or change in rating, or an increase salary. Only the department head and his assistant were recognized in the Lab's personnel structure and the rest were responsibilities that Sid had assigned. Since there was never a formal Lab announcement for each of the changes in responsibilities, I couldn't show or tell Yo, "I've been promoted." However, I was glad that Sid never micromanaged and our new roles were left for us to define. In my new assignment, I would be interacting closely with the programs and project I was supporting.

One day, I was talking to a programmer supporting chemistry, who I remembered from my earlier supervisory assignment of the IBM 701, and asked her how the new department reorganization was working out for her and others. When she said her new supervisor had never stopped by, I was stunned. Later, I talked to Sid and said that since the other supervisor hadn't bothered to look after the programmers supporting chemistry, I would gladly take over that responsibility. The treatment and the well-being of people were important to me and I wanted no one left to wither on the vine.

The Computation Department had a certain minimum requirement of math or science courses for hiring college graduates as math/programmers. Sid had created the category of computer technician and computer operators, people who had at least two years of college; to meet the need to operate and support the scientists with their computer related workload. These individuals could apply for advancement to math/programmer provided they completed their college degree with math and science courses. The advancement was not automatic. It had to be earned. While I was the supervisor for Earth Science support, I promoted one technician to math/programmer for he met the requirements and demonstrated in his programming skills.

At the time of the promotion, I explained to him danger of promotion from technician to programmer. "As a technician, you are currently evaluated as excellent. However, when promoted, you will be ranked with the rest of the programmers, and most likely be placed initially at the bottom of the heap."

"Do you really want to take that step and compete when there are other avenues of promotion in the technician grades?" I asked him.

"Yes," he said. "I want to be a programmer."

Later when I reviewed his performance, the physicist he worked with gave him more programming responsibilities, and he met every challenge. I had no doubts that he would be successful as a programmer and I was right. The project he supported was pleased with his work as a programmer and his dedication to their effort. It was a promotion well deserved.

Around 1970, another individual, working in the same group, had attended the same local college and graduated with a BA degree. After noting that his co-worker was promoted to math/programmer, he assumed that he was next in line for promotion. I reviewed his qualifications with his lead programmer and determined that he didn't qualify.

He said, "You promoted another computer technician in the same group after he got a degree from the same college. I graduated too and I should be promoted like him."

I had to explain to him that he had no knowledge of the other technician's qualifications on which to base his claim. I was forced to review his record. His performance as a technician was satisfactory, but the classes he took did not meet Computation Department's hiring standard. He had taken no math or basic science classes. I saw only crafts, arts, and Hispanic studies in his college transcript. LLNL was a science and engineering research laboratory and his classes reflect nothing to support them in their work. It was my responsibility for each one in my division for their welfare and future. I told him I could not promote him on his qualification.

After hearing my words, I saw the employee's expressionless face as he walked out of my office.

Later, I received word from the scientists he supported attempting to pressure me for his promotion. The politically correct do-gooders of the 1970's, who have no responsibility for his future, wanted me to concede with respect to affirmative action. I refused in his best interest, because he would surely fail as a programmer.

During another visit in 1971 with the Earth Science Division Leader, Joe Knox informed me that the Advanced Research Project Agency (ARPA) wanted his division to reprogram TENSOR, an unclassified hydrodynamics code for the ILLIAC IV that was being installed at NASA Ames, Moffett Field, California around 1970. He wanted my input on whether his group should become involved. Since I was studying large-scale scientific computers, I knew about the ILLIAC IV. It was parallel processing system that was a cousin to LRL's CDC STAR's vector processor. It was built with the same electronic technology of the STAR, discrete components. It was huge in size like the STAR and it had the same failure rate. System software was University born – esoteric but not practical. Except for an antiquated teletype, access to the computer was non-existent. It was during this era that ARPA was promoting the ARPA-net (birth of the internet) that was still being developed. After presenting the cold hard facts, I said to Joe, "At a minimum, you must allocate a physicist, two or more programmers, and a computer technician from your limited staff." I told him with only a Teletype, at 10 characters per second, accessing and looking at output on a two –dimensional code would tie up his Division's resources for years. There was no provision for storage and visual or printed output to be productive. I watched Joe's expression while gave him the facts. He seemed non-committal, but I noted later that Earth Science had declined ARPA's request. At least that's what I thought.

I've been Gored to death
ARPA not user friendly
Job tried by Satan

ARPA/ILLIAC IV

It was several months later during 1971 when Sid called me into his office and said, "Tad, I want you to give up your supervisory position and take on another job." I thought, *here we go again. What's next Sid?*

"I want you to take charge of programming the TENSOR code for the ILLIAC IV under an ARPA contract," said Sid.

That was a bombshell dropped on me! I had to think fast to get out of this nightmare.

"Sid," I said, "There are more qualified programmers than me to do this job. In fact, I told him Val Kransky had been working with the TENSOR code from the very beginning from the IBM 704 to the CDC 6600 for almost fifteen years. In fact, he and Jerry Owens had been studying how to vectorize the code. Surely, he can get the job done quicker than I can."

I was pacing in front of Sid's desk like a cornered animal in a cage. It must have been an amusing sight for Sid to observe for I saw a slight grin on his face that he normally didn't show.

Sid leaned back and said, " No, Tad, I want you to do the job!"

I thought for a moment, there's one other poor guy who could do the job.

"Sid, I said, "How about Harry Nelson. I heard from other programmers that he did a superior job with CORONET for the STRETCH!"

"No, Tad, I have selected you to do the job."

Then, I decided to tell him why I was so reluctant to do the assignment. I told him about my conversation with Joe Knox.

Several months ago, I told Sid, I had had a conversation with Joe Knox, Division Leader of Earth Science, about the use of the ILLIAC IV for the TENSOR code. He told me that the Advanced Research Project Agency (ARPA) had approached him to take on a contract to program the TENSOR code for the ILLIAC IV and he asked me for my advice. I advised him not to assume the burden of programming for the ILLIAC IV. He'd need a full time computational physicist. Second, he'd need one, but most likely, three programmers, and eventually, a production assistant. In addition, I told Joe that my final assessment was even worse because he could only access the ILLIAC IV system remotely by means of a Teletype at ten characters per second. I had seen no provision for storing the mass of data from the code or any provision for hardcopy output. It was a losing proposition.

Sid let me rant on and on with my reluctance for the assignment. Then he said, "APRA has a number of contracts with the Laboratory and they are pressuring the Directors to take on this task or they will have to reassess some of their contracts with the Lab."

He reached into his desk and handed me a memorandum from ARPA to Mike May, Director of LLNL. ARPA was indeed pressuring the Lab to take on this task at all cost.

"OK, Sid, I'll do it but I need fixed target, code and problem, with all the current documentation to proceed with the job," I answered reluctantly.

"Sure, Tad," he said and got out of his chair, turned around and picked up an armful of FORTRAN listing of the TENSOR code. It was fourteen inches high of solid computer printout.

"Here Tad, this is your documentation of the code," he replied.

I thought this is not exactly what I wanted. What I needed was a write-up of the code and the numerical equations to begin preliminary mapping of the code on a multi-processor computer. I reached over and took the pile of FORTRAN listings and left.

It was apparent that Sid had made up his mind long before because when I returned to my office, I received a call from his secretary (Administrative Assistant) that I was expected to leave for ARPA's Headquarters in Washington DC to present a talk on the Laboratory's ARPA/TENSOR project. This was an unpleasant turn of event for me. However, ARPA had the Lab by its contracts and, consequently, Sid had already decided that I was the one who could fulfill the contract for the Lab.

The trip back to ARPA Headquarters in Washington DC was a big surprise since I would have assumed that the presentation should have been the responsibility of the TENSOR code physicist. I had no other directives about the meeting and I was to report immediately. Programming the TENSOR code did not scare me, but the eighty thousand lines of FORTRAN listing was useless input to assess the numerical model for the ILLIAC IV. I left the listings in the corner of my room. Then, I quickly made contact with Val Kransky, the programmer, and Ted Cherry, the code physicist for the TENSOR code. Ted was already aware of the ARPA contract and gave me UCRL documents for the code. He said the unclassified version of the code would be used for seismic studies but the numerical technique was the same for the classified and unclassified versions. We discussed what might be a reasonable test program to consider for the ILLIAC IV.

With the information at hand, I mapped out the memory requirements based on my knowledge of how many instructions a typical hydro-code executes during one cycle of computation. The ILLIAC IV placed certain limitations on the computation and storage since it consisted of sixty-four processors running in lock step fashion. I drew my view graphs, and wrote my presentation.

I had to hurry home to tell Yo about the bombshell dropped on me and that I had to fly back to Washington DC. There wasn't time to rest or tell Yo the whole story since I had a red-eye flight out of San Francisco that night. I flew into Dulles Airport, rented a car, and headed for Department of Defense ARPA Headquarters. After going through the usual red tape of clearances, I headed for the conference room. There I met my contract sponsor, Col. Russell. I waited for my turn to present my TENSOR Project. There couldn't have been more than two dozen attendees, majority in uniforms with fruit bowls full of medals showing. They were attentive, but when I asked if anyone had any question about my project, nobody raised a hand. I was puzzled to know if anyone actually understood what the ARPA/TENSOR project was about or what was sort of effort involved. I left quickly feeling a bit frustrated and knowing that this trip was a waste of my time.

When I returned, I asked Sid for at least two additional programmers to tackle this eighty thousand lined behemoth. This time he didn't hesitate and allowed me to choose my assistants. From my previous supervisory assignment, I had a good idea who I considered to be good candidates to work with me. I met with Landon Bruce, who was assigned to Bio-Med and had worked with Stuart Stone on a digital analysis of chromosomes, and asked him if he would join me on the TENSOR Project. Over the years, I had observed Landon working with Stuart and, if you knew Stone and managed to take his overly demanding abuse, you were indeed a dedicated programmer. There was one other individual who had joined my previous assignment but I had very little knowledge of him. He was just starting an assignment for chemistry so I hooked him. He was Bill Derby.

Little did Landon or Bill knew what they were getting into on this assignment. Neither had any experience with large-scale numerical code like the TENSOR two-dimensional hydrodynamics model. My own experience was "Cherry Pie," a two dimensional Lagrangian Hydro-code which I programmed for the IBM 701 for the physicist, Bob Jastrow when I started working at the Lab in 1953. The document, a ton of FORTRAN listing, gathered dust in the corner, and useless for planning the programming for parallel computer architecture.

In the meantime, Ted Cherry was busy reviewing the TENSOR code and its probable use as a seismic computational model on the ILLIAC IV. The TENSOR code had a long history with most of the effort dedicated to the Weapons effort. Many changes were made on the spur of the moment and, therefore, little if any documentation of the addition or changes were ever recorded. The listing showed very little clues to changes. The usual scenario for changes occurred as follows: the physicist would worked furiously to make changes in the physics and, about four thirty in the afternoon, rush into the programmer's office and pressure him to make the changes and run the code on scheduled production time that night. The programmer would sweat the time out to make the changes, recompile or patch the code, and set up the production run in time to go home for the day or miss dinner with the family. Under those conditions, it was always foreseeable that the names of variables would become jumbled. After all, who could remember all of the symbolic names used in eighty thousand lines of FORTRAN statements?

Ted Cherry intended to do it right this time. The dual-purpose model for weapons and seismic applications wouldn't do for the ARPA application. He decided to write a new numerical model reflecting more accurate modeling of seismic application by changing the coordinate system. Each coordinate would be replaced by an origin and a displacement variable. However, this computational model was a two-dimensional finite difference scheme whose independent variables were distance and time. Every equation had to reflect Ted's new approach.

My fixed target for the assignment was shot full of holes. Even worse, the three of us waited while Ted made his changes and provided us with is new equations. The whole process was a nightmare. Meanwhile, we began to examine some of the so-called documentation that Val Kransky and his associates provided us. There was some attempt to document part of the code, but the write-up proved worthless because the writer, a computer technician, used variable names that often matched nothing within the code.

Then only one month into the project in 1971, the next bomb dropped! Ted Cherry must have been frustrated with this ARPA assignment and decided to quit! He left for a company near San Diego called S^3.

I had just started this contract, and now I was left holding this bag empty of anything useful to carry out my assignment from Sid. There were three options: 1) Quit. 2) Go to Sid and ask for another job. 3) Go back to Joe Knox and ask for another physicist. Without an ace in the hole, a firm offer from outside of the Lab, the first two options for me were fraught with danger, for I would have to be prepared to leave the Lab. Finding a job was not the problem. Uprooting the family and home that Yo and I had established in Livermore would have been devastating for us. We had been through so much to create the two most important things in our lives: a stable and secure family life for our children. If I had to move, I would again be faced with the bane of my life, housing. The third option would mean months before Earth Science could find a new physicist to take on the job. What physicist would consider an assignment that was going nowhere? When I told Landon and Bill, I could see a drain of their lifeblood in their faces. However, there was a fourth option. I would not accept *shikata ga nai*, can't be helped, but do what was instilled in me from my parents, *Gaman*, endure this unforeseen event. I would not be defeated. I would take on the responsibility of the Physicist in the third option. I met with Sid and told him what had happened and said, "I will carry out the Lab's commitment to ARPA by taking on the role as Computational Physicist and finish the job."

Sid looked at me and, with his deep words of wisdom and a man of few words, doubtfully he said, "Ok."

From my previous work with "Cherry Pie" for Bob Jastrow, I had a firm understanding what the job would require. I had no doubt that I could do the job as code physicist because, from the day I started my career, I had continued to study numerical methods, attended lectures at the University of California Extension in the evenings on computational methods, gave seminars on computational techniques to my programmers, and attended graduate classes on computational physics at various universities. There was nothing magical about the finite difference scheme. Starting with Ted Cherry's partial effort on his new scheme, I began my task with Ted Cherry's UCRL report on the Tensor code. I rewrote all three phases: Equations of Motion, Constitutive Equations, and Slide Lines. While all three require adjacent points in the finite difference scheme, the slide line calculation required search for nearest neighbors and construction of equivalent point values followed by calculating the first two phases. The task was a challenge, a task that I had not envisioned. I was confident that I would succeed.

I was fortunate that I did not have to worry about the family, since our family life was stable, and that Greg and Glen were doing well in their respective schools. Yo, in the meantime, was occupying her free hours by pursuing her sewing interest. Once she told me her class was held at Camp Parks in one of the abandoned barracks building. Because the old barracks provided no privacy, she said there were some hilarious and embarrassing moments when they had to try on their sewing projects in class. I saw Yo, true to form, keeping meticulous notes and sewing samples that others in the class treasured.

I assigned Bill Derby to program the Equations of Motion, Landon Bruce the Constitutive equations, and I took on the challenge of the Slide lines, which was the most difficult phase of the TENSOR code. All three of us worked on the plan of attack, but my new job also required me to prepare and present reports for ARPA Progress meetings. Meanwhile, Sid would slip data for me to prepare for his COCOM meetings. I had undertaken a huge task, but I was determined to meet the challenge. I read and reread Ted Cherry's technical report on the slide lines, because it was an unusual computational method.

There were two options for us to program the code. First was an assembly program called ASK. The second was a higher-level language call GLYPNIR. Both were ALGOL based since Burroughs Corporation was always ALGOL based. Students at the University of Illinois had programmed both. We discarded GLYPNIR because the results from users indicated that the compiler produced such a large code that either the code ran at snail pace or memory was swamped with little room for data.

Once we were at the stage of checking our code, ARPA provided all ILLIAC IV users computer time to simulate the ILLIAC IV by using the Burroughs 6000 series computers at several locations: University of Illinois, University of California San Diego, and UC Davis. The disadvantage was that the simulated code ran 400,000 to one slower in code execution. While simulation went at snail pace, just to look at the output was horrendous. A hydro-code can have as much as twenty variables while sixty-four processors of the ILLIAC IV are chomping on the data in parallel. Without some judicious approach, the output from sixty-four processors would swamp all of the output resource of the three University computer facilities.

There were several other limitations that made our life difficult. We had no computer at the Lab to check out our programming and required traveling to a university site where we had no priority. Until the start of this project in 1971, all of my program compiling and check-out had been with "hands on" experience where I was in absolute control of operating the computer. This was the first experience of handing my program on punched cards across a counter to an operator to run my code. I was at the operator's mercy. On our first try, the operating system rejected our program deck because of the inconsistency of character representation on the punched cards. We were faced with three character sets: Burroughs BCL, IBM's EBCDIC, and standard ASCII. In order to set up the runtime code with punched cards for the Burroughs B6700, we had to make sure that we were using Burroughs character representation, BCL. Not all keypunching equipment punched the same code on the IBM cards. Most of the Lab's keypunchers were set to ASCII, but there was EBCDIC also. It was frustrating; because it was difficult to know which character representation was on the card until you submitted your program to the operator to run. That led to a series of comical errors that cost us valuable machine time. This was also the first time I learned the term "Flakey" for a computer running with errors. We also had to contend with "Bomb Threats" because there were rumors at the universities that the three of us were from Livermore Lab developing a nuclear bomb code. The cloud of the Vietnam War was haunting us everywhere we went when we went to use the university computers. This was in spite of the non-weapons application of the TENSOR code.

While LLNL was vilified as the Nuclear Weapons laboratory, the threat of nuclear war had been a primary concern of the United States since World War II. I remember when I was with ATIS/MIS in Tokyo, Japan in 1948; our MIS interpreters questioned ex-Japanese soldiers returning from Siberia about Soviet Russia military installations, especially, nuclear facilities. My COCOM assignment for Sid had been to assess the capabilities of computers system that should be banned for use by Soviet Bloc nations to develop nuclear weapons. To believe that nuclear threat was impossible was pure fantasy.

During the 1970s, on every August 6, the anniversary of the first atomic bomb blast on Hiroshima, a small crowd would gather in the open lot in front of our house and march down East Avenue to demonstrate against nuclear weapons research. There were odd looking people with banners, caskets, grim reaper costumes, and a mock atomic bomb marching in a straggly line towards the Lab. Sometimes I heard a Buddhist monk beating a drum with one note, "bong, bong," as he walked with the crowd. A few brought little toddlers to march with them. When they reached the Lab, they would try to intimidate people from going to work. Some would line up together and try to barricade the access to the Lab, only to be arrested. The Lab was not a bomb factory, but a Federal Government research and development facility for nuclear weapons under the patronage of the University to keep America safe. All of these demonstrations that occurred year after year were amusing if not sad, for their naiveté.

In the meantime, Mel Pirtle and his crew were busy trying to get the ILLIAC IV up and running with the help of Burroughs Corporation engineers. The crew was highly unprofessional.

Each time we went to the ILLIAC IV Project office, the sweet smell of marijuana wafted in the air. We also heard from the CSC representative, who was assigned to the ILLIAC IV project, the rumor of the day, "Who's sleeping with whose wife or secretary?"

After two long years, we completed our programming and simulation. We were anxious to use the computer, even in its unfinished condition. It was nothing new to me since I had been there with the IBM 701, the LARC, and the CDC 6600 before they were completed. We even volunteered to use the ILLIAC IV in whatever state they were available to help them debug the system.

Our offer was rejected. In fact, one of Mel Pirtle's programmers wanted to change the programming language that would negate two years of hard work for every one with an ARPA contract. I immediately drew up a straw-man memorandum addressed to Col. Russell, set up a meeting with all ILLIAC IV users, and finalized our protest to the extreme programming changes.

For the last ARPA progress meeting, I asked my sponsor, Col. Russell whether I should tell it like it is. He agreed that I should.

At the meeting, all hell broke loose when I told the truth about what was happening to the software. In rebuttal, Mel Pirtle talked about "Wholesalers and Retailers." I wasn't sure if I was a wholesaler or retailer because his gibberish made no sense to me. The project then put pressure on ARPA to terminate our contract. They thought they had me by the "contract." Col. Russell didn't have the guts to talk to me. After all, I had asked him before the meeting to tell what the changes in software meant to the users. I did not point a finger at any one person. It was the first time in my whole career that I stepped forward, proposed a meeting of the users. I drew up a preliminary document in order to save two years of effort by those all ready committed towards making the ILLIAC IV project a success. I had not taken my assignment lightly for the Laboratory. The job required each of us to spend time away from our families to use computers at UC San Diego, UC Davis, and as far as the University of Illinois, and even deal with bomb threats. All of this sweat was for naught. All I could say was thank goodness for releasing me from a useless effort!

Colorless Rainbow
My world is for the better
Glad you came my way

The Best in People

Sid wasn't too concerned when he heard that ARPA had cancelled the TENSOR contract, for he had been pressured to take on the task and the effort that did not help the Computation Department in any way. I was not disappointed or disheartened that the contract was terminated, but I was angry with my sponsor Col. Russell for his non-support when he agreed that I should be forthright with my presentation. I had not taken my commitment lightly to meet LLNL's obligation. I had no regrets about the cancellation of the contract, for I was satisfied that I had put my best effort forward and had met the ARPA/ILLIAC IV assignment in spite of all of the obstacles and disappointment I faced from the start.

Yet, I gained something from this software effort. First, I found that the quality of programming that was given to me was worthless. While the programs were supposedly written in the higher-level language, FORTRAN, it was, in fact, a brute force conversion of assembly code into FORTRAN. There was no attempt to utilize the advantage of FORTRAN or use simple mathematical techniques that would have enhanced the performance of the code. In addition, the documents proved totally useless. Finally, by studying the set of partial differential equations, I found that vectorizing and/or parallel processing for this application could be better achieved by applying the physics together with mathematics to the application.

Not all was lost. My experience with programming for the ILLIAC IV led me to write a paper for the February 1975 IEEE/COMPCON Computer Conference in San Francisco on my experience to write parallel/vector code of the TENSOR code. I named my talk, "STAR TREK," as a play on the words for my arduous journey to program for the vector computer, CDC STAR. I had to battle "Klingons," rather "cling on" to destroy obsolete programming. I had my audience mesmerized; yet I was still surprised when I won the best paper for that conference. I was also invited to Texas A & M to give that same paper.

As usual, Sid was busy with a proposal to establish a national computer center for magnetic fusion research at the Laboratory. Sid asked me to write the computer specification and conduct an evaluation of a vendor's computer operating system for the center. One day, after Livermore was selected for the computer center and the contract was signed, Sid came to my office and said, "Tad, I have to post this position for Magnetic Fusion Energy Computer Center Software Supervisor." At first, he seemed reluctant to let me read it, but he handed to me and said, "Read this, Tad, but I don't want you to apply."

That was the first time I had seen a posting for a position at the Laboratory where I wasn't qualified before it was posted. It was too bad that I didn't have an ace up my sleeve to tell Sid, "Thanks, but no thanks. I'm quitting."

Throughout the specification and evaluation of the computer center effort, I worked with Dieter Fuss and Hans Bruijnes. I had sensed that both of them wanted a share in the Magnetic Fusion Energy Computer Center operation. On the other hand, I had no interest in running the computer center, but it would have been nice for Sid to give me a choice. Physicist, John Killeen, was named the director, Hans as his assistant, and Dieter for software development.

It seems that Sid had something else in mind for my next assignment. In 1974, I had been assigned the Principal Investigator for Energy Research and Development Administration (ERDA), Division of Physical Research. The task, to investigate problem formulation and advanced computer architectures using parallel and vector processors. That did not release me from Sid's COCOM work. In fact, my new assignment would complement the COCOM effort. In retrospect, maybe Sid had been worried that I would no longer be able to assist him on his pet projects if I had applied and accepted for the MFECC posting. However, I recall that there were two other individuals that were assigned to evaluate the various vendors' software and operating system with me who dearly wanted the newly created position. Sid always had an open door policy and sometimes things happened without the full knowledge of the rest of his staff. I am sure if I had applied, he would have had a difficult decision to make based on qualifications of the applicants. The MFECC was national center for research and the posting was required formality, but Sid had the power to choose.

Then in 1976, came a *tsunami* through the Computation Department. The major user of the CDC STAR continued to express their frustration with the CDC STAR's poor reliability and the difficulty of programming for it. From Sid's point of view, the STAR was an experiment: the first step into vector and, therefore, parallel processing. In the late 1960's, design of computers to achieve higher and higher performance had reached a level of complexity, and only the next step of vector processing could bring about significant gains in computational throughput. However, we were naive. Our early studies of vector concepts were conducted by using IBM's Array Processing Language, APL. It did not give the user any realistic idea of the throughput on execution since it was an interpretive language. Soon the studies became how clever you could write your code in APL rather than a deeper understanding of how well it executed on our numerical codes. We had a lot to learn and had unwittingly based our assessment on the simple assumption about our computational models and mapped it onto the vector processor. When CDC offered a second STAR as a consolation for the poor performance, Sid couldn't resist the bargain. Sid was now in the hot seat. One STAR was bad enough. Two STARs dimmed Sid's future. Politics loomed its ugly head. There were always subtle rumors about why Sid had not been promoted to Associate Director when clearly his role and contributions to the mission of the Laboratory deserved that status. People who were jealous of Sid's power in his position as Computation Department Head began a movement to replace him. The Director of the Laboratory, Roger Batzel, formerly Associate Director of Chemistry, placed his successor, Gus Dorough, Associate, Director of Chemistry, over Sid. The axe fell and the reorganization of the Department was announced.

I had watched the whole ugly scene unfold. When I visited Sid's office, Sid was sitting quietly with a stern look listening to Gus Dorough and his Assistant Associate director. It was a difficult moment for me to see my boss, who had led the Laboratory to be the foremost computer center of the world, treated so poorly. There had been bad blood between the Chemistry Department and Computation Department before all of this happened. At one time, Sid had asked me, together with Bill Wattenburg, an outside consultant, to assess the Chemistry Department's request to establish their own computer center. The consultant had recommended against their proposal because it would require manpower and resources that would eventually reduce the effectiveness of the Laboratory's Computer Center to support the Weapons Program. So now here was the Chemistry Department Head exacting a kind of revenge and now dictating the demise of Sid's future. When the reorganization had been officially announced at the Department meeting, I had only heard the focus of the Department was simply on computer reliability and not one iota on providing more powerful and capable computer systems for the primary computational needs of the Laboratory: Nuclear Weapons Research and Development. I was stunned because the Computation Department would be without a rudder, sitting in still waters, and going nowhere.

When I returned home and told Yo the terrible thing that had happened to Sid, she was shocked and asked me what Sid was going to do? Yo had met Sid at one of the Computation Department picnic and he was cordial and very friendly towards her. At the time, I too worried about his future, but Sid was well known in the computer industry and the government. He was the icon in advancing our country toward more powerful and capable computer systems. Later, he worked with Control Data and was an advisor for IEEE, and when I became Division Leader, I kept close contact with him and supported his effort with the IEEE supercomputer conferences.

Dr. Teller and Sid had always persuaded and encouraged computer companies to push the state of the art in order to provide the Laboratory with the most powerful computer for weapons design. Faster and faster has been the goal because there has been no upper bound for supercomputers for scientific applications. The LARC and the STRETCH was beginning of the thrust for supercomputers. Without Sid's help for Seymour Cray to find the backing to produce the CDC6600 for LLNL and followed by the CDC7600, the Laboratory's supercomputing capability would not have advanced significantly and Livermore's timesharing system may not have been realized for sometime later.

After Sid was sidelined, the Division Leaders, who had been selected by Sid, immediately abandoned the torpedoed ship. Bob Lee, who had been the supervisor for graphics group, was selected to replace Sid as Department Head. He announced that his mission was to bring stability into the Department's computer system project and reliability to the STAR computers.

Now that Sid had been ousted, I was in an awkward position because I had devoted twenty-three years helping Sid as supervisor, Project Leader, and with his vital COCOM effort for the US Government and all that undoubtedly would mean nothing to the new Department Head. I had to review my options and make an immediate decision. I even wondered if I should have been more selfish about my own future rather than believing that I was doing something productive for the Laboratory. My roots were firmly established in Livermore when our two sons had been just reaching their high school years when I had first considered quitting. Changing jobs would not have been an easy one or my first choice. Surely, a decision to leave the Lab would have been devastating news for Yo. However, my old supervisory position, which I had left five years before to take on the ARPA contract in 1971 for the Laboratory Directors, had been upgraded to the Division status as Application Programming Division 1 (APD1). I saw this as an opportunity to regain the position of Division Leader. It was August 1976 when I submitted my resume to the new Department Head, Bob Lee, who subsequently accepted me as the new Division Leader of APD1.

Under the circumstance, the appointment could not have been better for my family, for Greg and Glen were attending UC Davis. Our lives would not be upended and our sons would have a stable home to rely on a place where their roots had taken hold. In addition, I had returned to a familiar territory.

This time, the Division Leader status gave me limited autonomy, with an office, administrative staff, and a modest operational budget. When I visited my new office, it was empty, and Pat Gray, the former Division Leader and his administrative staff placed all files in locked cabinets. They had not had the courtesy to bring me up to date on the Division's status. They had simply abandoned ship without consideration for the welfare of the personnel they had been supporting. Rather than dwelling on the poor communication from the previous APD1 staff, I had more urgent things to take care of. I immediately posted positions for secretary and administrative staff in order to bring life back to the Division.

Meanwhile, Bob Lee was making some changes of his own in Sid's old office. Bob Lee immediately asked the Department Secretary to find another position. He summarily dismissed her, not because of her performance, but he said he didn't like her life style. I was appalled.

I was aware that she was trying to find her way after a difficult divorce, but her actions away from the Laboratory had never affected her performance as the Department Secretary for Sid. When she saw my posting, she applied. The Department Head's loss was a gift, for I filled the most important position for my Division with a dedicated and excellent secretary. We talked about what had transpired and that she might look ahead for herself. I told her, "I had observed over the years at the Lab that, when reorganization occurs, the secretarial staff was treated poorly or ignored." I suggested that maybe I could work towards enlarging her responsibilities to advance her to a higher classification. After our discussions, she entered a degree program with the local college in the evenings and received a BA. I followed through with my promise to enlarge her responsibilities.

When the Department change took place, Bob Lee terminated the RISOS security project and ERDA's advanced high performance project that I had been working on for Sid. I took a tour of my building to see what space was available for my Division. The rats had abandoned ship. Among the discarded computer output, manuals, and supplies strewn carelessly about, I saw a young woman busy trying to make headway with all the discarded items.

"Hi," I said. "What happen here? Where is everyone?"

She said, "The Department terminated the RISOS Project (a security software project) and everyone left. Some quit the Laboratory and others were transferred to other positions."

"What about yourself?" I asked. "Didn't someone from the Department come to see you about another assignment?"

"No. No one has said anything to me. In fact, no one from the Department has called me or bothered to tell me anything." She replied. "I'm just trying to clean up the mess."

I was shocked once more at the *haji* of managers. How could the Lab treat people so poorly? I mused while I was angered in my heart for this disgraceful behavior.

"Sherry, pick up your things and forget the mess. You are working for me as of now."

At home, both Greg and Glen were doing well in school and Yo, with time on her hands, enrolled at our local Chabot Community College and signed up for a few courses in homemaking and sewing. Throughout the 1970's, she concentrated on her interest in tailoring. She took meticulous notes and made samples of each new topic in the class. She told me that members of her class wanted to use her binders full of examples because she had taken the time to detail each step. She was exacting in her sewing just like her writing that was letter perfect. I couldn't help but notice how animated and an expressive face she had when she talked about her sewing class, teachers, and students. I was somewhat jealous to know what went on in those classes, but happy to know that she filled her empty hours with what she enjoyed doing. It was also the period when I was pleasantly surprised with our sons' achievements in school.

Around 1981, the era of Personal Computers was also just beginning, but software was lacking. I had acquired an IBM personal computer for processing salary data. When office staff saw the PC, they were curious about the new beast. One day, I took a few minutes to introduce the IBM PC to the secretarial staff. I pointed out to them that they had been doing the equivalent of programming but didn't realize it. For instance, the scheduling of daily activities, the decisions, and results they expected from their effort was just the same as what programmers do, only the language was different. The simple explanation must have had some effect on the young woman that I found abandoned that one day. The next day she told me she had enrolled in a computer class at the local community college after I had explained about programming and the PC. I never had any doubts about her as a dedicated and excellent employee and never regretted extending a helping hand.

I was at odds with the new Department Head from the get go. He wanted to fire me on the day I went to thank him for selecting me as Division Leader. I had innocently said to him, "I would like to continue supporting the advanced research project under ERDA."

"Tad, do you want the Division Leader job or not? You can't do both!"

I said, "All I want to do is to give it direction. If you have a problem with that then I will just drop it!"

I was told to drop it. As a result, the Department never pursued advanced computer technology, and from then on it became a second-class computer center. From the beginning of the reorganization, the Department Head was focusing on two things: reliability of the existing systems and "The Mission Statement" for the Department. Every Monday morning, the staff listed items to go into the mission statement. Every verb and adjective was subject to review. I often wondered if the Head knew what job he had been hired to do. If he didn't know, then we were in trouble! It was a painful boring exercises to wordsmith every word to the bitter end.

In our one-on-one meetings, I would try to keep the boss aware of what was going on in my user community so that there would be no surprises for him. More than once, I would nearly have to grab his hand and say, "Don't phone them now! I just want you to be aware of what might need attention in the future! I will take care of it!" Walking on eggs would have been an easier exercise for me than talking to the boss.

From the start, I began to assess the Division's strengths and weaknesses. I noticed someone from the past, who had applied to be advanced to a programmer and was declined, was now assigned as programming support to The Earth Science Division. I assumed he had taken my previous advice and taken math and science courses at the local college. I reviewed his yearly performance report. There were no statements about his programming assignment, only non-committal words: He didn't work out. I couldn't find a spot for him. I don't need him for my project. I conducted an off-the-record, one-on-one interview with the evaluators and determined that he could not program, but that the scientist had left out the details for fear of legal consequences. Frustrated, each one had passed this employee onto the next person. One physicist told me the employee couldn't do a simple programming task. He had falsified his work in an unprofessional manner at the expense of the physicist who had counted on the results for a scientific conference. All of the fears I had had before about promoting this man had been verified. The previous Division Leader had accepted him on affirmative action and had not taken the responsibility for the person's non-performance. I was now responsible for the previous Division Leader's poor judgment. A tedious paper work and review process had to be set in action in order to take proper action to remedy the case. The unqualified man was called in my office with his group leader as a witness to review, specify the options, and choose a course of action: reclassification back to technician, red lined in salary, dismissal, or resignation. The employee chose to resign.

The most painful experience came at salary review. Placing employees into peer groups for salary review was the order of the day. Those closest to the heart received the gold! The first impression never faded. While every organization struggles to achieve an objective performance evaluation, the results remain subjective in the end. I was shocked and angry when the rest of the department supervisors told me outright that my division belonged to the bottom peer group! I was shocked again when the department head heard that denigrating statement of the people he was ultimately responsible for and said nothing. I said my piece and raised such a storm over the discriminating statement that the department head called in the associate director the next day. The department head made a concession to me, but my name was mudd. Even at my own expense, I was not going to shirk my responsibility for my division. I went to work improving our department.

When I took over APD1, I found that the division had failed to fill a number of positions supporting the users. I also noted that a few of the programmers were not suited for scientific applications. The status quo would not do, I needed to act quickly. First, I called the group leader and told them that we are going to begin an active campaign to attract better qualified programmers. I wanted each of them to contact professors at the colleges they had graduated from, give talks about scientific programming, and participate in the recruiting at the colleges. I had already given talks at the University of California Davis and begun an association with their Computer Science and Math programs. I also gave talks at Chico State and at Northern Arizona University.

Additionally, I invited professors in the Math and Computer Science Department to participate in our Summer Program to learn about the Laboratory's work. The Laboratory, as well as the Department, gained significant benefits from my aggressive effort to recruit and promote people for the Laboratory's work. We invited a professor from Boston College who made a significant contribution to the Magnetic Fusion Project, and consequently, received an open invitation to return the next year from the Project. A professor from the University of Hawaii who we had invited for the summer, designed and implemented a control system for the Mechanical Engineering Department's High Pressure Containment Project. The Mechanical Engineering Department also invited him to continue his effort the following summer. I personally invited a Computer Science professor at the Northern University of Arizona to participate in various unclassified projects for two summers. The invitation would help enhance his Computer Science curriculum with real examples for a minority college. Each effort had opened the door wider to access each university's top students for the Laboratory. It was a win-win situation. I could have said *shikataganai*, and done nothing. The challenge was there and I dared to take it. It meant added responsibility for me and for my group leaders. Nevertheless, we did meet the challenge and attracted outstanding students from the respective colleges. The effort benefited both the Laboratory and the University by providing real experiences from Laboratory, enriching their courses through their experiences, as well as contributing to the Laboratory's effort.

While we did have a personnel representative in the department working with the Lab's personnel department, he chose to sit in his office and review files submitted to him. I went to him and told him about our plans to be actively engaged in the recruiting process. He seemed relieved because he did not want the job in the first place. Sid delegated it to him in lieu of supervising.

By taking over the recruiting task, I had made it possible for me see Greg and Glen on my recruiting trips. When Glen was attending the University of California Davis, I had given talks to math classes and recruited for Computer Scientists. The travel allowed me to share a few minutes with him. Later I also recruited at Arizona State University in Tempe, Arizona where Glen was an internee doctor at Maricopa County General Hospital. The University of Arizona, Tucson, Arizona was one of several places I recruited for Computer Scientist. At Tucson, I was able to see Gregory where he was working for the IBM Company. We spent several dinners together while I enjoyed the southwestern Mexican food that I had missed in Livermore.

Our efforts proved even more effective when LLNL took on new programs involving dynamic systems and controlled laboratories. When the first, minicomputers built by Digital Equipment, Hewlett Packard, and Data General appeared, the engineering department purchased and used the minicomputer to control experimental devices. Initially, the electronics department assigned technicians to program these one-of-a-kind systems. Later, the electronics department asked the Computation Department to carry on the assignment. When I reviewed the request, I found that the technician wrote the control program in assembly language and patched many times over as the project developed. There had been no updating of documentation as the changes occurred. The electronics department wanted an APD1 programmer to clean up the running program. In short, they expected miracles from a programming mess. Our programmers made the best of it and began learning about system programming for computer-controlled minicomputers.

While APD1 provided programmers to the magnetic fusion program, around 1980, the Laboratory was beginning to set up a tandem-mirror facility designated as MFTF-B. I heard from my group leader that the electronics department was specifying and designing the hardware and software that controlled this large test facility. I made a bold decision to get involved rather than sit on the sideline. I immediately set up a meeting with the electronics department project engineers to see if we could provide software support.

The project manager said, "Tad, go away! The electronics department intends to do all of the necessary planning and implementation."

I did not want to hear a "No" for an answer. I said, "I know the project involves software and we would like to participate in it. We have the expertise and know how to do the software. In fact, I have Walter Ng here who is between assignments. He is an excellent programmer and worked with small systems. Why don't you let him work with you, at no cost to your project, for six months and see how it works out?"

I charged Walter's time to my overhead account, and after six months, we reviewed the progress. Walter was instrumental in designing the system software and, from his excellent effort; they added twelve programmers from APD1 for the MFTF-B project. However, this project was only one of several systems software that APD1supported. With our bold attempt to share the system programming with The EE Department, I saw a growth in my Division that doubled every two years for small system software. I needed to act to meet the demand. I convinced Bob Lee to allow me to add a Deputy Division Leader to meet the growth. It was now time for the Group Leaders to focus on Computer Science graduates, especially with system design on their interview trips.

Meanwhile, I learned about a programmer in my division who was providing excellent software in graphics with his scientific programming. I encouraged him by having him present his work to the division meetings, allowing him to visit outside vendors to enlarge his knowledge, and asked him to join me in the interview process at the University of New Mexico where he had graduated.

"Why are you encouraging him and promoting him?" a Group Leader asked me in one of our group leader meetings. "He'll probably leave."

I gave him no comfort in his fear. I had always believed that a leader brings out the best in people. If he grew with our help, then he was more valuable to us.

In our weekly Division meetings, we did not talk about mission statements but focused on how we could do a better job in peer review for performance evaluation and salary management. Everyone wanted an objective method of evaluation, but no one could agree what the elements were. I observed the process at the Department level and found it not based on merit but a bidding war. In our own salary review, I noticed a young woman who was an outstanding programmer, but recommended only an average merit increase by her group leader.

"How come you suggested such a low increase when she is the best of your group?" I asked the group leader.

"Well, she only works 90%," he said.

"Yet she produces more software and user support than your so-called best paid programmer." I said.

I told him she was too low on our salary curve for her excellent programming. This is where she should be in our salary grouping, and this is what I propose she deserves. I put down a number large enough to make the group leaders eyes open wider.

The young woman was a recent mother, and she would get up early in the morning, take her child to her mother's home in San Francisco, and drive to LLNL. Because she did not always arrive at LLNL at 8:00 A.M, she asked to set her effort at 90%. She happened to be Chinese American, but that had no bearing on my decision. I had seen her work, and it surpassed anyone's that I knew of. I guess I had gotten to a point where I was weary of people rewarded by anything but merit or *shikataganai*.

Because the division was growing too rapidly, the Group Leaders were concerned about their own voice in our general division meetings. In response, I chose my deputy, Ted Michels, to head the small system effort with the thought that eventually we would split into two divisions at some appropriate time. The splitting of effort by the group leaders was never clean because the support of FTE for user's Division, Projects, and Programs overlapped in many ways.

During the years I was division leader, I learned that Control Data Corporation at the Sunnyvale site hired Sid as an advisor. He was also still active with advanced computer technology and had been a driving force as chairman of IEEE Conferences on scientific supercomputers. He was also recognized as playing a key role in shaping our government's policy on supercomputing and security. When he asked me for some help with the conference arrangement, I offered my administrative assistant to help him. I was convinced that this was a good opportunity for her to participate and grow professionally. For several years, she had helped IEEE in their conference arrangements. I saw a great change, for she was very enthusiastic about what she was accomplishing, and IEEE recognized her efforts. I was hoping it would open some doors for her.

Meanwhile, Bob Lee had decided to step down as department head citing that he had accomplished his mission with the center's computer systems reliability. He suggested that a committee from the entire department select the new department head. This was the era of choosing a leader with "fuzzy" feelings. The new department head was John Ranelletti, who was the former division leader for USD, User Systems Division. The newly appointed Computation department head saw our numbers grow and began to be concerned because we were now bigger than combined FTE's of the Department and Nuclear Weapons support. The change did not occur through a natural progression of events. It had happened because we made it occur by our bold step forward. Yet the department head considered the programmers supporting applications as "second class citizens" when compared to the department's systems programmers. "We tried to address those feelings," was a quote from Ranelletti much later, but his answer was without substance. Without telling me, John Ranelletti, the department head began a series of meetings with the group leaders and facilitated by the Human Resource department. I sat in the meetings quietly and heard all of the concerns. I heard nothing new, and I saw no consensus from the meetings. One day, John Ranelletti came to me and said he was dividing our division into SSD and ASD. Then, he looked at me slyly and said, "You know why, Tad." I looked at him but said to myself, "No, I don't, because you didn't have the courtesy to talk to me first."

The split created a problem for my new smaller division because the arbitrary split did not reflect the proper support for projects and programs, especially the Laser Project. If John Ranelletti had been more forthright in discussing his fixation on dividing my division without examining the consequences of his action, I could have provided support that is more meaningful to the Laser Program. After the split, I sat week after week with my programmers and the Engineering department's personnel in their group meetings about the software for the Laser Enrichment Project. I was disappointed in the meetings, for I considered it a waste of everyone's time. I did not interject myself as the group leader, for that was not my role. The meeting should have been reserved for top down discussions rather than nitty-gritty details of instruction-by-instruction presentations. The de facto group leader was not my choice. Since the Engineering department had the primary role of controlling the project, their staff recruited both engineers and programmers for their project. When they failed to find programmers, they came to my division for instant support. My agreement with the Engineering department called for joint support, not after the fact and finger pointing at my division. John could have prevented this if he acted responsibly. John had cut me off at the knees and had the audacity to ask me why I could not walk?

It was 1985, and I had been working for 35 years with computer related efforts since I first started at LASL in 1951. The Computation department had become a second-class computer center that was dead in the water with direction towards advance computer systems for the Laboratory. It was time to think of retiring. One day I visited the Personnel department class on retirement options. When I saw one of their representatives, she spent much of her time with pencil and paper trying to show me my options. After seeing her struggle so hard and spend so much time scribbling and writing the options, I asked her, "Have you ever considered using an IBM PC? " No," she said. "In fact, the Personnel department has no PC's."

"I have a consultant working for my division. Why don't I let him program your procedures and loan my PC to you for a while," I said.

Later, I talked to her and she was beaming with joy. "I can type in a few numbers and have more time to talk to my clients about their retirement she said. " I do more interviews that I did before." After that, I saw that Personnel department had ordered more than a dozen PC's for their work.

Before I retired, a group leader said to me, "Did you know the graphics software programmer that you were encouraging and promoting left the LLNL to work with Lucasfilm?"

Then he added, "Did you know he was gay?"

He waited for my reaction. He was smugly waiting for me to say I had been wrong to encourage him – and that if I had not known he was gay that proved somehow that I had made a miscalculation about him in general.

I looked at him in disbelief.

My world is colorless. I am glad the graphics programmer came my way.

Division Leader – APD1

Home, where the heart is
Humble place for all seasons
Timeless memories

Home

Where will I rest my weary head?
When thoughts of home come to mind
Where familiar faces can be found
Where warmth of human kindness be
Where, oh where can home be?

From that Day of Infamy
One last look that was my home
'Twas roots of my past,
Where the warmth of family blessings,
Raised my spirits and hope
For another day.

Guiding words of my father,
Raised us to be good citizens.
Bring no shame
Upon Our Family Name
Watchful words to live by

My mother's love
A gift of life
Gentle soft-spoken
Warm with every word
Lost in infinity

With brothers and sister
Each day an adventure be
Laughter, smiles, and pleasures
One last look
Fades into the past

Memories shuttered from light of day
No time to think about the past
No time to reminisce
No time for memories
No heart, no soul, no warmth can be

Bring the gift of life into this home,

Lady on the Bridge

With warmth of love
In this humble house
Let memories be born again
Home is where the heart is.

Set roots on this land
Sow the "American Dream
Home, where the heart is

Roots

Like nomads, Yo and I had moved hither and yon seeking a place to set our roots. Several times, we were denied buying a house. All we wanted to do was to realize the American Dream: to settle down and to be free and equal. Finally, it seemed that the dream was possible here in Livermore. Because the Housing Office of the LLRL arranged for a rental in a newly opened housing tract, I did not faced the frustrating task of finding housing. It was the first of its kind in the East Bay Area valley and anything but luxurious. The construction was as bad as the house in the "Three Little Pigs;" "I'll huff, puff, and blow your house down." Everything in the house matched the chintzy construction. They hastily built the house on top of a slab floor without any seals to protect the inside from the outside. When the wind blew, dust turns the floors into a gritty ash brown mess just like Manzanar.

We had moved into a two-bedroom house on a corner lot of a cul-se-sac and most of the renters were young people with small children or had just started a family. An Air Force officer stationed at Camp Parks rented the house next to us. We were surprised when we saw his wife with five youngsters in the small house. The children were in a stair step array except a void where the husband had undoubtedly been on duty elsewhere. When I saw the mother, she moved about without energy. She looked lifeless, a shell of a young woman, and worn to a frazzle bearing and doing all of the household chores without help. In addition, it seems that she had hardly any time left to keep track of them.

One day, my wife was ready to back the car out of the garage to do some shopping. No sooner had she reached the ignition to start the car, than she heard a strange noise by the garage door. She got out of the car and looked. There under the car was the neighbor's three-year-old child lying on the garage floor trying to drink whatever remained in an empty soda bottle. Quickly, she grabbed the child from under the car and marched him to the neighbor's house.

Concerned about the neighbor, Yo said she asked the mother if she had any friends or relatives to help her. She replied that they were devout Catholics, but with her husband in the Air Force, they have never been able to set roots anywhere. The Catholic Church had promised to help, but no one had ever come to visit her.

It was a wakeup call for us, and we began looking for a home to buy. Again, we were frustrated in our search. During the war, the President, Congress, and community leaders had done their job well –"No Japs Allowed." The home developers in town feared that we would scare away prospective homebuyers and would not dare to admit it to us. One well-known developer in town said, "Why don't you wait awhile because we will be building suitable (cheaper) homes later." I remembered President Truman's tribute to the most decorated all *Nisei* Unit in the US Army history, the 100/442 Battalion. He had said, "You fought not only the enemy but you fought prejudice -- and you won." How hollow those words sounded as my wife and I pursued "the American Dream" of owning our own home.

Lady on the Bridge

Frustrated in our search, I began contacting builders as far as across the bay that would require commuting fifty miles. I wrote letters to building contractors that I was interested in buying a home and asked if they would consider my application to purchase one of their houses. In the letter, I specified that I was a Japanese American, an ex-US GI, and fully employed. Only one developer responded, Eichler. The reply was a cordial and heart-warming letter stating that they never discriminate based on race and would be happy if we would consider buying their homes. I have forgotten many names, but never his.

Meanwhile, the manager of our tract homes had heard that we were looking for another place to live. We were on good terms with him and he knew we were good tenants. He visited us one day and said he was building a custom home on the outskirts of town for his family. Because he was managing the tract homes, the company had stipulated that he had to live in one of the units so he would not be able to live in the custom house. He asked if we would consider a lease with the option to buy. The house was on a half-acre of a one-acre plot, had three bedrooms, one bathroom, a large living room, and a detached garage. A barbed wire fence enclosed the acre lot since the owner had previously had a horse. Every day when I went to work, I had seen the house under construction but had never thought that it would be mine someday.

Other *Nisei,* who worked at the Lab, had the same discriminatory problem with builders in Livermore. They asked, "How about the *Nisei* couple on East Avenue?" The builder replied that we had purchased our home from a private party and it was not a tract house.

For several years, we were without neighbors until a young *Nisei* couple asked if we minded if he bought the adjacent property. They had lived in the same tract that we had just moved from to our new home. When I met them, they impressed us as a friendly *Nisei* couple with a young daughter that was just learning to walk. They wanted to build a custom home. Recalling our own rejections with housing, we welcomed him to be our neighbor. During the construction of his house, we helped him by giving him free use of our electrical connection. We watched every phase of the construction. Upon completion, the husband asked us, "Can we continue to tie into your electrical power line?"

I said, "I don't think that's a good idea. It would be impossible to sort out our individual usage and, furthermore, it would put an extra load on the power supply."

He looked put out and said, "But, *Nihonjin dooshi,* as fellow Japanese."

I looked at him and walked away.

The price of living
No crystal ball to see with
Life is not dirt-cheap

500 dollars

You must be kidding, "500 dollars an acre! You should have bought 10 acres back then," said a casual acquaintance when I told him what property was worth at the time I settled in Livermore in 1953.

I remember the land around me was mostly dry hayfields growing on rocky soil. Here and there were a few acreage plots with remnants of grape stock that had been neglected and showed no sign of greenery, a couple of chicken farms with chicken coops ready to fall apart, a farm, Wagoner Farm north of East Avenue that had ceased operation, and a few horses and some stray cattle corralled behind barbwire fences. South of East Avenue, there was Wente's Vineyard on a large acreage, and Concannon Winery on Tesla Road, but this was not the fertile farm land like my father-in-law's farms in Reedley, California. What would I do with ten acres of dry rocky land without utilities or water? I was not raised to be a farmer nor did I have a crystal ball to speculate on the future of Livermore, let alone money to burn.

I hesitated to tell him that I had only recently graduated from college and had no spare cash to invest in anything. Yo and I were brought up during the 1930's, the Depression years. If we did not have the money, we did without and did not rely on anyone else for help. Early on, we had even flipped coins to see who would get to see a movie in town on some weekends. We were trying to establish our home and family, consequently, we had priorities that are more pressing. Yo and I talked about our need to take care of our own health and later of our children. We had worried about medical care if anyone needed extended hospitalization. We looked at what Livermore could offer for emergency care, and found only a small community hospital, St. Paul, in a residential area. Livermore was once a place for long term care of tuberculosis patients recuperating in sanitariums near College Avenue. However, new drugs had made these facilities obsolete. There was also the Veteran's Hospital on Arroyo Road near Del Valle Dam, but it hardly qualified for our family care.

We had decided to join the Kaiser Foundations' medical care, because, when I was attending UC Berkeley, I had taken coverage under their medical plan, and found their facility excellent and low cost. There was only one drawback for us living in Livermore; the closest facility for us was thirty miles away in Walnut Creek, California. In order to avoid the long travel to Walnut Creek for routine medical care, we had decided to pay and augment our medical plan by selecting a family doctor in Livermore. We found Dr. Jerry Schwartz, who was just establishing his practice in town. We told him that we were members of the Kaiser plan, but we wanted him to be our doctor for minor and routine medical care. Dr Schwartz was grateful that we were up front with him about our Kaiser plan and agreed to provide medical services for us. There was another bonus for us having a new doctor in town. Whenever I was on travel for the Lab, he made house calls when Yo needed help. Of course, all of the extra medical cost came out of my wages, but the choice was our first priority and ours to make.

We were not alone worrying about the lack of adequate hospital service in the valley. As soon as Lab employees started to buy homes in Livermore, they sought medical facilities outside of this town as far as Oakland, CA. Then, around 1960, an active campaign for donations to establish a hospital on a site donated by the Kaiser Gravel Company started in Livermore. Even though I continued with my Kaiser Medical Plan, I volunteered with other Lab employees to pledge money from our wages for this important cause. In 1961, the Valley Care Center opened to provided emergency care for valley residents. Forty years later, I was still a charter member even though I had never used the hospital facility.

During the first two years, Lab employees were apprehensive about the permanency of their job with the Lab. When the Atomic Energy Commission (AEC) extended the contract for the University of California to manage the facility, Lab employees began to look for homes to settle down in the area. In Livermore, the options were almost non existent. Quickly, builders and contractors began to meet the demand and soon open space began to disappear. Our house, surrounded by hayfields, stood naked on East Avenue for several years. To the north of our house, Mt. Diablo that loomed high above the dry valley landscape soon began to fade from our view. Every day, it was reassuring to hear the lonesome sound of the train whistle as it traveled to and from Stockton. Soon the whistle sound muffled into silence by homes gobbling up the hayfields to the north. Old chicken farms disappeared as builders bought out the owners' property.

At first, builders constructed modest single story homes with backyards and spaces between houses. The cost of homes matched the income of a single wage earner. Then families qualified for larger loans based on two income families. Quickly, bulldozers began plowing up fields, scattering all life forms in the land, and building monstrous two story homes. Three-car garages replaced the two-car garage and the space between homes gradually disappeared. Land values escalated and the $500 dollar an acre plot disappeared. We were lucky for a while because in front of our home and along the north side of East Avenue, there was one large open field, owned by an old German family that remained untouched for several years.

Every spring in those early years of 1960's, I heard the "pop, pop, pop" of the farmer's shotgun hunting down jackrabbits on the open field across from us. Then one spring, I was surprised to hear the roar of a plane buzzing close to our house. Not knowing what was happening, I rushed outside. It was a biplane flying low northward towards Jackson and Perkins rose growing land. The plane was so close to our house; I could see the pilot with his goggles on. Suddenly, the pilot let go a cloud of insecticide over the rose patch, zoomed upward, turned half-circle to the right, and headed back towards us. Then I heard the plane turn back once more to make another pass at the rose plants. I saw a cloud of insecticide suspended in the air above the roses after he finished his runs. Later, as I drove to the Lab early in the morning, I was not surprised to see the same biplane dusting Wente's vineyards with insecticide. This time he was even more daring. I watched with fascination and anticipation as the pilot swooped down under the power lines without extra room to spare and sprayed the field.

This was a great way to exterminate insects, for I remember *Otoosan* spraying his roses with a two-gallon hand sprayer. I saw him vigorously pumping the plunger to keep the pressure up. Occasionally, he would brush his brow with shirtsleeve for he was sweating. I have had to often use a hand sprayer just like my father to kill aphids, thrips, moths, fungus, and all of the other Natures' soldiers trying to ruin my garden. However, I was surprised when I read the label of the insecticide Father was using. I remember name; it was Black Leaf Forty - a derivative of nicotine.

Then it dawned on me that smoking can kill you, but I was thankful that I did not take up that bad habit.

However, years later, I lost the excitement of watching the barnstorming over the vineyards forever because the government banned spraying insecticides by airplanes.

While we moved to this place called home in 1955, my yard remained dormant for the two more years. Of course, my appendectomy contributed to the delay. Then again, I had no idea how I wanted to landscape it. It was, after all, a quarter of an acre of rocky dry soil with stubby weeds that I saw waiting for me to act on every day. While our house was in Alameda County proper, we had all of the city facilities except for a line to the sewer so we had a septic tank. Water, however, was a problem. The builder connected our water to the Livermore City water line at Livermore City Limit, Nielsen Lane. Then he laid a one-inch galvanized pipe on top of the open field all the way to our house. I thought nothing about this arrangement until one summer I had to take a shower before leaving on travel. I had my first big surprise when I turned on the cold water. I was almost scalded to death. I quickly lathered myself, washed, and turned on the hot water faucet to rinse myself with the water still the hot water line. I was red as a lobster plucked from a pot of hot water. The first freezing day in winter was also a big surprise for us: No water. The water pipe on top of the ground from Nielsen Lane remained frozen until 10:30 in the morning. We quickly learned to save water at night for washing and for our breakfast. Meanwhile, our yard suffered with stubby weeds around us and it looked like a fire hazard. I tried my luck with a sickle, but the blade kept bouncing off the rocks. When I looked at the blade, it was either dull or bent in spots where it hit a rock. Rocks, rocks, they were everywhere. Finally, I had to hire a local farmer to plow the stubby weeds that continued to invade my garden.

It was a busy period for me since I was in charge of the Lab's new acquisition of the IBM 701 and the IBM 704. We were also expecting our first child, and Yo was having trouble with the pregnancy that forced her to rest most of the day. I learned that there are so many things to do when you move into a new house. I parked the family car outside, because I had set up a table saw from Sears Roebuck in the garage to work on an endless number of projects such as shelving, bookcases, and patio. Most nights, I worked in the garage until midnight. Sawdust was flying all around me, and in my hair and nostrils. Every so often, I would stop and gather up the sawdust that was piling up under the saw. I purchased most of my lumber from Diamond Lumber Company and Livermore Lumber Company on North L Street and Railroad Avenue. I chose redwood for outside projects because it was the easiest to work with and was as cheap as Douglas fir. For my cabinetry, I chose Philippine mahogany that was very popular during the late 1950's. It was also easy to work with but required extra care in finishing the cabinetry because of its porous grain.

One day before Greg was born, Yo and I saw an announcement from the Livermore High School offering a night class on wood crafting. We both enrolled and Yo decided she would make a wooden sewing box that she needed for her sewing projects. I decided to make a coffee table. With the help of our woodshop instructor, Mr. Hunter, I saw Yo carefully cutting pieces of wood with a band saw and shaping it for her project. I had never seen Yo swing a hammer before, but there she was busy working with all of the woodshop equipment. She did not hesitate one bit and was thoroughly engrossed in her project. I remember when I was attending the Santa Monica High School, SAMOHI, I had signed up for woodshop as an elective class. A vocational class would train young people to become productive citizens. I did receive some basic knowledge of using woodshop equipment, but my big class project was making a laminated cutting board in the shape of a pig. I thought I had done a nice job making it, but I cannot recall *Okaasan* ever using it when she was preparing dinner. This time, I was more ambitious. I decided to make a coffee table out of a solid-core door. I searched several lumber companies and found a door with mahogany veneer on both sides. It was heavy with the solid core. The width was just right, but I needed to shorten the length. For the legs, I decided to make then with wrought iron, but I had never used an acetylene welding tool. Mr. Hunter showed me the fundamentals of welding, and I did a few practice runs before trying my luck with the wrought iron legs. I had a hard time trying to see my welding with the heavy helmet on and trying to look through the helmet's small window. My product was not professional looking, but the defects were unnoticeable unless you turned the coffee table upside down. We both looked forward to this night class, for we were having great fun, learning new things, and spending the time together. I was surprised and marveled at the work Yo did on her sewing box. After I brought my coffee table home, I finished it with five coats of lacquer. It was a prize to behold in the family room until Greg, when he was about a year old, found it to be just the right height and a wonderful object for teething.

It was hot here in Livermore, but it was dry heat with the humidity around 5%. Since the temperature soared as high as 120° F, I tried installing a swamp cooler, but that proved too unsightly and messy. Instead, I bought an air conditioner, but I had no place to install it because I did not want to cut a hole in the wall or block out a window. In desperation, I replaced my front door with a ¾-inch plywood, cut a hole to fit the air conditioner, made a bracket to hold it up, and placed it there. It worked fine, but I worried that I had eliminated one entryway that made it hazardous for us in case an emergency. After a second thought, I decided it would be safer to cut a hole in my living room wall on the south side of the house and place the unit there.

Meanwhile, I was dabbling in landscaping the backyard, but I had no firm plans. I bought a number of Sunset Magazine booklets to get an idea of planning the yard. My backyard was over a quarter of an acre with weeds, rocks, and earwigs. Although my family had been in the nursery business during 1930 – 1941, I had never dealt with landscaping. For my yard, I did not want a ticky-tacky looking garden that had a sharp rectangular form. I saw some free form arrangements in the Sunset book, and I decided that was what I should do. Then I thought about my Japanese heritage and began to think what influence it would have on my project. However, a formal Japanese garden was not what I had in mind. A Japanese garden was nice to look at, wander through leisurely and enjoy for the beauty of nature, but it would not be functional for children to run and play in. I made a compromise: I would highlight the shrubbery, with screens like *shoji,* using black painted posts, red frames and yellowish reed paneling. I would keep one area of the yard for a children's play yard. However, I needed a lawn to cover a large open space. Yet, I did not want spend my life mowing a lawn, so I decided I would sow dichondra seeds in place of Kentucky Blue grass. I had my plan laid out, but it lay dormant for a while.

In October 1955, I had to visit Poughkeepsie with a team of programmers to make use of our IBM 704 during its final stage of construction. Yo was expecting our first child who was supposed to be born in late November, and her doctor assured us that my trip would not be a problem. However, since she would be alone, we arranged for Yo to stay with her brother's family in Berkeley. Everything seemed to be working out well, but Mother Nature has a strange way of surprising us. On 25 October 1955, around 8:00 p.m., Yo fell off the sofa that she was resting on, because an earthquake shook the Bay Area that night. My brother-in-law rushed Yo to Kaiser Walnut Creek since her fall from the sofa appeared to affect her pregnancy. I heard nothing of the

244

complication until I received a telephone message that Yo had gone into labor and had given birth to our son, Gregory. I received a garbled phone message: a call that went to someone else until it finally reached me at midnight. I quickly changed my travel plans and hurried back to California. Before going to the hospital, I bought roses at a florist and visited Yo and my new son at Kaiser Permanente in Walnut Creek. Yo was groggy since she said she had been in labor for twenty-seven hours. Greg was born one month earlier than scheduled, but he was eight pounds at birth. I guess he was just anxious to get out into the world because his quarter was too small. I remember seeing Yo's body stretched to the limit, and her doctor had prescribed a corset to help her carry her baby. I had even kidded that she should push a cart or a wheelbarrow to help carry the bulging stomach. Before Greg was born, I always had pictured myself pacing the floor while waiting for Yo to deliver her baby, but none of it was true for me. In addition, our priority of hospital coverage had paid off for us.

Greg with Grandparents

A chronic problem
Oh, how does your garden grow?
It's a rocky life

The Garden

My well-laid plans for the garden had to wait once more until we could adjust to our wonderful and joyous birth of Greg in October, 1955. We were very fortunate that *Okaasan* came to help us for a few weeks and followed by Yo's mother. It was a busy time for all of us while Yo and I were learning to be parents and contend with all the feeding and changing diapers that came with it. We were managing, but soon another surprise was in store for me.

One day after our mothers left, I was feeling lousy, but, in my customary Japanese attitude of *gaman,* I still went to work. Yet, I could not concentrate or shake the queasy feeling. I kept thinking that I was suffering from my mother-in-law's rich food that she had cooked for us. I must have over indulged with her delicious Japanese cooking that we had been missing. Just to be on the safe side, I decided to call the Lab medical office for appointment. I waited patiently until 1:00 p.m. to see the Lab's doctor on site. He was not a practicing physician, but an industrial doctor who was available in case of medical emergency at the Lab. He examined me while I explained my nausea and the lack of energy. He performed a cursory examination without any tests and said to me that I might be coming down with a stomach flu that was common during the winter season. Then he added, "I would advise you to see your regular doctor."

It was early afternoon, and, since it sounded to me to be something minor, I decided to drive to Walnut Creek Kaiser for a routine check-up. Since I was sure I would be home in time for dinner, I did not let Yo know of my plan. For spontaneous appointments, I had to wait and wait for my turn. The first doctor went through his routine examination, and when he finished, he said I was to wait in the room until another doctor would come to re-examine me. This time the doctor ordered a series of blood test and told me to wait in the waiting room until the test results were ready. About 4:30 p.m., I saw the third doctor. He said my white blood count was extremely high. Then he lowered the boom. You have a ruptured appendix. We have to operate as soon as possible.

I told him that I had driven up here by myself and did not tell my wife. "Can I drive home and come back?" I asked.

He said I was scheduled for an appendectomy at 7:30 p.m. and that I had to wait here at Kaiser for pre-op. Yo was home with our one month old infant, Greg, and no way to reach me since I had driven our car to Kaiser. It was winter and the weather had turned ugly. Meanwhile, while the nurse prepped me, she asked if I wanted to be awake during the operation. I had remembered back in Santa Monica, a friend of the family died of a ruptured appendix. I surely did not want to be awake to learn of my demise. I had heard that a routine appendectomy was a simple operation, but my better judgment told me to decline the offer. They turned me over sideways, hunch my legs up, and gave me a spinal.

I have no memory of what happened after that until I woke up in the recovery area. Someone said the simple operation took four hours. They said they joked with the surgeon that he was excising a big length of my intestine. I was lucky to be alive, for my appendix had ruptured. Fortunately, the rupture was contained in a localized area. The doctor was very careful to clean the ruptured area so that I would not develop peritonitis. Because my appendix was unusually large, the surgeon believed that my appendicitis attack was chronic rather than acute. When he told me about the chronic condition, I though back to my earlier days and remembered that every once in while, I would get a sharp pain where my appendix was located, but the pain did not last very long. On this last experience, I never thought that I had appendicitis, because the people I saw with acute appendicitis attack would double up, unable to move, and turn green at the gills. That never happened to me. However, appendicitis may be a family trait, for I do remember that my uncle and my brother Frank both had an appendectomy and survived.

I was in a bad way: numb and groggy. Worse still, the nurse wanted to insert a catheter. My manhood was now at risk. I protested vehemently and told her I did not need it. I said I would take care of my normal functions by myself. I was in for a long recovery, but the hospital food is hardly a gourmet fare. I had survived a couple of weeks, but they wanted to keep me in the hospital past Christmas Holidays for full recovery. I was determined to leave before then. With a bit of *Gaman,* I was able to walk the floors with my IV's dangling at my side. Later, I managed to convince the doctors that I was ready for discharging before Christmas 1955.

I was glad to return home, but the doctor who discharged me warned me not to exert myself physically for several weeks. I heeded that advice because I remembered what my Uncle did after his appendectomy and suffered the consequence. He had decided to drive his truck just after his surgery, ended up holding his intestines that protruded from the torn sutures, and had to drive back to the hospital for help. While I was resting, my brother, Frank showed up at our home with one of his workers and a truckload of plants. He told me he saw my yard unlandscaped and decided to help me with my yard.

Okaasan had also added plants for my yard: *Sakura*, a flowering cherry tree, Japanese Yew, Bamboo stalks, Heavenly Bamboo (Nandina Domestica), and Pittosporum. These were plants from the West Los Angeles Nursery. Frank asked me if I had any ideas of landscaping my yard. I showed him my rough plans for the back yard and that I had decided to place a semi-circle driveway in front so that I would not have to back out into the traffic to drive out. When he looked at my sketch with the three loops for the lawn area, he said laughingly, "Hey that looks like Mickey Mouse's head!" Sure enough, it did look like Mickey Mouse.

I had an even bigger surprise. Frank and his worker proceeded to unload the plants and began planting them following my rough sketch. This was a bigger gift than I had expected. There were Junipers, Cypress, pines, bottlebrush, acacia, and many other plants that they planted in our yard. They made sure to plant *Okaasan's* gifts also. I was happy but at a loss for words to thank Frank. He did not stay that day, for he said he had to rush for an appointment with a nursery in Sacramento, CA.

A few weeks later, I felt full of energy and decided to start my garden. It seemed like a daunting task. First, I whacked the weeds down as much as I could. Hoeing the weeds was almost impossible task because rocks of all sizes were everywhere: on the surface and embedded in the ground. Each time I lowered the hoe, it would simply bounce off the rocks. In desperation, I resorted to using a shovel to dislodge the weeds and rocks together. The process made music of its own; sound of metal scraping along the pebbles followed by clunks against rocks, and a display of sparks flying off when the shovel blade hit something solid.

As I looked back at my effort, I was sure a goat or sheep could have done a better job. At this point, I had decided that if I planted my lawn quickly, I would remove most of my unsightly weeds. However, there was one big drawback. I had to prepare the ground first. I marked off the outline of the lawn into three adjoining circles of different sizes that I had sketched out earlier. I did not want a rectangular garden. After all, it would not reflect my Japanese heritage of a free form found in Nature. I began digging the ground because covering the plot with topsoil was not feasible with so many rocks underneath and, besides, too expensive. I took careful aim with my shovel, lowered it, and placed my food down hard on the spade. It pierced the soil a few inches and then I heard a sound, "clunk" while refusing to go any further into the ground. I repositioned the shovel a few inches away and repeated the digging. I failed again. I dug carefully around the spot to see what the matter was. Right there staring at me was a solid rock! Simply spading or picking up some rocks was not going to work.

In my youth, I worked in my father's nursery and helped working on landscaping projects, but never like what I was facing for my own home. I decided the only way to prepare the soil for seeding was to remove most of the rocks and gravel by screening. I stopped my work, went to Nelson's Hardware store, and bought galvanized screens of various sizes for my screening box. All I could see in my mind's eye was a horrendous task facing me.

For several weeks and months, I used a pickaxe and mattock to loosen the soil, tossed a shovel full of soil and rocks against the screen slanted to allow the dirt to fall through while the rocks rolled down to the ground. I kept repeating the process until there were enough rocks to dump into the wheelbarrow. The first time I tried to lift and move the wheelbarrow, I thought I would end up with a hernia. I was just too gung ho and did not realize how heavy a wheelbarrow loaded with rocks could be. I wheeled the rocks and placed them into piles along the border of my yard. It was a slow and backbreaking job. However, a few swigs of Budweiser saved the day for me.

Sweat did not have time to roll off my back because the valley temperature rose above one hundred degrees. When I finished, I had over a dozen big piles of rocks: small rocks, big rocks, smooth rocks, jagged rocks, black rocks, red rocks, white rocks, quartz rock, and multicolored rocks. Some rocks were so beautiful, smooth and round that, I stopped for a moment and wondered where they came from? There was no river in the valley that I knew of that could tumble rocks and smooth them so round over the years. When did this happen? However, enough daydreaming for the moment, for I had no time to think about how I would dispose of those rocks once I finished my landscaping job. My arms hung like two limp rags too worn out and sore from shoveling and hauling dirt and rocks.

In this merriment
When Old Glory passes by
Fill your heart with pride

Livermore Rodeo Parade

The whinny of horses awakens us
Hearing the Clip-clop, Clickity-clop,
the staccato of hooves
playing on the pavement nearby
Each anxious for the parade
Touting Livermore's greatest
Fastest Rodeo in the West

Peeking out the window
It's our neighbors we see
Old time ranchers and cowboys too
Cowboy hats and Stetsons
Western shirts and Bolo ties
Sitting tall on their steed
Jockeying and ready to go

Hurry we must
Our son, with clarinet in hand,
in the East Ave. School band
At Fifth Street School
Band Master Viera anxiously wait
Leave the son and find a place
on Livermore's First Street
A nice little spot with the sun to our back
Sit and wait for the parade to start
Crowds are forming crowding our space

Old Glory comes into sight
Proudly held by Color guards
The sharpness of each step
taken with pride
Rifles firm at angle forty-five
Crowd stands proudly
Some salute sharply
But most with a hand over heart
There is silence that shouts out loud
We are one in this moment in time
As eyes follow that flag of mine

Lady on the Bridge

Quickly,
the sound
of the marching band
the twirling batons
of majorettes
Keeping the beat
To the marching band
Brasses sounding
Drums rumbling
Clarinets resonating
Cymbals crashing
Crowds clapping
As they pass by

On this day, the parade
stretching far
Old Timers on a stagecoach
Peeking out
Children in a prairie schooner
Waving happily
Carol Jean's dancers' sequins sparkling
strutting their stuff
Old timers on horses
Prancing about
Motored floats with bright colored streamers
fluttering around
Vintage car tooting its horn
beeping loudly
Straw hats and pretty bonnets
waving hands happily
Livermore fire truck in the parade
Shining brightly

Band and more bands
Vying for a prize
Lost is the reason
For this parade
'Twas twelve hundred C's
Livermore's quota
For Red Cross needs
To help our brave soldiers
Of World War I
So revel this day

Lady on the Bridge

And remember the reason;
For our brave young men
who have marched for our Freedom

Yellow butter cups
The tasty morsels of life
Why not go for it

Playland

   This one-horse town had begun to morph into a different social makeup when scientists and engineers of the Lawrence Radiation Laboratory began to set their roots in Livermore. When I came to Livermore in 1953, I had seen no school nearby or a park for children to play. What I had seen were open fields covered with grasses that quickly turned dull brown, but, of course, I told my friends it was golden brown. Shortly after Lab employees began to settle down in this town, Livermore changed drastically from a rural ranch and cowboy atmosphere to a more sedate bedroom community. Concerned Lab employees wanted an orderly growth of the town and pushed for a slow growth initiative. A few ran for City Council and for the Mayor's office. They wanted to restrict heavy industries from establishing within the city to mitigate the problems associated with an industrial city like Detroit, Michigan. Many of the employees were recent graduates of colleges and who were just starting a family or had young school-age children. Many wives were also well educated with college degrees, but chose to be "stay-at-home moms." Besides, this town did not offer any meaningful employment for the highly qualified wives nor did the lab with its strict nepotism ruling. With the surge of preschool children from the young families, Livermore had no facility for the toddlers. Soon a Livermore preschool formed, but Yo and I believed it was more convenient and better to have our children stay at home.
   Since Greg had begun to walk, it was time for me to think about the children's play yard. I thought about my childhood and tried to remember what I enjoyed. I remembered when I was a child; my play yard was my father's nursery. However, as I grew up, I followed my brother, Frank around the neighborhood, because Frank seemed to know where the fun places were. There was even a public playground in West Los Angeles where I learned to slide down a big tall slide, and learned how to use a swing. Then later, when our family visited our good family friends in Norwalk, Frank and I played with their son, Jiro on his father's farm. Jiro had shared his toy cars with us, and we made roads and hills on their farm's sandy soil. We played for hours pretending we were drivers and truckers - even accompanied by our voices sounding like big trucks.
   With that in mind, I sketched a plan for a sand box, but not any old sand box. My sand box was triangular shaped with the sides made into a form of a box that could contain all of the children's toys, and a hinged cover for a place to sit. There were dump trucks, cars, buckets and shovel, and other toys stored away for playing. I had also made a screen frame so that stray cats would not use the play area as their litter box. Because our lot was completely out in the open with no shade tree and with the temperature in Livermore sometimes rising above 100 degrees, I had to construct a shade for the children. First, I sunk two redwood posts in the ground to support a shade. Next, I constructed a large rectangular frame, and covered it with reed fencing for a shady roof. I suspended the frame between the two posts by means of a pipe through the center of the frame. Then, at Nelson's hardware store, I found something that I could make into a crank so that the children could easily tilt the frame and provide shade as the sun moved overhead. I tied the rope to both ends of the frame and wrapped rope around the axle of the crank that allowed the frame to tilt east and west and still be taut and secure.

Next, I wanted the children to learn to climb. One day, I saw a schematic of a climber cottage in a pamphlet that had open sides in the form of ladders. It was just right for kids to climb and scan the horizon. I added cleats on the roof for the children to hang onto while climbing onto the roof. Even I, with acrophobia, could climb it.

The children could see so many things in the distance from the roof of the climber house. On most days, if we looked northward, we could see the smoke coming out of the smokestack as a train was passing. Sometimes we could hear the fire engines as they rushed to put out fires started by the train's hot boxes. On rodeo weekend, we could hear the crowd and the announcer from the rodeo stands blaring through the speakers. "Contestant number 6 in chute 3, riding the world famous bucking bull, Dynamite Buckaroo," shouted an announcer. Shortly afterwards you would hear the roar of the crowd or a groan if the cowboy failed. The rodeo was about two miles from the house on South Livermore Avenue near Rodeo Lane. All the while we lived in Livermore, I never took the family to see the rodeo because the rodeo was not only dusty and dirty, but also some of the events were cruel to animals.

On the Fourth of July, when we did not go to see the fireworks at the Alameda County Fair grounds in Pleasanton, we would climb on top of our climber house and look westward. We could see the fireworks propelled high into the sky then bursting in so many beautiful colors. We could hear the boom of the canon firing, but the fairgrounds were too far to hear the "oohs and aahs" from the crowd.

Since the ground was dirt, pebbles, and rocks, I needed to cover it so that the children would not hurt themselves. Sawdust was inexpensive, so I ordered ten yards to cover the area. The lumberyard quoted that thirty yards was as cheap as ten yards. I was worried that it was an over kill but I agreed to the delivery of thirty yards of sawdust. When I spread it out, there was almost six inches of sawdust on the play yard, and some overflowed into other areas. But, at least, the children would not get hurt if they should fall. The sawdust, however, created another problem. We had to be careful that the children did not bring the sawdust into the house. We had already taught them the Japanese tradition of removing our shoes before entering the home. Brushing off the sawdust or changing clothes was just an added inconvenience.

For some time, there were no houses nearby and our place visible to everyone that passed by on East Avenue. Yet it seems that people were attracted to our yard, especially the play yard, and they wanted to drop by and leave their kids. We had to discourage their visits, because they wanted Yo to babysit while they went off to do personal errands or just to be free of their kids for a while. I assuredly did not build the play yard for someone else's convenience or for Yo to babysit for others. One day, Greg's schoolmate came over to play without our approval. When Yo asked the children if their parents knew where they were, they said they did. Yo was about to let them stay, but asked them to be careful so that they would not get hurt. The eldest kid said, "Don't worry. If we get hurt, my mother said she would sue you." Yo immediately escorted them out of our yard and told them not to come back.

Frank planted a few pyracanthas in front along East Avenue, and, while it was attractive, it produced red berries in the winter. Then one day, I noticed pyracantha seedlings growing everywhere in my small patch of dichondra lawn in front. Just above that piece of lawn was our neighbor's electric power line that stretched from a telephone pole to their house. During early winter, redwing blackbirds would feast on the berries, sit on the power line, and, every so often, deposit the encapsulated fertilized seeds onto my pretty dichondra lawn. Then as winter progressed, I saw birds eat the over-ripe berries and fly erratically, for the berries had fermented. At times, the birds would crash against the house and drop dead onto my yard. The prettiness of the berries had turned into a disastrous condition. I had to stop it. First, I dug up my dichondra lawn and replaced it with big Yuba rocks with plastic sheeting underneath. Then, I dug up all of the pyracantha and decided to plant colorful annuals, gladiolas, and mums. When the flowers were in full bloom, people would remark that they enjoyed the color splash that I provided as they traveled to and from the Lab.

But my efforts were also an attraction to critters. We lived by open fields, and we had changed the balance of nature with the landscaping. I planted daffodils, narcissus, and gladiolas near the open field. Everyone enjoyed the combination of the colors at springtime. But there was one critter in particular that was a nuisance, a gopher. Yo said one day, when she was outside with Glen observing the plants in front, she noticed the yellow daffodil plants wiggling. It was a nice sunny day with no breeze. Why was that daffodil moving? She kept watching, and the daffodil plant gradually sunk into the ground. While she was surprised with this disappearing act, she saw some dirt pushed outside the hole. Yo saw Glen nearby and shouted to him, "Glen, see that shovel over there? Quickly, go for it."

Yo held the shovel high and waited near the daffodils. The gopher pulled another daffodil down, then stuck his head out.

WHAM!

When I returned from work, Yo said she had something to show me - a fat gopher that had met its maker

On other occasions, I had tried to drown out gophers by pouring water down each gopher hole with my garden hose. All that I accomplished was water down the hole. Once I followed the gophers' tunnels and found their labyrinth of interconnecting runways and air pockets. Sometimes I set up gopher traps, but they are nasty things to set. I cringed every time I set those traps, but I gradually won the battle.

One other critter needed watching. One spring day in 1965, I was roto-tilling the front section to plant chrysanthemums. I had stopped for a moment and started walking towards the house to pick up another set of tools. Yo happened to be watching where I was working that day. She yelled, "Stop!" She went running towards the place I had just left. There were two men, who had stopped their pickup, got out, had latched onto my roto-tiller, and had started to pick it up and steal it. Yo's yelling startled them and they dropped the roto-tiller, jumped back into their pickup, and took off.

From that day, I had to carry my tools in a wheelbarrow, and wheel them away from the roadside whenever I had to leave the area for even a second. Civilization had indeed come to this small town; it was not always pretty.

Lonesome to be one
There's someone to share life with
Welcome, my brother

Out of the Blue

It was out of the blue, when Greg was about two years old and walking, that Yo said Greg should have a brother or sister. This was not typical of her family playbook, for both of her sisters, Michiye (Michi) and Matsuko (Mat) had only one child each. She must have sensed that it must have been a lonesome life without another sibling. I remember the stories she told me about her nephew, who was sent by his parents in Denver, Colorado, to her parent's farm in Reedley during the summer time. Her parents and the *Chonan*, Charlie, were trying to reestablish their farm and livelihood after interned at Poston, Arizona during World War II. Summer was the busiest time for her parents growing peaches and table grapes for a living. The timing of harvest is of the utmost importance. Thus, when the crop was ripening, her parents must pick the crop or lose the profits. Her parents had no time to babysit. They were up before sunrise and had work to do even at night. Yo's other brothers were still in the US Army or relocated elsewhere. Thus, there was no other small child around for her nephew to spend the time with or toys to play with. Worse still, tractors and trucks were always present during the harvesting and moving right along with the pickers. The equipment was especially attractive to a curious and active grandson who thought they were fun things to climb on and ride. Her parents were in constant fear that the grandson, who was too young to help, was in constant danger of the moving equipment. The Reedley farm was not the place for her nephew to be running around, especially in the way of the workers. But her sister and brother-in-law did not seem to understand the inconvenience and responsibility they were imposing on their grandparents in Reedley. She said her parents finally had to send him back home to Colorado every time he visited in the summer.

I remember seeing Sharon, Mat's daughter, when she was a little girl attending the University of Minnesota Child Center when I was among the *Nisei* teaching Japanese at the university during World War II. I met her mother there. Because Sharon's father was a U.S. Army officer during World War II, she moved many times with her father's reassignment. Sharon was a bright, lovely person, and headstrong, not in a pejorative sense, but self-assured like her mother, Mat. But I do not recall that Mat foisted Sharon onto someone else while growing up. Still, I often wondered what her life was like, and if she had had a sibling if her life would have been different.

When Yo told her obstetrician that she wanted to have another child, the doctor said he was concerned because she was past thirty-five years old. He cautioned her that there might be complications in her pregnancy because of her age. But Yo would have none of that, for she wanted a sibling for Greg, now that both of us had the hang of conceiving. Somehow, Glen had not heard of the normal nine months pregnancy term either. He decided petite mother's womb was too small. The doctor had placed Yo on a 1,200-calorie diet, but she was just as round and bulging as much as she was when she had Greg. Glen was born on August 6, 1958; he was also born a month early. When I rushed Yo to Walnut Creek Kaiser, the doctor told me that there was no sense in me waiting because the doctor was going to make sure that Yo would not suffer giving birth as she had with Greg. The doctor told me to go home and come back in the morning. Again, I was spared having to pace around in the waiting room while Glen was born. Like Greg, he was about eight pounds at birth.

Once we had gone through the process of raising our first child, we had learned that in spite of all the worrying we did, the child would somehow survive our ignorance of child raising and stumbling around for answers. Thus, we just went through the motions of child rearing. In addition to commemorating the dropping of the atomic bomb "Little Boy" on Hiroshima, Japan, on August 6, 1945, Glen did have a surprise for us.

A cold blue terror
Forever a second be
Children all alone

Defining Moment

Don't any one dare move
Booms a hostile voice
Under his jacket
A Cold Blue Pistol
This is a Holdup!
Man shouted gruffly
The Gun held menacingly
Slid back the cover and armed it
Give me your money or I'll shoot
The Cocking sound echoed his threat
Dear God we're in deep trouble

Shopping for Christmas
Is such a big chore
Stretching the dollar
What we always do
Shop in Livermore
Is the town merchant's lackluster cry
J C Penney is the best we can offer
In this one-horse cowboy town
Whatever we choose
The size is too small the color wrong
Stetson hat or saddle is not on our list
Escape this town for Christmas shopping

Twas a sunny day
List of lists in hand
For early shopping
Is on our minds
Oakland Capwell seemed too far
Try our luck at new Bayfair's Mall
Macy east and Monkey Wards west
Not much else but there's a bank
Banks in our town never get it right
This might be worth a try
Let's drop in and see

Lady on the Bridge

Please watch your brother
innocent request
But not to worry
Be back very soon
Over there, we can see you too
In the bank, two tellers working.
We crowd the teller's window
asking questions about this bank
Enters a Burly Crew Cut Man
Our Fate now is almost doomed
A silent vow this defining moment
Never again,
leave our children alone

Sit with me awhile
This key will open the door
To World's Wonderland

Wonders of the World

"What's wrong with our kids?" My wife would give me this questionable look as if my side of the family's genes were the source of our child rearing discrepancies. Of course, I was sure the dilemma wasn't on my side of the family. Our first child presented the greatest anxiety because we wanted to do the right thing, but we didn't know how. We bought Dr. Benjamin Spock's bible, "Baby and Child Care," but our children never seemed to fit the mold in their development stages whether at one month, two months or any other month. We turned to the pages in the book and wondered, "Where did they come up with this data?" Of course, I could have spared myself the agony of child rearing if I had followed my parents' culture and left the responsibility of raising the children to my wife.

But somehow, I didn't fit the mold of my parent's culture because I wanted to share joy of rearing the children with Yo. I would feel cheated if I were to miss the opportunity to be involved in my children's lives from the day they were born. Both of our children must have been on an accelerated schedule or we lost count of the days because they were both born a month early. Greg was never satisfied with his normal feeding schedule and the amount didn't seem quite enough. I remember our kitchen was a sauna bath. Steam poured out constantly from the stove as we sterilized bottles to fill milk and extra bottles for sugared water to keep him happy. I was always afraid to look up at the ceiling because the paint might fall off from the water spots from the steam. Somehow neither one of our sons knew about Dr. Spock. Our second son, Glen, was colicky. The book said the condition would last about two weeks - a condition that usually occurs at nighttime. Since Yo was with the children in the daytime. I felt it was only fair that I get up at night and try to comfort Glen through his difficult period. I thought, "Two weeks, my eye! Dr. Spock, his colic lasted six months!" I would have sung a lullaby to soothe him, but I feared he would develop neurosis from hearing my gravelly singing voice. Somehow, both children survived our blind trial and error procedures.

While they were growing up, I wanted my children to enter the world of wonders through reading. Most of all, I wanted reading to be an enjoyable part of their life. After dinner, I would sit each of my children on my lap and read simple stories with them. My wife was an integral part of this process. When Yo went shopping, she took our sons to Sprouse Ritz, a five and ten cent store in town, and let them select a little reading book for daddy to read at night. I would look for signs that alerted me that my son was ready to read. I would carry my son, look at the photos and pictures hanging on the wall, and ramble on and on about each one, "Look, that's your grandma and grandpa. They live far away in Los Angeles.... See that pretty red flower ..." When I saw a sign that they were recognizing the pictures with my words, I began reading through phonics. It was later that I became aware of the Dr. Seuss storybook, "Cat in the Hat" that mimics what I was already doing.

When my first son started kindergarten, the teacher saw that he could read, so she let him begin the day by reading the school announcements. Her good intentions met with adverse reaction from parents who in turn pressured their children to compete with my son. Jealousy reared its ugly head, and my son was the target of name-calling, dirty tricks, and even rocks thrown at him.

One night, Yo told me that one of the *Nisei* mothers came storming into our home, grabbing children's books and quizzing Yo on what we were doing to teach Greg how to read. Yo said she stood by flabbergasted not knowing what to say or do with this mother's frantic state of mind. While Yo was talking, I thought back to understand who this young *Nisei* was and where she spent her childhood. She was born in Hawaii and her father was a Buddhist priest. I heard from Yo's cousin, whose family lives in Hawaii, that Japanese families are highly competitive with each other in Hawaii. Over forty percent of the population was of Japanese descent and no Japanese wanted to be less than their neighbors were. I just shook my head and thought, "How small minded."

The incident did not end there. The jealousy tainted the minds of the children and jealousy turned to hate and discrimination. Later, I talked to Greg and Glen about the Manzanar experience and discrimination. I explained how people who cannot compete on the same level use any means to try to even the odds: Name-calling, dirty tricks, and outright discrimination are their weapons.

I said, "Your classmates are mad at you because their parents want them to read like you, but they can't right now. It's not your fault. But," I said, "I will not accept that kind of behavior from either of you. I don't want you to treat anyone poorly because they are different from you."

I started the exciting adventure with my children and I would not lose the opportunity. I opened them up to the wonders of the world. I gave them the tools for learning. No one can take that away from them. I believed that without being able to read, writing is impossible, and success in doing math goes hand in hand with being able to read. From that point on, I never needed to help them with their schooling. I would, however, look over their shoulder once in awhile and ask a question or two to see if they were on track. Most important, if they had a question about anything, I would stop whatever I was doing and listen. Not listening would erode a vital link between us. The link is still vibrant, except I am now the one who needs all of the help I can get.

It's a doggone shame
Dog is man's best friend I read
Why can't I have one?

Petty thoughts

"Dad can I have a dog for a pet?" son Greg asked excitedly as he put aside the little Golden book he was reading.

It was one Saturday morning, I was watching the children while Yo was hanging the daily laundry outside. I answered hesitantly, "Why don't we ask your mother because it's a big decision for the family to make, especially, how to take care of a pet?"

"Gee, why do I have to always ask Mom?" son asked inquisitively.

I didn't want to make the decision, because I remembered when I was about my son's age, I never had a pet. However, I once saw a scrawny tan colored dog running among the rows of plants and shrubs in the family's nursery yard, but I never had a chance to play or pet the dog. If the dog was somebody's pet, I didn't see anyone looking for it. "Maybe I remember seeing a stray dog in the yard and not a family pet. I certainly don't know the first thing about taking care of a pet," I thought.

"Greg, mother's outside hanging clothes and she should be finished pretty soon. Why don't we go outside and find mother and ask what she thinks about having a pet?" I was trying to dodge the issue.

Greg got up from his chair and walked with me to look for mom. We walked out into the garage, removed our slippers, and put on our outside shoes as we normally did. Outside, I looked at Yo busily hanging the laundry. I remembered very vividly that I had tried to help her hang the washing once but was chided for doing a sloppy job. Even later, if I wanted to help, I could hand her the washing or select the clothespins for her. Yo was a stickler for exactness on stretching each piece, placing the next one with the tip overlapping just enough for the clothespin to hold them on the line.

Every day, besides the children's clothes, there were dozens of diapers that needed rinsing, sterilized in Clorox, laundered, and hung out to dry on the clothesline. While a young girl, Yo learned that the only sanitary way of drying clothes was on a clothesline. But for rainy days, there was the Kenmore dryer installed in the garage. One day, when the sky was cloudy and looked iffy as to whether it would rain, I saw Yo hanging the clothes outside, I asked her, "Why don't you put the wash in the dryer?" "It'll save you a lot of time from running in and out to keep the wash from getting wet." Yo said, "No, the sunshine is the best dryer. That's how my mother dried her clothes. When I take in the clothes, they always smell so clean. Thus, the extra time hanging the laundry outside is worthwhile. I just love the smell of the outdoors in my washing." From that point on, I learned about clothes drying and never mentioned the dryer again.

Greg also saw mom busy back then, almost every morning, while eating breakfast, the washing machine in the kitchen would go thump-swish-thump-swish, washing dozens of diapers and the clothes of his younger brother. Sometimes the washing machine would dance around on the floor and suddenly go thump and stop. Dad would jump out of his chair, open the lid, even the load and let the washing finish.

"Mom, when you're finished, I want to ask you a big favor." said Greg.

She looked at Greg and said, "I'll be finished in a little while. Why don't you go inside and play with your brother."

We headed back into the garage, sat by the steps of the family room, and went through the family ritual of removing the shoes, brushing the clothes to shed any dirt or sand, and donning slippers to enter the house. Yo was fussy about keeping the house clean. Removing the shoes before entering the house is something she learned to do when she visited Japan with her mother as a youngster. She told us one day that every home had a wooden platform in front of the entrance where people left their shoes before going into the house. At our home, the ritual of removing shoes was a must because the backyard was a big play yard and the children could track in dirt.

As soon as Yo finished hanging the laundry and entered the playroom, Greg said, "Mom, can I have a dog for a pet? Dad didn't answer me when I asked him first, but he said I should ask you." There was a moment of silence while Yo and I looked at each other as if muttering, "He's your son, so why don't you answer him?" Then Yo said, "Greg, do you remember when we spent a day at Oakland's Children's Fairy Land? While I was minding your brother, you and Dad saw all of the Fairyland displays; Little Red Hen, Blue Whale, the Cuckoo Clock on a lopsided building?"

"Yes, Mom," Greg answered, "I also saw so many other things with dad. I remember standing in front of the wall where Humpty Dumpty was sitting on top and I had fun reciting Humpty Dumpty sat on a Wall with dad."

"But, afterwards, you were so happy riding the Jolly Trolley around and through the Fairyland that you wanted one more ride," Yo replied.

"Mom, will we go again when my brother can walk with me?" asked Greg.

"Yes, but let me finish what I want to say," continued mom.

"Afterwards we walked towards Lakeside Park, spread our blanket under a shady tree, and ate our picnic lunch. We decided to see the ducks at the Lakeside Park pond. Greg, you were having fun petting the ducks. Dad was acting silly and having fun quacking and making noises like a duck. But do you remember what happen when you came home?"

"I remember you called the doctor and we went to his office," said Greg.

"The doctor gave you a medicine because you broke out with hives after petting the goats and ducks. I remember you had big red spots all over your body. Do you remember trying to scratch the red spots, Greg?" asked Yo.

"And, do you remember when your younger brother broke out with ring worm after playing with your cousin's kittens? I'm afraid both of you are allergic to furry animals and having a dog for a pet just won't do," said Yo.

Greg didn't pout or leave in a huff after Yo had finished talking. I said a silent, "Thank you" to myself, and we never mentioned pets again.

Nature's harvest gift
Pilgrim's festive Thanksgiving
Thanks go a long way

Thanksgiving Turkey

I wish there were more thanks in Thanksgiving. When I was in McKinley grammar school in Santa Monica, California during the late 1920s, I had dreaded the day after Thanksgiving. At school, we had learned about the Pilgrims and about how they had shared their harvest with our native Indians at that first Thanksgiving day. It was a lesson of thanks and sharing our good fortune with others. The teacher had given us supplies to act out Thanksgiving Day. Some children had drawn pictures of the Pilgrims and Indians while others had cut out pictures of the turkey from magazines. But when we had returned from the holiday, the teacher would ask each of us about Thanksgiving. In those days, I had tried to imagine I was a small mouse in the corner of the room just hoping that the teacher would not call on me. Mother ruled the kitchen and roast turkey with all the trimmings were not on her menu. A bowl of rice and pickled horseradish for Thanksgiving dinner wasn't what I had wanted to share with the class.

It was after I was married that we began to celebrate Thanksgiving with our children. My task was to clean the turkey while my wife prepared her special stuffing and all the trimmings. I had often seen my mother clean the inside of a chicken by scraping out what looked like purplish red innards. "*Okaasan*, what's that you're scraping out of the chicken?" I once asked. "It's best to remove these parts inside because sometimes the chicken can carry some sickness," she replied. I followed mother's advice and scraped out the vital organs inside the turkey until it was squeaky-clean.

My wife always out did herself. There was always too much food for the four of us. But the kids had always looked forward to Yo's special Thanksgiving stuffing made of rice, ground beef and pork, and spices all cooked together. One year, my wife said, "Why don't we celebrate this Thanksgiving Day with the grandparents since they are all alone? I'll ask my brothers and their families to join us. I'm sure my parents will be happy to see their family together."

We had decided to make the arrangements and provide all of the food. We left for the grandparent's house a day early to prepare everything. Grandparents' home was a long drive out into the "Fruit Basket of California" in Central Valley. We had traveled this three-hour route many times before. It had never failed; as I drove out to the highway, the kids would say," Are we there yet?" Every fifteen minutes the same question would come up. "No, pretty soon," we answered each time. Finally, I had decided to let my wife drive while I sat with my sons and kept them occupied by playing a game of being the first person to call out out-of-state license plates of the cars passing by.

As soon as my wife turned east from Highway 99 onto Manning Ave., the kids would be excited because they knew we were getting closer to grandma's house. Still, it would be at least twenty minutes more before we would turn into the grandparents' driveway. My in-laws' home was an old farmhouse typical of the early 1900s. It was a single story house with a porch in front and a screened porch in back. It was white but weathered and the dust had dulled the siding. Inside, there was a kitchen, and a large room that was a dining area and a parlor. The house had

263

two bedrooms but the floor of the second one did not match the rest of the house. And the room didn't seem to set on any permanent foundation. In winter, sleeping in that bedroom was like sleeping in an icebox. There was no insulation or sheetrock on the inside, and the ceiling was just the roof by itself. Summer was no better because the valley was sweltering hot, and I could hear the high-pitched "bzzzz, bzzz" as the mosquitoes zoomed down out of nowhere, for they seemed to relish my blood.

The original farm had been a turkey ranch that left the land very fertile. Yo told me that when her father had first moved here, he planted a melon patch where the turkeys had grazed while his fruit trees and grape vines matured. The melons had grown so large that the buyers prized them and wanted every one of them. On site, there were several old buildings left from the former turkey ranch that were dilapidated and severely weather worn. The boards were so dry and split that I could see through the sidings. There was a tall barn, a shed for storage, a pump house, an outhouse, and old building that housed a *furo*, Japanese bath. Of course, using the outhouse was for the last desperate need, but even entering the other old buildings was hazardous. I tried never to stay inside any one of the old buildings more than I needed to.

When we entered the driveway, the dust followed us all the way to the house. The grandparents, who were working outside could see that someone had arrived. They quickly put their tools away and welcomed us into their home. As soon as we had settled in, my wife said to her mother, "*Okaasan*, we're going to the grocery store to buy all of the things for Thanksgiving. Do you need anything?" We headed for the Japanese grocery store in Reedley since her mother had nothing in mind for shopping.

While shopping, a friend, Yo knew from childhood saw her, and soon the gossiping started that brought each up to date on what had happen and who had done what since last time they had seen each other. I, of course, had no idea of the people they talked about, and stood by looking dumbfounded and watched. I could see from my wife's reaction, for sometimes she would raise her eyebrows, act surprised and acknowledged her friend's news as, "Oh, really?" Finally, after she caught up on all of the local news, we continued with our shopping for Thanksgiving. There was one item that my wife was sure to buy. It was either a pie or cake; that had always been grandmother's weakness.

I remember the story that my wife told me about an event that had happened to her when she was at Poston, Arizona during the war. In camp, earning extra money had been almost a non-existent opportunity. One day, she said, there was a posting for internees to harvest cotton. Not wishing to go by herself, she had coaxed one of her friends to take the job with her. They rode on an Army truck outside the internment camp and through the dusty Arizona desert to a cotton field. At the site, they each received a long canvas bag that each would fill with the cotton they picked. My wife was less than five feet tall, and the bag was at least ten feet long. Worst of all, she had to pick what had been left after the cotton-picking machine had made its run through the field. She dragged that heavy sack between the rows of dried up cotton bushes for hours until she was exhausted. The foreman kept yelling, "A'ndale, a'ndale (Hurry up)!" She ignored the prodding, sat down and quit, and waited for the weigh-in to collect her pay. When she returned to camp with the work crew, she went directly to the Poston canteen to buy something for her mother. Her cotton-picking wages had been barely enough to buy a small cake. She said the cake was dry and stale, but her mother still enjoyed it. On this Thanksgiving holiday, grandma would be sure to have sweets.

As soon as we returned to the farm, we spent the rest of the day preparing everything except the turkey. My wife was slaving over the stove preparing our children's favorite stuffing. Instead of bread, she used cooked rice mixed with ground beef and pork, and herbs. First, she cooked the ground meat and drained the fat over and over. Then she mixed ingredients together and let it cool until the next morning. While Yo was busy, I plucked out the hair feathers and cleaned the turkey for stuffing early Thanksgiving Day.

In the morning, we never had needed an alarm clock since the grandparents were always up before dawn. Without fail on our visits, grandma would usually fuss with the pots and pans in the kitchen to make sure we would hear that they were up already. We would moan and groan, turn around, and cover our ears because we wanted a few more winks. However, this morning was special, for we needed to stuff and prepare to roast the twenty-pound turkey. At the minimum I had estimated that it would take at least five hours to roast Tom.

Around noon, her brothers and their families arrived. Our sons went outside to play ball with their cousins while the adults turned on the TV and watched football games. The wives were in the corner somewhere chatting. However, Yo and I were too busy to listen to the gossip. When five hours had passed, I checked the thermometer and it was 165 degrees in the center of the stuffing. It was time to serve. There were enough places and chairs for all of us to sit together, and grandma brought out her best tablecloth. In the meantime, my wife had finished preparing the vegetables and the rest of the food. I was busy preparing the gravy. We called the children to come in and wash up for dinner.

Since space was limited on the dinner table to place the turkey and other food, I had decided to carve the turkey in the kitchen. As soon as I had filled a big serving platter, Yo hustled the servings to the dining table. I must have lost track of how long I had been in the kitchen until I realized that I had better join everyone. I put some slices of turkey and mashed potatoes on my plate and walked into the dining room. Surprise! Everybody had finished and left the table. I looked and saw them all gathered around the TV. Only the dirty dishes with remnants of eaten food left there to accompany me with my Thanksgiving dinner. I pushed some plates aside and shoveled my food into my mouth. It was the loneliest Thanksgiving I ever had. However, it was just as lonely afterwards, because nobody offered to help us clear the table or help with the dishes. I did not hear one "Thank you" that day. Thanks is such a small word but big in heart even at Thanksgiving.

God's wondrous gift, life
A dream, a blue print of life
Vision from within

Dreams

It was not my dream, a blue print of life that I had wished upon my children. A dream is a spark that could glow brightly but it would sputter unless fueled by energy within. Yo and I had been careful not to dictate our children's future, for without that inner spark, it would not glow. There was, however, one thing constant that Yo and I had stressed to our children as they grew up; go to college and get a degree. It was the catalyst for success. Remembering my own past, I know that it was my parents' fond hope that someone in our family would go to college. They came from a troubled time of feudal Japan, gave up on their own educational aspirations, struggled hard in a land foreign to them, and often found it unwelcoming, they wanted us to have a better life that could come with higher education. I remember *Okaasan* always hinted that it would be nice if one of us would become a doctor or a lawyer. However, I had no idea about or desire for these two professions, because I had no role model to motivate me or guide me. I was naive, because I grew up in the era that did not necessarily open the door of opportunity for me, a *Nisei* with a college education. On the other hand, I am sure what my parents observed was that a *Nisei*, who had become a doctor or a lawyer, could provide professional service to a Japanese community.

While it may not have concerned me at that time in my life, I did not hear those same words of advice, "Go to college" given to my sisters. It was after I was married that I learned why. Yo had once told me that, upon graduating from high school, she wanted to enter the business college at Fresno State. Somehow, her parents were against her going to college. "You are a girl. Girls don't need a college education." was the attitude of her *Issei* parents. Instead, after she graduated high school in 1939, her father sent her to a Japanese Finishing School in Fresno, California conducted by an elderly *Issei* couple. While the goal of the schooling was teaching Japanese etiquette, social skills, flower arrangement, and even the archaic customs like Tea Ceremony, the couple, in fact, ran a marriage arrangement service for *Issei* families. Because the *Issei* had to hold fast to their culture in order to survive in America in the face of discrimination and anti-Asian laws forbidding them to become citizens, they must have believed that *Nisei* would meet the same fate. Girls were like chattel that must imbue traditional Japanese culture to make them more attractive as wives. Somehow, Yo must have missed some of her finishing classes, for she had never entertained me with *cha-no-yu*, a tea ceremony or decorated our home with an *ikebana,* Japanese flower arrangement.

Since Yo was a stay-at-home mom, she paid close attention to Greg and Glen growing up. What we both cared about was who our children's friends were because sometimes jealousy showed its ugly head towards our sons. Because both Greg and Glen did well in school, it seems that a few parents put pressure on their children to do better than our sons did. We talked to both of them to cast what was happening in its proper light and explain to our children that it was not because of what they had done. We were always interested and supportive of their education, and attended all of the parent-teacher conferences to meet the teachers. I found that the quality of the teachers ranged from superb to "Why are they teaching?"

One day, after I had returned from work, Greg, who was attending Almond Avenue Grammar School and never needed help with his math, brought his textbook and math papers for me to help him with a particular math problem. I saw his worried look, and he seemed hesitant to ask. He showed me a problem that he had completed and said that the teacher told him his answer was wrong. I opened his math book to the particular chapter, glanced at the topics, and read the exercise he had worked on. The chapter was on measuring objects, and the problem asked to calculate a volume of a given object. Greg's answer was correct. He said he went over and over his calculation, but the teacher kept insisting his answer was wrong. The teacher had confused the calculation of surface area for volume. I told Greg he was right, but I said he would have a hard time correcting the teacher. In fact, I said it could be detrimental for him to do so. I said, "Know that you are right, but just let the teacher believe she is right." Later, I heard that she had become the supervisor for advance mathematics for the Livermore Schools District.

Without any professional qualification, she also had the audacity to say that Greg needed psychiatric treatment at our parent teacher conference.

Because playing basketball was never my greatest achievement, Greg and Glen must have inherited my poor basketball ability. One day, Greg came home from East Avenue Middle School looking a bit disappointed. The coach tested the student's ability to shoot baskets that day. There were several boys that did not shoot baskets very well; a few were Orientals. He said the P.E. teacher told them they would never amount to very much in the future, because they could not shoot baskets very well. I was completely flabbergasted and could not give any excuse to Greg for that misguided statement.

Years passed, and Yo was working at a bistro to fill her empty hours because our two sons had graduated UC Davis, and had established their own careers: Greg was an IBM Senior Engineer, and Glen was an OBGYN doctor. One day, she saw the ex-P.E. teacher at a bistro sitting with several women teachers from the East Avenue School for lunch. She had heard that the group was celebrating his promotion as the principal of the East Avenue School. The moment seemed ripe to talk to him about the past. She approached him and repeated what he had said to Greg and the other East Avenue students who could not shoot basketballs very well. Then she let go forcefully telling him that those students who he said would not amount to anything had graduated various colleges. She told him that our sons were a senior engineer for IBM, and one was a doctor. Other students that he had denigrated became a practicing psychiatrist, another was a doctor, and one other became a research post-doctorate. As his faced turned red and he became speechless, she turned and walked away.

Ever since Russia had launched the first man into space, I constantly read that America's educational system was failing our children in math and science to meet the challenge. From the stories, I heard from my sons, I could understand why. When Glen was attending East Avenue School, he said two of his teachers amused him on how they conducted themselves in the classroom. One was a science teacher nearing his retirement and his enthusiasm for teaching had retired years before. His exams were a re-hash of prior years, and, if a student had siblings that had him as a teacher, the pupil would know all the questions in the test. The other person was a math teacher who taught the slower achieving math students. He had convinced the principal to let him teach the advanced students. One day, Glen said the teacher wanted to demonstrate on how to solve a problem on the blackboard. The students watched him as he fumbled around trying to find his way. He stopped for a moment and uttered, "This is a tough problem." When the bell rang, Glen said he was still at the blackboard unable to solve the problem.

Yet both Greg and Glen were fortunate to have an outstanding teacher at East Avenue. He was Mr. Immel who must have left a great impression on my sons, because Yo had heard that they both visited him after they attended their Livermore High School classes on many occasions. Each advanced further in mathematics at Livermore High School when they attended and participated in the multi-media math program at the math learning center, which Mr. Al Ofiesh and assisted by Mr. Graham had developed a new curriculum. Both of our sons became student teachers in the program to assist other students with their individual assignments. At first, I thought the learning would be superficial, but I learned otherwise. It was one day at the Lab when a physicist saw me talking to someone in my group and he asked, "Are you Greg Kishi's father?" Then he said that he wanted to thank Greg and me, because his daughter was having a hard time with math that she was ready to give up her goal of going to college. She signed up for the Math Learning Center and was still having difficulties until Greg assisted her. She said that Greg was very patient with her, explained math in a way she could understand, and had helped her overcome her fear of math. He said excitedly with a glow on his face that she was now enthusiastic about applying for a college education.

Before the days of the personal computers, students at Livermore High had the opportunity to learn IBM's FORTRAN, FORmula TRANslator, a higher level programming language, and use a CDC 3400 computer system to compile, debug, and run their programs. The CDC 3400 was part of the Department of Applied Science at UC Davis' LLRL site for their graduate program. Greg and other Livermore High students were eager to learn FORTRAN and utilize the CDC 3400. The FORTRAN program used IBM cards for compiling. Greg showed me the program he had designed, programmed, and was eager to compile and run it. It was an ambitious endeavor. At the time, I hated to tell him I had an aversion to FORTRAN because I was a purist believing that assembly language programming was the only way to go. Actually, I hated reading a computer manual, because they can be very dull. Every Thursday after school, Greg would offer a ride in our station wagon to any student who wanted to use the CDC 3400 computer at the CDC Building on East Ave. and Research Drive. I remember Yo had mentioned that one Livermore High School student was Anne Perlman. I recognized the name Perlman, because I knew her father and respected him highly. He was a member of LLNL's Engineering Department that I interfaced at LLNL. I had also seen Greg leaving early for school to use the High School's keypunch for his FORTRAN program. I was surprised when I learned that his teacher had given him the key to the room so that he could come before school started, open the room, and use the school's equipment. He had earned the trust of his teachers, and they knew he was a responsible individual.

One day, Greg told me about new equipment that the physics class had received. It was a portable CO_2 laser. He was excited about tinkering with the laser and dreaming about a project to use it. Some days before, I had cut out an article in the local newspaper reporting that the American Heart Association would sponsor a high school student's science project by providing a stipend up to seventy-five dollars. I showed him the article and encouraged him to contact them and see if they would consider his project. Greg received approval, and his next step was to carry out his project as promised. He had arranged with his physics teacher, Mr.Trimingham, to use some equipment from the physics lab supplies for his project. I had to move my car out of the garage since he needed space to set up his project. I also gave up my precious coffee table top so that his equipment would be set on a solid level platform. I was amazed how focused he was on his project, and all of the extra procedures he had to take, from setting up the lens and mirror, aligning the laser system, taking pictures of his laser application, and developing his own films. He did all of this with rudimentary equipment. After Greg finished, I saw him over several nights assembling his snapshots and writing a final report for the American Heart Association sponsorship. One Saturday, Greg went to UC Berkeley to talk with his sponsor about his project. When Greg returned, he told me that the sponsor, who was a professor at UC Berkeley, had commented that the level of his accomplishment was equal to some of his graduate students' projects. He had also asked Greg if he would be interested in applying to UC Berkeley.

After Greg had graduated from high school and entered UC Davis, he continued using the CDC 3400 on his semester breaks. On those occasions, Glen had also accompanied him to use the CDC 3400 in the evenings. One day, two individuals, Lowell Woods, head of the Lab's "O" group and Andrew Porter, a graduate student of the UC Davis' LLNL site had been impressed with the level of their FORTRAN programs and had offered them the use of the CDC 3400 anytime in the evenings. Later, Greg and Glen had permission to power up the system by themselves, run it, power it down, and close the facility. Lowell Woods had also invited Greg to participate in the Lab's summer program for college students. However, the Lab was reluctant to allow him to be in the summer program even though Lowell had argued before the Laboratory's directors for his case. At the time, I had known nothing about Greg's invitation by Lowel. It seems the denial was due to my supervisory position at the Lab that would seem to be preferential treatment for Greg. The Lab did allow him to work in Lowell's "O" group without any stipend. But then, I did recall that even Dr. Teller's son, Paul was once denied participating at the Lab because inviting him might have reflected undue influence by Dr. Teller.

Over the years, I had often heard of Lowell Woods and Andrew Porter spoken with great respect by my two sons. I had also observed that Lowell had hired college students into his "O" group to further their interest in science by challenging them with creative projects. Greg described to me the solar energy project Lowell Woods had assigned him for the summer. He was to write a program for a PDP11 mini-computer to control a solar panel and follow the sun for maximum energy input. One day, Greg came home with a handful of motor parts. Lowell had told him he had to assemble the step motor to control the solar panel. The solar panels were set on a pole with the cables connected from the solar panel to the PDP11. First, the pole holding the solar panel had to be set in the ground. Lowell was undoubtedly the Lab's best equipment expediter, and he had often bypassed the Lab's red tape for acquiring supplies. I chuckled when Greg said that Lowell bought cement, rented a post hole digger, brought all of it into the Lab at night, Then he dug the hole for the solar panel post, cemented it, and returned the post hole digger all in one night. He had cut the Lab's red tape by at least six months. One day, I visited the site where Greg's project was located, and I saw the pole with the solar panel on top, cables dangling down and into a trailer. Inside the trailer was the PDP-11 system that Greg was writing the software for to control the solar panel. From my supervisory experience being responsible for programmers and technicians, I could see that Greg was not only programming a real-time data acquisition and control system, but, also, he was involved in all aspects of the project: assembling motors to control the panel, hooking up the system, and programming. It was a dream project from beginning to end.

For Glen, the spark must have been there the day he started kindergarten. Yo told me Glen never wanted to go to pre-school and was completely happy to be at home. On the first day of kindergarten, Yo walked with Glen towards the East Avenue School. When they reached Hillcrest Street, Glen told Yo not to walk further with him to the kindergarten class because he could do it himself. From then on there was never a need to show him the way. However, in the shadow, Yo was always near to make sure everything was ok. One day, when Glen had forgotten his lunch, Yo took it to the Livermore High School office for him. She met Mr. Reginato, the principal, and he said Glen was probably at the Student Union. A crowd of students were watching Glen and his classmates playing "Dungeons and Dragons". Sure enough, when Yo went to see Glen, she said he was down in front in the middle of the crowd.

Glen pointed out to me several times that he and his classmates grew up in a time and place that was unique. His friends were the off spring of goal oriented, highly motivated parents that worked at the Lawrence Livermore Lab. They were all members of the math club that competed with other high schools in math contests. He had nothing but praise for his teammates. I remember meeting Greg and Glen's classmates, and without exception, they were outstanding students, who respected each other as classmates, and enjoyed their off hours with each other. However, they were youngsters who earned the teacher's respect and not automatically given to them.

One day, when Yo and I opened our local newspaper, there staring at us was a photo of Greg and another student, Pat Duletsky from Livermore High who each won the Pacific Gas and Electric scholarship. The award must have been newsworthy because their pictures appeared for several weeks. Yo and I were honored to attend the awards ceremony held at Jack London Square, California. However, Glen was not to be outdone. His picture also appeared in the local Livermore Herald newspaper. The Herald interviewed him about his Livermore High School experience. He had won the CSF Seymour Award for excellence as an outstanding student. Yo and I knew nothing about their pictures appearing in the newspaper. No sooner had we seen Glen's picture, than Yo received a call from a mother whose son was in the same class as Glen. Yo said she could hear the rage in the mother's voice as she accused us of promoting Glen's picture in the newspaper. She shouted through the phone that her son had done better on the SAT tests and he should have been the one in the newspaper. Yo told her that we knew nothing about the article until we saw it that morning. The mother quickly hung up the phone, but we were amused to hear later that she had stormed over to the Livermore Herald Newspaper Office, and raised a ruckus over the whole affair.

Many wonderful people had kindled the dream, the inner spark of our children, and especially their teachers who found Greg and Glen worthy of recognition as outstanding students: diligent, trustworthy, and studious. It glowed brightly in the "Wonders of the World" opened by the key: reading.

In summertime heat
She's a red-hot tomato
Enough to jar you

Gentleman Farmer

If *Otoosan* had only taught me how to farm and warned me of the pitfalls I would face, then maybe my attempt to grow vegetables in my garden would have been easier. It was only after Greg and Glen had outgrown their swing and slide that I began to think about growing my own vegetables in the backyard. The thirty yards of sawdust that I had spread had packed down or blown away to other parts of the yard. The sawdust was a constant reminder that I needed to do something with that empty space. Fortunately, there were no weeds to hoe because sunlight didn't penetrate the layer of sawdust. However, the rocks and pebbles were still waiting underneath to challenge me.

I gathered as many pamphlets as I could about vegetable gardening from Sunset, Ortho, and handouts from the local garden stores. The whole process looked simple enough: dig the area up, cultivate the soil, and level the area, dig rows of trenches, smooth the planting area, and dig pockets for seeds or plants and pre-water the seeding area. However, the hardest part was to know how many seeds to put in each planting spot. I was overly generous, for if three would do, then five or six must be better odds for success. It was a tough decision to make to thin out the seedlings, for I was greedy and tended to leave more than I should have.

My first attempt was growing cucumbers and squash. That year the weather was nice and balmy at the end of February and early March. I got excited and prepared the vegetable bed, and planted my seeds. I was happy to see the seedlings sprout. Success was at hand I thought. While feeling smug about seeing the plants poking out, I began to notice a few toppling over. I gently pulled the broken ones out of the ground and noticed something chewed the delicate stems. Earwigs had snuck into my vegetable bed from the neighbor's hayfield and snipped some of my seedlings. I had to find something to deter the ugly looking earwigs. I decided to cut the bottom off used tin cans and place them over the seedlings as barriers. Then I doused the area with DDT. I knew insecticide was safe because I had seen a photo of our US Armed Forces delousing refugees with DDT during World War II.

My seedlings seemed happy, as they grew bigger. Then the weather turned cold as the temperature dropped below fifty degrees. Every day I looked at my prize, but they just refused to grow and eventually rotted. For several years, I would get excited when the weather turned warm before spring, but I was always defeated in starting my vegetable garden early. Eventually, I learned the hard way not to get excited until sometime in April for sowing seeds in the Livermore Valley.

Finally, my cucumbers and my squash began growing nicely. At first, the cucumbers would be straight and vibrant looking. They were delicious in our salad, but gradually some turned bitter. Yo tried her magic of cutting off the ends and then rubbing them against the cucumber. It must have been an old wife's tale - still bitter. Slowly the leaves began turning yellow and the ends of the cucumber shriveled up. I looked under the leaves and it was full of little bugs. Some were aphids, ants, and thrips that were sucking the life out of my plants. I had noticed the ants herding the aphids to produce more sweet liquid. The sweet honeydew left by the aphids soon caused the leaves to form sooty mold fungus that turned black. It was disheartening. Once I tried spraying the plants, but I was against the odds of success and I had to yank the plants out of the ground.

Squash was another curious gardening experience for me. I was delighted to see the bright yellow flowers with bees busy with pollen covering their legs. I believed that the yellow blossoms would all fruit. I was wrong. I learned that there are male and female flowers even though they look the same. When the squash began to grow, I could swear that I saw them grow by inches every day. I should have picked them early, but I thought, "Why not wait and get more for your money?" Zucchini were prolific producers that had their good and bad points. They were good because I got many zucchinis. It was bad because I hated to throw them away and my friends and neighbors didn't want my prize zucchinis either. It was even harder to take when Greg and Glen grumbled at dinner and said, "Zucchini again?" Finally, when I had to yank them out, there staring at me was a big fat zucchini that had managed to hide under a leaf. It must have been at least six pounds. For amusement, I carefully picked it and took it to Yo. When she looked at it, her eyes opened wide and gave me that questioning look, "What do you expect me to do with this monster?"

I ventured into growing other vegetables with varying success. My experience of growing carrots was the worst, because they came out of the soil in deformed corkscrew shapes as the roots sought out nutrients in the hard rocky soil. I also tried cantaloupes and watched the plants produce a few nice melons. I was waiting patiently for them to ripen when, one morning, the prize melon I had been watching had a big gash raked over it. I was stunned to see the beautiful orange colored flesh inside exposed. I was puzzled for several days, for I kept thinking that it was a neighborhood cat that had clawed at it. Then, I looked carefully at the soil near by. There were animal tracks but not tracks of a cat. Later, I found out that there were possums in the neighborhood. My one and only neighbor loved cats and always left food out on his porch for stray cats to feed on. The possums must have loved him for his free meal.

Two things that I loved growing: tomatoes and strawberries. With tomatoes, I had never figured out how many tomato plants I should plant. Strawberries, on the other hand, there just weren't any limit because they were my weakness. I still remember when Joe had started the nursery in Santa Monica on Wilshire Blvd, and my sister-in-law, Yo invited me for a slice the fresh strawberry cream pie. It makes my mouth water when I think about that sumptuous delicious flavor of strawberry smothered with whip cream.

It's hard to imagine a world without tomatoes. They were once called love apples, but the vine is poisonous. Some say the tomato is a fruit and some say vegetable, but it doesn't matter to me. Sliced, diced, cooked, and even from the ketchup bottle, the tomato is forever tasty. I have watched kids slather ketchup on French fries, eggs, hamburger, steaks, and any other edible food. I have read that Baskin and Robbins once made ketchup ice cream but it didn't "ketch-on." Tomato is not only tasty food, but it has other uses. It may be insanity, but in Spain an annual tomato fight takes place. Anything that moves is a likely target. It is messy: soft and squishy. Why, it could even restore your copper pots and pans to nice even glow if you daubed some on the copper metal and rubbed it vigorously.

"She's a red-hot tomato! What an eye-catcher!" Can something as red and luscious as a tomato have a dark past? Imagine in Europe, around 1500's, people did not believe the tomato was edible. They thought it was poisonous since it belonged to the nightshade family, *Atropus belladonna.*, The name, Belladonna or "beautiful woman" seems so appropriate. Even though Peru and Mexico claim its origin, the tomato took a long roundabout way to reach America. It was the colonists who had brought the tomato plants from Britain to the New World and, even then, people were afraid to eat it.

One year, I decided to grow my own tomato plants in my garden. I measured a four by twelve foot plot, roto-tilled the soil, prepared it with fertilizer and humus, and set two rows for planting. I had no knowledge of how much fruit each plant would bear. I had guessed that a dozen tomato plants would be enough for our family.

Rather than sow seeds and wait anxiously, while I twiddled my thumbs, for the tomato seeds to sprout, I decided to plant seedlings from a nursery. I watered and watched the seedlings grow day after day. The tomato plants had bushed out and looked beautiful and green. Still it was at least two months before I saw any bloom. Somewhere I had read that tomato blooms were self-pollinating. I thought if I tickled each bloom of the tomato blossoms, I could help pollinate the blossoms. It seems silly but I buzzed around each blossom like a busy bee pollinating my tomato plants. It worked, for every blossom set. Slowly but surely, little round green orbs of tomato started to form.

After seventy days, the tomatoes started to ripen. Not one at a time, but the dozen plants, decided to lavish me with tomatoes. I filled one bucket in no time. My wife saw the tomatoes and panicked. "We better can them," she said. "Bring them inside. I have Kerr jars and some quart mayonnaise jars to can them."

Why did this always happen at the hottest days of the year? I waited until Yo started boiling a big pot full of water on the stove then I dumped my first batch of tomatoes into the sink, pulled the stems off, and washed them. When the water boiled, I dumped the tomatoes into the pot. Then I watched for the first sign of the skins splitting; out they came, and dumped into the sink for peeling. It was hot and humid as beads of sweat formed and ran down our bodies like a waterfall. There was no time to worry about sweating, for we are too busy: peeling the skins, cutting out the stem part, squeezing, and tossing them back into another pot for cooking. There was no need to add water because we crushed the tomatoes for juice. After we had cooked the tomatoes down, our jarring process began. We sterilized the jars and lids by boiling them in a large pot. First, we filled each jar with the processed tomatoes and added two tablespoon of bottled lemon juice per quart for acidification. Next, we capped the jars and placed them back into a pot of boiling water until the first sign of boiling. We retrieved the hot jars and set them aside to cool. Then, we waited to hear the "Pop" sound signifying that the vacuum had sealed the jar.

This hot sweaty process went on for days and our house retained a distinct smell of tomatoes. We had boxes of canned tomatoes in quart jars. Kerr had become a household name. Year after year, I could never correctly estimate the number of tomato plants I would need to be in happy equilibrium with the number of tomatoes for eating versus no more canning. The boxes of canned tomato began to swamp the space in the garage. I do not recall *Okaasan* using tomatoes in her cooking. Cooking *sukiyaki* with tomatoes as one of the basic vegetables would not only dominate the delicate flavor, but also change the appearance of this simple dish. Again, cooked tomatoes on top of a bowl of rice may look like the *Hinomaru*, a Japanese flag, but it just would not look appetizing to me. Because we had ended up having so many boxes of tomatoes piling up in the garage, I had to build an extra shed for storing them. Some twenty-five years later, I still had canned tomatoes in my shed waiting to share their red juicy flavor.

While Greg and Glen were growing up, I did not pay any attention to planting fruit trees except a Navel and a Valencia orange tree. However, around Memorial Day, we always looked forward to picking our own cherries. It was a nice drive down Vasco, a two-lane road, to the small farming town of Brentwood where several owners of cherry orchards would allow people to come and pick their own cherries. They would hand you a bucket and let you use their ladder to pick your own, and charge at the end by the weight of your booty. I remember when we were picking cherries; we would be up on the ladder giving in to the temptation to eat as many cherries as we were picking to keep. Even with a bucket full of cherries, they did not seem to last too long.

While picking our own fruit at Brentwood was fun, it seemed to me that I could enjoy fruit longer at home if I planted a few fruit trees. Again, the perils of a gentleman farmer hit me. First, I planted a dwarf apple tree that had two varieties grafted on to the main stalk. I was happy to see the tree blossoming. Then my troubles began. Little nodules were forming on the trunk of the tree. Gradually the branches began to stop growing. I kept cutting back the branches until it was almost bald. I finally dug it out, stuffed everything in my fifty-gallon oil can, and burned all of it. With that big oil can, I never had to haul trash to our local garbage dump, for I was able to burn most of my garden trimmings. There was nothing closer to nature than to start a fire in that fifty-gallon oil can on a freezing cold early morning, hug close to it to warm up, and then start work in the garden before feeling cold again.

After the loss of the apple tree, I decided to try my luck with plum and peach trees. I had purchased a Santa Rosa, a soft fleshy fruit, a Satsuma plum, a firm blood red fruit and a freestone peach. All three were bare root trees, took hold quickly, and bore fruits the third year. I was happy for the moment then my troubles began. Borers attacked each one and the sap oozed out. I cut away the infected areas and applied an insecticide. It was a constant battle. The peach tree succumbed. Both plum trees were vigorous growers and survived the attacks with my constant scraping and spraying. Then I was shocked when I saw the fruit on the Satsuma plum. Instead of red, it was yellow. Someone had put the wrong tag on the tree. I was devastated!

It seems that everyone plants Santa Rosa plums, because they are vigorous growers and they bear many fruit. I was in trouble again, for most of the fruits ripen all at once. When I picked a bucket full and took it to Yo, she decided to try her luck making plum jam. If luck was what she needed, then it was not always there. There must be some magic in adding the right amount of pectin because some jams were loose and some would hardly shake in the jar. While completely immersed in jarring plums, we forgot that we did not need so many. The fruit began to drop to the ground since we could not keep up with the ripening fruit. Then, one day, our neighbor brought us a bucket full of his ripened Santa Rosa plums. I told him that we had more than enough from our tree. He went away a bit unhappy for not being able to unload his over ripened fruits. Before he left, I took a quick look at what he had in the bucket and I was shocked. He must have picked many of the fruits from the ground. I was sure I saw some gravel and leaves mixed in with the fruits. Yo and I would have never offered any fruit that was not the best of the crop. It was Japanese etiquette taught to us by our parents. Surely, it would have been *haji* to do otherwise.

Even with my unlucky first experience with an apple tree, I was willing to try again by planting a Golden Delicious and a Red Delicious apple trees. This time they took hold and produced a bountiful supply of apples. Still, I had to be vigilant and spray to deter coddling moths. It was no small chore. By the time I finished spraying with a two-gallon sprayer on trees over ten feet tall, my left arm hung like a limp rag and the right arm was sore from pumping the sprayer for pressure.

As time passed, as more and more homes built around our neighborhood, and other critters appeared in our yard. Our first next-door neighbor hired a Japanese gardener to landscape his yard. He did a well-planned garden but it required regular maintenance of the plants to keep the landscape in balance. However, my present neighbor had a different view of gardening – he did not like to cut or trim any plants. Consequently, his hedges had resorted to their natural growth: sky-high. Unaware at the time, a blue jay had planted acorns and almonds in his yard and ours. An acorn sprouted in his yard and next to our fence and the oak tree has now grown to forty feet high. With the prevailing westerly winds, two thirds of the oak tree branches hung over the fence. Raucous blue jays had made their home in my neighbor's yard, and it had been a constant struggle to remove acorns and almonds planted by them. On the bright side, the blue jays had planted two almond trees that were producing almonds for us. For a while, we were able to gather almonds until I saw a squirrel sharing our crop. For some reason, Yo wanted me to cut down one of the trees even though it was bearing almonds. Without hesitation, I brought out my chain saw and cut the tree down to three inches from the ground. This time, I could not burn the trimmings because the city banned burning within its jurisdiction. I piled all of the branches and trimmings in the back yard to haul them to the Livermore Disposal Site. The next day, as I wandered to the backyard, I was surprised to see a squirrel sitting and looking at the place where once there was an almond tree. I stayed in the background quietly and watched. The squirrel was motionless and staring at that empty spot for the longest time. I stared and was amazed that the squirrel could remember that an almond tree was once there. The squirrel turned suddenly, scampered up the other almond tree, and began munching.

It was a race to see who could harvest the most almonds from the lone almond tree. Then, a few years later, there were two new little squirrels scampering about in our yard. The almond tree was always the first fruit tree to blossom before spring. Even when the weather was windy and raining, the blossoms usually set and produced a good crop of almonds. Every year, we looked forward to the almonds ripening to harvest them. I noticed, however, that the almonds on the tree were disappearing before the outer covering turned yellowish, signaling that the almonds were ready for picking. When I looked around the tree, I saw bits and pieces of almond hulls on the ground. I thought that surely the squirrels would not eat green almonds. I checked the almonds on the tree, they were still green, and the insides were soft and immature. Yet the squirrels did not seem to care, for I caught them eating every green almond in sight. Yo thought she would outsmart the squirrels by picking as many as she could of the green almonds on the tree and storing them away. Months later, they shriveled up and dried into a small hard shell. I smashed one with a hammer to see what was inside; all I saw was a brown sliver of what should have been an almond nut. The squirrels had won the race and harvesting almonds for us had become outdated.

I had been noticing for a long period that my garden was marked with strange diggings, especially where the ground was cultivated. Even my large potted plants were disheveled with holes and flowers dug up. When I first started my garden, I was happy to see a family of quail sauntering through my garden as if they were on a family picnic. They had visited quite often until the new housing went up and the Church of Christ erected buildings around us. However, gradually a host of critters: stray cats, crows, rabbits, blue jays, squirrels, possums, and rats, invaded my yard. The neighbor's shrubbery has grown so tall that my plants have become tall and spindly as they reach for sunlight. The oak tree sheds leaves so often that I spend my weekends just raking the dead leaves. A parasitic mushroom had appeared from nowhere, and it attacked the roots of anything I wanted to plant. It was hard to be a Gentleman Farmer.

From my window, I heard a blue jay squawking away and saw it pecking at the loose soil. It stopped and picked up a peanut shell and deposited it in the hole it had just dug up. It kept flying back and forth from the neighbor's yard and planting the unwanted peanuts in mine. One day, I happened to look over the neighbor's fence, and I saw the neighbor holding a peanut between her fingers and waiting for a blue jay to come and pick it. I thought I solved the mystery, but I noticed the squirrels were scratching the loose soil. It came up with a peanut and off it scampered. I watch from my window now and see life's symbiosis – not always favorable.

Some work for peanuts
Symbiosis Nature's work
Thing to crow about

From the window

Looking out the window
I marvel at what happens outside
A neighborhood cat prowling
A blue Jay hiding peanuts
A crow perched on a limb
A squirrel scampering on my fence
Their lives intermeshed

Watching a cat behind a trash bag
Crouching low
Carefully m o v e s
One front paw f o r w a r d
Crouching still
The other paw f o r w a r d
Head low
Sideway look
Nearby a bird is busy
Scratching the soil
A peck peck here
A peck peck there
Unsuspecting
A SUDDEN POUNCE
FEATHERS FLY
A SQUWAK
The frightened bird eludes
This is not the cat's day

Marveling at a blue jay flying low
I see peanut in his bill
Landing quickly on my flower pot
Peck peck peck
Dig a big hole
Drop the peanut in the hole
Scrape scrape with the beak
Plant the peanut
Hope it grows
Blue Jay nature's seeder

Lady on the Bridge

Digging in my garden row
My neighbor's squirrel
Finds the blue jay's hidden stash
Peanut in his mouth
Scampering along the fence
Jumps
Upon my roof
Climbs atop my neatly trimmed yew
Looks a moment for a spot
Scratch the branches
Digs a hole
Quickly
Buries his ill-gotten booty
A tasty morsel for a wintry day

Soaring high above
A lone crow
Sees a squirrel digging the soil
Eyes the morsel in its mouth
Follows his scampering
Perches nearby
Waits patiently for the squirrel to leave
Quickly
Robs the squirrel's winter stash
An easy grub to crow about

Looking out the window
Marveling at nature's way
No books
No teachers
How do they know?
Their lives intermeshed
Symbiotically

Food for thought on mind
Some things in life are not free
Got to have it now

Got to Have

Today, I had succumbed to my wife's request to shop for her "Got to Have" item. She needed twelve place mats. I had decided to go to Wal-Mart, even though it was the most vilified store in the US. I had read where City council members of several cities had voted down Wal-Mart's intrusion into their districts. They even changed the zoning laws to protect their action. Yet Wal-Mart started from humble beginnings in Arkansas. However, none of this mattered to me now because I was on my wife's "Got to Have" errand. It was a well-intentioned idea, but somehow, it got lost in its actualization. Possibly a life example may clarify the phrase, "Got to Have."

One year on our Christmas holiday, we were visiting our grandchildren in Tucson, Arizona. They live in a big two-story southwestern motif house in a gated community. Even in this wide-open desert land, the backyard was the size of a postcard. Behind the house was wide river wash filled with southwestern shrubbery, willow, cottonwood, and sagebrush. There were packrats, ground squirrels, foxes, coyotes, rattlesnakes and other living animals hiding in this wash. Our daughter-in-law, Melanie, had cleared a large area of the shrubbery in the wash for the children's play yard. Then she bought CBs to keep in contact with them. On our visit, she demonstrated how each could communicate with one another. I saw my wife listening and watching intently at what was occurring.

When we returned home to Livermore, my wife said, "We got to have one of those CBs so I can call you when you're working in the yard."

I concurred that having CBs was a good idea. Certainly, CBs were better for keeping track of someone than wearing a restrictive electronic ankle bracelet like the one Martha Stewart wore when she was under house detention for violating insider-trading laws. The next day, I went to Best Buy and looked around the electronics department for that "Got to have" item. Normally, a sales person would be hounding me, but for a small item like a CB, I was on my own. There were so many choices it was intimidating. I read the package info: made in Thailand, India, China, and..., but not one made in USA. One type would operate within two miles and another five mile limit. Then I read the directions for the five-mile brand: An FCC license approval was required before operating the set. I certainly did not want deal with obtaining a license. Besides, I could almost hear my wife say, "Take it back. I won't answer any question for the government." I bought a pair of two-mile limit CBs made in China.

When I returned home, I carefully opened the package, loaded the batteries, and tested the equipment. It worked as stated. Then, I took the pair of CBs to my wife and said, "Here's your CB. This is how you operate it. First, you turn this dial to turn it on or off and to talk; you push this button that I labeled and speak. I will leave mine on so that you can contact me at anytime."

She looked at me with a horrified look and said, "I have to do all that?"

For months on end, the "Got to Have" C's were on our dining room table gathering dust like other "Got to Have" items. However, even the steps to operate the remote for the TV had intimidated her.

Back at Wal-Mart, we were looking for place mats.

"Oh," I said, "I thought I saw some in your kitchen drawer."

"Yes, but," she answered. "When someone spills anything on them, I have to wash and iron them."

I was not about to challenge the response. We headed for the dry goods section: beddings, towels, pillows, and, at last, place mats.

While I was checking one section, my wife was wandering around touching this item, picking up another, and decided they were not what she wanted. Since it seemed obvious that she wanted something that was soil proof, I focused on synthetic material or plastic. The plastic items all had gaudy looking pictures on them that would look unattractive on the table. All of the ones that looked pretty were either all-cotton or a combination of cotton and synthetic polyester.

Finally, after rummaging around for a while, I found some plastic ones that had a picture of apples painted on it.

"Look! These are not too bad. And you get two for one," I said.

"Two for one?" she asked.

My thrifty wife took the two for one and we were off to the checkout stand.

I had noticed that my wife was having the same trouble with the shopping cart as I had when I was pushing it. The handle was gooey with something left by a previous kid or customer. After paying for our "Got to Have" item, I said, "Leave the shopping cart for the next poor soul. Let me get some wet towels to wipe our hands."

In the men's room, Instead of a washbasin with a regular faucet with handles, I found a sensing device. I stuck my hands under one spigot. Nothing happened. I poked the black sensing device and tried it again. Nothing happened. After a frustrating few minutes of trying two more spigots, I saw a man go to a different washbasin, stick his hands underneath the spigot, and lo and behold, it worked. I waited for him to leave and quickly tried my luck. A small stream of water squirted out, but it shut off in about two seconds. I stuck my hands in and out from underneath the spigot to get enough water to rinse my hands. When I had finished, I grabbed some paper towels, moistened them, took some dry paper towels and returned to my wife.

"Here, wipe your hands. That shopping cart was real dirty. Hopefully, it wasn't dirtied by a kid with a cold." I said to her.

Finally, we were returning to our car. As I approached our vehicle, I had noticed an angular face middle-aged woman standing near our car. She was dressed in a royal blue dress with small flowery print. Her hair was dark brown-haired and curled. She stood behind her small new silver Toyota Scion and next to her shopping cart. She was munching feverishly on something. Her mouth was moving so fast and enjoying her eating that she did not even flinch as we walked by. Her behavior was just like my neighbor's squirrel never intimidated by me watching while it munched almonds from my tree. In the cart, I noticed what looked like a ten-pound bag of Purina Puppy Chow. I did not want to be intrusive. Surely, I thought, she must have a bag of cookies behind the pet food bag.

While we were leaving, my wife asked, "Did you see that lady eating from that pet food bag?"

I answered, "Oh, I thought she was eating something else."

"No," my wife said. "She kept reaching into that pet food bag."

I shook my head and thought; I hope she has her own doggie dish. Otherwise, there is Hell to pay if she has a pet waiting at home!

Day in and day out
A world sensed without meaning
Homeless and hopeless

Homeless

Walking towards the bus stop
I seek a place to sit
Warily a big lump I see
A brown disheveled cover
Draped over a narrow bench
Wishing not to get too close
I quickly walk away
Shake my head in disbelief and think
Leave it alone -It's not my problem

Yet, I look once again and wonder
Will my world come to this?
A place to rest my weary bones
Place my worldly things by my side
Wrap myself in this cocoon
To keep the stardust out of my eyes
Rest, rest till the next morn
Just another weary day
Homeless-To wander once more

The rumble of my bus ride
Breaks my pensive moment
Quickly aboard, I step
The door closes sharply behind
Sitting but cannot shake the thought
One last look I must
There, a haggard rumpled woman
Appears from beneath the lump
A silent prayer-May the morning light bring hope

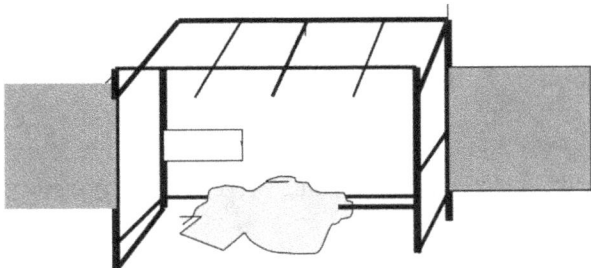

Worries on my mind
Please I'm reading poetry
What's that all about?

What in the World?

It was the third Monday in 2005, Martin Luther King Holiday, and I was in deep trouble. I was supposed to order my wife's medication as soon as we returned from our Christmas holiday in Arizona with the grandchildren. I must have been losing my mind. I had forgotten all about her being out of it until last Friday. Since Livermore Kaiser Medical facility was never open over the weekend, I surmised that I had just enough pills until Monday if I cut her heart medication in half. I was unnerved today because I found that Livermore's Kaiser Facility closed on this holiday.

Darn it, this emergency would never have happened if my wife had continued keeping track of our medications. Now she has a hard time remembering her daily medicines. To think, yesterday, when I gave her the beta-blocker, she asked me, looking confused, "What's this?"

"It's your heart medicine," I said. "You can't go without it,"

"I thought I took one this morning?" she questioned me.

"You take one in the morning and one in the evening," I answered. I took a deep breath for this was not the first time this conversation had taken place.

It had been so simple before. She had always had everything listed so that all I had to do was pick it up at the Pleasanton Pharmacy. Her writing was impeccable and complete. I didn't even have to phone in ahead of time for the items. Now, the responsibility was on my shoulder, another thing to worry about without her help. It was lucky I phoned Kaiser's hot line this morning. The woman on the phone said she would forward the request to Pleasanton Kaiser since it was open on this holiday. It's another day on the road, another day lost.

It was ten o'clock Saturday morning and this pharmacy was busy. I approached the counter, reached into my pocket for my wallet, extracted my Kaiser membership card, and handed it to the clerk. She swiped my card through the reader to verify my membership. Then she asked me for some identification. As I handed her my driver's license, she glanced at it and scanned my face, returned my driver's license, and then, pointed to a display panel on the wall and said, "Look for your name there."

It was a good thing I brought this book on poetry, The Force of Few Words by Jacob Korg. It might be a long wait with this large crowd today. As I was trying to skim through this book of poems, I heard a voice that sounded as if he was addressing me. I looked and there was an older man, gray hair, ruddy complexion, and deep lines across his face sitting in one chair away from me. He bent his head towards me and began saying something. I put my book aside for a moment and a bit puzzled, because I didn't recognize him. I asked, "Are you talking to me?"

"I haven't seen you here before. Are you new here?" the ruddy-faced man asked.

With a questioning look at the man, I replied, "I live in Livermore but our Kaiser Pharmacy was closed on the weekends and this one was open today on Martin Luther King holiday."

"Well, I live here in Pleasanton. I'm eighty-four years old and I live in a senior home," he said.

Well, ok. So what? I thought. "Well, I'm about your age too," I replied as I tried to return to my reading.

"I live alone because I lost my wife thirty-five years ago. In the senior housing, the residents are mostly older women. But I don't intend to get married again," the man continued trying to keep my attention.

"I grew up on the East Coast near Boston," he continued. "How about you?"

A bit perplexed at this conversation, I closed my book and said, "I was born in California and you might say I could belong to the 'Sons and Daughters of the Golden West' if that means anything to you.'"

The man seemed not to hear me and continued his chatter. "Did you notice how crowded everywhere is getting these days? It seems more people are coming here without anything. I remember when I was young, I said to momma, 'Momma, can't we bring our cousins to America?' Do you know what she said to me?"

"Momma said, "They can't come here just like that. They have to wait and have to be able to live on their own."

"Today, I see people come without anything or even work," he spoke raising his voice a bit.

"I own an American car but I see lots of people buying foreign cars. That's wrong! They should buy American made cars." He continued to raise his voice.

Not understanding what his conversation was about, I said, "Well, I own a Toyota. Do you know why?" I questioned the man.

"You shouldn't buy Japanese cars," he answered. "Remember, we fought a war with them."

What's his problem? I thought. "I bought the Toyota because of its quality. The American car makers forgot quality," I replied.

"Did you know that during the war, we had imprisoned Germans on the East Coast? America shipped the prisoners from Europe," the old person continued after mumbling further about cars.

"Well, I'm a citizen and my parents were Japanese and I was also imprisoned during the war," I replied looking a bit puzzled at the man's conversation.

Suddenly I heard my name called out. I quickly waived my hand goodbye at the inquisitive man and left.

Whew, what a day, I thought. What was that all about? What was his problem all about? Why did he single me out? That talk about immigrants, prisoners, and American cars --come to think about it, I was the only oriental in this place. Nah, that can't be. I'd be paranoid to think that at this day and age.

This had been a day to remember. A day lost and I know even less about poetry because of that puzzling intrusion. Why me? This day had been a hassle but I'm glad I'm able to be responsible for the medications for both of us. I will gladly accept this responsibility since Yo is having a hard time even remembering what and when to take medicine for her health. She can't last very long without following the doctor's order. We need each other now more than ever.

Forever gridlock
Made in America lost
Nation's future hocked

Gridlock

Gridlock! It was 1955, when Yo and I had gone to Tahoe over the Memorial weekend with our friends, and on our return, we encountered the worst holiday traffic between Tracy and Livermore. It was stop and go all the way on the two-lane highway from Tracy. At times, I was sure I was in a parking lot instead of the freeway. A few motorists, looking smug, cheated and tried to pass the line of traffic by driving along the right shoulder of the roadway. I almost followed them, but my better judgment told me not to! I was relieved when I saw that they received their due, because two miles ahead, the CHP had stopped them and were ticketing them. As we moved slowly past them, we all felt vindicated as we waved at them a laughing goodbye. Yet we were in the jam-packed motorcade for over one hour to travel just ten miles as the speedometer hardly moved. After that, Yo and I vowed never to travel on a holiday or allow us to be in a gridlock on the highway.

Gridlock was unheard of when Yo and I first set our roots into Livermore Valley in 1953. We traveled many times on what was once a part of Lincoln Highway. That old highway twisted and turned through the valley. It skirted along Portola Ave passed by the old "Highway Garage," traveled along First Street, turned into Greenville Road, drove over the winding Altamont Pass, and up through the town of Mountain House, followed Grant Line Road and down Byron Highway, rode through Tracy town along 11th Street, crisscrossed over the low lying farmlands to Modesto and turned into Highway 99. Even on this entire two-lane highway, traveling at the posted speed limit had hardly ever hampered us.

This semi-agricultural and ranching community of four thousand people hadn't changed very much after World War II until the Lawrence Livermore Laboratory was established in 1953 at the abandoned Naval Preflight Station at East Avenue and Greenville Road. But soon afterwards, builders started new housing on the northwest side of town. Besides the new housing tract that H & L Homes had built on Adelle Street and Elizabeth court, I also saw flat roofed duplexes scattered here and there as if they were jammed into any available empty lots. Maybe it was the ready-mix concrete readily available from Livermore–Pleasanton Sand and Gravel companies, or maybe it was just the cheapest way to construct a house by pouring a concrete floor as the foundation. When I opened the door of my rental house and took my first step on that hard concrete floor, I had assured myself that this would be temporary; just a roof over our head. But I did feel lucky that the Lawrence Livermore Laboratory Housing Office had arranged our housing, for I didn't have to look for one by myself. I had heard that the house we rented was priced under $8,000, but I believed it was overpriced after seeing the cheap construction. Even though the temperature in the valley rose to over 110 degrees in those early years, there was no air conditioning installed in the houses. Except for the time I was interned at Manzanar, I had spent most of my life in mild coastal climates. I soon found out how unbearable the inland heat was in the summertime. Every time I passed by those flat top duplexes, I was glad that our rental wasn't one of those, for I wondered how anyone could survive the hot Livermore summer temperature in those stuffy low roof houses.

Our rental home had no landscaping: just rocky soil and scrubby weed patches. After all, this valley was grazing land for cattle. This kind of rickety shack was a humble start for a lot of new young people fresh out of college who were employed at the Lab. During the early days, over fifty percent of the Lab employees commuted to Livermore. While many Lab employees drove from Berkeley, some commuted from as far away as Palo Alto, San Enselmo, Sacramento, and it was rumored that somebody commuted from as far as Fresno, California. It was mind boggling to think that anyone would travel over 150 miles from Fresno for work. In contrast, our last move to our East Avenue home was a just a mile and a half to work.

Owning a home had posed many problems, especially in a small town where there were very few choices for shopping. There would be no more makeshift furniture that we put up with when I was going to college. This was our home now that we were furnishing, and I had looked forward to buying tools for gardening and home projects. If JC Penny was the best that Livermore could offer, the neighboring town of Pleasanton had even less. We had headed towards downtown Oakland to shop at the big stores. Except for the holidays, traffic was never a problem during the 1950's. We had never given a second thought to jumping into our Plymouth station wagon, merging onto US Highway 50 from Portola Avenue, and heading for State Route 17 (Now known popularly as the Nimitz Freeway, I-880) to Oakland. For several years, we had shopped at Sears Roebuck, Emporium Capwell, and Payless; all on Telegraph Blvd. Sears was our store for the Kenmore washing machines and dryers. We had always parked at the Payless parking garage and did our Christmas shopping at Emporium Capwell. Sometimes we would shop at Montgomery Ward, but it was further away and inconveniently located. We never bought anything on credit, for that was what we had learned from our parents. It was simple: if we didn't have the money, we didn't need it.

Then there was a time when discount stores appeared: Affiliated Government Employees (A.G.E.), a non-profit membership store, and A/C, and soon followed by White Front, a large low-cost store. While we tried to find bargains, we were never satisfied with these stores, because of poor merchandising, quality, and selection. Worse still, the sales clerks often didn't know their merchandise. Then, as the population increased, shopping malls appeared. First, the Bayfair Shopping Mall in San Leandro, and then one was constructed southwest of Hayward, the Southland Mall (1961). The latter became a convenient location for our shopping for home appliances and my tools and equipment since it was relatively close and easy driving on the roadways. Even Yo had no trouble driving to Southland Mall. But coming home posed a dilemma for her. One day, while I was working on our patio roof, Yo went to Sears in the Southland Mall to pick up some items for me. I was so busy with my project that I hadn't noticed that she was late returning. Finally when she drove in, she said," I'm sorry I'm so late." She said she didn't realize that she was headed towards Berkeley instead of Livermore. She knew she was lost. She kept driving and looking until she found a kind person who directed her back to the right road for Livermore. I never pursued the topic further after she told me.

When our sons were growing up, Yo and I decided that the family should go out to dinner together. For dinner we drove to the East Bay area since the only place to dine in Livermore that we knew about was Yin Yin, a Chinese restaurant. We wanted to sit at a table with cloth napkins and not in booths and vinyl-covered seats. On our first outing around 1960, Glen was still in a stroller, and we all went to Anchor's Inn on University Avenue in Berkeley that was replete with linen napkins, table settings, and a waiter eager to serve us. During the children's early years, we often drove to San Francisco, visited the San Francisco Zoo, spent hours at the de Young Museum/Planetarium, relaxed at the Japanese Tea Garden, and enjoyed the salt air breeze at Fisherman's Wharf. Then, after our outing in the Bay Area, we often went to Spenger's Restaurant in Berkeley. Spenger's was always busy with the hustle bustle of people talking, and like many crowded restaurants, they seemed to herd you to the bar first. But we waited patiently with our children to be seated at a table. While Yo and I chose Spenger's Captain's Choice, our sons loved the Spenger's scampi. Once seated, the waiting for service was still long. However, their generous serving of sourdough bread mitigated the long waiting. My mind has still captured the fresh smell of their crisp sourdough bread liberally spread with real butter and not oleo. We would always catch the attention of our waiter for more servings of their delicious sourdough bread.

The Hickory Pit near MacArthur Blvd and Telegraph was another favorite place for us. I remember the shiny stainless steel kitchen, the busy cooks tending to the open pit for cooking, and bibs to sop up any drippings as we ate barbecued ribs. But when Greg and Glen were teenagers, we looked for a place to satisfy their big appetites. On the eastside of San Leandro on old MacArthur Blvd, we found Piper's, an all you can eat smorgasbord restaurant. The place was owned and run by a Greek family that I met some years later at my Greek friend's home. They kept the place neat, and the food was fresh and satisfying. Yo and I were always proud of our two sons because they always conducted themselves as gentlemen at the restaurants. One day, we were in for a big shock. We were sitting in a booth and enjoying our dinner when we all looked in surprise at a lady sitting alone and eating fried chicken. She was big. Her body overlapped the chair generously on both sides as she sat there. Her table was strewn with the aftermath of her gobbled fried chicken that she chomped on non-stop. It was gross! We had suddenly lost our appetite.

Later I had found an advertisement of an all-you-can-eat Chinese smorgasbord restaurant in east Oakland near the Montgomery Ward store. While the menu had traditional American-Chinese food, they served shrimp scampi on Friday night. Dinner was $1.85 around 1975. We all skipped the Chinese food and waited for the freshly cooked scampi. I had noticed that most of the patrons were older couples, but I learned later that the demographics would change over the years. When Glen was at UC Davis, he said that he and his college friend, Jerome, went to George's to eat one night. He said they were a bit uneasy since they were the only light complexion customers in the restaurant that night. Our family had the same experience when we went to Oakland City's Fairyland to see the Crooked House, Humpty Dumpty, and all of the other Fairytale characters that I read with the children. At first, the place was neat, but gradually graffiti and broken displays began to take over. Soon, it was no longer fun or safe to visit anymore.

While most of the roads during the 1950's were two lanes, the traffic was never bumper-to-bumper. The scariest road was the one between the Dublin grade and Castro Valley, where Caltrans had installed a three lane highway. People called it "Blood Alley," because careless impatient drivers met head-on with other fools using the middle passing lane at the same time. One of the worst accidents I had heard about was a Greyhound bus crashing head-on with an oncoming car in the middle passing lane. Left were death, destruction, and carnage. Every time I had to travel along that stretch, I kept my eyes wide open looking in front for drivers impatient enough to veer into the middle lane, or took a quick glance in the mirror to give room for someone who might want to pass me. There were crazy impatient drivers that I had to be cautious about to avoid crashing. It was with a sigh of relief that I would reach the top of the Dublin grade and see the Tri-valley come into view on our return trip at night from the Bay Area. There were no bright lights seen, for the valley was still the sleepy dry farming land. Even Camp Parks (Historic Military Posts) that had been bustling with activity during World War II lay silent with "lights out." Far to the east, I could barely make out lights from the homes in Livermore, but to the south, the few floodlights of the gravel and sand companies outlined structures like skeletons. However, I knew I was close to home.

When Greg started attending UC Davis, we loaded our station wagon with his belongings and headed for Davis, California. At first traffic was light as we drove north on US 680 to Walnut Creek, branched northward to the Benicia Bridge, skirted along Suisun Bay past the "Moth-ball Fleet," and joined eastward on I-80 to Davis. The only bottleneck occurred at the connection with Highway 24 at Walnut Creek, for the interchange was still under construction. The toughest part of this excursion was helping Greg carry things up to the third floor of his dorm. Every semester when I looked at his dorm, I kept wondering why someone didn't think of rigging a boom out the end of the dorm to haul heavy things up to the top floor. It sure would have helped parents who were past their prime to lug heavy things.

On our return, I noticed that the bottleneck at the I-680/24 interchange was worse because we were merging with the commuters returning home. Greg suggested traveling on a country route from Dixon, to Rio Vista and across the Sacramento River, down southward across the San Joaquin River to Oakley, through Brentwood and along Vasco Road to Livermore. His suggestion had saved about twelve miles from the 90-mile commute we made to Davis from Livermore. There was, however, one blind spot on a bending road, and I always gave a big sigh of relief when I passed it without meeting someone head-on who had taken a shortcut around the curve in the road or passed on a hill. I was right to be cautious, for around 2007, some thirty years later, that stretch down Vasco Road had become the new "Blood Alley" created by impatient drivers from Brentwood. I usually chose to return via the freeways for safety's sake. Then I began to notice that the bottleneck at Walnut Creek became progressively worse each year. First, I had to drive past that junction by 3:30 p.m. going in either direction. Then the next year, it was 2:30 p.m. Since the situation was so irritating, I tried a different route through the Central Valley on Interstate 5 and branched towards the Tracy I-205/5 cutoff. It had added more than 10 miles to the travel, but it was less nerve-racking. Glen had also started at UC Davis, and our hauling service continued. He was also on the third floor of his dorm. By the end of our two sons' UC Davis careers, my arms had grown a few inches longer from carrying the heavy concrete blocks used for bookcases.

Since the 1920s, gasoline taxes have helped California improve its roadways. During the late 1950s, Highway 50 between Livermore and Dublin had problems with flooding during heavy winter storms. One afternoon, I heard over the seldom used intercom blast warning to Lab employees, who lived in the Bay Area, to leave work and return home before Highway 50 flooded over. I had always noticed that one section of Highway 50 near Camp Parks was low and the land around the north side was always swampy. Soon afterwards, CalTrans made major improvements along this route and with the roadway to Tracy. The new highway spanned Greenville Road and routed directly over the Altamont Pass. Not only was the deadly "Blood Alley" near Castro Valley eliminated, but also a major interchange at Dublin-Pleasanton had been constructed that connected I 680 north/south with I 580 east/west. I always wondered, "Was there a threshold for the number of fatalities before a major highway improvement? And what was that number?" One of the amazing aftermaths of new highway construction of the I-580/680 crossroad was that it had transformed the sleepy town of Pleasanton into an affluent bustling city.

While the employees at the Lab had changed the balance of social structure of Livermore, some had entered the town's political scene to influence the town's future. They had proposed to limit the commercial and industrial sector for light industries. They moved for slow growth for the housing sector. However, I had watched builders and construction companies steadily gobbling up empty spaces. Bulldozers with their giant jaws had gouged the land, and scrapers had leveled the site while animals fled their humble burrows. In their place, builders erected huge two story houses with three car garages. The "slow growth" was laughable since the builders had been able to borrow quotas from future home constructions. However, the city was able to negotiate with the builders for city amenities like parks, and space for schools. The city council encouraged parks for the community and moved for a better a community library. With the Lab's increased role in nuclear weapons research and development, more than fifty-percent of the Lab's eight thousand or more employees had chosen to live here. The growth was not without problems for there had been great impact on the schools, because LLNL was a federally funded laboratory that did not contribute taxes toward schools. School assignments had become a nightmare at times for the parents. One of the important contributions towards this community by Lab employees was the pledge from their salary to establish a local hospital. Even a Provisional League of Women's Voters started here. Livermore was no longer just a cowboy town.

While changes in Livermore were taking place, other events were shaping the future of this valley and the Bay Area. The Lab was foremost in advancing the state-of-the-art large scale scientific computers. However, when the USSR successfully launched Sputnik on October 4, 1957, the race to dominate space was on. When the National Aeronautics and Space Administration (NASA) formed, the need for computers to guide and control the space modules accelerated the advance of miniaturized computers and Integrated Circuitry (IC). Neither NASA nor the Department of Defense (DOD) invented the IC's, but they helped to accelerate their development and usage. While the beginning of Silicon Valley started from Hewlett-Packard's humble laboratory beginnings in a garage, in reality, it was the steady advancement of the technology occurring at universities and in the computer industry. Silicon Valley industries grew steadily to provide the components and continued to evolve as new technology gave birth to new manufacturers. Venture capitalists looking for potential profits poured money into innovations. A vicious cycle began. The need for people was on. Prices for housing began to skyrocket. Roadways and traffic jams grew progressively worse. While most of the people who commuted lived near the Silicon Valley, the housing crunch forced people to commute even farther from the industries.

Meanwhile CalTrans had constructed freeways in the Bay Area that made it possible for people to commute from outlying communities as far away as 100 miles where housing was less crowded and less expensive. However, the impact was even greater because of the high cost of living, affected workers in other enterprises as well. More and more people eyed homes in the Tri-Valley. The supply and demand raised prices of homes and land. Builders looked even farther out to the San Joaquin Valley for cheaper land. I remember when Tracy was low-lying land where tomato crops were one of the main farming products. Whenever I drove through Tracy, I could smell the spicy aroma of the Heinz 57 variety tomato processing factory. Land was dirt cheap back then. When home pricing went up in Livermore, houses in Tracy were almost one-half of that of Livermore's homes. Builders went even farther away from the Bay Area. At first, people who commuted from the outlying district tolerated travelling in exchange for buying into the 'American Dream', of a big house, yard, and even a swimming pool. The downside was that they needed to carpool or buy an additional car in case of car trouble. There was no infrastructure in the outlying communities, which imposed further outlays for the family. Still they had the 'American Dream'. However, the price of everything continued to climb with the age-old rule, supply and demand.

Once again gridlock became commonplace. The commuting that was tolerable at first now was jammed with cars of people owning the 'American Dream'. Even worse a new phenomenon occurred. America was losing its dominance in the auto industry. My first car was a Chevrolet and I was at the Chevrolet garage almost every weekend to find out what was wrong with it. I was also surprised one day when I was cleaning the inside of the car and found a handful of nuts and bolts stuffed behind the car seat. I always wondered if any of those pieces belonged in my Chevrolet. Now I own a Toyota, a Japanese auto, and all I needed to do after I bought it was fill my gas tank and change oil once in awhile. I remember when I was in Japan, I had heard stories that Japan had a hard time assembling parts for its war equipment because they had no standards or quality control. However, after losing World War II, Japan hired America's Quality Control expert, Dr. W. Deming, and adopted his efficient manufacturing methodologies. This led to Japan's industrial revolution that allowed Japanese automakers to produce better and lower cost automobiles that competed favorably with America's auto industries. Soon our auto companies were unable to meet this competition, lost ground and even closed factories. Furthermore, because of the high cost of American labor, government requirements, and health and benefit packages, American companies began outsourcing manufacturing products to utilize cheaper foreign labor costs. Ironically, Japan had later found itself needing to outsource its production to Korea, Malaysia, and other Asian countries to cut its costs.

It seems that our social downfall happened when Sony produced the Walkman in 1979 with the miniaturized computer chips. People with a handset tied to their ears were listening to music blaring out. This was also the period of launching of personal computers (PCs) and the birth of Bill Gates' MSDOS (1980) operation system with the blessing of IBM. The age of software development surged on. DARPA (Defense Advanced Research Project) in 1969 originated the early concept of the Internet. The concept and implementation had gone through several evolutions. This was the period of innovations and mass production of electronic components: laptops, cell phones, iPods, and the list goes on. Once a product caught on, companies looked to cheaper production costs by moving their manufacturing to Asian countries. People were yakking with these gadgets held close to their ears on the streets, at the stop sign, in the stores, and worse still while they were driving. The innovation had even led to "texting" with these gadgets that had made riding on the roads even more hazardous for the unwary travelers. Everyday an accident occurred on highways because some driver was unaware that he had more than two tons of plastic and metal under his control and yet was not mindful of the heavy crowded traffic. I have shuddered when I have seen drivers, speeding in the fast left lane, suddenly decide to cut across three lanes of traffic to veer towards an off-ramp. In their wake, I have heard drivers braking and seen big rig drivers trying not to crash. These big rigs are monsters that are forty feet long and weigh up to thirty-three tons. Many wait at the ports to load shipping containers on foreign ships and transport them to distant distribution locations. There is never a day when I do not see three or more big rigs lined up and speeding on the highways. My heart has skipped a beat and adrenaline flowed when I was in traffic with these monsters, for I know that I don't want to be behind them or in between them. Forget the speed limit! I speed up to distance myself from the thought of being crushed to death between two big rigs.

Lady on the Bridge

In 2007, the housing bubble burst, including here in Livermore. Builder speculating in this vicious cycle kept building bigger homes for more profit. However, land is finite; its value rises many-fold, and escalate the cost of homes beyond people's means. Greed and fraud inflated the bubble. Predatory lenders had dreamed up innovative schemes like 'interest only', low down payment, adjustable rate mortgage, balloon loans that allowed people who could barely scrape up enough money to make the initial monthly payments only to be faced with huge payments a few years later. Entire housing tracts now stand empty and invite vandalism and crime. Even Livermore has not been exempt from this fiasco. No matter what street I travel on, I have seen at least one house up for sale. The crisis has resulted in at least ten percent of the households faced with foreclosures, bankruptcies, and tax liens on houses. However, this dilemma has far-reaching consequences on the economy, slowing down manufacturing, dragging down construction, and declining revenues for local and state governments.

Was it boom or bust in the year 2008? As I watched the bubble grow, greed fueled it. Much of the fast growth built on speculation had defied reality and led to grief for workers and investors. Rather than the traditional merchandise, the Internet has now become the vehicle to promote soft merchandise using broadband, online shopping, digital media, game playing, and whatever innovative minds can provide. Money made of plastic seems to be no problem. Credit card companies have no shame. Time and again, I have received a credit card from loan companies even though I had not requested one. Their hope is that I will never pay off my balance, whereupon they can charge their exorbitant interest rates. People have been spending as if there were no tomorrow on items for the good times.

Still in the year 2008, almost every day on I-580 the traffic mixed with autos and semi trucks grind to a halt. Gridlock! I no longer jump into my Toyota when I think about traveling on the freeways, for I ask myself, "Do I really want to face that gridlock? And although the whole world is trying to go green, do I want to inhale the smog while I am sitting in a virtual parking lot?" It is a jungle out there!

Chapter 10: Finale

Oh serenity
Refuge ruptured forever
My hole in the ground

Earthshaking news

Monstrous metal giant
opens its gargantuan jaw
claws the field with a
grinding sound
burrowing animals flee with fright
dust flies and dirt dribbles
weeds, dirt, and debris
feeds its hungry mouth
dump trucks wait to devour the load
When one belly is full
one more is ready for its meal

Little sticks with red markers
jammed into the ground
marks the way for the
Monstrous metal giant
to claws and claw until
the field is ready to
erect man's humble abodes
Watching from across the way
long ear cotton tailed rabbit
sitting on it haunches
looks with disbelieving eyes

Nothing's forever
For God will be my witness
Dusts to dusts are we

Ever Changing

Life is full of surprises
Can man control earth's destiny?
Some do think so

How naive can they be?
Born of the Sun
Our constant energy source

Earth whirling around the sun
Spinning on its axis
Cloaked by an atmosphere

We were whole millions of years ago
But there are forces beyond our control
Thrusting continents into pieces

What are today were not yesteryears
Dinosaurs roamed the earth
Glaciers carved the earth

Heated by decaying radioactive elements
Cauldron boils beneath the soil
Held together by gravity

These are forces beyond our control
Convection, radiation, and Coriolis too
Known and yet unpredictable

Solar heating causing air mass flow
Moisture evaporating from land and sea
Coriolis forces affecting the flow

We have seen Mother Nature's wrath
Earthquake, Tsunami, and hurricanes upon the land
Havoc and death we cannot comprehend

Lady on the Bridge

The fastest computer is no match
Nor all data known to man
For Computational Physics is not exact

People talk, rant, and rave
Earth is doomed they say
You must make a change today

We postulate on such small scale
When millions of years have gone by
Making our answers so miniscule

Death and destruction by man's own hands
From wars, genocide, religious intolerance
Far more insidious than any change man makes

Dust to dust
That's what it shall be
For the present will be just the past

Omoide (Memories)

Standing at the crest
Of Taiko Bashi
The Lady on the Bridge
Looks once more
The long hard Journey
She has taken
My three sons
Have come to see me
She cries with joy
She hears the voice
Of one who reminisces
With her
Nostalgia of yesteryear
Of her Motherland
No tears to shed
On this way
There is a glow
On her face
For she knows
Her Lord
Waits for her

But, one last wish
She asks
A statue of Nimomiya Kinjiro
I have saved
Through that terrible time
For my son
To remember me by

Trip into the past
Nostalgia of old Japan
Sealed in bronze statue

China Cabinet

Okaasan, from that day on the bridge, we have traveled a long way together. Let me share with you once again some moments that I remember. One day when I was visiting, I noticed a beautiful cherry wood china cabinet along one wall of the dining room filled with a few objects that you saved from the bonfire we started to rid ourselves of everything Japanese. In Japan, your most treasured objects would surely be in the *tokonoma*, a Japanese alcove but then, I could have missed seeing those things so close to you and dad.

Besides the family pictures, I saw dishes I sent you when I was a member of US Military Intelligence Service (MIS) stationed in Japan during World War II. I was looking for some nice pottery but many of the shops in the Ginza district had many items that stamped with "Made in Occupied Japan." Finally, I found a shop that carried Noritake pottery. My eyes caught sight of a set of fine bone china dishes. It was unusually delicate shaped white porcelain with a single branch of lovely cherry blossoms imprinted on it. I thought it was perfect for a sashimi dish. On my military assignment to Kyushu, Japan, I found a set of rice bowls made by the famous Arita pottery factory. I read that pottery from this region was world famous for its blue and white porcelain. The color and simplicity of the pattern was so beautiful I had to buy it for you. When I asked for six pieces, the proprietor looked at as if I were crazy or just plain stupid because I looked Japanese. I forgot that you once said something about settings things in odd numbers. Now I realized that what you meant when you said, "Japanese are superstitious about numbers." I learned that a set of four pieces was unacceptable because in one form of the word it has the same sound as death, *shi*. Thus, each set consisted of five pieces since I learned that odd numbers three, five, and seven are good while even numbers in our culture are bad.

In the corner was another item that caught my eye, a grotesque shaped piece of metal that you retrieved from the family home in Tokyo, Japan after a devastating earthquake that laid waste to the entire Kanto region in 1923. When you told us how the family fled to a park to escape the devastating fire that destroyed your family home, it was the first time I felt an emotion of fear in your voice. While stationed in Japan, I saw the devastation that fire can cause on the wood and paper houses of Japan. As I traveled the countryside, I saw miles and miles of empty space as far as my eye could see. Here and there, a few smokestacks stood as a silent reminder that people once lived and worked here. The scene was such vast emptiness that I could not visualize or begin to comprehend the horror and chaos that must have occurred during the incendiary bombing of this countryside. Was it collateral damage? No. It was strategic bombing targeting civilians and small factories in order to bring the fear of God and destroy the will of the people to resist. Even those escaping to open spaces and rivers did not escape the horrendous firebombing with napalm. The firestorms raged for five days sucking the very life out of the region. Hundreds of thousands died and millions of people left homeless. The devastation was ten-fold greater than the Earthquake of 1923. Where did people go? What happen to all the charred ruins and ashes left behind? Even the smell of death of burning flesh was gone. What I saw was a landscape picked clean as if vultures had dined on a carcass and even the smokestacks looked like bones picked clean of life. But then, everywhere I traveled through your motherland, no trash could be seen anywhere and although the buildings showed the ravages of the war, they were always swept clean. With only one exception, the cigarette butts GIs flipped out of their fingers.

Okaasan, among your treasured items, I recognized in your china cabinet the statuette of Ninomiya Kinjiro, the statuette you had given me. During that chaotic period after the FBI took dad away, I had lost track of many personal things including Ninomiya Kinjiro. All those many years before our world blew to splinters like those paper and wood houses outside Tokyo. He was born in a poor family during Japan's feudal era and Ninomiya always displayed reading a book while collecting firewood for his family. Everywhere I traveled in Japan, a statue of him stands, especially at schools. He had become the symbol of diligence, learning, and hard work that helped Japan recover from its terrible wartime disaster.

One day, I was walking through countryside of Japan towards dusk when I saw near the skyline of a small hill, children walking the skipping. I could almost hear their voices singing happily, as they played. In my mind, I was in a nostalgic place of old Japan, *Furusato*, a time and space where you, *Okaasan,* must have enjoyed your childhood. I thought, at that moment, is this idyllic place that the lady on the bridge left to start a new life? I wonder too, what life might have been for me if I had been born in your motherland?

I close my eyes and reach into the deep recesses of my mind seeking a vision of my own childhood. I cannot see the lady on the bridge for I am an infant. It is not the warmth of mother's bosom that still lingers there but the sound of a soft tender voice singing and humming, "*Nennen kororiyo okororiyo. Boya wa yoiko da nenneshina* ..." "Sleep, sleep, little one. You're a good baby, now go to sleep..." It is comforting. It is mine.

Togetherness fades
When Mother, the glue, is gone
Her heartbeat remains

The Heartbeat

The mother is the glue that keeps the family together. Once she is gone, togetherness seems to fade away. After my father passed away, it was Frank, Stella, and Kazumi who looked after mother. Later, when her health was declining, they had to place her in a convalescent facility because she needed more help than they could provide. Frank called me one day to spend some time with her. On September 5, 1984, I had quickly arranged to visit *Okaasan*

Okaasan, Kaz; in front. Frank and Tad; from left

the next day, and let Frank know of my flight plans. Through the years, I had been deeply grateful of Frank and Stella thoughtfulness that had always made sure that my ties to *Okaasan* would never be lost.

The call had come at a chaotic period for me, because the Computation Department Head had just cut my division in half. I had worked hard, had taken risks, and had taken the initiative to build my division to meet new challenges in software development and applications for the Projects and Programs that I supported at the Lab. Through my endeavor, my division had almost doubled its size. But my department head only looked at the size of my group and feared that it had become larger than the rest of his department. Never once did he have the courtesy to sit with me and find an amicable solution to how best to reorganize and still provide the support for my users. It was a difficult time, for he had simply cut me at the knees. However, to be with *Okaasan* was more important to me than to dwell on my own problem.

On my flight down to Los Angeles, I could still remember hearing my mother's soft voice singing a Japanese lullaby, "*Nen nen kororiyo okororiyo Boya wa yoi ko da nenneshina*…." When I saw her at the convalescent home, she seemed to be in good spirits. She said, "One day I fell down at home and I couldn't get up to call Frank. The next day, he found me on the floor and called for help. I didn't break any bones, but I'm too weak to move around easily." Then she said, "I dread this place but I know that there is no one that can take care of me every day." I sat with her and we chatted about old times, the people we knew, and the friends who had passed away.

Only the setting made it clear that she was not the resilient mother that I knew. This time I did not see the mask.

I could not help but see a feeling of happiness in her spirit and a glow in her face. When mother was at Manzanar, she had embraced the Catholic faith that had helped her find strength through that terrible period. I sensed that she had come to terms with her Maker. When it was time for me to leave, I heard her last words of joy, "*Hontoni ureshii. Sannin no kyodai ga mimai ni kite kuremashita (*I'm really happy. My three sons came today to see me)." Yes, she had fulfilled her destiny.

One day, after mother had passed away at the age of ninety-two, my brother called me and said, "Mother asked me to be sure to give Tadashi the statuette of Ninomiya Kinjiro." Frank and Stella made a special journey to bring mother's final request to me.

"*Okaasan*, I have the lovely stature of Ninomiya Kinjiro. When you first gave it to me in recognition of my achievement as the outstanding student in the Japanese school, I was too ignorant to understand its full meaning. He was the symbol of *giri* and *gaman* that shaped your life. It is only now I understand what this gift means: It is your life. It may be made of bronze but when I hold it, it is warm. I feel your heartbeat."

Ninomiya Kinjiro, Patron Saint of Japan, Statuette-Okaasan's gift

Wheel of Justice creeps
Redress and Reparation
Too late for parents

Epilogue

The wheel of justice turns very slow indeed. The seed of "Hate" that was sown by President Franklin Delano Roosevelt never died even though many young *Nisei* and *Kibei* fought valiantly against the enemy and prejudice to prove that he was wrong and that we belong. Slowly a redress movement began to compensate for the injustice, but it wasn't until 1978 that legal proceedings began to occur. By the actions of many *Niseis* and championed by Senators Daniel K. Inouye and Norman Mineta, together with House Representatives, Norman Mineta and Masayuki Matsunaga pushed for the Redress action. On the 200th anniversary of the signing of Constitution, the House of Representative of the 100th Congress passed the House Resolution 442 by a vote of 243 to 141. In 1988, the Senate passed its version by 69 to 27. While the Senate passed the joint Senate/House Bill unanimously, the House not fully convinced about the injustice and need for reparation, finally agreed to the Bill 243 to 141.

On August 10, 1988, President Ronald Reagan signed the "Civil Liberty Act of 1988" legislation stating that a grave injustice was done motivated by racial prejudice, wartime hysteria, and the failure of our elected representative to uphold the Constitution. Yet, even in this millennium year 2000 there are those still in doubt that I am an American, full dream of freedom and justice in this great nation of immigrants and, therefore, deserved no apology.

One day in 1989, Yo and I each received formal letters signed by President George H. W. Bush with an apology and Government checks for $20,000 each.

As I held the checks and looked at Yo, I could sense that she was thinking and feeling as I was at the moment.

There were no hurrahs; just a silent reflection on the terrible consequences perpetrated on our families by our government.

When I said, "This really should have been for our parents," she nodded her head in silent approval.

But there was sadness for both of us, because our parents would never see this day to receive the reparation for their loss and sufferings. We were the survivors. The right to become citizens denied by law, vilified for not assimilating into America's mainstream, survived through their heritage of "*Gaman*," only to have their dreams of a better life for the family shattered by Executive Order 9066.

"Let's each give our sons the checks in memory of our parents," I said to Yo.

She agreed wholeheartedly.

But no reparation will right the loss of our family life that was torn asunder by this unjust and hateful act of our elected representatives. I am saddened that *Otoosan*, who I had proudly looked up to, had become a ghost of himself after his imprisonment. Then years later when he passed away, *Okaasan*, who had tried to hold the family together, held steadfast to her culture that was one constant of her life. She could not speak forcefully about what was right for her children, for fear that, she would bring "*Haji*" to her husband's name.

Lady on the Bridge

Now she is gone and my heart is torn because there is a great divide within the family and I do not know how to bring them together. If only I could share my letter with *Okaasan* to let her know the sadness I bear in my heart about what has happened to our family and with the in-laws.

From the feudal lands
A seed from Cherry Blossoms
Sterile, will not grow

Letter: Lovely Cherry Blossom – Sterile

Okaasan, ogenki de irrashaimasuka, Mother have you been doing well?
Gobusata shite orimasu, I'm sorry I haven't written to you for a long time.

Okaasan, I want to recall when I sat with you at your home, you were talking about your heartfelt wishes for the welfare and the well being of the family after you were gone. I sensed that you wanted to speak out and make things right for the family situation but your strict adherence to the Japanese way of life didn't allow you to supersede *Otoosan's* role as master of the household. Now that I have grown older, I have a greater appreciation of your world and that you feared you might shame his memory. When you spoke about the Boyle Heights property purchased in Mabel's daughter's name for the family, I heard in your voice a betrayal by your son-in-Law of its ownership. But *Otoosan* had no other choice. I was naïve to believe that *Otoosan* had the opportunity to set roots in this land and achieve the American Dream. I thought that "Jap" was just a slur, but it was our imprisonment at Manzanar that opened my eyes that racists and politicians vilified all Japanese.

Okaasan, when I was in my high school civics class, I was awed by the Constitution of this great country. "Freedom and justice for all" always inspired me to be a good citizen. But I had never learned in my civic's class about the Alien Land Laws that denied *Issei* civil rights and the right to become naturalized citizens. And consequently, the government denied *Otoosan* the right to purchase the property in our family name. My world was not what I believed it to be. It was a hard lesson for me to learn about equal rights behind barbed wires in Manzanar.

I heard in your voice, *Okaasan*, your anguish how Joe had to struggle to restart a nursery in West Los Angeles when denied the Boyle Heights property as collateral. I have nothing but great admiration and thanks for my brother Joe. As *Chonan*, he has never shirked his duty to the family. After working so hard to establish the nursery business, you told me that Joe had to move the West Los Angeles nursery to his home property and growing yard in Malibu because the owner had sold the property to a land developer. I couldn't help feel the disappointment in your voice when you said that, in the meantime, Joe and Yo had divorced. Now I understood why I didn't see Joe at the West Los Angeles nursery on my visits and why nobody invited me to see the Malibu property on which Joe and Yo had built their home.

I learned from Frank that Joe had lost interest in the nursery business after he lost his nursery brokerage business as well, and decided to devote the rest of his life to golf. Frank also said that Joe started a rental concession for golf carts with the Los Angeles County California Golf Courses. It seems that Joe's divorce settlement must have been amicable since Joe was able to use the Malibu property as collateral to start his new venture. I chuckled at that idea that Joe was devoting his full effort towards golf. It seemed so contrary to what he said one day when we were delivering plants from our Santa Monica nursery to the Brentwood Country Club. One day, after we made our delivery, we watched golfers teeing off on the green, pick up their golf clubs, and chase after the golf ball. Joe said at that time, "You'll never catch me chasing after that small white ball." Now, his life is nothing but chasing that little white ball.

Okaasan, you had said that Joe left the nursery business in care of his ex-wife Yo and Frank. When you said that Joe wanted to sell the nursery eventually, you did not speak to me directly and your voice drifted away as you said, "Joe promised to share the proceeds of the sale with the rest of the family." I was puzzled because your words sounded as a wish rather than a firm assurance of his promise. I assumed that Frank would share equally in the ownership of the nursery since he devoted his entire life to it. You also hoped that Joe would leave something for his younger sister and me. If you remember, "*Okaasan*, I said, "I don't expect or deserve anything, since I have received more than enough from the family. Besides, I haven't devoted any time to the nursery after being interned at Manzanar. If Joe is going to be generous, then my share should go to my younger sister, Kazumi." "But," you answered, "all of your life you never asked for anything for yourself. Your reply was always 'I have more than enough and someone else needs it more than I do.' I feel that, since all of you worked hard when you were young and we used your savings to help buy the family property, each one of you deserves something in return."

Your indecisive statement about Joe and Frank puzzled me. *Okaasan*, while you were talking, my mind was racing through past memories to understand your anxiety about the future of our family. *Ie*, family is the bedrock of our culture set firmly on ancestral ground. What did I miss? Did the internment change the importance of family or our attitudes toward each other? I remember what *Otoosan* said once, "I want each of you to stand together as *kyodai's,* brothers." Of course, those words didn't have full meaning for us as youngsters.

I remember one day, I was puzzled when father took on odd jobs, rather than devote time at the nursery. Only now, I realized that both of you had sheltered us from the hard times of the depression. That day, a customer contracted my dad to landscape his new home in Malibu. He asked him if he would also clean up the mess the contractors left in the new house. One Saturday, we traveled from Santa Monica along the coast highway to Malibu. A nice two story home was right on the beachfront property. The yard was small but you could see and hear the ocean from the large window facing the water. The painters did a quick and dirty job because they left splotches on the windows. Dad assigned Frank and I to clean the windows while he and Joe did the heavy work of cleaning up the debris outside. Scraping paint off of windows with a razor blade is tough on your fingers. Every once in a while, I had to flex my fingers for they seemed to be frozen in one position. Just about noon, *Otoosan* said, "Let's stop for a while and eat lunch." He handed Joe some money and said, " Why don't you drive down the road to that store we passed on our way up and buy some food?" About a half an hour later, Joe returned with some sandwiches and drinks. We sat on the floor and ate our sandwiches. It wasn't the lunch that I remember so well. It was enjoying each other's company. There were never any put-downs. No one said, "You were doing your job wrong." I learned to appreciate the importance of *Ie*, family working together as one even in my world.

Okaasan, let me reminisce about Joe and me. It was Joe's senior year in high school and his college years at UCLA that he said he received a harsh education about life in America. When I was in my freshman year at SAMOHI, "Oh, you must be Joe's younger brother," a teacher said. I thought, "What was I in for? Was I expected to live up to his reputation?" Later, I learned that Joe was popular with his schoolmates and he was active in sports. He was the pitcher for the high school baseball team and a member of the swimming squad. One day, there was a swimming meet scheduled at a private club in Santa Monica since the high school didn't have a swimming pool. I was puzzled why Joe was home that afternoon. I asked, "Aren't you suppose to be at a swimming meet today?" Suddenly I realized that I stuck my nose into something I shouldn't have. I saw the disappointment in his face. There were no tears but a hesitation in his voice as he said, "The owners of the private club found out that there was a Jap on the swimming squad and told the school that no Jap is allowed on this club property." That day, Joe learned that "Jap" was no longer just a slur.

Okaasan, you always encouraged us to get an education and go to college. *Otoosan* said, "People can take everything away from you except what you have in your head, your education. So study hard." I often heard you hint that it would be nice if one of the sons could become a doctor or a lawyer. Joe was an excellent student and he entered UCLA and majored in Business. It was three years later when I enrolled in UCLA but I majored in Math and Sciences the subjects that I excelled in at school. In all of the semester I attended in my classes, I saw only one other *Nisei*. On the other hand, most of the *Nisei* majored in general education or business. Through his association with other *Nisei*, Joe learned that a degree in business could be a dead end. One day, I saw him talking to *Otoosan* and I wondered why he wasn't at UCLA that day? Again, I stuck my nose into his affair and asked, "Aren't you in class today?" Then I learned the next reality of being a *Nisei*. He said, "Even if I graduate from UCLA, the prospect of using my degree is almost zero." Then he added, "Have you noticed that fruit stand about a half mile down the road on Wilshire Blvd? Did you know the *Nisei* running that store has a Ph.D. in engineering and can't find a job as an engineer? In fact, most of the *Nisei* working there are college graduates. That's why I told dad that I wanted to start a new nursery a few blocks away on Wilshire Blvd and use this place as the growing yard."

With dad's blessing, I saw Joe designing and setting up the new nursery. It was in an ideal location visible from either direction on the busy Wilshire Blvd. Instead of the makeshift arrangement of dad's nursery, Joe planned an office, a store for seeds and other products, storage for large supplies, a greenhouse for shade plants, planting area, and an easy access into the yard for deliveries. The nursery business showed great promise.

While the business drew from the local area, customers came from such places as Hollywood, Bel Air, Beverly Hill, Brentwood, and Malibu. There were also a number of celebrities that were our customers. I remember making several deliveries to Walt Disney's home in Santa Monica. His house, typical of the era and neighborhood, was located in a middle-income residential area. Another celebrity I saw one day at our nursery was Will Rogers. He had just finished selecting some nursery items and having a great time laughing and joking with my father and Joe. The following day, I help deliver plants and supplies to his ranch in Pacific Palisades.

If you will remember, *Okaasan,* within two years Joe had paid back more than half of his loan. Because the retail nursery business is labor intensive, the success of our family business was largely due to all of us working without salary. Until he was drafted in October 1941, Frank worked full-time at the nursery after graduating high school. I was in college but I helped on the weekends. I'm sure that you remember me working at the nursery during one Christmas vacation. I was hauling a wheelbarrow load of plants from the back of the yard to the front when all of a suddenly everything went blank. I passed out. It must have been the stress of final exams that caught up with me. When I came to, the wheelbarrow was on its side and the five-gallon plants were scattered around me. Joe heard the wheelbarrow fall, came running over, helped me up, and told me to take it easy for the rest of the day. I also remember another time when the work overwhelmed me. On that day, I was squatting and bending over pulling weeds in and around the plants when, all of sudden, the whole world seemed to fade away. I had passed out with sunstroke. I decided then and there that I better take my parents advice and use my brain instead on my brawn as you had always encouraged us to study hard.

When President Roosevelt declared Executive Order 9066, the fate of the nursery was sealed. Joe had heart wrenching decisions to make. First, he had to find someone to take over the nursery business. Not an easy task to find someone suitable or someone you could trust. I saw him rushing in and out of the office to meet with buyers and lawyers while we tried to keep the business going. Then, he had to worry about and make arrangements for his own family, the father-in-law, and the rest of us. I saw the disappointment in his face when he had to sell his new car for half of its value. He shouldered all of these burdens by himself for I knew nothing about the business to help him.

I remember at Manzanar, you told me that we lost our family nursery. The worst had happened to Joe because of the internment at Manzanar. The individual who negotiated to carry on the nursery business, reneged on the contract saying that he could not make the payments. Joe, unable to leave Manzanar in order to protect his business, lost the nursery.

Looking back, I wondered, "How does Frank fit into this picture since he didn't suffer the pain and humiliation of internment?"

Hence, the whole issue of family business is difficult to comprehend that it is beyond my understanding. *Okaasan*, is that why you were so uncertain? It seems that Frank was content to spend his whole life with the nursery business. He told me, when he returned to California after leaving the Army, he worked at the old nursery on Wilshire Blvd currently owned by a *Hakujin*, Caucasian. He quit after a year or so and rejoined with Joe because the new owners didn't know how to run the nursery business.

When I returned from Minnesota, I rode with Frank from our home in Boyle Heights to the nursery in West Los Angeles. What amused me at the time, Frank still loved sporty souped-up cars even though he was a family man. I can still hear the *rumph, rumph* of his motor ready to go to work. On the way to the nursery, I had to hang on tight to my seat because he gunned his motor and barreled out at every stop sign. I can still hear the tires screeching as he raced to the next stoplight. Sometime later, he told me that he quit doing this jackrabbit start and stop. He said he realized that he wasn't getting to work any faster than just cruising at the set speed of signals. But that's Frank. *Okaasan*, you used the word, *nonki*, carefree, because he would be late to work often. I understand. I also had a hard time getting Frank up in the morning to catch the bus for school.

There was one other word that bothered me, *shinyou,* trust and/or confidence. The word has so many meanings that I'm having trouble associating it with Frank. Is it confidence in Frank? Is it lack of dependability? Or is it that Joe can't rely on Frank? Maybe you mean Joe can't give Frank credit for his contributions. Frank is content to do his work diligently. What he does is not half measure but he doesn't extend his thinking beyond the immediate. Joe, on the other hand, is not content with the status quo. But both had their carefree moments. Frank loved to gamble at times at Reno. One time, he had to pawn his watch to buy gas to come home. He caught hell when the wife received the watch from the pawnshop through the mail. Joe loved the horses. I heard that he would leave work early in order to place his bet on the last race at Del Mar which was 100 miles or more from West Los Angeles. One day, he said to me, "I finally quit feeding hay to the horses!"

Shinyou and *Nonki*, does each of these underlie your doubtful words?

Okaasan, if there was doubt in your wishes, I'm afraid the worst did happen after you were gone. When you and dad came to America, you brought a seed from your motherland. You smothered it with attention as we looked on. You expected it to flourish but it would not survive on this soil without your attention. It all happened when Joe decided to sell the nursery business in Malibu. I thought Frank was a full partner but it was only on paper. I heard that Joe set up a corporation but never asked Frank to participate in any decisions with Joe and his ex-wife. When we were growing up, I remember clearly the value of family as told to us by our father, especially, brothers standing together as one. The seed you planted was "*chonan*." He was the eldest male child that was treated and pampered more than the rest of us. Joe was "*chonan*" and you counted on him to look after the interest of the family. I have no quarrels with him for he treated me well.

We had lost the nursery while we were interned at Manzanar, but Joe was never content to take the Japanese attitude, *Shikataganai* (Why try because that's fate). Joe was determined to establish the business once more for the family. There was never any doubt in my mind that Joe carried out his responsibility for our family as *chonan*.

Maybe Joe characterized Frank as lazy or irresponsible since he didn't do well in school or maybe he felt he wasn't aggressive enough. Frank was just a happy go lucky guy and always contented with whatever he was doing. Yes, he wasn't aggressive but he had a keen sense of responsibility for the family. While Joe took care of your well-being, it was Frank and Stella, as well as Kazumi, who spent their life looking after you and *Otoosan*. Frank knew that I couldn't be there all of the time so he kept me informed and called me when he needed moral support. Was Frank, irresponsible? No. Caring? Yes. I always looked up to Frank as my *niisan* because he was always there for me looking after my welfare and well being.

The final chapter of the selling of the nursery is hard for me to stomach. Joe's ex-wife did the books as usual and Frank had total management responsibility for the nursery while Joe was off on his newly found business. Surely, without Frank, the business would not have prospered at Malibu. Before closing out the nursery, Frank said he drafted a letter to his business associates to thank them for their support over the many years. When he showed the letter to Joe, Joe said, "I'll take care of it." Later, when Frank asked a business associate if he received a letter from the nursery thanking him for his business. He said, "Yes, I did, but I didn't see your name anywhere in the letter." As I listened, I was stunned when I heard that *Niisan* had taken all of the credit when it was Frank's suggestion to write the letter. It was Frank who had devoted his life to what he believed was our family nursery. I thought, "How low can you, Joe, stoop to take credit away from your brother, Frank who devoted his life to our nursery business?" While I was telling my wife about what Frank told me, I was so heartbroken I could not hold back the tears. I cried through the night. I could not understand how my brother Joe, "*chonan*," who I looked up to, steals the dignity of his younger brother.

Okaasan, there is more to this heart wrenching story. Frank felt that his share of the business he received was unfair for what he had contributed over the years. He filed a civil suit against Joe for his fair share of the sale of the business. He based his argument on the seed that you planted, "*chonan*." Frank asked me to be his witness. I was now between two brothers in their financial problem. I had no quarrel with Joe for he had always been good to me, for I remember how he and Yo included me in their lives. He was always supportive and encouraged me to continue my college education. And Frank has always been there for me too. I told Frank that I would be a witness about what our parents believed with respect to their culture of *chonan*, but I would have no part in what is an equitable share in the money matter. The whole legal process seemed to take a long time and the lawyers agreed to accept my deposition in place of appearing as a witness. It was slow and bitter fight and Joe could not come to terms with the suit. I learned latter that statements made in the heated argument between them that left a bitter taste. A few months after the trial started, Frank informed me that Joe collapsed on the golf course and died. Without Joe, the suit closed. Even if he had survived, the suit based on the cultural concept of *"chonan"* was without merit. Now, there is animosity and a great divide between family and in-laws. I have a heavy heart because I do not know how to heal this wound.

But our family is not alone on this tragic state of affairs, the cultural concept of *"chonan"* that *Issei* were determined to pass on to their children. Even my wife's family has not escaped this tragedy. The seed you have planted brought ill will and jealousy between son against son, daughter against son, and even daughter against daughter over a fair share of family possessions. It is not what you and *Otoosan* had struggled so hard to leave for us.

It would be sad if this were the only legacy left by your generation, the *Issei*. *Okaasan*, you and *Otoosan* you have given us values far greater than this. Your generation, the *Issei*, who left Japan for America, was promised great opportunity for the future. Politicians spouted lofty words of equality and freedom from our Constitution, but they say it was not for the Asians. At every turn, you met with disappointment and even hate for you are Japanese. *Gaman* was the way you persevered over adversity; accepted the disappointment as *shikataganai*; taught us right and wrong and never to bring *haji*, dishonor to the family by our conduct. While you clung to your culture, a safe place, you gave us core values: education, respect for teacher, *Sensei*, ethics and morality that are congruent with Judea-Christian values. But I am a *Nisei* who lives in two worlds. I will not choose one over the other. I will be Japanese, who, since the beginning of time, accepted way of life from other lands: philosophy and religion from Buddhism and Confucianism to augment Shintoism; writing and words from China to enhance the Japanese language. I will choose what will be my legacy for my children.

Family is core of our culture and that *kyodais* should stand together and have fundamentals in our beliefs and not just lofty ideals. I remember the wonderful event with our children. It was one day when we were ready to sell our rental home in Tucson, Arizona. My sons, Greg and Glen called me and said they would help me ready the house for sale. We stayed at Greg's home so that we could get an early start the next day. We assessed what we needed to do and each of us selected our share of the work. We talked and joked while we worked and never criticized anyone's work. Somehow we missed lunch because we wanted to finish the job that day. At last, it was time to quit. We were grubby and sweaty so we chose KFC (Kentucky Fried Chicken) as our dinner fare. It wasn't the greasy chicken that I remember and hold dear. It was that special moment when I sat on the floor, shared, and enjoyed my sons company. But there is a story that is even more heartwarming that you would be proud of the grandsons. One day, Greg told us this story: It was one Thanksgiving Day when Melanie and Greg invited Glen and Margaret for dinner. During the dinner, Glen said, "Greg, I want to thank you because you have been so good to me over the years when I was a poor college student and always included me in your gifts to the parents." I was moved and speechless when I heard those words. These are values you instilled in us and are alive. But Glen did not wear a mask. His feelings were open, honest, and unashamed to share them with his brother.

Lady on the Bridge

Okaasan, the seed that you and *Otoosan* brought to this land is sterile. In my world that Yo and I live in, we have strived for a legacy from our hearts, a love that knows no less than a hundred percent for each of our sons.

O-karada ni ki wo tsukete kudasi, Please take good care of yourself.

Your son, Tadashi

April blossom time
Captures Mother's nostalgia
Sakura Spirit

Sakura, Sakura (Cherry Blossom)

In my garden
Time has taken its toll
A cherry tree grows weary
A gift from *Okaasan (mother)*
Some years ago

Plant the *Sakura* my son
For at cherry blossom time
You can enjoy with me
The beauty of the pinkness
The delicateness of the petals
Sakura, cherry blossom
Of my childhood

I saw the full bloom
Of those same cherry trees
When I was a little girl
I laughed and sang
Danced around as blossom fell
Like pink snowflakes
The fragrance still last in me
Sakura, Sakura
Of my childhood

Okaasan
Your generous gift, *Sakura*
Flourished in my garden
Delicate pink in April bloom
Its fragrance waft in the air
Ethereal double pink blossoms
Brighten the days there after
Then gently floated to the ground
Into a sea of dainty pink petals
Sakura, Sakura
I see your spirit there

I am sadden though
A raucous Blue Jay

Lady on the Bridge

Planted an acorn
By my neighbor's fence
A towering oak now in place
Sucking the nutrients from the garden
Casting shadows on the cherry tree
The rays of the Sun Goddess, *Amaterasu*
Screened from sight
Sakura, Sakura
Fighting for its place

Sakura, Sakura
While the rogue oak tree
Usurp your right to be
You have brought days of joy
The beauty, delicateness of another day
Sakura, Sakura
Okaasan's nostalgia

Bibliography

Unran, Harlan D. Manzanar: Historic Study/Special History Study, *The Evacuation and Relocation of Persons of Japanese Ancestry During World War II: A Historic study of the Manzanar Relocation Center*, United State Department of the Interior National Park Service, 1996

Williams, Carey. *Prejudice: Japanese Americans Symbol of Racial Intolerance*, Little, Brown and Company, Boston, MA, 1945.

Appendix

Historical periods

Many dates are approximate and precise dates for events before A.D. 600 are guesses.

JOMON (10,000? - 300 B.C.) Prehistoric period of tribal/clan organization.

This period is identified by the *Jomon* braided pattern pottery made by Mesolithic to Neolithic hunters

660 B.C. Mythological Jimmu ("Divine Warrior"), descendant of sun goddess Amaterasu Omikami, founds empire.

YAYOI (300 B.C. - A.D. 300) Era named "Yayoi" after the place in Tokyo where wheel-turned pottery was found.
Rice cultivation, iron and bronze making.

Large settlement in Kyushu Island.

In Shinto, Japan's oldest religion, people identify *Kami* (divine forces) in nature and in such human virtues as loyalty and wisdom. 100-300: Local clans form small political units.

KOFUN (YAMATO) (300 - 645) Unified state begins with emergence of powerful clan rulers; Japan establishes close contacts with mainland Asia.

Yamato clan rulers, claiming descent from Amaterasu Omikami, begin the imperial dynasty that continues to occupy the throne today. Japan adopts Chinese written characters. Shotoku Taishi **(574-622)** begins to shape Japanese society and government more after the pattern of China. He also calls for reverence for Buddhism and the Confucian virtues.

(645 -1185)
New aristocratic families are created. Especially powerful is that of Fujiwara no Kamatari, who helped push the reforms.

710, Imperial court builds new capital at Nara.

Buddhism, in combination with native Shinto beliefs, continues to flourish. Establishing classical Japanese culture aided by invention of *kana* (syllabary for writing Japanese language).

KAMAKURA (1185-1568) Military government established in Kamakura by Minamoto no Yoritomo.

1192: *Bushi* become new ruling class.

1274, 1281: Kublai Khan's Mongol invasions are repelled with help of *kamikaze* ("divine winds," or storms).
Zen and spontaneity in ink painting, garden design, and the *chanoyu* (tea ceremony).

(1543) Firearms introduced by shipwrecked Portuguese soldiers.

(1549) Christianity introduced by Francis Xavier.

MOMOYAMA (1568 -1603)

Oda Nobunaga starts process of reunifying Japan after a century of civil war. He was followed by Toyotomi Hideyoshi (1536-1598). Foundation of modern Japan is laid.

Arts such as painting, monumental decorative designs, and the tea ceremony continue to flourish.

EDO (TOKUGAWA) (1603 -1868) Japan enters an age of peace and national isolation.

Tokugawa Ieyasu founds new *shogunate* at Edo (now Tokyo). Christianity is suppressed. Establishment of rigid social hierarchy ensures peace and stability throughout Japan. (Samurai are ranked highest, followed by farmers, artisans, and merchants.)

1700s, cities and commerce flourish. A growing merchant class enjoys Kabuki and Bunraku theater. Printing and publication of books increase; education becomes available to the urban population.

(1853) Commodore Matthew C. Perry and his steam frigates arrive in Japan the United States wants to use Japanese ports as supply bases for its commercial fleet. Japan accepts the U.S. demands and opens its door for the first time in two centuries.

MEIJI (1868 -1912) The emperor is restored; Japan makes transition to nation-state.
Dispossessed *bushi* become soldiers, policemen, and teachers with fall of feudal system and political reform. New national policy is to make Japan a rich and powerful country, to prevent invasion by Western powers. Emphasis is on building a strong military and strengthening industries.

1882: US/Chinese Exclusion Act prohibits naturalization – Angel Island is set up

1884: Japanese government allows voluntary emigration to Hawaii.

(1895, 1904-05) Japan becomes world power through victories in Sino-Japanese and Russo-Japanese wars.

1907-1908: US/"Gentlemen's Agreement" prohibits secondary migration of Japanese from Hawaii to the mainland.

(1910-45).Korea annexed.

TAISHO (1912-1926) Japan expands economic base within Asia and the Pacific.

1913: US/California Alien Land Law prohibits "aliens ineligible for citizenship" from owning property or land.

1921: US/The Immigration Act of 1921: The national-origins quota system established. Alien Land Law prohibits non-citizens from owning land.

1922: **US/** U. S. Supreme Court affirms ban against naturalization of Japanese immigrants.

1924: US/Johnson-Reed Act initiates "ineligibility to citizenship."

SHOWA [1926 -1989] Japan experiences World War II and its aftermath, as well as economic recovery.
Japan's liberal rulers replaced; military-run cabinets make imperialistic inroads in China. Manchuria taken over in **1931**.

1937-1945: World War II; war in China followed by invasion of Southeast Asia.

1940: Japan joins the Axis powers.

December 7, 1941: Pearl Harbor brings United States into war in the Pacific.

November 1, 1941, Military Intelligence Service (MIS) formed to train *Nisei* and *Kibei* in Japanese Military Language at Presidio San Francisco, California.

February 19, 1942: President Franklin D. Roosevelt issues Executive Order 9066 (Exclude Japanese from designated areas and remove people of Japanese ancestry from the West Coast.

1942-1945: Japanese incarceration into concentration camps.

1943: *Nisei* recruited from Concentration Camps to form all Japanese unit, 442nd Regimental Combat Team.

1943: Immigration act of 1943 repeals Chinese Exclusion Act

1945, January to November final phase of Relocation Program

August 1945: first atom bomb is dropped on Hiroshima, the second on Nagasaki. The emperor airs by radio a statement of unconditional surrender.

November 21, 1945, last evacuees left Manzanar.

1945-1952: Allied occupation of Japan

HEISEI (1989-) In **1989** Prince Akihito succeeds to the throne.

1988:The Civil Liberties Act authorized apology and $20,000 reparation to American citizens

Glossary

Japanese Word in Romaji (transliteration of Japanese into Latin alphabet) Long o= oo/ou	Pronunciation "()" silent "-" implies sound tied closely together Note: tsu =t(sk)-(c)hew R and L sound alike	Definition
Abunai	Ah bo(o) na(w)-e	Dangerous
Amaterasu	Ah ma (s)te(p) ra(h) sue	Sun Goddess
Ammasan	A(l)m ma(w) son(g)	Masseur but in lowest class
Anata no	Ah gna(w) ta(w) no	Your (No=of)
Ari	Ah ree(d)	Have, exist, are:from verb *aru*
Arimasen	Ah ree(d) ma sen	Doesn't exist
Azuki	Ah zoo key	Pinkish purple beans
Baishakunin	Buy sha(h)-coo nin(ja)	matchmaker, go-between
Banzai	Ba(lk)-n za-e	Hurrah, cheers, congradulations
Benjo	Ben jo(e)	Toilet, bathroom
Bentoo	Ben to(e)	Lunch
Booya	Bo(w)-o ya(w)	Boy
Botchan	Boat chan(ce)	Small child
Bukkyo	Book ke(y)-yo(del)	Buddhist religion
Bushi	Boo she	Warrior class (i.e., knight)
Chazuke	Chaw zoo ka(y)	Bowl of rice with tea poured on top
Chonan	Cho(sen) non(e)	First born son
Dakara	Da(w) ca(w) ra(h)	Because
Dansu	Dawn Sue	Dance (Japanese phonetical form of dance)
Doomo	Do(ugh) mo(e)	Very, quite, somehow
Doozo	Do(ugh)-o zo(ne)	Please (i.e., request)
Doshite	Do(ugh) she (s)te(p)	Why
Ebi	Eh-b	Lobster,shrimp
Enryo	En(d) lee-yo(del)	Timidity showing restrain or being reserved in feeling and action
Eta	E(h) ta(lk)	Non class individual
Furi	Foo ree(d)	Shake
Furo	Foo ro(w)	Bath
Furoshiki	Foo ro(w) she ke(y)	Cloth wrapper
Furusato	Fo(od) rue sa(w) to(e)	Old (nostalgic) Japan, Edo Era
Gaman	Gau(dy) mon(gol)	Repress, endure feelings and pain
Gambaru	Gau(dy) um bah roo	Persevere
Genkan	(a)gain kahn	Entranceway
Giri	Gi(ld) ree(d)	Obligations

Gochisoosama	Go chee(se) so sa(w) ma(w)	Expression: Thank you for the dinner
Gohan	Go hawn	Cooked rice, meal
Ha	Ha	Well, Indeed, Yes, Ha!
Hai	High-e	Yes
Haji	Ha gee	Shame, dishonor
Haji wo shire	Ha gee wo(e) she ra(y)	Know shame
Hajimemashite	Ha gee ma(y) ma(h) she te	Greetings: Nice (for the first time) to meet you
Hayaku shinasai	Ha ya(w) coo she na(h) sa(w)-e	Hurry up
Hakujin	Ha coo jean	Caucasian
Hinomaru	He kno(w) ma(h) roo(st)	Japanes flag = round like the sun
Hoito	Ho(e)-e to(e)	Greedy
Hontooni	Hon(e) to(e)-o knee	Really, very
Ie	E-a(ble)	Home (see *Kazoku*)
Ii	Ee	Good, fine
Iikoto	Ee co(at) to(e)	Good thing
Ika	E ca(w)	Squid
Ikebana	E ka(y) bah nah	Flower arrangement
Imooto	E mo(e)-oo(h) to(e)	Younger sister
Inu	E Ne(w)	Informer, dog
Issei	Eas(t) say	First generation
Itadakimasu	E ta da key ma(w) sue	Expression to start eating
Itoko	E to(e) co(ld)	Cousin
Ittemairimasu	Eat te(d) ma(w)-e lee ma(h) sue	Expression: I'm leaving
Kabe	Ca(w) be(th)	Wall
Kagami	Ca(w) ga(ll) me	Mirror
Kakei	Ca(w) kay	Ancestors
Kazoku	Ca(w) zo(ne) coo	Family
Kekko	Ke(tch)-ick co(ld)o	Splendid
Kekkon	Ke(tch)-ick con(e)	Marriage
Kibei	Key bay	*Nisei* who returned to US from Japan
Kite kure mashita	Key te(ch) coo ra(y) ma(h) she ta(h)	Came (kureta= to do for me)
Kooden	Co(ld)-o den	Monetary obituary gift
Kodomo	Co(ld) do(ugh) mo(e)	Child, children

Kodomo no tamme ni	Co(ld) do(ugh) mo(e) kno(w) ta(w) ma(y) knee	Sacrifice for the children
Koko wa anata no shorai de naiyo	Coco(a) wa(h) Ah na(h) ta(w) Kno(w) sho(w) lie da(y) nigh-E Yo	This place is not your future (i.e., Your future is not here)
Konnichiwa	Con(e) knee che(ese)wa(h)	Good afternoon
Kore wo	Co(ld) la(y) who(a)	(with) this
Kozukai	Co(ld) zoo ca(w)-e	Small expense money
Kyoudai	Ke(y)-yo(del) die	Sibling
Maguro	Ma(w) gu ro(w)	Tuna
Makizushi	Ma key zoo she	Wrapped sushi, usually seaweed
Manjuu	Mon jew-u	Steamed yeast bun with filling
Matakoiyo	Ma(w) ta(lk) co(ld)-e yo(del)	Come again: *Mata*=again, Koi=come, *Yo*=must (implied)
Me	Me(dic)	Eye
Meshiagari nasai	Me(dic) she ah ga(ll) ree(d) nah sa(w)-e	Please eat
Mikan	Me kahn	Mandarin or tangerine orange
Mimai	Me my-e	Visit
Mimi	Me me	Ear
Mochi	Mo(de) chea(t)	Sticky rice for pastry
Nai	Gna(w)-e	Nothing, doesn't exist
Nakoodo	Gnaw co(de)-o do(ugh)	Matchmaker
Naika	Nigh-e ca(w)	Do you have?
Nandemonnai	Gna(w)-n de(bt) mo(w) gna(w)-e	Nandemo=anything, nai=doesn't exist
Nanimo	Nah knee mo(e)	Nothing
Ne	Ne(st)	Is it so
Neisan	Ne(st)-e son(g)	Older sister
Ni	Knee	In, on, for
Ni yotte	Knee yo(ke)t te(t)	According to
Nihon	Knee hon(e)	Japan
Nihonjin	Knee hon(e) jean	Japanese (see Nipponjin)
Niisan	Knee-e son(g)	Older brother
Nipponjin	Nip-pon(e) jean	Japanese (See Nihonjin)
Nisei	Knee say	Second generation
No	Kno(w)	Of
Nomi nasai	Kno(w) me nah sa(w)-e	(do) Drink
Oishikatta	Oh-e she caught ta	Delicious
Ojisan	Oh ge(e) son(g)	Uncle
Okaasan	Oh ca(w)-ah son(g)	Mother (honorific mode)
Okayu	Oh ca(w) you	Soft (mushy) cooked rice
Omoide	Oh mo(w) e da(y)	Remembrance

Omiyage	Oh me ya(w) ga(te)	Gift (note: O=honorific)
On	O(w)n	Filial piety, obligation
Onna	O(w)n nah	Female
Onsen	O(w)n sen(t)	Hot Spring
Osoku naru	Oh so coo nah ru(le)	Late become (i.,e you'll be late)
Otoko	Oh to(e) co(ve)	Male
Otooto	Oh to(e)-o to(e)	Younger brother
Otousan	Oh to(e)-o son(g)	Father (honorific mode)
Oyakoko	Oh ya(w) co(ld) co(ld)	Loyalty (parent child)
Ozouni	Oh zoe knee	Vegetable stew with *mochi*
Ryokan	Re(ed)-yo(del) kahn	Inn
Sakanatsuri	Sa(w) ca(w) nah t(sk)che(w) ree(d)	Fishing (sakana=fish) (tsuru=suspend)
Samurai	Sa(w) moo rye-e	Warrior class, soldier for a *Shogun*
Sannin	Sahn knee-n	Three (person)
Sansei	Sahn say	Third generation
Sensei	Sen(d) say	Teacher
Shibaraku deshta	She ba(h) la(w) coo desh-ta	Greetings:It's been a while
Shikata	Shee ca(w) ta(lk)	Way, method
Shikata ga nai	Shee ca(w) ta(lk) ga nah E	That's fate, nothing you can do about it, hopeless
Shimpai shinaide	Shim pa-e she na(h)-e da(y)	Without worrying
Shinsei	Shin say	Newly arrived Japanese
Shinto	Shin to(e)	Religion native to Japan
Shiri	She ree(d)	Fanny
Shogatsu	Sho(w) go(d) t(sk)-che(w)	New Years
Shogun	Sho(w) goon	Top of *Bushi* class
Shoji	Sho(w) gee	Door
Shokugyokikai	Sho(w) coo gee(se)yo key kay(ak)-e	Job opportunity
Shoyuu	Show you-u	Soy sauce
Somatsu	Se(w) Ma t(sk)-che(w)	Humble or crude
Soochishimasu	Se(w) che(ese) she ma(h) sue	Will do so
Sore wa	Se(w) la(y) wa(h)	That (is)
Sushi	Su(e) she	Cooked rice with vinegar and sugar flavor and various ingredients added, such as, fillet fish, other sea foods, …
Tai	Tie	Carp
Taiko Bashi	Tie co(ld) Bah she	Drum Bridge (symbolizes hardship reaching Pardise)
Takagi	Ta ca(w) gi(ld)	Firewood
Takagi wa naika	Ta ca(w) gi(ld) wa(ll) nigh-e ca(w)	Do you have any firewood?
Tako	Ta co(ld)	Octopus

Lady on the Bridge

Takuan	Ta(lk) coo awn	Pickled Japanese horse radish
Tame	Ta(ll) ma(y)	For
Tatami	Ta(lk) ta(lk) me	Straw floor covering
Torii	To(e) ree(d)	Shinto shrine archway
Totemo	To(e) ta(ste) moe	Very
Tsukemono	T(sk)-che(w) ka(y) mo(e) no	Pickled things: *Tsuke*=pickle, mono=thing
Unagi	Oo(p) na(w) gee(k)	Eel
Ureshii	Oo(p) re(in) she-e	Happy
Wa	Wa(ll)	As to
Yari	Ya(w) lee	Spear
Yoi ko da	Yo(del)-e co(ld) dah	Good child
Yonsei	Youn(g) say	Fourth generation
Yoroshii	Yo(del) ro(w) she-e	That's fine, good
Yukata	You ca(w) ta(ll)	Informal summer kimono, bathrobe
Yuutousei	You toe say	Honor student
Zabuton	Za boo ton(e)	Cushion

318

The Author

Tadashi Kishi, a Nisei (second generation Japanese American) was born in Culver City, California, December 11, 1921. He spent most of his childhood in Santa Monica, California and graduated from Samohi, Santa Monica High School in 1939. He was attending UCLA majoring in Physics when the war broke out. After President Roosevelt issued Executive Order 9066, he was uprooted and interned at Manzanar, California with other Japanese in the Santa Monica area.

While interned at Manzanar, he took 24 units of Educational courses at night under the University of California's Extension School in order to qualify to teach high school physics at the Manzanar High School. After teaching one year op Physics, he applied to teach conversational Japanese at the University of Minnesota as an opportunity to seek freedom from internment.

Later, he was inducted in the US Army, trained in Military Japanese at the Presidio of Monterey, California, and served in Occupied Japan as a soldier and interpreter for MIS/ATIS assigned to General Macarthur's GHQ.

After his discharge from the Army, he continued his college education at UC Berkeley and graduated with a MA degree in Math. He began his career at the Los Alamos Scientific Laboratory (LASL) and transferred to the Lawrence Livermore National Laboratory (LLNL) at Livermore, California. He was a Math/Programmer, System designer, and supervisor for large-scale scientific computers: IBM 700 series, LARC, and CDC 6600. He was the project manager for the LLNL's commitment to utilize the ARPA ILLIAC IV for scientific application. He returned from the ARPA assignment and was a staff member of the Computation Department investigating special system for large-scale scientific applications. His last assignment was the Division Leader for programmers and technicians for scientific applications, small computer systems for the Magnetic Fusion Test Facility (MFTF), and the Laser Project.

He has written several technical papers, given seminars at universities and won the best technical paper at the IEEE Computer Conference in San Francisco, California.

www.ingramcontent.com/pod-product-compliance
Lightning Source LLC
Chambersburg PA
CBHW081820280526
45789CB00007B/2271